Contents

*Here are
the Michelin maps
to use with this
guide :*

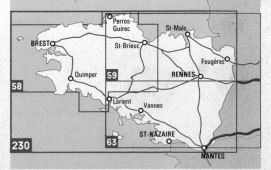

BRETON NAMES

Place-names. – In Brittany, as in other French provinces, place-names have meanings that are often easy to find. Most of them are formed from a root to which the name of a saint is added.

Ploe, plou, plo, or **pleu,** which means parish, has given us: Ploudaniel (Daniel's parish), Plogoff (parish of St Cof), Ploërmel (parish of St Armel), Plougastel (parish of the castle), Pleumeur (great parish), Plounevez (new parish), etc.

Tre or **Tref** (parish subdivision) has given: Tréboul (place of the pool), Trégouet (place of wood), etc.

Loc (holy place) gives: Locmaria (Mary's place), Locronan (place of St Renan), Locquirec (place of St Guirec), Locminé (place of monks), etc.

Lann (church) gives: Lannion (church of St Yon), Lampaul (church of St Paul), Landerneau (church of St Ternoc), Langoat (church in the woods), etc.

Ker (village or house) gives: Kermaria (Mary's village), Kerjean (John's village), Kerguen (white village), etc.

Guic, gui (town) gives: Guimiliau (town of St Méliau), Guisseny (town of St Seny).

Traon, trou, tro (valley) gives: Tromelin (valley of the mill), Tromeur (great valley), etc.

Coat, goat, goët, hoët (wood) appears in: Huelgoat (high wood), Kergoat (house in the woods), Penhoët (end of the wood), Toulgoët (hollow in the wood), etc.

Family names. – Many are formed from the word Ker (house) followed by a distorted Christian name: Kerber (House of Peter), Kerbol (House of Paul), Kerjean (House of John), Kertanguy (House of Tanguy), etc.

Other names indicate professions: Le Barazer (cooper), Le Goff (blacksmith), Le Goffic (tinker), Le Gonidec (ploughman), Quémeneur (tailor), Le Tocquer (hatter), Le Trocquer (second-hand dealer), etc.

Nicknames are also widely used: Le Bihan (small), Le Braz (big), Le Bail (marked on the forehead), Cudenec (mournful), Cosmao (jolly old man), Le Fur (wise man), Gallouédec (powerful), Le Moigne (one-armed), Le Troadec (man with big feet), Le Guen, Guennec, Guennoc (white man), Le Dantec (toothy), Le Cornec (horned), Le Pennec (obstinate), etc.

(Dupont/Explorer)

Join us in our never ending task of keeping up to date.

Send us your comments and suggestions, please.

Michelin Tyre Public Limited Company
Tourism Department
Lyon Road – HARROW – Middlesex HA1 2DQ

4

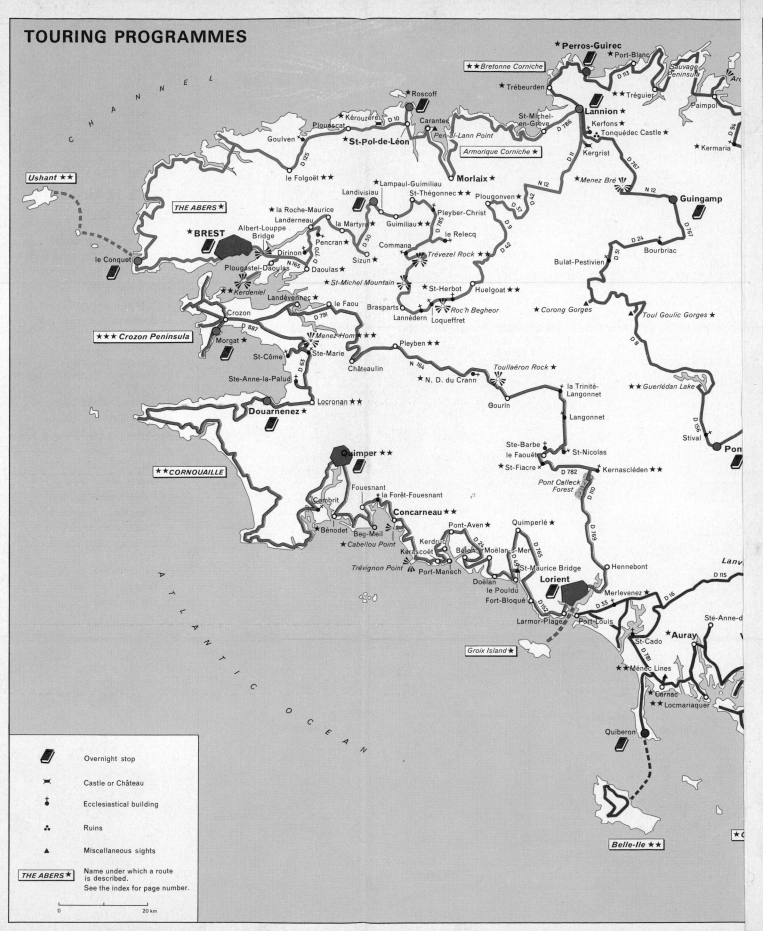

TOURING PROGRAMMES

★★ *Bretonne Corniche*

THE ABERS ★

Ushant ★★

★★ *Armorique Corniche*

★★ *Crozon Peninsula*

★★ *Menez Hom*

★★ *CORNOUAILLE*

Key (left map)

- Overnight stop
- Castle or Château
- Ecclesiastical building
- Ruins
- Miscellaneous sights

THE ABERS ★ — Name under which a route is described. See the index for page number.

0 ——— 20 km

9 10

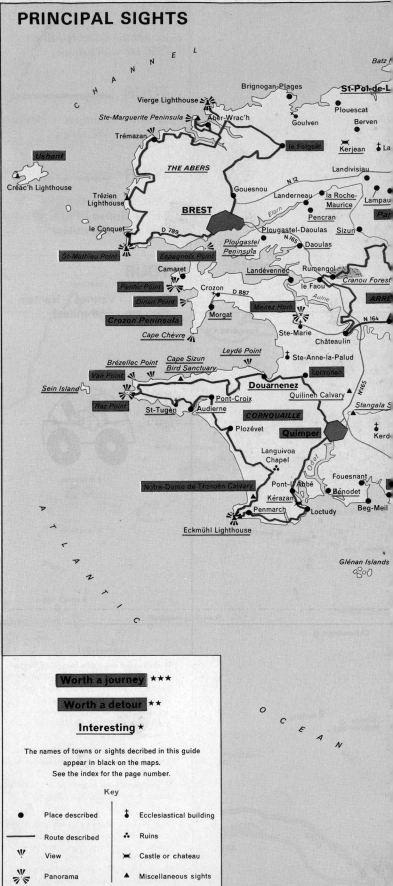

PRINCIPAL SIGHTS

Ushant

THE ABERS

BREST

Crozon Peninsula

Cape Chèvre

Brézellec Point
Cape Sizun Bird Sanctuary
Van Point
Raz Point

Sein Island

CORNOUAILLE

Eckmühl Lighthouse

Key

Worth a journey ★★★

Worth a detour ★★

Interesting ★

The names of towns or sights described in this guide appear in black on the maps.
See the index for the page number.

Key

- ● Place described
- ⚐ Ecclesiastical building
- — Route described
- ⚒ Ruins
- ⚑ View
- ⚔ Castle or chateau
- ✺ Panorama
- ▲ Miscellaneous sights

0 ——— 20 km

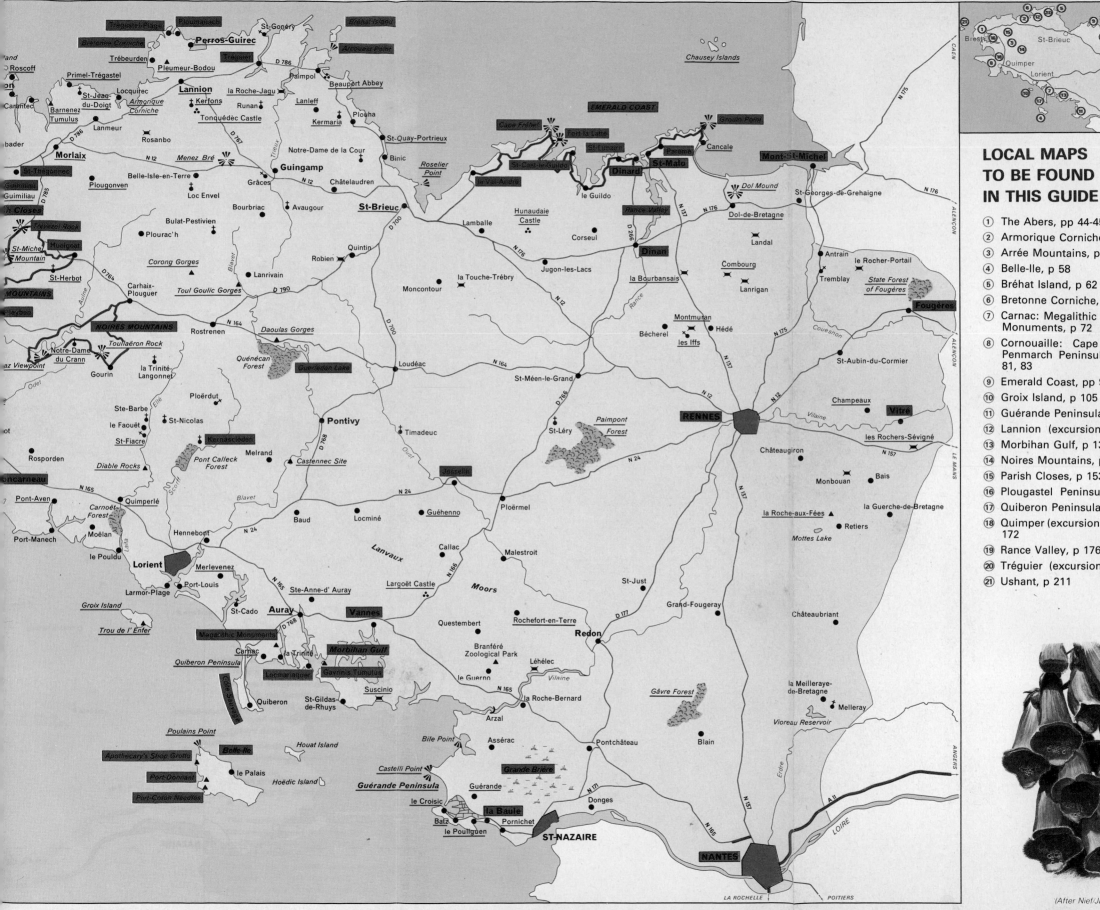

(After Nief/Jacana photo)

PLACES TO STAY

The mention Facilities, under the individual headings or after place names, refers to the information given on these pages.

The map on pages 14 and 15 indicates towns selected for the accommodation and leisure facilities which they offer to the holidaymaker.

To help you plan your route and choose your hotel, restaurant or camping site consult the following Michelin publications.

Accommodation

The **Michelin Red Guide France** of hotels and restaurants and the **Michelin Guide Camping Caravaning France** are annual publications which present a selection of hotels, restaurants and camping sites. The final choice is based on regular on the spot enquiries and visits. Both the hotels and camping sites are classified according to the standard of comfort of their amenities. Establishments which are notable for their fortunate setting, their decor, their quiet and secluded location and their warm welcome are distinguished by special symbols.

The Michelin Guide France also gives the address and telephone number of local tourist offices and tourist information centres.

Planning your route, sports and recreation

The **Michelin Sectional Map Series** at a scale of 1:200 000 covers the whole of France. For those concerning the region see the layout diagram on page 3. These give a general idea of the resources of a particular locality. In addition to the wealth of road information, the touristic details include beaches, bathing spots, swimming pools, golf courses, racecourses, air fields, panoramas and scenic routes...

LEISURE ACTIVITIES

For addresses and other details, see the chapter "Practical Information" at the back of the guide.

On the coast

To savour the charm of Brittany to the full, take note of the sea.

Learn how the fishermen live; watch the traffic of the ports, great and small. Go to the early morning fish auction *(la criée)*, watch for the return of the fishing boats. Even if you are not a good sailor do not be afraid to leave dry land in a fishing or excursion boat. The sight of the coast from the sea will be a revelation to you.

Follow the changing moods of the sea and sky. Admire the sunsets – they are unforgettable. Go for a walk by the sea at full moon; or when there is no moon, take a look at the lighthouse beams as they pierce the darkness. By day these lighthouses make wonderful observation points. A tour of the lighthouse equipment is an added attraction when it is allowed.

Become hardened to the wind. Sea going folk smile when landsmen call what seems to be a fresh breeze, a gale.

In windy weather do not stay shut up in your hotel or in your car. Walk boldly along the points or the capes. Take the lash of the sea spray with a smile; enjoy the salty tang on your tongue when you lick your lips. It is a great thing to have seen from close to, a rough sea crashing on a world's end cape: it verges on the sublime.

Seaside cures. – The special characteristics of sea water and the mildness of the climate are particularly beneficial for certain illnesses: rheumatism, arthritis and certain states of shock.

Sailing

The indented coastline provides many sheltered bays which are ideal for this sport. Plenty of sailing clubs, such as the well known centre on Glénan Islands, provide instruction. Large resorts hold regattas throughout the season. There are also various international events.

Yachting

Sailing and motor craft cruise off the Channel and Atlantic coasts with the islands offering good anchorage in numerous harbours, creeks and bays. The principal pleasure boat harbours are indicated on the map on pp 14-15. They have been selected according to their capacity and the facilities provided: refuelling points, drinking water, electric points, toilets and showers, handling and repair facilities, warden in attendance, etc.

(J. Gauthier/Azimut)

Brittany also offers canal boating. To travel from the Channel to the Atlantic, take the Ille-et-Rance canal then the Vilaine passing through Dinan, Rennes and Redon. Starting from Lorient, take a trip up the Blavet, the eastern section of the Nantes-Brest canal and the Edre, passing through Josselin and Redon on the way to Nantes. From the head of the Brest roadstead, go up the Aulne and the western section of the Nantes-Brest canal to Châteaulin and Carhaix-Plouguer.

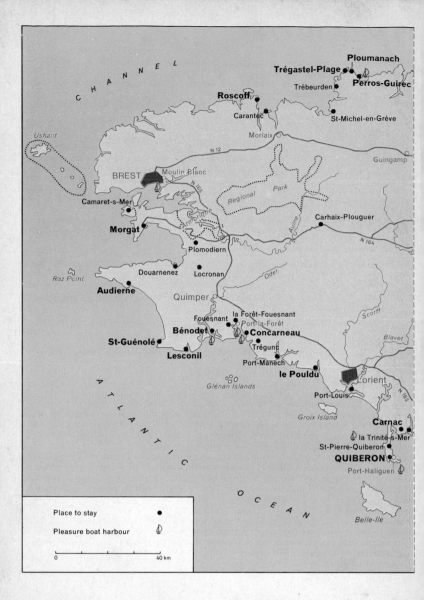

Amateur fishing

In the sea. – Fishing enthusiasts will have every opportunity to practise the sport, whether from the shore, out at sea or underwater, all along the coast from the Mont St-Michel bay to the Loire estuary. The angler may use a line with one or two hooks; if more are used, the Harbour Office (Inscription Maritime) must be told. A permit is necessary if a net is used. Float fishing, using a line with a lead sinker is allowed from rocks and quays and from the shore. Shrimps and prawns are caught with a long-handled net; the best time is at low tide. You may dig for clams, cockles and sand eels with a spade or rake and among the rocks you may hunt for mussels, crabs, winkles and conches.

In rivers. – Brittany's estuaries, rivers and brooks teem with trout, pike, salmon, mullet, shad, etc., and are particularly favoured by fishermen.

Anglers must observe the fishing regulations and should obtain particulars from the local angling associations or tourist information centres.

Skin diving

This sport is gaining in popularity in Brittany. The southern coasts (Port-Manech, Port Goulphar at Belle-Ile) with creeks of cystal clear water, an abundance of fish and seaweed, provide an ideal setting to practise underwater fishing or swimming to marvel at the beauty of it all. The diving centre at Glénan Islands has superb facilities for indoor training in winter.

The Michelin Regional Map Series (1:200 000) covers the whole of France. They show

> *golf courses, stadiums,*
> *racecourses, beaches, swimming pools,*
> *high altitude mountain airfields, long distance footpaths,*
> *viewpoints, scenic routes, state forests, interesting sights.*

This is the perfect complement to the Michelin Green Guides.

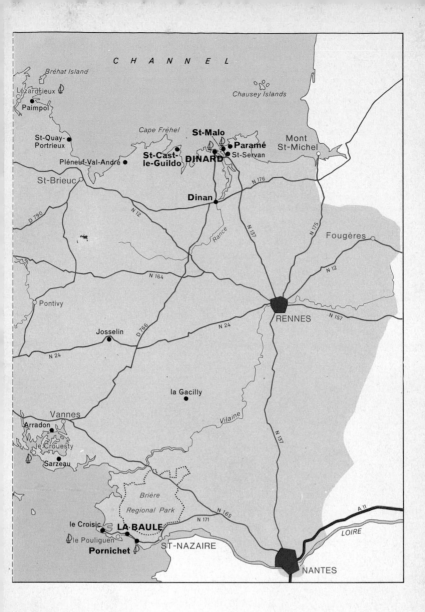

Inland

The **Argoat** *(p 21)* was off the beaten track for so long that it remained silent, melancholy and rural in character, but schemes such as the Armorique Regional Nature Park (1969) in the Arrée Mountains *(p 49)* draw an ever increasing number of tourists.

The Argoat is the ideal stopping place for lovers of nature to stand and stare, for naturalists to watch hundreds of birds and discover a wide variety of plant life and for those who like to walk alone. To these, turning off the beaten track will often reveal a former manor now become a farm, or following a scarcely perceptible path across the fields, the presence of a megalith or a little chapel standing alone and noticeable from a distance only by its pointed steeple. There are gorges too, where waters leap from rock to rock before disappearing into depths below. Poets and romantics who love the simple charm of nature will be transported into a world of fantasy and, often in hazy surroundings, conducive to dreams and mystery, will be able, at leisure, to weave anew the rich store of Breton legends.

Rambling

Many long-distance footpaths enable ramblers to discover the region covered in this guide. Topo Guides give detailed itineraries and useful advice to ramblers.

The GR 37, 38, 39, 380 crisscross the Argoat and will delight trained ramblers and less experienced walkers alike.

*The **Michelin Guide France** revises annually its 500 town plans showing:*
- *throughroutes and by-passes,*
  new roads, car parks and one-way systems
- *the exact location of hotels, restaurants and public buildings.*

With the help of all this updated information take the harassment out of town driving

SEASONS

Brittany's climate is both mild and invigorating.

Spring is the time when gorse and broom flare golden. The countryside, flowered and scented, noisy with birds of every species, is delightful when the sun shines. It is the time when the nature lover can enjoy the country almost undisturbed.

A characteristic of the Breton **summer** is its moderate warmth, due to the bracing sea breeze (average 17 °C - 64 °F) which blows from the ocean.

Occasional showers keep the fields green, the foliage fresh and the mosses flourishing. Rare spells of heat come with infrequent light winds from the east. The hazy light has a special quality. Scores of painters come to capture the Breton scenes.

In **autumn,** the russet tints of the trees sometimes make splendid pictures at sunset.

Northwesterly and southwesterly gales are frequent: for those who like to watch rough seas, the gales, however, provide a wonderful spectacle!

The **winter** is mild, with a mean temperature like that of the Mediterranean coast. A bitter wind may come from the east, but not too often. During these "dark months", as they are known locally, the northwesterlies and southwesterlies often rage.

(After J.-L. Lemoigne/Azimut photo)
Cape Sizun Bird Sanctuary. – A cormorant

Introduction
to the tour

The most vivid memory left after a visit to Brittany is that of the coast, with its many coloured cliffs, scarred, rent and crumbled by a pounding sea; a chaplet of islands and a multitude of reefs; piles of rocks and impressive headlands.

To the tourist who has had his fill of seascapes, the Breton hinterland offers melancholy heaths covered with gorse and crests with rocky slopes from which wide panoramas open out.

Mysterious megalithic monuments, a multitude of chapels with delicate steeples consecrated to a host of local saints, parish closes and pardons which give glimpses of the pious fervour of the people, add to the attraction of one of the most original regions of France.

Trévezel Rock

Times and charges for admission to sights described in the guide are listed at the end of the guide.

The sights are listed alphabetically in this section either under the place – town, village or area – in which they are situated or under their proper name.

Every sight for which there are times and charges is indicated by the symbol ⓥ in the margin in the main part of the guide.

APPEARANCE OF THE COUNTRY

SOIL FORMATION

The relief of Brittany is the result of an evolutionary process which has taken place over millions of centuries. The planet earth, a fiery globe, is assumed to have detached itself from the sun over four thousand million years ago. This period is divided into eras.

Primary era. – It began some 600 million years ago. Water covered the whole land mass of France. It was at this period that the earth's crust was forced upwards: the fold, known as the "Hercynian fold" which appears in the form of a V and is shown in shading on the map, made great mountains rise up (Armorican Massif, Massif Central, the Vosges and Ardennes). These mountains of impermeable, crystalline rock – granite, gneiss and mica-schist mixed with volcanic rock such as prophyry – appeared in Brittany as two massive chains stretching from east to west and separated by a central furrow.

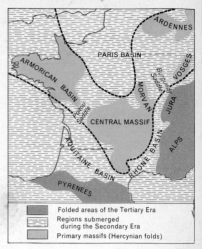

Folded areas of the Tertiary Era
Regions submerged during the Secondary Era
Primary massifs (Hercynian folds)

Secondary era. – It began about 200 million years ago. Since the beginning of this age, the Hercynian relief was levelled by erosion forming the Armorican peneplain. Erosion, or the constant destruction of the soil by alternating rain, sun, frost and the action of running water, wore away rocks as hard as granite or sandstone.

Tertiary era. – It began some 60 million years ago. The altitude of the Armorican Massif rose only slightly. The highest point is the Toussaines Beacon – Tuchenn Gador – in the Arrée Mountains (alt 384m - 1288ft). The deep cuts into the coastline were formed by rocking movements of the earth.

Quaternary era. – It began some 2 million years ago. This is the present age during which the evolution of man has taken place.

Changes in the sea level, due to the waters freezing over during the Ice Age followed by a rise as the ice melted, brought about the flooding of valleys, thus forming the deep estuaries known in Breton as **abers.** The inland mountains became steep cliffs (Cape Fréhel, Penhir Point, Raz Point) and the hills turned into islands (Batz, Ushant, Sein, Groix, Belle-Ile, etc.).

LANDSCAPE

The Armor

The name of **Armor,** which means "country near the sea", was given to the coastal region by the Gauls; the interior was Argoat, "country of the wood" *(p 21).*
The Breton coast is extraordinarily indented; this makes it 1200 km - 750 miles long whereas it would be half that without its saw-teeth. The jaggedness of this coastline with its islands, islets and reefs, which is due only in part to the action of the sea, is one of the characteristics of Brittany.

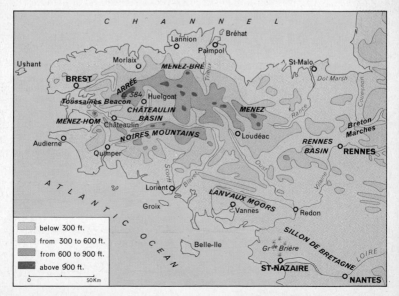

below 300 ft.
from 300 to 600 ft.
from 600 to 900 ft.
above 900 ft.
0   50 Km

The most typical seascapes are to be found at the western tip of the peninsula. Sombre cliffs, rugged capes 50 to 70m - 160 to 224ft high, islands, rocks and reefs give the coastline a grimness which is reflected in local names with a sinister ring: the channel of Great Fear (Fromveur), the Bay of the Dead (Baie des Trépassés), the Hell of Plogoff (Enfer de Plogoff).

There are many other impressive features, too: piles of enormous blocks of pink granite sometimes rising as much as 20m - 64ft as at Ploumanach and Trégastel; the red sandstone promontory of Cape Fréhel standing 57m - 182ft above the sea; the brightly coloured caves of Morgat. The Brest roadstead, the Bay of Douarnenez, the Morbihan Gulf and its islands are unforgettable.

The successive estuaries between the Rance and the Loire offer magnificent views at high tide as one crosses the impressive bridges that span them (Albert-Louppe and Térénez bridges).

Some low-lying sections of the coast contrast with the more usual rocks. In the north, the Bay of Mont-St-Michel is bordered by a plain won from the sea; in the south, the inhospitable Bay of Audierne, the coast between Port-Louis and the base of the Quiberon Peninsula, and the beach at La Baule give a foretaste of the great expanses of sand which predominate south of the Loire.

Wherever the coast is directly open to the sea winds, it is completely barren. This is so on the points and on the summits of the cliffs: the salt with which the winds are impregnated destroys the vegetation. But in sheltered spots there are magnificent flowering shrubs which bloom profusely. Arum lilies, camellias, hydrangeas and rhododendrons which would be the pride of many a skilled gardener, bedeck the smallest gardens. The climate is so mild that plants which grow in hot countries flourish in the open and mimosas, agaves, pomegranates, palms, eucalyptus, myrtles, oleanders and fig trees may be seen.

The tides. – Visitors should first learn the rhythm of the tides, a division of time as regular as that of the sun. Twice every twenty-four hours the sea advances on the coast – this is the rising tide. It reaches high water mark, stays for some time at full stretch and then drops back – this is the falling or ebb tide – until it reaches low water mark. After remaining flattened for some time, the cycle begins again.

The timetables for the tides are displayed in hotels, on the quays and in the local papers. Look at them before deciding on your programme, bearing in mind how long you have to spend.

It is at high tide that the coast of Brittany is most beautiful. The waves advance on the coast, break on the rocky outspurs and surge in parallel crests into the bays; a shining liquid carpet fills the estuaries. This is the time when a journey along a coast road or a walk to the harbour is the most rewarding; it is also the time for aquatic sports and pastimes.

At low tide the uncovered rocks, stained with algae and seaweed, are often dirty and can be disappointing. At the mouths of the great coastal rivers there is only a poor thread of water winding between mudflats. The greater the tide and the gentler the slope, the greater is the expanse of shore uncovered; in Mont-St-Michel Bay the sea retreats 15 to 20 km - 9 to 12 miles. On the other hand, low tide is the joy of anyone fishing for crabs, shrimps, clams, mussels, etc.

On the north coast, the tide sweeps in, in exceptional cases to a height of 13.50m - 43ft in the Bay of St-Malo and of 15m - 49ft in the Bay of Mont-St-Michel. When the wind blows, the battering ram effect of the sea is tremendous. Sometimes the shocks given to the rocks off Penmarch are felt as far off as Quimper, 30 km - 18 miles away.

Attacking the softest parts of the cliffs, the sea makes fissures and brings down slabs of rock. In this way caves (Morgat), tunnels and arches (Dinan "Château") are formed. Peninsulas joined to the mainland by strips of softer material are turned gradually into islands.

The waves do not only destroy; they also have a constructive effect. The sand they carry, added to the alluvial deposits brought down by the rivers, forms beaches, gradually silts up the bays (Mont-St-Michel Bay is a striking example), and connects islands with the mainland; this is the case at Quiberon and it will also be the same, in due course, at Bréhat.

The waves. – Waves are an undulating movement produced by the wind. Even after the wind has dropped, the movement continues; this is the swell. The impression that the water moves forward is an optical illusion: by watching a floating cork one can see that the up and down movement does not displace the water.

Near the shore the undulation of the waves, which reaches to a depth of about 30m - 100ft, is braked by the bottom. The balance is upset and the crest collapses, thus forming rollers of foam and giving out a dull, rhythmic sound: this is the surf. When the wave meets a steep obstacle, such as rocks or cliffs, it seems to recoil, shoots up, flinging spray into the air, and then falls with all its weight. On stormy days the spectacle can be awe-inspiring.

A land of sailors. – The Bretons, if one is to believe a well-known proverb, "are born with the waters of the sea flowing round their hearts". Whether they are engaged in coastal or deep sea fishing, fishing for cod or crustaceans, they have kept up with the latest techniques.

Lorient and Concarneau are the two most important fishing ports in France after Boulogne and consequently Brittany is the greatest fishing region both in monetary value and size of the catch.

Coastal fishing. – All along the coast there is inshore fishing. Boats which sail and return with the tide, bring in fresh fish such as sole, mullet, turbot, skate, bass, sea-bream, mackerel, crustaceans, scallops, etc. Even so the catch is not nearly enough for local needs and a town like St-Brieuc on the north side of the peninsula receives supplementary supplies from Lorient in the south.

On the Atlantic coast, the season for sardine fishing lasts from June to September. In winter the sardine boats are used for trawling, lobster or crab fishing.

Deep sea fishing. – Trawlers operating in the Bay of Biscay, the Irish Sea and off the coasts of Iceland bring in most of the fresh fish, especially the kinds of fish in great demand. Trawling is the main activity of big ports like Lorient, Concarneau and Douarnenez.

For **tunny** fishing both live bait and nets are used in the Bay of Biscay and seine nets along the African coasts.

The white tunny is fished from June to October: starting somewhere between Portugal and the Azores, the season ends in the Bay of Biscay. Tropical or albacore tunny is the quarry of a fleet of some thirty boats with refrigerated holds, equipped at Concarneau and operating from the ports of West Africa during the season.

Cod fishing. – The **cod** fishing fleets operate in the fisheries of Newfoundland, Labrador and Greenland. Paimpol and St-Malo were once renowned for their cod fleets but now only St-Malo has connections with cod fishing. The fleets are currently undergoing reorganization since public preference has shifted from salted to frozen cod. The trawlers have become veritable factories with mechanical filletting and freezing equipment on board.

St-Malo is the number one port for frozen cod and third in importance for the salted product.

Crustaceans. – Most crustacean fishing takes place along the rocky coasts using lobster pots and traps, but long distance fishing using all the modern equipment is also common. The lobster boats with refrigeration plants, leave from Camaret, Audierne and Douarnenez for the coast of Mauritania for several months at a time. The boats are equipped with tanks as well as freezing plants.

When the boats return to harbour, part of the catch is put into storage beds. These are situated at many points round the coast, the most important lying between Primel and Audierne.

Oysters and shellfish. – Conchyliculture or oyster or mussel breeding has now become commercially important. Brittany, which has for long been the great production region for flat oysters (Belons), has also developed its Portuguese oyster beds. The biggest maturing beds on the Channel coast lie off Cancale and Morlaix and on the Atlantic in the Belon and Pénerf river estuaries. Mussel breeding on poles known as "*bouchots*" is carried out along the coast from the Mont-St-Michel Bay to St-Brieuc Bay and in the Vilaine estuary. Mussel farms are also to be found in the Aven estuary, at Tudy Island and Le Croisic.

Fish processing. – Sardines, mackerel, white and albacore tunny are all canned in the factories round the coast, particularly in the Penmarch region, at Douarnenez, Concarneau, Quiberon and Nantes. Brittany produces two-thirds of the national total.

Algae. – Algae, a raw material for the chemical industry (iodine, soda, alginates, etc.), and above all ordinary seaweed, have for long been harvested and used as fertilizers.

The Bretons also use shelly sand from beaches, sea mud and maërl (sand from banks containing calcified algae, found around Paimpol) to improve the soil. According to a local saying these sands change "gorse to clover and rye grass to wheat"; they can be used either in their natural form or as a processed product.

Vast plants (the largest is at Pleubian) process seaweed and alginates which are found in a diverse range of products such as foodstuffs (biscuits), cosmetics and plastics. Other plants along the coast manufacture iodine and soda, refine marl and process fish offal for use in fertilizers, animal feed and pharmaceutical products.

(Michel Guillard/Scope)

Naval dockyards. – Half of all the ships built in France come from the Breton yards: the Atlantic Dockyard at St-Nazaire for merchant vessels and Brest and Lorient Dockyards for ships for the French Navy.

The Golden Belt. – In addition to the sea-related activities, market gardening in the sheltered rich, alluvial coastal areas between St-Malo and the Loire, which is known as the Golden Belt (Ceinture Dorée), makes an essential contribution to the Breton economy. Potatoes, cauliflowers, artichokes, peas, French beans, carrots, cabbage, onions and garlic are all grown in the open fields. Part of the production supplies the large consumer markets, notably the Paris region, and the rest is sent to the local canneries and exported to Great Britain.

The Argoat

Although less picturesque than the Armor, the Breton interior or "Argoat" is very attractive.

The Plateaux. – Plains cover most of the country, although you must not expect to find great expanses extending without a break, to far horizons. Instead you cross a series of rises without any clear idea of their general direction. Between these uplands flow deeply sunken rivers with brown, rushing waters. The land is usually cut up into a chequerboard pattern by banks and dry stone walls which form the boundaries of fields and pastures. Pollarded oaks grow on most of the banks and it is these which make the countryside, seen from a distance, seem heavily wooded.

The mountains. – Mountains! The word rather overpowers the Breton hills. But this is what the coast dwellers call the central part of Brittany. It must be said that in many places the barrenness and loneliness of the heights, the saw-toothed crests contrasting with the undulating plains that they overshadow and the strong wind give an impression of high altitude. In clear weather a vast expanse can be seen from Trévezel Rock (384m - 1229ft), the Ménez-Hom (330m - 1056ft) and the Menez Bré (302m - 966ft).
The rivers flowing down from the hills to the Channel or the Atlantic offer pretty scenery. The fresh vegetation in their valleys contrasts with the barren lands of the heights.

Forests and moors. – Brittany once had immense forests of oak and beech. Successive generations since the Romans have wielded the axe in these woods, and there are now only scattered strips of woodland: the forests of Paimpont, Loudéac, Huelgoat, Quénécan, etc. These woodlands are very hilly and intersected by gorges, ravines and tumbled rocks. A perfect example of this type of country is to be seen at Huelgoat. Unfortunately most of the woodlands would appear to be neglected and brushwood predominates. The fine forests are rare and these Breton woodlands owe their picturesque quality more to their relief than to their trees.
Untilled moors succeeded the forests. Near the summits they still form great empty stretches whose gloom is relieved for a time only when the gorse wears its golden cloak and the heather spreads a purple carpet on the hills. Elsewhere, moors have yielded to the efforts of the peasants and have become tilled fields. Such are Lanvaux Moors, where the visitor, misled by the name and expecting rough ground, finds reclaimed land, rich in promise for the future.

Economic activity. – For a long time the Argoat was essentially an agricultural and stock rearing region but a great stimulus has been given to its industrial development as a result of a decentralization policy adopted by many large firms.

Agriculture. – Although Brittany is said to be a harsh and poor land, it is, nevertheless, one of France's foremost agricultural regions.
Nearly half the land under cultivation is given over to cereal production together with fodder crops (cabbage, sugarbeet).
There are still many apple orchards in Ille-et-Vilaine and in the south of the Finistère but a certain decline is noticeable in Morbihan. The apples are used in the making of cider, apple juice and concentrate.

Stock rearing. – The Argoat is especially known for its dairy cattle, which produce about 20 per cent of French dairy products. There are many large dairies in Ille-et-Vilaine and Finistère. The subsistence farm style of pig rearing has been replaced by intensive rearing units. The Argoat is now an important pig producing region which meets local demands and supplies national markets and the many firms which produce fresh, canned or salted pig meat products.
Poultry farming is suitable to small holdings and has been increasingly successful, meeting a third of national requirements. The Côtes-du-Nord which has a poultry research centre at Ploufragan, and the Finistère head the list in the production of chickens and eggs.

Industry. – It is particularly successful and active in central Brittany. At Rennes and in the surrounding area there are two Citroën factories, printing plants, factories manufacturing packaging materials (also in Finistère), building materials, hosiery, and military workshops. Redon manufactures gas lighters, Châteaubriand nearly one third of all French ploughs, Fougères shoes and glass, Dinan hosiery. Cigarette paper is made at Scaer, Quimperlé and Ergué-Gaberic.
Though there are few mining industries, they have maintained a certain importance. The most noteworthy are the kaolin works and slate quarries at Châteaulin and Carhaix-Plouguer, the tin mine at St-Renan (Finistère), the copper, lead and zinc deposits in the Noires Mountains, titanium in the south of the Ille-et-Vilaine, and the granite quarries of which the best known is at Kersanton near Logonna (Finistère) – its stone was much used in Breton statuary.

The Michelin Map of Greece no 980
at a scale of 1:700 000 has
all the practical information needed to make driving a pleasure.

HISTORICAL FACTS

BC	**Ancient Armor**
6C	The Celts arrive in the peninsula and name it Armor (country of the sea). A little known people who set up many megaliths were there before them.
56	Caesar destroys the fleet of the Veneti, the most powerful tribe in Armor *(details p 137)*, and conquers the whole country.
AD	For four centuries Roman civilization does its work. Then the barbarian invasions wreck Armor, which returns almost to savagery.

Armor becomes Brittany

460	Arrival of the Celts from Britain, driven from their homes by the Angles and Saxons. Immigration continues for two centuries. These colonists revive and convert Armor and give it a new name, Little Britain, later shortened to Brittany. The Breton people make saints of their religious leaders, who become the patrons of many towns in the peninsula *(details p 25)*. The political state, made up of innumerable parishes, remains anarchic.
799	Charlemagne subjugates all Brittany.

The Duchy of Brittany

826	Louis the Pious makes Nominoé, a noble of Vannes, Duke of Brittany *(p 213)*.
845	Nominoé throws off Frankish suzerainty by defeating Charles the Bald, near Redon. He brings all of Brittany under his authority and founds an independent ducal dynasty which lasts for more than a century.
851	Erispoë, son of Nominoé, takes the title, King of Brittany. He was later assassinated by his cousin Salomon who reigned from 857.
874	Assassination of Salomon (the Great, or St Salomon). During his reign the kingdom of Brittany reached its zenith embracing both Anjou and Cotentin.
919	Great Norman invasion. Rapine and pillage.
939	King Alain Barbe-Torte drives out the last Normans.
952	Death of Alain, the last King of Brittany. In the fortresses built all over the country to resist the Normans, the nobles defy the successors of Barbe-Torte. There follows a period of disorder and poverty which lasts until nearly the end of the 14C.
1066	William the Conqueror lands in England.
1215	Magna Carta.
1337	Start of the Hundred Years War ending in 1453.
1341	The War of Succession begins at the death of Duke Jean III. His niece, Jeanne de Penthièvre, wife of Charles de Blois, supported by the French, and her brother Jean of Montfort, ally of the English, contend for the Duchy.
1351	Battle of the Thirty *(details p 118)*.
1364	Charles of Blois, though aided by Du Guesclin *(p 24)*, is defeated and killed at Auray *(details p 52)*. Brittany emerges ruined from this war.

The Montforts

1364-1468	The Dukes of the House of Montfort restore the country. This is the most brilliant period of its history. The arts reach their highest development. The dukes are the real sovereigns and pay homage only in theory to the King of France. Constable de Richemont *(p 215)*, the companion in arms to Joan of Arc succeeded his brother in 1457 as Duke of Brittany.
1488	Duke François II, who has entered into the federal coalition against the Regent of France, Anne de Beaujeu, is defeated at St-Aubin-du-Cormier and dies. His daughter, Anne of Brittany, succeeds him.

Reunion of Brittany with France

1491	Anne of Brittany marries Charles VIII *(details p 178)* but remains Duchess and sovereign of Brittany.
1492	Christopher Columbus discovers America.
1498	Charles VIII dies accidentally. Anne returns to her Duchy.
1499	Anne again becomes Queen of France by marrying Louis XII, who had hastily repudiated his first wife. The Duchy remains distinct from the Crown *(details p 213)*.
1514	Anne of Brittany dies. Her daughter, Claude of France, inherits the Duchy. She marries François of Angoulême, the future François I.
1532	Claude cedes her Duchy to the Crown. François I has this permanent reunion of Brittany with France ratified by the Parliament at Vannes.

(Museum of Brittany, Rennes)

Anne of Brittany

French Brittany

1534	Jacques Cartier discovers the St Lawrence estuary *(details p 193).*
1588	Brittany rebels against its governor, the Duke of Mercœur, who wants to profit by the troubles of the League to seize the province. Bandits like the famous La Fontenelle ravage the country *(details p 93).*
1598	By the Edict of Nantes, Henri IV puts an end to religious strife *(details p 142).*
1675	The "Stamped Paper" revolt *(details p 164)* which develops into a peasants' rising.
1711	Duguay-Trouin *(details p 193)* takes Rio de Janeiro.
1764	The Rennes Parliament and its Public Prosecutor, La Chalotais, oppose Governor Aiguillon *(p 179).* The authority of the Crown is much weakened. The Revolution is near.
1765	Arrival on Belle-Ile of many Canadian families of French origin from Nova Scotia *(p 56).*
1773	Birth of Surcouf, the Breton pirate *(p 193).*
1776	American Declaration of Independence.

(St-Malo Museum)

Surcouf

1789	The Bretons welcome the Revolution with enthusiasm.
1793	Carrier executes thousands by drowning in the Loire near Nantes *(details p 142).*
1793-1804	The Laws against the priests and the mass levies give rise to the *Chouannerie* (revolt of Breton Royalists).
1795	A landing by Royalist exiles is defeated at Quiberon *(details p 166).*
1804	Cadoudal *(details p 52),* who tried to revive the *Chouannerie,* is executed.
1826	René Laënnec *(p 168)* the great physician died.
1832	Another attempted revolt, organized by the Duchess de Berry, fails *(details p 142).* This was the last rising.
1861	Start of American Civil War.
1909	Strikes and riots among the Concarneau cannery workers.
1914-18	Brittany pays a heavy toll in loss of life during the First World War.

Brittany today

1927-28	The Morbihan aviator Le Brix, accompanied by Costes, are the first to fly round the world.
1940	The islanders of Sein *(p 205)* are the first to rally to General de Gaulle's call.
1942	An Anglo-Canadian commando raids the St-Nazaire submarine base *(p 199).*
1944-45	The end of the German Occupation period witnesses a wake of destruction, especially at Brest, Lorient, St-Nazaire.
1951	Formation of the organization Comité d'Études et de Liaison des Intérêts Bretons (CELIB) to safeguard Breton interests, is an initial step towards the rejuvenation of the local economy.
1962	First transatlantic transmission by satellite of a television programme by the station at Pleumeur-Bodou *(p 156).*
1966	The opening of the Rance tidal power scheme *(p 175)* and the Arrée Mountains nuclear station near Brennilis.
1967	The *Torrey Canyon* disaster off the English coast, causes great oil slicks to hit the beaches of Brittany.
1969	Creation of the Armorique Regional Nature Park *(p 49).*
1975	First search for oil in the Iroise Sea off the Finistère coast.
1978	Establishment of a charter and council to safeguard the Breton cultural heritage. *Amoco Cadiz* oil spill on Brittany beaches.

Green Tourist Guides.

Scenery, Buildings,
Scenic routes,
Geography, Economy,
History, Art,
Touring programmes
Plans of towns and buildings

Guides for your holidays

Principal Campaigns of Du Guesclin

Bertrand Du Guesclin, born at La Motte-Broons Castle, near Dinan, was one of France's greatest warriors.

Entering the King's service (in 1356), he was dubbed knight at Montmuran Castle *(p 113)*, on the capture of Rennes. Subsequent victories brought further titles and honours: Governor of Pontorson (1360), Count of Longueville (1364), Duke of Molina and Transtamarre (1366), King of Granada (1369), High Constable of France (1370). His campaigns, waged mostly against the English and their allies had brought about considerable expansion of the crown lands by his death in 1380 *(p 86)*.

(Museum of Brittany, Rennes)
Du Guesclin

①	1356	Capture of Rennes.
②	1359	Liberation of Dinan.
③	1363	Capture of Breton towns. From St-Pol Du Guesclin sends ships against the English.
④	1364	Capture of Mantes and Meulan.
⑤	—	(May 16) Victory of Cocherel.
⑥	—	(Sept. 29) Defeat of Auray. Du Guesclin made prisoner.
⑦	1366	"The Great Companies", commanded by Du Guesclin, march into Spain. A series of victories over Peter the Cruel and the English brings the French to Seville.
	1367	(April 3) Defeat of Najera: Du Guesclin made prisoner and taken to Bordeaux.
	1369	(Jan. 17) Du Guesclin ransomed and returns to Spain.
	—	(March) Siege of Montiel Castle; Peter the Cruel killed; Du Guesclin returns to France.
⑧	1370	Capture of Moissac and liberation of Périgord.
⑨		Liberation of Le Mans. Victory of Pontvallain. Liberation of Maine and Anjou.
⑩		Capture of Bressuire.
⑪		Defeat of Pont de Juigné. Du Guesclin made prisoner.
⑫	1371	Capture of Briouze.
⑬	1372	Victory of Mortain. The Norman Bocage is freed.
⑭	1372-1373	Capture of towns in Poitou, Saintonge and Angoumois.
⑮	1373	All Brittany conquered except Brest and Derval.
⑯	1374	Capture of St-Sauveur-le-Vicomte.
⑰	1378	All Normandy conquered except Cherbourg.
⑱	1380	(June 27) Capture of Chaliers.
⑲	—	(July 13-14) Capture of Châteauneuf-de-Randon. Death of Du Guesclin.

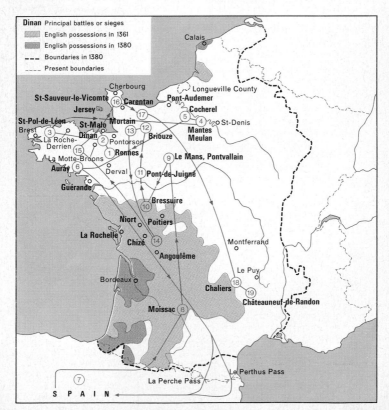

(From documents supplied by the Museum of French Monuments at the Palais de Chaillot, Paris)

TRADITIONS AND FOLKLORE

A LAND OF LEGENDS

The Breton soul has always been inclined to the dreamy, the fantastic and the supernatural. This explains the astonishing abundance and persistence of legends in the Armor country.

The Round Table. – After the death of Christ, Joseph of Arimathea, one of His disciples, left Palestine, carrying away a few drops of the divine blood in the cup from which the Redeemer drank during the Last Supper. He landed in Britain according to some legends, in Brittany according to others, lived for some time in the forest of Brocéliande (now the forest of Paimpont) before vanishing without trace. The precious cup was lost.
In the 6C King Arthur and fifty knights set out to find it. For them it was the Holy Grail, which only a warrior whose heart was pure could win. Percival (Wagner's Parsifal) was such a man. In the Middle Ages the search for the Grail gave rise to the endless stories of adventure which formed the Cycle of the Round Table. The most famous version of the tale in English being, of course, Sir Thomas Malory's *Morte d'Arthur* (1471) and Alfred Lord Tennyson's *Idylls of the King* (1859).

Merlin and Viviane. – One of King Arthur's companions, Merlin the sorcerer, came to the forest of Brocéliande to live there in seclusion. But he met the fairy Viviane, and love inflamed them both. To make sure of keeping Merlin, Viviane enclosed him in a magic circle. It would have been easy for him to escape, but he joyfully accepted this romantic captivity for ever.

Tristan and Isolde. – Tristan, Prince of Lyonesse, sent to Ireland by his Uncle Mark, King of Cornouaille, brought back from Ireland Isolde, whom Mark was to marry. On board their ship Tristan and Isolde accidentally drank a philtre which was intended to bind Isolde to her husband in eternal love. Passion stronger than duty sprang up in both their hearts. There are several versions of the end: sometimes Tristan is slain by Mark, furious at his betrayal; sometimes he marries and dies in his castle in Brittany. But Isolde always follows him to the grave. Wagner's opera has made the love story famous.

The town of Is. – At the time of good **King Gradlon**, about the 6C, Is was the capital of Cornouaille; finds claimed as belonging to Is have been discovered in Trépassés and Douarnenez Bays and off Penmarch Peninsula. The town was so beautiful that, according to a Breton tradition, the inhabitants of Lutetia, seeking a name for their own proud city, chose Par-is ("like Is"), whence the name: Paris. The town was protected from the sea by a dyke, opened by locks to which the King always carried the golden key.
His daughter, the beautiful Dahut, also called Ahès, who led a dissolute life, met the Devil in the form of an attractive young man. To test her love he asked her to open the sea gate. Dahut stole the key while the King was asleep, and soon the sea rushed into the town. King Gradlon fled on horseback, with his daughter on the crupper. But the waves pursued him and were about to swallow him up. At this moment a celestial voice ordered him, if he would be saved, to throw the demon who was riding behind him into the sea. With aching heart the King obeyed and the sea withdrew at once, but Is was destroyed.
For his new capital Gradlon chose Quimper; this is why his statue stands between the two towers of the cathedral. He ended his days in the odour of sanctity, guided and sustained by St Corentine. As for Dahut, she turned into the mermaid, who is known as Marie-Morgane and, by her beauty, still lures sailors to the bottom of the sea. Everything will stay exactly as it is until the Good Friday when Mass is celebrated in one of the churches of the drowned city. Then Is will cease to be accursed and Morgane will no longer be a siren.

THE SAINTS OF BRITTANY

Brittany, with its magicians, spirits, fairies and demons – both masculine and feminine – has also known more haloes than any other part of France. Its saints are counted by hundreds; their painted wooden statues adorn chapels and churches. Truth to tell, those (St Yves for example) who were canonized by the Vatican authorities can be counted on one's fingers. The most "official" among them were simply recognized by the bishops; the people adopted others. Their fame goes no farther than the borders of the province, or even the limits of the villages where they are venerated. (For the purposes of this guide the names of saints of purely local standing have been left in their original form).

Patrons of towns. – The Celtic religious leaders who landed from Britain in the 5C *(p 22: Historical Facts)* became the patron saints of the seven former bishoprics: St-Malo, St-Brieuc, St-Pol-de-Léon, Dol (St-Samson), Tréguier (St Tugdual), Quimper (St Corentine) and Vannes (St Patern). The same applies to many other localities: St-Efflam, St-Lunaire, St-Briac, St-Gildas, etc.
Until the 16C, tradition demanded that every Breton should make a pilgrimage to the cathedrals at least once in his life; this was called the Tro Breiz (tour of Brittany). Whoever failed to observe this rite was bound to make the journey after his death, when he could cover only the length of his coffin every seven years!

The "healing saints". – The Bretons have always been on trustful, friendly and even familiar terms with their saints.
There are saints who are invoked on all occasions. Innumerable others are invoked against specified ailments: rheumatism, baldness, etc. For centuries they took the place of doctors. Horses and oxen also have their appointed saints (St Cornély and St Herbot).

Saint Yves. – "Monsieur Saint Yves" is the most popular saint in Brittany. He is the righter of all wrongs: whoever suffers injustice turns to him. He is the comfort of the poor.
Yves Helori, the son of a country gentleman, was born at Minihy-Tréguier in 1253. When quite young he had a taste for the ascetic life. He came to Paris to study law, and unravelled its subtleties for thirteen years. On his return to Brittany he became a priest, and at the bishop's palace of Tréguier acted as a magistrate in one court and as an advocate in others.

He won unheard-of popularity by his spirit of justice and conciliation, the rapidity of his judgments and the brevity of his pleas. One day a *bourgeois* summoned before him a beggar who came every day to the grating of his kitchen to enjoy the smell of cooking. Yves took a coin, made it ring on the bench and dismissed the plaintiff, saying: "The sound has paid for the smell."

In order not to "cut out" the barristers Yves always chose the most wretched cases, and thus became known as the "poor man's counsel". In fact, he was a precursor of free legal aid. He was canonized in 1347.

As the patron saint of advocates and men of law, his cult has spread all over Europe and even to America. And within the last few years delegations of barristers from many foreign countries have joined the unceasing stream of pilgrims who attend the blessing of the poor *(pardon des pauvres)* at Tréguier *(p 226)*.

The calendar saints. – Mystical Brittany has made a place among its innumerable saints for the great figures of the Church.

Statues of the Apostles line church porches and stand on Calvaries; St Michael is the patron of high places; St James, that of sailors; St Fiacre of gardeners. St Barbara, who is invoked in stormy weather, is the patroness of corporations which handle explosives (her father, who had her martyred, was killed by lightning). St Apolline protects people from toothache, and many others have an established cult. The Virgin Mary is the most fervently invoked of the saints.

Saint Anne. – The cult of Saint Anne was brought to western Europe by those returning from the Crusades. Her eager adoption by the Bretons was in part due to the popularity of the Duchess, Anne of Brittany and her later renown.

Patroness of Brittany and mother of the Virgin Mary, Saint Anne was originally invoked for a good harvest.

The most famous *pardon* in Brittany, that of Ste-Anne-d'Auray, is dedicated to her, so is the very important one of Ste-Anne-la-Palud. These colourful events which express the Breton religious fervour have given rise to the local saying, "Whether dead or alive, every Breton goes at least once to Saint-Anne."

A doubtful legend makes St Anne a Cornouaille woman of royal blood who was taken to Nazareth by angels to save her from her husband's brutality. After having given birth to the Virgin Mary she returned to Brittany and lived there till her death. It was Jesus who, when visiting his grandmother, called forth the sacred spring of Ste-Anne-la-Palud.

The statues usually portray her alone or teaching Mary to read, very often wearing a green cloak symbolizing hope for the world.

COSTUMES AND HEAD-DRESSES

Costumes. – Brittany possesses costumes of surprising richness and variety. The fine clothes passed down from one generation to another were to be seen at every family festivity. It was customary for a girl at her marriage to acquire a costly and magnificent outfit that would last many years. Today the traditional costumes are only brought out on great occasions such as *pardons*, First Communions, weddings, baptisms and sometimes High Mass on feast days, and even then few young women are to be seen in them.

In spite of attempts to modernize the dress, and the efforts of regional societies over the last few years – and they have had some success – to make the young appreciate the old finery, the tourist who travels quickly through Brittany is not likely to see many of the rich, traditional dresses made familiar by picture postcards and books on the subject.

Here and there a few old men have remained faithful to their beribboned felt hats, and more rarely, to their embroidered waistcoats. The costume for the women is a plain black dress.

(Dupont/Explorer)

Bigoudènes

The women's traditional costumes attract above all by the brilliance of their aprons which reveal how well off the family are by the richness of their decoration. The aprons are made of satin or velvet, are brocaded or embroidered or are edged with lace and are of every size and shape: at Quimper they have no bib, at Pont-Aven they have a small one, while at Lorient the bib reaches to the shoulders.

Ceremonial dresses are usually black and are often ornamented with bands of velvet. The finest examples are those of Quimper which are adorned with their many coloured embroideries.

Head-dresses. – The most original feature of the Breton costume is the *coiffe* or head-dress, now worn mostly in Finistère and Morbihan.

One of the most attractive is the *coiffe* of **Pont-Aven** which has as an accessory a great starched lace collar.

The **Bigoudène** *coiffe* from the **Pont-l'Abbé** area is one of the most curious: it used to be quite small but has since 1930 become huge.

In **Quimper** the *coiffe* is much smaller and is worn on the crown of the head; in **Plougastel**, where tradition is still strong, the *coiffe* has a mediaeval appearance with ribbons tied on the side *(illustration p 218).*

In **Tréguier** the plainest of materials is allied to the most original of shapes. The **Douarnenez** *coiffe* is small and fits tightly round the bun on the back of the head, that of **Auray** shades the forehead and that of **Huelgoat** is almost like a lace hair-net.

In order to get a complete picture of the richness and variety of Breton costume the tourist should visit the museums of Quimper, Guérande, Rennes, Dinan, etc., all of which have fine collections of traditional dress.

(Hervé Coataner/Scope)
Cape Sizun

◄ *(Christiane Olivier, Nice)*
Pont-Aven

THE PARDONS

The Breton *pardons* are above all a manifestation of the religious fervour of the people. They take place in the churches and chapels, sometimes consecrated by the tradition of a thousand years. There the faithful come to seek forgiveness for their sins, to fulfil a vow or to beg for grace.

The great *pardons* are most impressive, while the smaller events, though they may be less spectacular, are often more fervent. It is well worth the tourist's while to arrange his trip so that he may be present at one of them *(Principal Pardons and Festivals p 226).* It is also one of the rare occasions when he will see the old costumes, perhaps slightly modernized.

The procession, which begins in the afternoon, is the most colourful ceremony: candles, banners and statues of saints are carried by men and girls; with pilgrims singing hymns, priests, the Blessed Sacrament, and sometimes even several bishops.

After the procession, the lay festival is given free rein. As a rule this is a rather ordinary fair.

(Dupont/Explorer)
Pardon at Ste-Anne-la-Palud

EVOLUTION AND REGIONALISM

The two Brittanies. – The map below delimits **Upper Brittany** (Haute-Bretagne), or the "Gallo" country, and **Lower Brittany** (Basse-Bretagne), or the Breton-speaking country.

French is spoken in the first, French and Breton in the second. Lower Brittany has four regions, each of which has its customs and brings shades of diversity to the Breton language. These are: the district of Tréguier or Trégorrois, the district of Léon, the district of Cornouaille and the district of Vannes or Vannetais.

Apart from the language, these limits conform with tradition. It is in Lower Brittany that one is more likely to find the old customs; in Upper Brittany they have hardly left a trace. And the delimitation has not remained fixed.

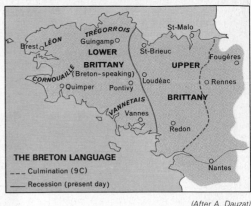

(After A. Dauzat)

The two Brittanies

The Breton language. –
From the ethnic and linguistic point of view the Bretons are nearer to the Welsh than to the French.
This is because in the 5 and 6C *(p 22)* Armorica (present day Brittany) was invaded by Britons driven from Britain (present day Great Britain) by the Anglo-Saxon invasion. Brittany was founded, and the Breton language opposed the French language, derived from Low Latin.
In the 9C the dynasty of Nominoé *(p 213)* marked the apogee of the Breton nation and the farthest advance of its language *(see map)*. The Norman invasions that followed and feudal rule harmed the unity of Brittany.
The annexation of the province to France in the 15C and the French Revolution enhanced the trend in favour of French.
An association called U.D.B. (Union for the Defence of the Breton Language), after a vigorous campaign for the optional teaching of Breton in Lower Brittany, secured this in the secondary and teachers' training schools. The University of Rennes has a chair of Celtic Language and there is a strong demand for the creation of an Institute of Celtic languages.

Breton names. – *P 4.*

Rapid development of Brittany. – Brittany changed more in the first half of the 20C than in the two previous centuries. Contacts of Breton soldiers with men from other provinces, and especially the return to their homeland of men who had held administrative or executive posts in the navy, the civil service, commerce and industry, hastened the evolution started by the tourists.
The distinctive character of customs, dress and furniture faded away. Villages no longer kept alive a mass of traditional customs and traditional beliefs. Less than half the population still know their own language.

Regionalism and Celtic Clubs. – For the past twenty years the provinces have cultivated regionalism. In Brittany a few folklore groups were active, but the movement did not spring from the soil.
Before 1939 the Bretons of Paris – who founded the first Celtic Club in 1917 – made it their business to spread an interest in Breton gatherings. At the Liberation the clubs grew; today more than 60 in Brittany revive and bring fame once more to Breton dances, music and costume. Sometimes girls, who want to look their best, wear the *coiffe* and embroidered skirt and apron. The "ringers" (bagpipe and bombard players), who numbered sixty-three in 1939, are approximately now 2500 and are in great demand at parties, weddings, festivals and marches.
The Lorient Interceltic Festival and the folk festivals give opportunities to bring these groups together and to make them compete and give displays greatly enjoyed by those who see them.
The vitality of clubs like these is being proved in every part of France and overseas. There are ninety-four associations in Paris and its environs. The Bretons of New York elect a "Duchess Anne" every year.

Make up your own itineraries

– *The map on pages 5 to 8 gives a general view of tourist regions, the main towns, individual sights and recommended routes in the guide.*

– *The above are described under their own name in alphabetical order (p 43) or are incorporated in the excursions radiating from a nearby town or tourist centre.*

– *In addition the Michelin Maps nos 58, 59, 63 and 230 show scenic routes, places of interest, viewpoints, rivers, forests...*

LEARNING AND LITERATURE IN BRITTANY

The Middle Ages and the Renaissance. – Learning was centred in the monasteries; the language used was Latin; the subjects studied were concerned, for the most part, with the history of the Church or of Brittany, moral philosophy and the lives of the saints. A life of St Guénolé was written by Wurdistein, Abbot of Landévennec, in the 9C and a life of St Pol by Wromonoc, a monk from the same abbey.

Authors are rarely known by name, but there are some exceptions such as, in the 12C: The philosopher **Peter Abelard,** one of the most brilliant figures of the Middle Ages, who was born at Pallet near Nantes and became Abbot of St-Gildas-de-Rhuys *(p 191).* He wrote an account of the hardships he endured.

Etienne de Fougères, who was created bishop of Rennes in 1168 and whose *Livre des manières* (Book of Manners) gave him free rein to lecture his contemporaries on moral issues.

Guillaume Le Breton, poet and historian at the court of Philippe-Auguste whose reign he patriotically eulogised.

Students from Brittany first went to the University in Paris, and then to Nantes when that establishment was founded in the 15C; schools were established to supplement the teaching provided by the churches and monasteries in out of the way parishes and yet it is not until the 15 and 16C that one begins to hear of names such as those of the historians Pierre Le Baud, Alain Bouchard and Bertrand d'Argentré, of the poet Meschinot from Nantes who wrote a series of ballads entitled *Les lunettes des princes* (the Princes' Spectacles), which became well known in his own time, of Noël du Fail, Councillor of the Rennes Parliament who depicted the world around him so well and of the Dominican, Albert Legrand, who wrote the *Vie des saints de la Bretagne armoricaine* (Life of the Saints of Armorican Brittany).

17 and 18C. – The best known figures of the 17 and 18C are Mme de Sévigné – Breton by marriage – who addressed many of her letters from her Château des Rochers *(p 184)* and wrote vivid descriptions of Rennes, Vitré, Vannes and Port-Louis –, **Lesage,** the witty author of *Gil Blas* who came from Vannes, and Duclos, moralist and historian who was Mayor of Dinan.

There was also Fréron *(p 168)* who became known only through his disputes with Voltaire and who was the director of a literary journal published in Paris and, finally, the Benedictines, Dom Lobineau and Dom Morice, historians of Brittany.

The Romantics and Contemporary Writers. – Three figures dominated literature in the 19C in Brittany:

François-René de Chateaubriand *(p 193)* who had an immense influence on French literature. The effect he had over his contemporaries arose from his sensitivity, his passionate eloquence, his fertile imagination, all of which were displayed with brilliant and powerful style; in his *Mémoires D'Outre-Tombe* (Beyond the Tomb) he recounts his childhood at St-Malo and his youth at Combourg Castle.

Lamennais *(p 193),* fervent apologist of theocracy who became a convinced democrat, reflects in his philosophical works the evolution of his thought.

Ernest Renan *(p 207),* philologist, historian and philosopher was a thinker who maintained that he had faith only in science. He wrote many books in an easy and brilliant prose and in one, *Souvenirs d'enfance et de jeunesse* (Recollections of Childhood and Youth), described his native Brittany.

(Bulloz)

Chateaubriand by Girodet
(St-Malo Museum)

Less important but nevertheless true interpreters of the native soil and turn of mind of Brittany are the sensitive poet **Auguste Brizeux,** author of *Marie* and the poems *Telen Arvor;* Emile Souvestre who wrote such stories as *Les derniers bretons* (The Last Bretons); Hersart de la Villemarqué who published a collection of poems based on popular folk songs; Frédéric Le Guyader, a poet who sang the praises of cider; **Anatole Le Braz** the folklorist; **Charles Le Goffic** the novelist; and **Théodore Botrel** the song writer.

Others who came from Brittany and should be noted though they did not write in praise of their native province are: the Symbolist poets, Villiers-de-l'Isle-Adam and Tristan Corbière; the novelists, Paul Féval, author of *Bossu;* **Jules Verne,** precursor of modern scientific discoveries; Zénaïde Fleuriot whom young people still read; Louis Hémon who became known through his *Maria Chapdelaine,* and finally **Pierre Loti** with his *Pêcheur d'Islande* and *Mon frère Yves.*

Alphonse de Chateaubriant born in Rennes in 1877, depicts the Brière, **Jean-Pierre Calloch** native of the Groix Island *(p 105),* a lyrical poet writes in the Breton language. The Surrealist poet **Saint-Pol-Roux,** Marseilles born but undying lover of Brittany, wrote works touched with Romanticism, *Les Féeries intérieures.* René-Guy Cadou (1920-1951), also a poet, sang praise of nature.

Today **Henri Queffélec** is one of the authors who have most lauded Brittany in his *Le recteur de l'île de Sein, Un homme d'Ouessant, Au bout du monde, Franche et Secrète Bretagne* and *Promenades en Bretagne.*

Another contemporary author Pierre Jakez Hélias recounts vividly in the *Cheval d'Orgueil* the traditions of the Pont-l'Abbé region (Claude Chabrol made a memorable film from the work).

Unfortunately few Breton authors have been translated into English.

ABC OF ARCHITECTURE

To assist readers unfamiliar with the terminology employed in architecture, we describe below the most commonly used terms, which we hope will make their visits to ecclesiastical, military and civil buildings more interesting.

Ecclesiastical architecture

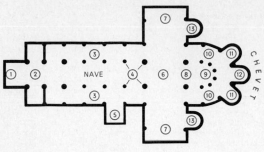

illustration I

Ground plan. – The more usual Catholic form is based on the outline of a cross with the two arms of the cross forming the transept: ① Porch – ② Narthex – ③ Side aisles (sometimes double) – ④ Bay (transverse section of the nave between 2 pillars) – ⑤ Side chapel (often predates the church) – ⑥ Transept crossing – ⑦ Arms of the transept, sometimes with a side doorway – ⑧ Chancel, nearly always facing east towards Jerusalem; the chancel often vast in size was reserved for the monks in abbatial churches – ⑨ High altar – ⑩ Ambulatory: in pilgrimage churches the aisles were extended round the chancel, forming the ambulatory, to allow the faithful to file past the relics – ⑪ Radiating or apsidal chapel – ⑫ Axial chapel. In churches which are not dedicated to the Virgin this chapel, in the main axis of the building is often consecrated to the Virgin (Lady Chapel) – ⑬ Transept chapel.

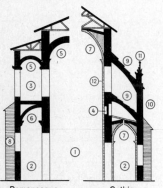

Romanesque   Gothic

◄ illustration II

Cross-section: ① Nave – ② Aisle – ③ Tribune or Gallery – ④ Triforium – ⑤ Barrel vaulting – ⑥ Semicircular barrel vaulting – ⑦ Ogive vaulting – ⑧ Buttress – ⑨ Flying buttress – ⑩ Pier of a flying buttress – ⑪ Pinnacle – ⑫ Clerestory windows.

illustration III ►

Gothic cathedral: ① Porch – ② Gallery – ③ Rose window – ④ Belfry – sometimes with a spire – ⑤ Gargoyle acting as a waterspout for the roof gutter – ⑥ Buttress – ⑦ Pier of a flying buttress (abutment) – ⑧ Flight or span of flying buttress – ⑨ Double-course flying buttress – ⑩ Pinnacle – ⑪ Side chapel – ⑫ Radiating or apsidal chapel – ⑬ Clerestory windows – ⑭ Side doorway – ⑮ Gable – ⑯ Pinnacle – ⑰ Spire over the transept crossing.

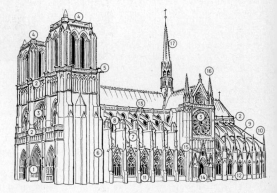

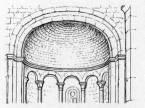

illustration IV	illustration V
Groined vaulting:	**Oven vaulting**
① Main arch – ② Groin	termination of a barrel
③ Transverse arch	vaulted nave

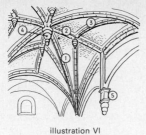

illustration VI

Lierne and tierceron vaulting:
① Diagonal – ② Lierne
③ Tierceron – ④ Pendant
⑤ Corbel

illustration VII

Quadripartite vaulting:
① Diagonal – ② Transverse
③ Stringer – ④ Flying buttress
⑤ Keystone

▼ illustration VIII

Doorway: ① Archivolt. Depending on the architectural style of the building this can be rounded, pointed, basket-handled, accoladed or even adorned by a gable – ② Arching, covings. Recessed arches or orders form the archivolt – ③ Tympanum – ④ Lintel – ⑤ Archshafts – ⑥ Embrasures. Arch shafts, splaying sometimes adorned with statues or columns – ⑦ Pier (often adorned by a statue) – ⑧ Hinges and other ironwork.

illustration IX ▶

Arches and pillars: ① Ribs or ribbed vaulting – ② Abacus – ③ Capital – ④ Shaft – ⑤ Base – ⑥ Engaged column – ⑦ Pier of arch wall – ⑧ Lintel – ⑨ Discharging or relieving arch – ⑩ Frieze.

Military architecture

illustration X

Fortified enclosure: ① Hoarding (projecting timber gallery) – ② Machicolations (corbelled crenellations) – ③ Barbican – ④ Keep or donjon – ⑤ Covered watchpath – ⑥ Curtain wall – ⑦ Outer curtain wall – ⑧ Postern.

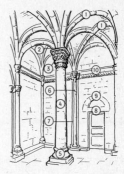

illustration XI

Towers and curtain-walls: ① Hoarding – ② Crenellations – ③ Merlon – ④ Loophole or arrow slit – ⑤ Curtain wall – ⑥ Bridge or drawbridge.

◀ illustration XII

Fortified gatehouse: ① Machicolations – ② Watch turrets or bartizan – ③ Slots for the arms of the drawbridge – ④ Postern.

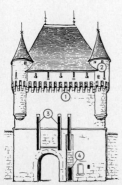

illustration XIII ▶

Star fortress: ① Entrance – ② Drawbridge – ③ Glacis – ④ Ravelin or half-moon – ⑤ Moat – ⑥ Bastion – ⑦ Watch turret – ⑧ Town – ⑨ Assembly area.

ARCHITECTURAL TERMS USED IN THE GUIDE

Aisle: illustration I.

Ambulatory: illustration I.

Apse

Apsidal chapel: illustration I.

Archivolt: illustration VIII.

Axial or **Lady Chapel:** illustration I.

Bailey: open space or court of stone built castle.

Barrel vaulting: illustration II.

Basket handled arch: depressed arch common to late Medieval and Renaissance architecture.

Bay: illustration I.

Bracket: small supporting piece of stone or timber to carry a beam or cornice.

Buttress: illustration II.

Capital: illustration IX.

Chevet: French term for the east end of a church; illustration I.

Coffered ceiling: vault or ceiling decorated with sunken panels.

Conical roof: sometimes pepperpot roof.

Corbel: see bracket.

Cradle vaulting: see barrel vaulting.

Credence: side table, shelf or niche for eucharistic elements.

Crypt: underground chamber or chapel.

Curtain wall: illustration XI.

Depressed arch: three centred arch sometimes called a basket handled arch.

Diagonal ribs: illustration VII.

Dome: illustrations XIV and XV.

Flamboyant: latest phase (15C) of French Gothic architecture; name taken from the undulating (flame-like) lines of the window tracery.

Fresco: mural paintings executed on wet plaster.

Gable: illustration III.

Gallery: illustration II.

Gargoyle: illustration III.

Glory: luminous nimbus surrounding the body; mandorla an almond shaped glory from the Italian *mandorla* meaning almond.

Groined vaulting: illustration IV.

Hammerbeam: illustration XVII.

High relief: haut-relief.

Jetty: overhanging upper storey.

Keep or **donjon:** illustration X.

Keystone: middle and topmost stone in an arch or vault.

Lintel: illustrations VIII and IX.

Loophole or **arrow slit:** illustration XI.

Low relief: bas relief.

Machicolations: illustration X.

Mandorla: see Glory.

Misericord: illustration XIX.

Moat: generally water-filled.

Modillion: small console supporting a cornice.

Overhang: see jetty.

Parapet wall: see watchpath; illustration X.

Parclose screen: screen separating a chapel or the choir from the rest of the church.

Parish close: p 37.

Pendant: illustration VII.

Pepperpot roof: see conical roof.

Pier: illustration VIII.

Pietà: Italian term designating the Virgin Mary with the dead Christ on her knees.

Pilaster: engaged rectangular column.

Pilaster strip: decorative feature characteristic of Romanesque architecture in Lombardy consisting of shallow projecting pilasters and blind arcading.

Pinnacle: illustrations II and III.

Piscina: basin for washing the sacred vessels.

Pointed arch: illustrations VI and VII.

Postern: illustrations X and XII.

Purlin: horizontal beams; in Brittany they are decorated with running carved ornamentation.

Recessed arches: illustration VIII.

Rood beam: sometimes tref; illustration XVIII.

Rood screen: illustration XX.

Rose window: illustration III.

Sacristy: room in a church for sacred vessels and vestments.

Semicircular arch: illustration V.

Spire: illustration III.

Squinches, dome on: illustration XIV.

Stalls: illustration XIX.

Tie-beam: beam connecting two slopes of a roof at the height of wall-plate; in Brittany tie-beams are often carved and painted into monstrous heads.

Tracery: interesting stone ribwork in the upper part of a window.

Transept: illustration I.

Transverse arch: arch separating one bay of the nave from the next; illustration IV.

Tref: see rood beam.

Triptych: three panels hinged together, chiefly used as an altarpiece.

Tunnel vaulting: see barrel vaulting.

Twinned: columns or pilasters.

Wall walk: see watchpath.

Watchpath: illustration X.

Wheel window: see rose window.

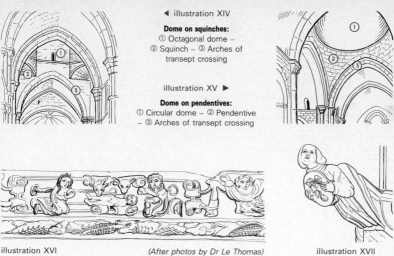

◀ illustration XIV

Dome on squinches:
① Octagonal dome –
② Squinch – ③ Arches of
transept crossing

illustration XV ▶

Dome on pendentives:
① Circular dome – ② Pendentive
– ③ Arches of transept crossing

illustration XVI

(After photos by Dr Le Thomas)

Tie-beam with carved decoration

illustration XVII

End of hammerbeam

◀ illustration XVIII

Rood-beam or tref: This supports the triumphal (chancel or rood) arch at the entrance to the chancel. The rood carries a Crucifix flanked by statues of the Virgin and St John and sometimes other personages from the Calvary.

illustration XIX ▼

Stalls: ① High back – ② Elbow rest – ③ Cheek-piece – ④ Misericord.

illustration XX

Rood-screen: This replaces the rood-beam in larger churches, and may be used for preaching and reading of the Epistles and Gospel. Many disappeared from the 17C onwards as they tended to hide the altar.

BRITTANY'S OUTSTANDING SIGHTS

Mont-St-Michel: abbey	★★★	St-Malo: ramparts

	★★	
Carnac: megaliths	Josselin: castle	Quimper: cathedral
Concarneau: walled town	Kernascléden: church	Quimperlé: church
Dol-de-Bretagne: cathedral	Locmariaquer: megaliths	Rennes: law courts
Le Folgoët: church	Locronan: church	St-Malo: castle
Fougères: castle	Nantes: castle	St-Pol-de-Léon: cathedral
La Latte Fort	N.-D.-de-Tronoën: calvary	St-Thégonnec: parish close
Gavrinis: tumulus	Pleyben: parish close	Tréguier: cathedral
Guimiliau: parish close	Plougastel-Daoulas: calvary	Vitré: castle
	Plougonven: calvary	

BRETON ART

Prehistoric monuments

The megaliths or "great stones". – More than 3 000 "great stones" are still to be found in the Carnac district alone. These monuments were set up between 5000 and 2000 BC by the little known race who preceded the Gauls. They must have had a certain degree of civilization to be able to move and set upright stones which weigh up to 350 tons. To give a simple comparison, the Luxor obelisk in the Place de la Concorde in Paris, weighs only 220 tons.

The **menhir,** or single stone was set up at a spring, near a tomb and more often on a slope. It must have had a symbolic meaning. In Brittany there are about twenty menhirs over twenty feet high; the biggest is at Locmariaquer *(p 128)*.

The **lines of menhirs** are probably the remains of religious monuments associated with the worship of the sun or moon. Most are formed by only a few menhirs set in line (many of the menhirs now isolated are the remains of more complicated groups). There are, however, especially in the Carnac area *(p 72)* fields of menhirs arranged in parallel lines running from east to west and ending in a semicircle or **cromlech.** In the Lagatjar area *(p 85)* the lines intersect. The lines of the menhirs appear also to be astronomically set, with an error of a few degrees, either by the cardinal points of the compass, or in line with sunrise and sunset at the solstices from which it has been concluded that sun worship had something to do with the purpose of the monuments.

As for the **dolmens** (the best known is the Merchants' Table at Locmariaquer – *p 128*), these are considered to have been burial chambers. Some are preceded by an ante-chamber or corridor. Originally all were buried under mounds of earth or dry stones called **tumuli** but most of them have been uncovered and now stand in the open air. The round tumuli found in the interior are of more recent date than the tumuli with closed chambers like the one of St-Michel at Carnac *(p 73)* and the former were probably built up to 1 000 BC.

Cairns are tumuli composed entirely of stones such as the ones at Barnenez *(p 53)* which dates back over 5 000 BC and at Gavrinis *(p 102)* which is not so old. Some tumuli without burial chambers probably served as boundary markers.

In northern Brittany **gallery graves** or **covered alleyways,** are formed of a double row of upright stones with flat slabs laid on them, sometimes engraved.

(Costa/Explorer)

Kerlescan Lines

Mystical tradition. – For long centuries the menhirs were connected with the mystic life of the people of Brittany. The Romans adapted some to their rites, carving pictures of their gods upon them. When the Christian religion became established, it sanctified many raised stones that people still venerated by crowning them with a cross or cutting symbols on them.

Churches and chapels

Nine cathedrals or former cathedrals, about twenty large churches and thousands of country churches and chapels make up an array of religious buildings altogether worthy of mystical Brittany.

The edifices were built by the people and designed by artists who transmitted to them an inspired faith. This faith appeared in a richness that was sometimes excessive – the exaggeratedly decorated altarpieces are an example – and a realism that was at times almost a caricature – as, for instance, the carvings on certain capitals and many church friezes, at the base of the vaulting. Only affected in part by outside influences, they always preserved their individuality and remained faithful to their own traditions.

Cathedrals. – These are inspired by the great buildings in Normandy and the Ile-de-France, although they do not rival their prototypes either in size or ornamentation. The little towns that built them had limited means. Moreover, their erection was influenced by the use of granite, a hard stone, difficult to work. The builders had to be content with rather low vaulting and simplified decoration. Financial difficulties dragged out the work for three to five centuries. Owing to this, every phase of Gothic architecture is found in the buildings, from the bare and simple arch of early times to the wild exuberance of the Flamboyant style; and the Renaissance often added the last touches.

The most interesting cathedrals are those of St-Pol-de-Léon, Tréguier, Quimper, Nantes and Dol-de-Bretagne.

The corresponding Gothic period in England, lasted until the end of the 13C and included in whole or in part the cathedrals of Wells (1174), Lincoln (chancel and transept: 1186), Salisbury (1220-58). Westminster Abbey (*c* 1250) and Durham (1242).

(Christiane Olivier, Nice)

St-Fiacre

Country churches and chapels. – In the Romanesque period (11 and 12C) Brittany was miserably poor. Buildings were few and small. Most of them were destroyed or transformed in the following centuries. It was during the Gothic and the Renaissance periods, under the Dukes and after the union with France, that the countryside saw the growth of churches and chapels.

Buildings constructed before the 16C are usually rectangular, though one also frequently sees the disconcerting T plan in which the nave, usually without side aisles, ends in a chancel flanked by often disproportionately large chapels. The chevet is flat; there are no side windows – light comes through openings pierced right at the east end of the church. Stone vaulting is rare and is nearly always replaced by wooden panelling, often painted, whose crocodile headed tie beams (cross beams dividing the roof timbers), wooden cornices at the base of the vaulting and hammer beams, are frequently carved and painted. When there is no transept a great stone arch separates the chancel from the nave.

From the 16C onwards there was a complete transformation in architectural design: it became necessary to include a transept which, inevitably, gave rise to the Latin Cross outline. The central arch disappeared; the east end became three sided; the nave was lit by windows in the aisles.

The tourist will be surprised to find in hamlets of a few houses only, and even in dreary wastes, chapels of which large places might be proud (Notre-Dame-du-Folgoët, Kernascléden, Notre-Dame-du-Crann, St-Fiacre-du-Faouët, etc.). The faith of the Breton communities has worked miracles.

Nevertheless there are many chapels where services are held only, perhaps, once a year on the occasion of a *pardon* or local festival, which leave a marked impression of spiritual as well as material neglect.

The belfries. – The Bretons take great pride in their belfries. The towers did not serve only to hold bells; they were also symbolic of both religious and civic life. In olden days the people prized them greatly, and it was a terrible punishment for them when an angry king had them laid low.

The belfries are usually square in outline and their position on the building varies considerably.

Small churches and chapels were often given the lighter and less costly gable tower in preference to a belfry. The tower was placed either on the west front gable or on the roof itself, at the intersection of the chancel and the nave.

It is reached by outside steps or by stairs in the turrets that flank it and are linked to it by a gallery.

Sometimes these little belfries become so reduced as only to be walls in gable form, pierced by arcades. This form of architecture, while fairly widespread in southwest France, is somewhat rare in Brittany.

Porches. – Breton churches have a large porch on the south side. For a long period the porch was used as a meeting place for the parish notables, who were seated on stone benches along the walls.

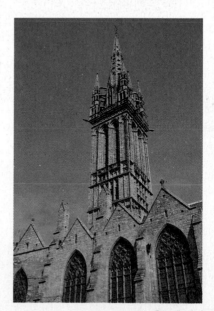

(Atlas/Parra Bordas)

St-Pol-de-Léon. – The Kreisker

A double row of Apostles often decorates the porch. They can be recognized by their attributes: St Peter holds the key of Heaven; St Paul, a book or a sword; St John, a chalice; St Thomas, a set square; St James the Elder, a pilgrim's staff. Others carry the instruments of their martyrdom: St Matthew, a hatchet; St Simon, a saw; St Andrew, a cross; St Bartholomew, a knife.

The fountains

There are innumerable fountains in Lower Brittany. Most of them are deemed to be sacred. Nearly all places where *pardons* are held have a fountain situated by the chapel where pilgrims come to drink. It is placed under the protection of a saint or of the Virgin, whose statues are set in small sanctuaries which are sometimes simple and sometimes very ornate. For great pilgrimages like that at Ste-Anne-d'Auray the spring has been arranged in modern fashion, with basins, troughs and staircases.

Many of these fountains which were once venerated are now used for domestic purposes.

Religious furnishings

Sculpture. – From the 15 to the 18C an army of Breton sculptors working in stone and especially in wood supplied the churches with countless examples of religious furnishings: pulpits, organ casings, baptistries and fonts, choir screens, rood-screens, rood-beams, altarpieces, triptychs, confessionals, niches with panels, Holy Sepulchres, statues, etc.

These works are as a general rule more highly developed than the figures carved on the Calvaries since it is much easier to work in oak, chestnut or alabaster than in granite.

(Atlas/Hureau)

St-Fiacre. – Rood-screen

Visits to the churches of Guimiliau, Lampaul-Guimiliau, St-Thégonnec, St-Fiacre at Le Faouët and Tréguier Cathedral (stalls) will give a good general idea of Breton religious furnishings.

The many **rood-screens** *(jubés)* to be found in the churches of Brittany are often of unparalleled richness. Some are cut in granite, as in the church at Le Folgoët, but most are carved in wood which makes them peculiar to Brittany. Their decoration is very varied and is different on both sides.

The rood-screen serves two purposes: it separates the chancel from the part of the church reserved for worshippers and completes the side enclosures of the chancel; the upper gallery may also be used for preaching and reading prayers. (The name derives from the first word of a prayer sung from the gallery.) The screen is usually surmounted by a large Crucifix flanked by statues of the Virgin and St John the Divine facing the congregation.

The **rood-beam** or *tref,* which supported the main arch of the church was the origin of the rood-screen. To prevent the beam from bowing it had to be supported by posts which eventually were replaced by a screen carved to a greater or lesser degree. It is to be seen mostly in the small chapels and churches where it serves as a symbolic boundary for the chancel; is usually decorated with scenes from the Passion and always carries a group of Jesus Christ, the Virgin and St John.

(P. Gaigneux/Azimut)

Lampaul-Guimiliau. – Rood-beam

Renaissance works are numerous and very elaborate. **Fonts** and **pulpits** are developed into richly decorated monuments.

Altarpieces, or retables, show an interesting development which can be traced through many stages in Breton churches. Originally the altar was simply a table: as the result of decoration it gradually lost its simplicity and reached a surprising size. In the 12 and 14C altars were furnished with a low step and altarpiece, the same length as the altar. Sculptors took possession of the feature and added groups of figures in scenes drawn from the Passion. From the 15C onwards the altarpiece became a pretext for twisted columns, pediments, niches containing statues and sculptured panels, which reached their highest expression in the 17C.

Finally the main subject was lost in decoration consisting of angels, garlands, etc., and the altarpiece occupied the whole of the chapel reserved for the altar, and sometimes even, joined up with the retables of side altars, decorated the whole wall of the apse as is the case at Ste-Marie-de-Ménez-Hom *(p 204).*

It is curious to find in Breton altarpieces of the 15C the influence of the Flemish craftsmen who excelled in this type of decorative carving, producing tiny figures in the minutest detail.

Devotion to the Rosary, which was promoted in the 15C by Alain de la Roche, a Breton Friar of the Dominican Order, gave rise from 1640 onwards to the erection of several altarpieces in which Our Lady is shown giving the chaplet to St Dominic and St Catherine of Siena.

Of less importance but equally numerous are the niches which, when the two panels are open, reveal a **Tree of Jesse.** Jesse, who was a member of the tribe of Judah, had a son, David, from whom was descended the Virgin Mary. Jesse is usually depicted lying on his side; from his heart and his body spring the roots of the tree whose branches bear the figures, in chronological order, of the kings and prophets who were Christ's forebears. In the centre is portrayed the Virgin representing the branch which bears the flower: Jesus Christ.

Among the many statues ornamenting the churches, such as the Trinity of St Anne and the Virgin and Child, are often to be found portraits of real people and items of great importance in the study of the history of costume in Brittany. Such representation, seen frequently in Central Europe, is rare in France.

The Entombment. – The Entombment which is often shown as part of a Calvary group in other parts of France is not often so seen in Brittany. The best depictions of the Placing in the Tomb or Holy Sepulchre with the group of seven round the dead Christ are at Lampaul-Guimiliau and St-Thégonnec.

Funeral statuary is represented in most masterly manner by the tomb of François II at Nantes and Olivier de Clisson at Josselin.

Stained glass windows. – Whereas the altarpieces, friezes and statues were often coloured, paintings and frescoes, as such, were rare; almost the only exception are those at Kernascléden. In contrast there are a great many stained glass windows, often Italian or Flemish inspired but always made in Brittany. Some are really fine: Dol Cathedral has a beautiful 13C window.

The three workshops at Rennes, Tréguier and Quimper produced stained glass between the 14 and 16C which should be seen; the most remarkable windows from these workshops are in the churches of Notre-Dame-du-Crann, La Roche and St Fiacre at Le Faouët.

In the 20C due to the restoration or the building of numerous churches and chapels the ornamentation of these edifices has been possible as in the colourful non-figurative stained glass windows. The cathedral at St-Malo is a good example.

Gold church plate. – In spite of considerable losses, Brittany still possesses many wonderful pieces of gold church plate. This was made by local craftsmen, most of them from Morlaix. Though fine chalices and shrines may be hidden away for security, magnificent reliquaries, chalices, richly decorated patens and superb processional crosses may be seen at Carantec, St-Jean-du-Doigt, St-Gildas-de-Rhuys, Paimpont and Locarn.

The parish close

The parish close is the most typical monumental grouping in Breton communities.

The tourist should not leave Brittany without having seen a few examples, and we therefore describe a tour of parish closes taking in the most interesting *(p 153).*

The centre of the close was the cemetery which was very small and with gravestones of uniform size. Nowadays this is tending to disappear. Around the cemetery which is often reached through a **triumphal arch** are grouped the **church** with its small **square** *(placître),* the **Calvary,** and the **charnel house** or ossuary. Thus the spiritual life of the parish is closely linked with the community of the dead. Death, *Ankou,* was anyway a familiar idea to the Bretons who often depicted it.

The extraordinary rivalry between neighbouring villages explains the richness of the closes which grew up in Lower Brittany at the time of the Renaissance and in the 17C. Competition between Guimiliau and St-Thégonnec went on for two centuries: a Calvary answered a triumphal arch, a charnel house a porch, a tower replied to a belfry, a pulpit to a font, an organ loft to a set of confessionals, an Entombment to chancel woodwork. The two finest closes in Brittany sprang from this rivalry.

Triumphal arches. – The entrance to a cemetery is often ornamented with a monumental gateway. This is treated as a triumphal arch to symbolize the accession of the just to immortality.

Some arches built during the Renaissance, like those of Sizun and Berven, are surprisingly reminiscent of the triumphal arches of antiquity.

Charnel houses. – In the tiny Breton cemeteries of olden days, bodies often had to be exhumed to make room for new dead. The bones were piled in small shelters with ventilating openings, built against the church or cemetery wall. Then these charnel houses became separate buildings, larger and more carefully built and finally reliquaries which could be used as funeral chapels.

Calvaries. – In these small granite monuments, episodes of the Passion are represented around Christ on the Cross. Many of them were built to ward off in 1598 a plague epidemic, or as an act of thanks after it ended. They served for religious teaching in the parish. The priest preached from the dais, pointing out with a wand the scenes which he described to his flock.

The distant forerunners of the Calvaries were Christianized menhirs *(p 34)*, which were still fairly common, and their immediate predecessors were the crosses, plain or ornate. Crosses along roads in this country-side are countless; there have been tens of thou-

(Christiane Olivier, Nice)

Notre-Dame-de-Tronoën. – Calvary

sands. In the 16C a Bishop of Léon boasted that he alone had had 5 000 erected. Ornate crosses were common in the 14C; many were destroyed. The oldest remaining Calvary is that of Tronoën, which dates from the end of the 15C. They were being erected as late as the end of the 17C. The most famous are those of Guimiliau with 200 figures, Plougastel-Daoulas with 180 and Pleyben.

The sculpture is rough and naïve – the work of a village stonemason – but it shows a great deal of observation and is often strikingly lifelike and expressive. Many figures, notably soldiers, wear the costumes of the 16 and 17C.

A lesson in sacred history. – Walking round a large Calvary, we see the history of the Virgin and Christ pass before our eyes: the Virgin's marriage, the Annunciation, the Visitation, the Nativity, the Adoration of the Shepherds, the Adoration of the Magi, the Presentation at the Temple, the Circumcision, the Flight into Egypt, the Baptism of Jesus, the Entry into Jerusalem, the Last Supper, the Washing of Feet, the Garden of Olives, the Kiss of Judas, the Arrest of Jesus, Jesus before Caiaphas, Jesus before Herod, Pilate washing his hands, the Scourging, the Crown of Thorns, the Carrying of the Cross, Jesus falling beneath the Cross, the Descent from the Cross, the Embalming, the Entombment, the Resurrection and the Descent into limbo.

Catell-Gollet. – The story of Catell-Gollet (Catherine the Lost) appears on several Calvaries (Plougastel-Daoulas, Guimiliau). Catherine, a young servant girl, has concealed her misbehaviour at confession. Embarked on the slippery slope, she steals a consecrated Host to give it to the Devil, who appears in the guise of her lover. The culprit is condemned to eternal fire. She is seen above (at the corner of the platform, below the right-hand cross) in the jaws of Hell; devils hold her neck with a fork and tear her naked body with their claws. The priest, when preaching, would draw a terrible lesson for flirtatious girls from this adventure.

No Calvary has all these scenes. The sculptor chose those that inspired him most, and arranged them without any regard for chronological order. Some can be recognized at a glance, others, more or less damaged or treated too sketchily, are a tax to sagacity.

① Cross of Christ. This is sometimes alone or flanked by one thief's cross.

② Thieves' crosses. Usually T-shaped and on either side of the Crucifix.

③ Horsemen (Roman guards) or the Holy Women, or St Peter, St John or St Yves.

④ Virgin of Pity (Mary holding the body of Jesus removed from the Cross) or angels catching His Blood in chalices.

⑤ and ⑥ Dais and frieze encircling the base of the Cross. They carry many figures, either isolated (Apostles, saints and holy women) or in scenes from the Passion. The four Evangelists are usually set in niches at the corners.

⑦ Altar on which is the statue of the saint to whom the Calvary is dedicated (sometimes there are several).

(After TCF Records photo)

Plougastel-Daoulas. – Typical Calvary

What is a Calvary?

Calvary is the name given to the hill, also known as Golgotha, where Christ was crucified. The hill took its name from its skull form (Skull: calvaria in Latin).

Breton Calvaries representing scenes from the Passion and Crucifixion are not to be confused with wayside crosses often erected at crossroads or near churches to mark the site of a pilgrimage or procession.

Breton domestic furniture

For centuries Breton artisans made box beds, chests, sideboards, dressers, wardrobes and clock cases. Repetition of the same models, differing only in small ornamental details, developed true mastery in them.

The **box bed,** an essential characteristic of Breton furnishing, afforded protection against the cold as well as privacy in the large common room. It sometimes has two storeys or bunks, one above the other, and two sliding doors, replaced by one large door in Leon and thick curtains in the Audierne region. There is also a bench-chest for easy access and useful for storage. The façade of the bed and the chest are richly decorated with lunes, garlands, religious designs, sometimes including the monogram of Christ, interlaced or adjoining geometrical figures, known as compass decoration. Wardrobes are decorated in a similar style. In Upper Brittany the box bed is replaced by the four poster bed with a canopy and curtains. As in most regions of France, the chest plays an important part. It is used to store linen or grain for everyday use.

The two-door wardrobe is also an important piece of Breton furniture. It is usually topped by a flat overhanging cornice or sometimes by a twin arched one as in the Rennes basin. Dressers are large with five doors and two drawers and some designs are picked out in copper studs as in the case of wardrobes.

Tables are large chests with sliding panels and are accompanied by carved seats.

Fine furniture and reconstructions of old interiors are to be seen in the museums of Nantes, Rennes, and Quimper and the Château of Kerjean.

(After Dupont/Explorer photo)

Breton interior

Castles and fortresses

Breton granite is somewhat daunting to the tourist coming to Brittany for the first time. Clean cut and hard, it does not age or weather and it would, therefore, not be possible to give a date to the grey buildings that blend perfectly into the landscape were it not for the architectural design and methods employed in construction. With the exception of the fortresses, most of which stood guard on the eastern border in fear of the kings of France or along the coast to ward off the raids of English invaders, there are few great castles in Brittany. This lack conveys perfectly the Breton character that turned all its artistic endeavour to the service of religion.

Nevertheless, it is easy to imagine Brittany in the Middle Ages. Few regions, in fact, had such fortresses and though many have been destroyed or have fallen into ruin, many are still standing. Before these walls the problems of war in the Middle Ages can be imagined. Although some fortresses fell at once to a surprise attack, it was not unusual for a siege to go on for several months. The attacker then sapped the ramparts, brought up machines which could hurl stones weighing over 100 kg - 200 lb, and tried to smash the gates with battering rams before launching the final assault.

In the middle of the 15C, artillery brought about new methods of attack and changes in military architecture.

At St-Malo and at Guérande the stone walls that encircled these towns can be seen in their entirety. Remains of ramparts of varying extent can be seen in many other places. Vannes, Concarneau and Port-Louis have ramparts that are almost complete. There are many fortresses: those of Fougères and Vitré are among the finest in France. Dinan and Combourg have fortified castles still standing; Suscinio, Tonquédec, etc., have impressive ruins; La Hunaudaye, though of lesser importance, the towers of Elven, of Oudon and Châteaugiron still stand proudly upright. La Latte Fort, standing like a sentinel, has a magnificent site.

Buildings, half fortress and half palace, like Kerjean, Josselin and the ducal castle at Nantes, are interesting to see, but there are few of them. The fact is that the Breton nobility, except for the Duke and a few great families, were poor. They included many country gentlemen who lived in very simple manors, which, nevertheless, retained their watchtower defences. They cultivated their own land, like the peasants, but they did not give up their rank and they continued to wear the sword.

Vitré. – The Castle

In some places these manor farms give a great deal of character to the Breton countryside. This is the case in Léon where they are numerous and where Kergonadéac'h, Kerouzéré, Kergroadès and Tronjoly together form a background setting to Kerjean, pride of the Province. Certain other châteaux, such as Rocher-Portail, were built later, and lack all appearance of being fortresses, but impress by their simplicity of outline and the grouping of the buildings; alternatively at such places as Lanrigan and La Motte-Glain it is the detail that charms the visitor. Landal is one of those that gain enormously from their surroundings; others take great pride in a well laid out garden or a fine park – these include Bonne-Fontaine, Caradeuc, Rosanbo and Couëlan.

Old streets and old houses

One of the charms of travelling in Brittany is to stroll in the old quarters of the towns. There is hardly a town or village which has not kept whole streets, or at least a few single houses, just as they were 300 or 400 years ago.

There you can conjure up the life of other days. On the ground floors of the houses the shops of tradesmen and artisans are indicated by sheet metal signs which creak on their hinges. Linen hangs out to dry on poles fixed to the windows along the façades. Heavy objects are hauled up with pulleys fixed to the gables. In the narrow streets, the roofs of overhanging houses almost meet; the roads are dark but at the back the dwellings give on yards which bring air and light to the rooms and the backs of the shops.

People worked long and hard: wages were very low. At the crack of dawn the watchman on the tower gave a trumpet call and the workers jumped out of bed. Every trade was thoroughly organized in a corporation which had its own street, its banner, its patron saint and its annual feast-day. There was no night life; at 8pm in winter and 9pm in summer the curfew rang from the belfry, the watch fastened chains across the streets, the lights went out and the town went to sleep.

Sunday brought rest. In a deafening chorus, the bells called the faithful to church. Masses, vespers and processions followed one another. Great occasions were the fairs, the harvest or wine festival, the corporation feast-days, the *pardons* and theatricals. People amused themselves with games of skill, like the *papegault* (a wooden bird to be shot at with a crossbow) and the *quintaine,* in which a jouster mounted on a donkey and armed with a lance charged a wooden dummy which he had to strike in the middle of its body. If he aimed badly, the dummy pivoted on its axis and hit the clumsy fellow with its staff.

Some picturesque old streets

Dinan: Rue du Jerzual (p 87)
Guingamp: Place du Centre (p 112)
Morlaix: Grand'Rue (p 141)
Pontivy: Rue du Fil (p 162)
Quimper: Rue Kéréon (p 170)
Quimperlé: Rue Dom-Morice (p 173)
Vitré: Rue Beaudrairie (p 217)

Modern towns. – It is difficult to find any basis of comparison between the old towns with their historical associations and the modern towns. And yet to cite only the chief ones, if Dinan, Locronan, Vitré, Morlaix and Quimper, as well as St-Malo which has been admirably reconstructed, have an undeniable appeal, it is impossible not to be struck also by the planning and grouping of buildings in such towns as Brest and Lorient. The wide streets and huge, airy squares are elegant and have obviously been built to achieve harmony and unity. The visitor may well be surprised by certain buildings, but he will find something to admire in the upward sweep of a tall bell-tower, the simple lines of a concrete façade, the successful decorative effect of stone and cement combined. Above all, if he has some slight appreciation of colour harmony, and goes inside any building he will be struck by the present day artist's skill in lighting.

BRETON FOOD AND DRINK

Breton cooking is characterized more by the quality of the materials used than by fine preparation.

Sea food, crustaceans and fish. – Shellfish, crustaceans and fish are all excellent. Particularly outstanding are the spiny lobsters, grilled or stuffed clams, scallops, shrimps, crisp batter covered fried fish morsels and crab pasties.

Belon oysters, Armorican oysters from Concarneau, La Forêt and Ile-Tudy, and Cancale oysters are all well known in France, but are not at their best until the end of the tourist season.

In Breton hotels the king of the table is the lobster. It is served grilled or with cream and especially in a *coulis,* the rich hot sauce which makes the dish called "Armoricaine" or "à l'Américaine" (the latter name is due to a mistake made in a Paris restaurant).

Try also *cotriade* (a Breton fish soup like *bouillabaisse),* conger-eel stew, the Aulne or Élorn salmon, trout from the Arrée and the Noires Mountains, or pike and shad served with "white butter" in the district near the Loire. This is a sauce made from slightly salted butter, vinegar and shallots, and its preparation requires real skill. Finally, there are *civelles* (elvers), which are a speciality of Nantes.

Meat, vegetables and fruit. – The salt pasture sheep *(prés-salés)* of the coast are famous. Breton leg of mutton (with white beans) is part of the great French gastronomic heritage. Grey partridges and heath hares are tasty as are the chickens from Rennes and Nantais ducks. Pork butchers' meat is highly flavoured: Morlaix ham, bacon, black pudding, smoked sausage from Guéméné-sur-Scorff and chitterlings from Quimperlé.

Potatoes, artichokes, cauliflowers and green peas are the glory of the Golden Belt. There are also strawberries and melons from Plougastel, cherries from Fouesnant and many other fruits.

Pancakes, cakes and sweetmeats. – Most towns have *crêperies* (pancake shops) where pancakes made of wheat or buckwheat are served with cider or, for those who like it, with yoghurt. In some of the smaller picturesque shops you may see them made. Others, more modern and with Breton furniture, offer more handsome surroundings, perhaps, but not better pancakes.

There is the plain, bare pancake the Breton has enjoyed for centuries, and also modern variations with jam, cheese, eggs, ham, salad, etc. The buckwheat pancake is eaten with salt and the wheat one with sugar.

Other cakes (lace pancakes at Quimper, Breton *galettes* or flat scones, Nantes biscuits, Quintin oat and cream cakes, *far* and *kuign aman*) find many devotees as do Rennes pralines, and Nantes *berlingots* (sweet drops).

Cider, Muscadet and Rhuys wine. – The local drink is cider. Except for that made at Fouesnant and Beg-Meil, however, it is inferior to Normandy cider.

The only Breton wine is Muscadet which is found all over Brittany. The people of Nantes guard it jealously and have founded the "Order of Bretvins" in its honour. The grapes are grown only around Nantes, on the slopes that border the Sèvre. This white wine, dry and fruity, is specially recommended to drink with oysters and shellfish, the *Gros-Plant* is also delicious with Breton specialities. The Muscadet Tour *(see Michelin Green Guide Côte de l'Atlantique – in French only)* takes in the best producing districts.

Vines still grow on the Rhuys peninsula, but the wine drawn from them is a subject of Breton humour. "To drink it", the Bretons say, "you need four men and a wall: one man to pour it out, one to drink, two to hold him up and the wall to stop him from falling backwards." Distilled, on the other hand, it produces an excellent brandy.

Key

Sights

★★★ **Worth a journey**
★★ **Worth a detour**
★ **Interesting**

Sightseeing route with departure point indicated
on the road   in town

✕ ∴	Castle, historic house – Ruins		Ecclesiastical building: Catholic – Protestant
⊥ ◎	Wayside cross or calvary – Fountain		Building with main entrance
☀ ·ᴠ	Panorama – View		Ramparts – Tower
⊥ ⵟ	Lighthouse – Windmill		Gateway
⌣ ⌘	Dam – Factory or power station	▪	Statue or small building
☆ ∪	Fort – Quarry		Gardens, parks, woods
▲	Miscellaneous sights	B	Letters giving the location of a place on the town plan

Other symbols

	Motorway (unclassified)	▢	Public building
◀▶ ▶ ❶ ❷	Interchange complete, limited, number	⊞ ✉	Hospital – Covered market
	Major through road	⍟ ⚔	Police station – Barracks
	Dual carriageway	⌖	Cemetery
	Stepped street – Footpath	✡	Synagogue
	Pedestrian street	⚘ ⛳	Racecourse – Golf course
	Unsuitable for traffic	≋ ⊡	Outdoor or indoor swimming pool
1429 → ←	Pass – Altitude	⛸ ⊤	Skating rink – Viewing table
▭ 🚌	Station – Coach station	⚓	Pleasure boat harbour
	Ferry services: Passengers and cars	⌁	Telecommunications tower or mast
	Passengers only	⬭ ♜	Stadium – Water tower
✈	Airport	B	Ferry (river and lake crossings)
③	Reference number common to town plans and MICHELIN maps	△	Swing bridge
		⊗	Main post office (with poste restante)
		ⓘ	Tourist information centre
		P	Car park

MICHELIN maps and town plans are north orientated.

Main shopping streets are printed in a different colour in the list of streets.

Town plans: roads most used by traffic and those on which guide listed sights stand are fully drawn; the beginning only of lesser roads is indicated.
Local maps: only the primary and sightseeing routes are indicated.

Abbreviations

A	Local agricultural office (Chambre d'Agriculture)	J	Law Courts (Palais de Justice)	POL.	Police station
C	Chamber of Commerce (Chambre de Commerce)	M	Museum	T	Theatre
H	Town Hall (Hôtel de ville)	P	Préfecture Sous-préfecture	U	University

⊙ **Times and charges for admission are listed at the end of the guide**

The practical information chapter, at the end of the guide, regroups:
— a list of the local or national organizations supplying additional information
— a section on times and charges.

SIGHTS

in alphabetical order

Brézellec Point

★ The ABERS

Michelin map 58 folds 3, 4 or 230 folds 2, 3

The northwest coast of Finistère, still known as the Coast of Legends, is broken up by estuaries called *abers* (Aber-Wrac'h, Aber-Benoît, Aber-Ildut), which create a fine sight at high tide.

The *abers* are different from the estuaries on the north coast (rivers of Morlaix, Tréguier or Trieux): their beds are not as deep and their slopes as steep. Beyond the high-tide mark the *aber* is prolonged upstream not by a small coastal river but by a tiny brook too small to dig a channel in the muddy estuary. There is no great port at the head of the estuary, as there is at Morlaix or Dinan.

The whole of this low and rocky coast, dotted with small islands, is particularly rich in different varieties of **seaweed**. Factories process most of it: the brown species in the manufacture of alginates and mannite, the fucus and floating weed as stock-feed; the remainder is sold as fertilizer *(details p 20)*.

ROUND TOUR STARTING FROM BREST

197 km - 122 miles – allow one day

★ **Brest.** – P 63.

> *Leave Brest by ② on the town plan, the D 788 towards Roscoff.*

⊘ **Gouesnou.** – Pop 4 101. The 16C **church** has a monumental south porch. The polygonal chevet (1615) surmounted by three pediments and the sacristy are good examples of the combined Gothic and Classical styles. Inside, note the modern stained glass windows by J. Le Chevalier (1970) and Renaissance niches on two tiers in the chancel. Under the trees below the church, to the west, is a fine Renaissance fountain with an altar adorned with a statue of St Gouesnou.

> *Take the D 13 in the direction of Lannilis and at Bourg-Blanc, turn right.*

⊘ **St-Jaoua.** – Standing in the centre of a shady parish close is a charming early 15C chapel which contains the tomb and effigy of St Jaoua. By the roadside, note the great 17C fountain built of large stones; curious semicircular shapes flanked by massive pinnacles crown the monument and pilasters.

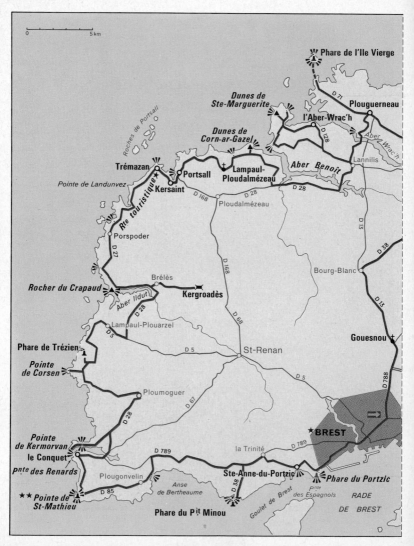

⊘**Plouvien.** – Pop 2 779. In the parish **church** is a tomb in Kersanton granite dating from 1555. The recumbent figure rests on the figures of sixteen little monks depicted at prayer, reading or meditating.

Leave Plouvien to the east by the Lesneven road.

⊘**St-Jean-Balanant.** – The 15C **chapel** was founded by the Order of St John of Jerusalem and was a dependant of the La Feuillée Commandery in the Arrée Mountains. At the tympanum, note the low-relief relating the Baptism of Christ. There is a fountain to the south of the chapel.

Continue towards Lesneven and at the fourth junction turn right towards Locmaria.

Locmaria Chapel. – In front of the 16-17C chapel with its square belfry-porch, there is a fine **cross★** with two cross-bars adorned with figures.

Go to Le Drennec and take the road on the left to Le Folgoët.

★★ **Le Folgoët.** – P 98.

Take the direction of Lannilis and at Croas-Kerzu, bear right towards Plouguerneau.

At the entrance of Le Grouanec, note on the right an eight-sided Gallo-Roman cross embedded in the wall of a farm.

Le Grouanec. – Beyond the village, on the right, in the small parish close (16C) is the ⊘fountain of Notre-Dame-de-Grouanec. Inside the **church,** the stained glass windows by Max Ingrand, sculptured frieze and beams in the south aisle are noteworthy; ceramic crosses mark the Stations of the Cross. The fountain, Notre-Dame-de-la-Clarté, may be seen 100m from the church.

Plouguerneau. – Pop 5 317. *Pardons (p 226).*

Make for the Lilia beaches.

Fine sheltered beaches of fine sand in a cove.

⊘**Vierge Island Lighthouse** (Phare de l'Ile Vierge). – Built between 1897 and 1902, this is the tallest lighthouse in France (77m - 247ft) and its beam has an average range of 52 km - 32 miles. From the top (397 steps) the **panorama★** extends over the Finistère coast, ranging from Ushant to Batz Island in fine weather.

Return to Plouguerneau and proceed on the D 13 in the direction of Brest.

2 km - 1 mile farther on, the former road is now a belvedere (small calvary) affording a good **view★** of the Aber-Wrac'h which is especially fine at high tide. Cross the *aber,* a pretty site where boats tie in.

Turn right at Lannilis.

The Aber-Wrac'h. – This little port, yatching centre and seaside resort has a sailing school overlooking the village.

The *corniche* road runs along the Baie des Anges; on the left stand the ruins of the 16C convent of Notre-Dame-des-Anges.

Bear right towards Ste-Marguerite dunes, then right again towards Cézon Fort.

From the platform by the roadside, there is an interesting **view** of the Aber-Wrac'h estuary, the ruins of Cézon Fort on an island commanding the approach to the estuary, and the lighthouse on Vierge Island.

Turn back and after Poulloc, bear right for the dunes.

(A.P. Sandford/Azimut)
Seaweed harvesting

Ste-Marguerite Dunes. – The roads through the dunes afford good views: to the left is the Aber-Benoît and in the distance the Portsall Rocks (Roches de Portsall), to the right the Aber-Wrac'h channel studded with islets. Seaweed is left to dry on the dunes for two to three days and then is sent to the processing factories *(p 44)*.

Make for the Brouënnou Chapel and turn left towards the St-Pabu Passage.

Half-way down, from the platform on the left, there is a good view over the Aber-Benoît and St-Pabu.

Go to Lannilis via Landéda and then, take the D 28, the Ploudalmézeau road.

Aber-Benoît. – The road crosses the *aber* and runs along it for a while giving good views of the pretty setting.

After 5 km - 3 miles, turn right for St-Pabu and after St-Pabu follow the signposts for the camping site to reach the Corn-ar-Gazel dunes.

Corn-ar-Gazel Dunes. – Beautiful view of the Ste-Marguerite Peninsula, the Aber-Benoît and its islets.

Turn round and follow the scenic road winding through the dunes and affording glimpses of the coast.

Lampaul-Ploudalmézeau. – Pop 610. The church has a Renaissance north door, a magnificent **belfry-porch★** crowned by a turreted dome, and a large chapel to the right of the chancel.

Proceed to Portsall.

Roads through the dunes lead to vast sandy beaches.

Portsall. – A small harbour in a sheltered bay. From a calvary-cross perched on a cliff at the far end of the harbour *(1/4 hour on foot Rtn, access via Bar-an-Lan on the Kersaint road)* a good **view** unfolds over the port, the coast and the Portsall Rocks in the distance where the tanker "Amoco Cadiz" ran aground in 1978.

Kersaint. – Beyond the village, towards Argenton, are the ruins of the 13C castle of Trémazan.

Trémazan. – From the car park past the village, the **view★** extends over the Verte Island, the Portsall Rocks and the Corn Carhai lighthouse.

★ **Scenic road** (Route touristique). – The *corniche* road follows a wild coast studded with rocks; note the curious jagged **Landunvez Point**. The road runs through several small resorts, Argenton, **Porspoder** where St Budoc, Bishop of Dol-de-Bretagne is said to have landed in the 6C, and Melon.

Turn right at the entrance of Lanildut.

Crapaud Rock (Rocher du Crapaud). – Overlooking the narrow channel of the **Aber-Ildut**, it offers good views of the harbour and the *aber,* a picturesque estuary accessible to boats regardless of the tides. The northern bank is wooded, the southern bank has dunes and beaches. The *aber* marks the notional boundary between the Channel and the Atlantic. However sailors consider this demarcation to be further to the south at Corsen Point *(below)* in view of the sea bed level.

After Lanildut, the road follows the aber as far as Brélès.

⊘ **Kergroadès Castle.** – *3.5 km - 2 miles from Brélès.* The castle built in 1613 has been restored. The main courtyard is closed by a crenallated gallery and is surrounded by an austere main building flanked by two round towers and two wings built at right angles. There is a pretty well.

Take the direction of Plouarzel and turn right after Lampaul-Plouarzel. The road then runs along Porspol Bay with Ségal Island in the distance, and through Trézien.

Trézien Lighthouse (Phare de Trézien). – The lighthouse (37m - 121ft high) has an average range of 35 km - 22 miles.

Continue towards Porsmoguer Beach (Grève de Porsmoguer) and after some houses turn right.

The road passes by the Corsen Maritime Station and leads to a ruined house on the cliff.

Corsen Point. – This 50m - 160ft cliff is the most westerly point in France. There is a fine view of the coast and islands.

Go to Ploumoguer passing through the Porsmoguer Beach, then turn towards Le Conquet. After 5 km - 3 miles, bear right for Kermorvan Point.

Kermorvan Point. – Its central part is an isthmus which gives a pretty view on the right of Blancs Sablons Beach and on the left of the **site★** of Le Conquet. At the tip of the point, to the left of the lighthouse entrance, the mass of rocks forms a splendid viewing-point.

The road goes round the great estuary, where the harbour is situated, to Le Conquet.

Le Conquet. – Pop 2 011. From this pretty **site★** there is a superb view of the Kermorvan Point. This is a fishing port for crawfish, lobsters and crabs and the departure point for the islands of Ushant and Molène. A pleasant walk may be enjoyed along the harbour *corniche* road which affords good views of the port and Kermorvan Point with the Ushant archipelago and its many lighthouses in the distance. The church which was restored in the 19C, has a fine 16C stained glass window depicting the Passion in the chancel and 15C sculptures under the porch.

The road from Le Conquet to Brest is described in the opposite direction on p 66.

ANTRAIN

Michelin map **59** fold 17 or **230** fold 27

Antrain overlooks rich farmlands bordered by hedges and trees and green valleys, lying as it does high on the promontory before the confluence of the Couesnon and Loisance Rivers. It is a market town with steep little streets.

Of its former Romanesque church there still remains a fine portal with a semicircular arch and buttresses on either side.

EXCURSIONS

⊙ **Bonne-Fontaine Castle** (Château de Bonne-Fontaine). – *1.5 km - 1 mile S. Leave Antrain by the Général-Lavigne and Bonne Fontaine Streets.*
Built in 1547 as a feudal manor house and remodelled in 19C, Bonne-Fontaine rises in the centre of a beautifully maintained park. The elegant turrets adorning the massive main range, the tall windows and the carved dormer windows balance the severity of the squat, machicolated pepper-pot towers.

⊙ **Tremblay.** – *4 km - 2 miles S by the D 155 and N 175.* Pop 1 653.
The **church,** which was built in 11 and 12C, modified in 16C and restored after a fire in 1801, is an example of Romanesque architecture. The solid square tower that rises above the transept crossing is topped by a pierced bell-turret. Notice the elegance of the canopy and the glory radiating outwards from the top of the great cross on the high altar, which bears three heads symbolizing the Holy Trinity at its centre, and at its foot the symbols of the Evangelists. The beam is ornate, entwined by a vine and ears of corn being pecked by birds. The six old wooden statues and the Christ, behind the entrance porch, are interesting.

⊙ **Le Rocher-Portail Castle** (Château du Rocher-Portail). – *14 km - 9 miles E by the D 155 and D 102 to the left.*
A drive bordered with chestnut trees leads to the castle set in a beautiful spot.
Gilles Ruellan, one-time pedlar who became a councillor of state, built the castle in 1608. A long façade and two wings at right angles to it enclose a big courtyard; along its fourth side runs a granite balustrade and beyond it is the moat spanned by a bridge which serves as the entrance. The ground floor of the wing on the left forms a beautiful arcaded gallery whose outer side looks out over a pool. An arched passageway through the right wing leads to a second courtyard closed by the outbuildings.

★ ARMORIQUE CORNICHE

Michelin map **58** folds 6, 7 or **230** fold 6

This short section of the Channel coast which is part of the Golden Belt *(p 21)* should be seen by all tourists who visit northern Brittany. The Lieue de Grève, a long, majestic stretch of sand, is followed by steep headlands skirted from a distance by the Armorican coast road proper.

FROM ST-MICHEL-EN-GRÈVE TO MORLAIX

59 km - 37 miles – about 5 hours – Local map p 48

St-Michel-en-Grève. – Pop 398. Facilities. A small seaside resort. The church and cemetery are nicely situated near the sea.

★ **Lieue de Grève.** – This magnificent beach, 4 km - 2 1/2 miles long, lies across the base of a bay which runs dry to a depth of over 2 km - 1 mile at low tide. Trout streams run into the sea through small green valleys. The road, which is very picturesque, follows the wooded coast and skirts the rocky mass of the Grand Rocher.

★ **Climbing the Grand Rocher.** – *3/4 hour on foot Rtn.* A road to the left, just before the Grand Rocher, leads to a car park nearby from which a path, runs to this 80m - 261ft vantage point. There is a very fine **view**★ of the Lieue de Grève; at high tide and especially with a northwesterly blowing in winter, the sight of the endless foaming rollers breaking on the beach and dashing against the seawall that protects the D 786 gives an excellent idea of the undertow *(see details p 19).*

St-Efflam. – Next to the St-Efflam Chapel, half hidden by lush vegetation, there is a fountain, which is surmounted by a massive dome. Efflam, a hermit who came from Ireland and landed with seven companions in 470 in the neighbouring bay of Porzmellec, settled in a place called Coz Iliz, 2 km - 1 mile beyond the Grand Rocher. Efflam died there in 512.

Bear left towards Plestin.

⊙ **Plestin-les-Grèves.** – Pop 3 447. The 16C **church,** which burned down in 1944, contains the tomb of St Efflam (1576) adorned with his recumbent figure. In the south aisle to the left of the altar, a statue shows him vanquishing a dragon, the symbol of paganism. Modern stained glass windows.

Return to the coast road.

★ **Armorique Corniche.** – Between St-Efflam and Locquirec the road picturesquely follows the much indented coast. After Plestin Point there is a fine view of the cove of Locquirec and its headland at high tide. Before reaching the village you will see, on your right and in the distance, the Bretonne Corniche *(p 67)* as far as Trébeurden; and on crossing the bridge, to the left is an attractive manor house.

Locquirec. – *P 129.*

Beyond the mill, Moulin de la Rive, take the corniche road overhanging the sea to the right in the direction of Poul Rodou.

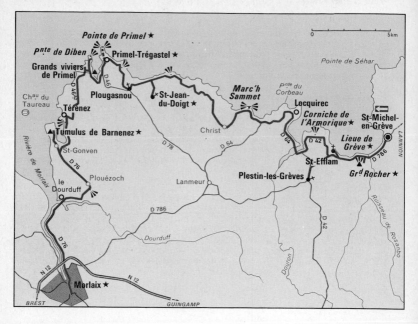

Marc'h Sammet viewing-table. – Built on a rocky headland, it commands splendid **views★**: to the east the beaches of Moulin de la Rive and the Sables Blancs and the rocky Corbeau Point; to the north Losquet Island dominated by the CNET (National Telecommunications Research Organisation - *see Lannion, p 125*); to the west the Poul Rodou beach (access 800m - 2 625ft below).

Go to Christ and turn right. Follow the signposts to the scenic road.

From the *corniche* there is a good view of the coast from Trégastel Point to Primel Point.

At the St-Jean-du-Doigt beach, bear left.

★ **St-Jean-du-Doigt.** – *P 192.*

Plougasnou. – Pop 3 434. At the centre of this small town, the **church** which is mostly 16C, has a Renaissance porch opening on to the square. In the chancel are two 17C altarpieces. In the south aisle, the Kericuff chapel closed off by an elegant Gothic arcade in oak contains a 16C wooden Trinity. A road from the church's east end leads to the **Oratory of Notre-Dame-de-Lorette** 300m - about 1/4 mile from the town, a granite building with a stone roof and two telamones framing the entrance.

Take the road passing by the Tourist Information Centre (Syndicat d'Initiative) and at the third junction turn right.

Go through Ste-Barbe. On the way down, the **view** extends over Primel, the beach, point and rocks.

★ **Primel-Trégastel.** – This resort lies in a good setting near a point dotted with piles of rocks comparable with those of Ploumanach and Trégastel. There are many hotels.

★ **Primel Point.** – *1/2 hour on foot Rtn.* The point is a jumble of pink **rocks**. From the central spur there is a fine **panorama** extending from the Bay of St-Pol-de-Léon to the Trébeurden coast. Out at sea are the Batz Island lighthouse and the Moines Island (Sept Iles). The tip of the point is separated from the rest of the peninsula by a fissure (which can be crossed at low tide) at the bottom of which lies a cave.

After 1 km - 1/2 mile turn right. The road passes near the fish ponds.

⊘ **Primel Fish Farm** (Grands viviers de Primel). – There are some twenty ponds full of crustaceans.

Diben Point. – At Le Diben, a picturesque fishermen's village, turn right in the direction of the fish farms and port; 100 m farther on take the road opposite towards the port which leads to a dyke. Just before this, bear left into a path leading to Diben Point: fine view over the bay and of Primel Point. Return to the D 46^A2 and follow a road to the right towards Port-Blanc which gives access to a car park from which a track *(1/4 hour on foot Rtn)* leads to a rock jutting out over the sea: lovely view of the islet of Port-Blanc.

The road passes on the right the attractive Guerzit beach and St-Samson beach.

Térénez. – This very pleasant and typically Breton little port is a sailing centre.

The coast road offers **glimpses★** of the Morlaix estuary, the Taureau Castle and the peninsula topped by the Barnenez Tumulus.

At the entrance to St-Goulven, turn right.

★ **Barnenez Tumulus** (Tumulus de Barnenez). – *P 53.*

Continue in the direction of Morlaix (p 140).

Beyond Plouézoch, a fine tree-lined road descends into the picturesque valley of the **Dourduff** with the colourful oyster-fishing port. After the bridge, the *corniche* road runs along the Morlaix River and gives views of the sand dredging port, the yachting port with its lock, and the charming setting of the town, river and viaduct.

★★ ARRÉE MOUNTAINS (MONTS D'ARRÉE)

Michelin map **58** folds 5, 6, 15, 16 or **230** folds 18, 19

The Arrée Mountains are the highest in Brittany, yet their topmost point is less than 400m - 1 200ft. They were perhaps proud peaks in the primary era *(p 18)*, but erosion has done its work. The sandstone or granite summits have been turned into rounded hills or *menez* (Menez-Bré, *p 59* and Ménez-Hom, *p 133*). The quartz formations, cleared by the action of water on the schist around them, have become sharp crests, fretted into saw-teeth and bristling with *aiguilles* (needles); these are the rocks or *roc'hs* (eg Roc Trévezel). The picturesqueness of these "mountains" is due to the grim and barren face of nature. The peaks often shrouded in mist afford fine views.

The mountain chain is wooded in parts, especially towards the east, but the summits are usually quite desolate. There is not a tree on them; the heath is pierced by rocky scarps; here and there are clumps of gorse with golden flowers in spring and purple heather in September. A few poor hamlets stand far apart. On the flanks of the hills small streams have dug valleys which are sometimes wild, sometimes full of freshness and verdancy. The whole area of the Arrée Mountains is now protected following the creation of the Armorique Regional Nature Park.

Armorique Regional Nature Park (Parc Naturel Régional d'Armorique). – The park - 65 000 ha - 160 550 acres - extends over 29 districts and comprises three zones: the Arrée Mountains, the Aulne estuary and the capes and islands (Roncavel and Camaret Peninsulas, the Ushant archipelago). Its aims are the protection of sites and of fauna and flora; the creation of activities to develop the economy (cooperatives, crafts); the preservation of aspects of rural civilization. Its main achievements are an information centre at Menez-Maur, museums in traditional houses (Brasparts, Kerouat, Ushant, St-Rivoal, Trégarvan) and the signposting of itineraries.

ROUND TOUR STARTING FROM HUELGOAT

122 km - 76 miles – allow one day – Local map p 50

★★ **Huelgoat.** – *Time: 1/2 hour. Description p 116.*

    Leave Huelgoat S by the D 14 in the direction of Pleyben.

2 km - 1 mile farther on, the road offers an extensive view of the Aulne Basin and the Noires Mountains.

★ **St-Herbot.** – *Time: 1/2 hour.* The **church**★ with its square tower, stands surrounded by trees in the middle of a desolate, arid countryside. It is mainly in the Flamboyant Gothic style. A small Renaissance ossuary abuts on to the south porch and on the north side a monumental horse-shoe staircase leads to the chapel. There is a fine Crucifix in Kersanton granite (1571) in front of the building.

Inside, the chancel is surrounded by a remarkable **screen**★★ in carved oak. Against this screen, on the nave side, are two stone tables for the tufts of hair from the tails of oxen and cows which the peasants offer on the *pardon (p 226)* to obtain the protection of St Herbot, the patron saint of horned cattle. Note also the richly decorated stalls (lift the seats) against the screen, the saint's tomb with a simple stone slab and recumbent figure on four small columns, the stained glass (1556) of the large chancel bay and the side windows depicting respectively the Passion, St Yves and St Lawrence.

Roc'h.Begheor. – *1/4 hour on foot. Car park to the right of the road.* A path amid the gorse leads to the summit at an altitude of 277m - 909ft, commanding a good **view**★ over the Arrée Mountains and the Noires Mountains.

⊘ **Loqueffret.** – Pop 482. The 16C **church** contains in the south transept, a 17C gilded wood altarpiece; in the north arm, an impressive Trinity housed in a niche with carved shutters. At the end of the nave, in the gallery are painted panels depicting Christ and the apostles. A fine cross adorned with figures stands on the south side of the church.

Lannédern. – Pop 361. In the parish close *(details p 37)* is a cross decorated with figures: ⊘ note St Edern riding a stag. Inside the **church** the saint's tomb (14C) and six low-reliefs (17C) illustrating his life are of interest. Note also in the chancel, the 16C window depicting the Passion and 17C statues of the Virgin and St Edern.

    Continue towards Pleyben and turn right after 1.5 km - 1 mile.

Brasparts. – Pop 1 115. The village has an interesting 16C parish close. On the calvary, note St Michael killing the dragon and a simple *Pietà* with the Virgin surrounded by the Holy Women. The **church,** remodelled in the 18C, has a fine pinnacled porch. In the entrance, on the right, is a **Virgin of Pity**★ (16C), and on the left of the chancel, an altarpiece of the Rosary dating from 1668. In the chancel, left of the high altar, a fine 16C stained glass window illustrating the Passion is noteworthy.

    Make for Pleyben.

★★ **Pleyben.** – P 157.

    Continue in the direction of Châteaulin.

Châteaulin. – P 76.

    Take the D 770 following the right bank of the Aulne.

(After Christiane Olivier, Nice, photo)

A house near Brasparts

49

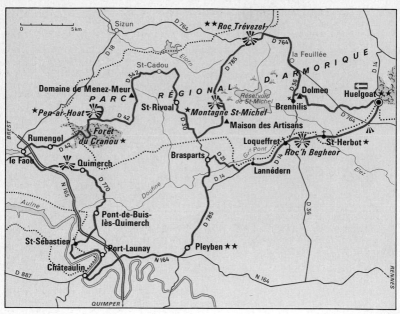

Port-Launay. – Pop 533. This is the port of Châteaulin, on the Aulne. The long quay makes for pleasant walks.

Leave the Brest road on the right and continue along the Aulne, pass under the railway viaduct, bear right at the roundabout and 100 m - 110 yds farther on, turn left.

The road climbs up the hillside and affords a lovely view over the verdant valley.

St-Sébastien Chapel. – The chapel stands near a farm. In the 16C parish close stand a triumphal arch surmounted by St Sebastian between two archers, and a fine calvary with figures including the saint pierced by arrows. Inside the rather dilapidated chapel, two 17C **altarpieces★** in gilded wood are to be seen in the chancel and south transept; in the north transept are panels recounting the story of Loreto, a small Italian village in the Marches region to which, according to legend, the angels transported Mary's house from Nazareth in the 13C.

Follow the small road over the railway line and the Quimper-Brest motorway and turn left into the D 770 towards Brest.

Pont-de-Buis-lès-Quimerch. – Pop 3 989. On leaving the village, below the road, on the left, can be seen an explosives factory, nearly three hundred years old. It produces also ammunition for hunting, plastic materials and pyrotechnic devices.

Quimerch. – *Up the hill, on the right, car-park and viewing-table.* The **view★** extends from the Ménez-Hom to the Cranou Forest taking in the Brest roadstead and the Plougastel Peninsula.

Le Faou. – *P 97.*

From Le Faou, take the D 42 to Rumengol.

Rumengol. – *P 188.*

★ **Cranou Forest** (Forêt du Cranou). – The road, hilly and winding, runs through the State Forest of Cranou, which consists mostly of oaks and beeches. Picnic areas.

On leaving Cranou Forest, bear right towards St-Rivoal; at the entrance to Kerancuru, turn left for Pen-ar-Hoat-ar-Gorré. In the hamlet (schist houses), turn left towards Hanvec and again left into an uphill road. Leave the car near a farm.

★ **Pen-ar-Hoat.** – Alt 217m - 712ft. *Time: 3/4 hour on foot Rtn. Walk round the farm and bear left towards the line of heights; after passing between low walls, the climb ends among gorse bushes.* The **panorama★** extends over the heath-clad hills: to the north are the hills bordering the left bank of the Elorn, to the east the nearer heights of the Arrée, to the south the Cranou Forest and in the distance the Noires Mountains and the Ménez-Hom, and, to the west, the Brest roadstead.

Return to Kerancuru and bear left and 3.5 km - 2 miles farther on, left again towards Sizun.

○ **Menez-Meur Estate** (Domaine de Menez-Meur). – The large estate is set in undulating countryside. The farm buildings are occupied by the Administrative Offices of the Armorique Regional Nature Park and a visitors' information centre. A small museum is devoted to the Park's activities and achievements, the flora and fauna, and the art of clogmaking, a popular craft in the local forests in the past. A nature-trail *(about 1 1/2 hours)* winds through the large enclosures where roam ponies, sheep, deer, horses, with panels giving information on the regional flora.

Go to St-Rivoal, passing through St-Cadou.

St-Rivoal. – Pop 208. After the village, below the Faou road, to the left, a small farm dating from 1702 is one of the many exhibits, dispersed throughout the park, which make up

○ the open-air **museum** showing the different styles of Breton architecture. The little house, built of schist and with a fine external covered stairway going up to the hayloft, comprises a large room with the living quarters for the farmer and his family round the great chimney and the domestic animals at the other end. Next to it is the barn with all the farming implements, and there are two bread ovens in the courtyard.

Take the D 30 in the direction of Brasparts

The road winds through a countryside of hills, and of green and wooded valleys whose freshness contrasts with the bare summits which are rocky and covered with heath.

After 5.5 km – 3 miles, bear left into the D 785 towards Morlaix.

⊘ **Craft Centre** (Maison des Artisans). – Housed in St-Michel farmhouse, it displays Breton crafts: paintings, sculpture, pottery, weaving, gold and silverware etc.

Continue in the direction of Morlaix.

★ **St-Michel Mountain** (Montagne St-Michel). – The way is signposted *(1 km - 1/2 mile)* leading off the D 785 to the left. From the top of the rise (alt 380m - 1 246ft) where there is a small chapel which reaches an altitude of 391m - 1 251ft at its summit, there is a **panorama★** of the Arrée and Noires Mountains. From the foot of the hill, a great peat bog called the Yeun Elez extends towards the east. In the winter mists, the place is so grim that Breton legend says it contains the "Youdig", a gulf forming the entrance to Hell. Beyond it may be seen the reservoir-dam of St-Michel which supplies the Arrée Mountains nuclear power station at Brennilis. Note the megalithic line on the rocky point to the right of the lake.

Views of the countryside, the mountains and the Brennilis basin from the road passing by the Toussaines Signal Station (Signal de Toussaines – alt 384m - 1 260ft).

★★ **Trévezel Rock** (Roc Trévezel). – *P 154.*

By the Roc-Tredudon pylon turn right into the D 764 towards Huelgoat and after 6 km - 4 miles bear right into the D 36 to Brennilis.

⊘ **Brennilis.** – Pop 573. This village has a 15C **church** topped by a delicate pierced belfry. Inside, seven polychrome panels (17C) at the high altar and a stained glass window (16C) in the chancel illustrate scenes from the life of the Virgin. In the south transept there is a fine 16C altar adorned with low-reliefs depicting the twelve sibyls.

Return to the entrance to Brennilis and turn right.

Dolmen. – 100m - 109ft farther to the right, a signposted path leads to a covered alleyway partly hidden by a tumulus.

Continue on the secondary road to return to Huelgoat.

ASSÉRAC   Pop 1 132

Michelin map 🔢 fold 14 or 🔢 folds 51, 52

Lying on the western periphery of the Brière Regional Nature Park *(p 103)*, this village has in the coastal waters a shellfish breeding centre. Nearby the Trait de Mesquer salt-marshes *(p 107)* extend from Pont d'Armes.

EXCURSIONS

Round tour of 35 km - 22 miles. – *W. Time: about 1 1/2 hours.*

Pen-Bé. – This vantage point affords a **view** of the bay with its profusion of upstanding poles for mussel rearing, Merquel Point and Dumet Island in the distance.

Return to Mesquery and bear left; bear left again in Kerséquin.

★ **Bile Point.** – The **view★** extends over two islets and the great ochre coloured cliffs.

Take the road leading to Pénestin and turn left in the direction of **Poudrantais.** The road follows the coast for a short distance giving glimpses of the cliff line.

Mine d'Or Beach (Plage de la Mine d'Or). – Two strange rocks, one in the shape of a menhir, interrupt this long stretch of beach at the foot of tall cliffs.

Once through Pénestin, branch off to the left. Le **Haut-Pénestin** has fine houses.

Halguen Point. – Heathland and pine trees cover this headland. Walk down to the rocky beaches which are backed by a short line of cliffs.

Return to Pénestin. The road then follows the Vilaine river.

Tréhiguier. – This small fishing port is a mussel breeding centre. Anchored in the estuary are pleasure craft mingling with the many motor and rowing boats used for the mussel fishing. Walk to **Scal Point★** to see the estuary widen between the Halguen Point, to the left and the Pen-Lan headland.

Return to Assérac by the D 192 and the D 83.

AUDIERNE   Pop 3 094

Michelin map 🔢 fold 13 or 🔢 fold 16 – Local map p 80 – Facilities

This bustling fishing port is on the estuary of the Goyen, at the foot of a wooded hill and in a pretty **setting★**. The beach is 1.5 km - 1 mile from the town, below Ste-Evette and near the pier from which boats leave for Sein Island.
Its main activity is fishing whether it be coastal fishing for lobster and crawfish or tunny fishing between June and October. *Pardon* on the last Sunday in August.

⊘ **Fish Farm** (Grands Viviers). – *Access by the Quai Pelletan and the corniche road.* There are some thirty pools full of crustaceans (lobsters, crabs, prawns).

⊘ **Thatched Cottage** (La Chaumière). – *Opposite the fish farm.* The cottage contains 17 and 18C Breton furniture as well as objects used in everyday life of that same period.

Michelin map 🔢 fold 2 or 🔢 fold 36 – Local map p 138

This ancient town is built on the banks of the Loch or Auray River near the famous sanctuary of Ste-Anne-d'Auray (p 204). The attractive harbour, as seen from the Loch promenade, and the town's old St-Goustan quarter are both of interest to the tourist.

The Battle of Auray (14C). – The town is famous in Breton history for the battle that was fought under its walls in 1364 and ended the War of Succession (p 22: Historical Facts). The troops of Charles of Blois, backed by Du Guesclin, held a bad position on a marshy plain north of Auray. Jean de Montfort, Charles's cousin, Olivier de Clisson, and the English, commanded by Chandos, were in a dominating position.

Against Du Guesclin's advice, Charles attacked. It was a total defeat. His body was picked up on the battlefield. On seeing the corpse of his rival, whom the Bretons made into a saint, Montfort could not master his emotion. But Chandos roused him, saying, "You cannot have your cousin alive and the Duchy too. Thank God and your friends." Du Guesclin had fought like a desperate man: having broken all his weapons, he felled his opponents with his iron gauntlets. The English leader saw him and persuaded him to surrender by saying: "The day is not yours, Messire Bertrand; you will be luckier another time." As for Olivier de Clisson, he lost an eye in the fight.

Cadoudal, or the last Chouan. – Cadoudal was a farmer's son. He was twenty-two years old when the Chouannerie (Breton royalist revolt) broke out in 1793. When the men of the Vendée were beaten he carried on the struggle in Morbihan. He was captured, imprisoned at Brest but escaped, and took part in the action at Quiberon (p 166), came away unhurt, submitted to Hoche in 1796 and reopened the campaign in 1799. The troops that hunted him undertook huge engineering works; the banks and hedges of the country, which the Chouans used as ramparts and hiding-places, were cleared away. Bonaparte offered the rebel a pardon and the rank of general, without success. The struggle ended only in 1804; Cadoudal had gone to Paris to try to kidnap Napoleon; he was arrested, sentenced to death and executed. His body was given to medical students for dissection. The remains were finally buried in a tomb built within sight of Cadoudal's house on Kerléano Hill, at the gates of Auray.

SIGHTS

Loch Promenade. – There is a good **view**★ over the port, the St-Goustan quarter and the Auray River, crossed by an attractive old stone bridge with cutwaters.

To explore the St-Goustan Quarter on the left bank, go down winding paths to the riverside quay.

Near the old bridge note the En-bas Pavilion, an attractive 16C house (restored).

★**St-Goustan Quarter** (Quartier St-Goustan). – From the Place St-Sauveur (**34**), a picturesque square with 15C houses, the Rue Neuve, a narrow alley edged with old houses, strikes off to the left and straight ahead is the steep Rue St-René.

Climb this street and turn right into Rue St-Sauveur. In front of St-Sauveur Church turn right again into Rue de l'Église downhill to Rue du Petit-Port.

This street, lined with picturesque dwellings, leads back to the Place St-Sauveur.
The quay to the left of the square is called after Benjamin Franklin. In 1776, during the War of Independence, the famous American sailed from Philadelphia to negotiate a treaty with France and landed at Auray. The house where he stayed, No 8, bears a tablet.

★**St-Gildas** (B). – This 17C church, with its Renaissance porch, contains a very fine **altarpiece**★ (1664) at the high altar, and a baptismal font with a carved canopy. Note the 18C woodwork in the side chapels and elegant organ loft (1761).

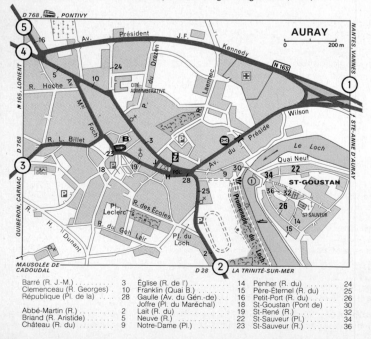

Barré (R. J.-M.)	3	Église (R. de l')	14	Penher (R. du)	24
Clemenceau (R. Georges)	10	Franklin (Quai B.)	15	Père-Éternel (R. du)	25
République (Pl. de la)	28	Gaulle (Av. du Gén.-de)	16	Petit-Port (R. du)	26
		Joffre (Pl. du Maréchal)	18	St-Goustan (Pont de)	30
Abbé-Martin (R.)	2	Lait (R. du)	19	St-René (R.)	32
Briand (R. Aristide)	5	Neuve (R.)	22	St-Sauveur (Pl.)	34
Château (R. du)	9	Notre-Dame (Pl.)	23	St-Sauveur (R.)	36

EXCURSIONS

Round tour of 23 km - 14 miles. – *Time: about 3 hours. Leave Auray by the D 768 towards Baud.*

⊙ **Carthusian Monastery of Auray** (Chartreuse d'Auray). – On the battlefield where he defeated Charles of Blois *(p 52)*, Jean de Montfort (who became Duke Jean IV) built a chapel and a collegiate church which was later transformed into a Carthusian monastery (from 1482-1790). In 1968 a fire ravaged this monastery. The funeral chapel, built in 1829 to hold the bones of exiles and Chouans who were shot on the Champ des Martyrs in 1795, after the unsuccessful Quiberon landing *(p 166)*, was restored as well as the black and white marble mausoleum, decorated with remarkable high reliefs and bearing the names of 953 exiles. The beautiful simple church is lit by modern grisaille windows. In the cloister galleries eighteen panels depict the life of St Bruno. A fine 15C Virgin in boxwood and an 18C Christ are of interest.

Turn round and take the D 120 opposite to Ste-Anne-d'Auray.

⊙ **Champ des Martyrs.** – The exiles and Chouans were shot in this enclosure during the royalist insurrection (1793-1804). A chapel, in the style of a Greek temple, stands on the site where they were executed and buried before the remains were transferred to the Carthusian monastery.

Follow the road to Ste-Anne-d'Auray.

The road skirts the Kerzo Bog (on the right) where the Battle of Auray was fought.

After 500 m - about 1/3 mile bear left in the direction of St-Degan.

The road climbs the leftward slope of the deep valley of the Loch.

⊙ **St-Degan.** – In the hamlet, turn left to see the **ecological museum.** Restored buildings, built of granite and with thatched roofs, surround the threshing area; you will see a house with furniture of the Bas-Vannetais, a building used both as living quarters and work place with everyday objects, ploughing implements and craftsmen's tools. An exhibition is devoted to Breton weddings.

Go to Brech and turn right into the D 19.

At the entrance to Ste-Anne-d'Auray, in a bend on the right, is a monument erected in 1891 to the memory of the Count of Chambord, the Pretender who narrowly failed to oust the Regime at the beginning of the Third Republic and who used to come on pilgrimage to Ste-Anne.

★ **Ste-Anne-d'Auray.** – *P 204.*

Pluneret. – Pop 2 334. In the cemetery, alongside the central alley, on the right, are the tombs of the Countess de Ségur, the writer of children's books, and of her son.

Proceed on the D 101 towards Bono and after 2 km - 1 mile turn left for Ste-Avoye.

Ste-Avoye. – Among picturesque cottages, near a fountain, stands a pretty Renaissance ⊙ **chapel** with a fine keel-shaped **roof★**. The fine oak **rood-screen★** is carved and painted to represent the apostles on the side facing the nave and the Virtues on the chancel side, surrounded by St Fiacre and St Lawrence on the left and St Yves on the right.

Turn back in the direction of Ste-Anne-d'Auray and take the N 165 to return to Auray.

★★ **Boat trip on the Morbihan Gulf.** – A pleasant excursion up the **Auray River★** as far ⊙ as Bono and round the gulf.

★ # BARNENEZ Tumulus (TUMULUS DE BARNENEZ)

Michelin map **58** fold 6 or **230** fold 5 – Local map p 48

⊙ This impressive tumulus, a mound of dry stones (**cairn** in Brittany and Scotland), stands on the Kernéléhen peninsula, dominating the Bay of Térénez and the Morlaix estuary. Discovered accidentally it is now possible to see this ancient burial place in cross section. Excavations between 1955 and 1968 revealed eleven burial chambers, two of which were roofed with great horizontal slabs. The entrances all faced south and were preceded by 7-12m - 23-39ft long passages. It would appear that there were two distinct periods of construction: the first tumulus in a local green stone is more than 6 000 years old while the second one, nearer the slope, is 300 years younger and is composed mainly of the light coloured Stérec granite, from an offshore island.

BATZ Island   Pop 744

Michelin map **58** fold 6 or **230** fold 5
Access: see the current Michelin Red Guide France

⊙ The island of Batz (pronounced Ba) 4 km - 2 1/2 miles long and 1 km - 1/2 mile wide is separated from the mainland by a narrow channel, notorious for its treacherous currents. The ferry arrives in Kernoc'h Bay which is fringed by the village and the modern buildings of the rescue station. This treeless – with the exception of the village – island has sandy beaches. To the north the island is fringed by offshore skerries. The mild climate is particularly suitable for market gardening. On Batz the men are either sailors or farmers and the women help in the market gardens or collect the seaweed.

⊙ **Church.** – The church in the centre of the village was built in 1873. Note in the choir the statues of the Virgin (14-15C) and St Paul the Aurelian (in wood, 17C), the Celtic saint of British origin, who died on the island in 573. In the north transept is a piece of oriental material dating from the 8C, reputed to be 'the stole of St Paul' *(p 54)*.

Lighthouse. – *On the west side.* 210 steps. The 44m - 144ft tall lighthouse stands on the island's highest point (23m - 75ft). View of the island and reef fringed coast.

The Monster's Hole. – *Go beyond the lighthouse and after the ruined house on the dune, take the path to the right.* The low-lying rock offshore is said to mark the spot where the dragon, who terrorised the island, is said to have landed, having been thrown out to sea by St Paul the Aurelian, with the help of his stole.

Ste-Anne Chapel. – *On the east side.* A ruined Romanesque chapel on the site of the monastery founded by St Paul. *Pardon* on the Sunday nearest to 26 July.
From the nearby sand dunes there are fine views of the coast and offshore islets.

★ BATZ-SUR-MER   Pop 2 591

Michelin map **63** folds 13, 14 or **230** fold 51 – Local map p 108

Bordered by the ocean and the salt marshes, Batz's tall church belfry acts as a landmark. The rocky coastline is interrupted by the sandy beaches of Valentin, La Govelle and St-Michel, the latter being protected by a breakwater beside which stands the Pierre-Longue menhir.

★ **St-Guénolé.** – It belonged to a priory in the 13C and was rebuilt in the 15-16C. Its **belfry**, 60m - 190ft high, surmounted by a pinnacled turret, dates from 1677.
In the **interior,** you will notice at once that the chancel is off-centre, that massive pillars support Gothic arches and that the wooden roof is shaped like the keel of a boat. The **keystones** of the arches in the north aisle are remarkably carved. One of the windows in the south aisle commemorates the consecration of the building in 1428.

○ **Ascent to the belfry.** – 182 steps. There is an extensive **panorama**★★ along the coast from the St-Gildas Point, south of the Loire, to the shores of the Rhuys Peninsula and, at sea, to Belle-Ile and Noirmoutier; you overlook the salt marshes *(details p 107).*

★ **Notre-Dame-du-Mûrier.** – The fine Gothic ruins of the chapel include a sculpted doorway which is flanked by a turret staircase with its granite covered roof. Legend has it that it was built in the 15C by Jean de Rieux de Ranrouët *(p 104)* to keep a vow he made when in peril at sea. He was guided to safety by a burning mulberry bush.

Customs Officers' Path (Sentier des Douaniers). – Take the path in front of the St-Michel beach, turning to the left. It skirts the cliff edge and offers a view of the Grande Côte and, later, of the Pierre-Longue menhir and impressive **rocks**★.

Return by the Rue du Golf.

○ **Salt Marsh Museum (Musée des marais salants).** – This museum of popular arts and traditions contains on the ground floor a display of 18-19C items: furniture, ceramics and salt workers' clothes. On the first floor in addition to an audio-visual presentation on salt marshes, there is a model of a salt pan and salt workers' tools.

BAUD   Pop 4 962

Michelin map **63** fold 2 or **230** fold 36

The village is built on a hill surrounded by a smiling countryside through which flow the Blavet, Evel and Tarun Rivers.

Notre-Dame-de-la-Clarté. – The 16C chapel with its venerated statue of Our Lady opens off the nave in the parish church (1927). *Pardon* on the first Sunday in July.

Fountain of Notre-Dame-de-la-Clarté. – It stands in the lower town, below the Lociné road, at the far end of the large car park.

○ **The Venus of Quinipily.** – *2 km - 1 mile SW. Leave Baud by the road to Hennebont. At a place called Coët Vin (1 500 m - 1 mile) bear left onto a narrow road; 500 m - 1/3 mile farther leave your car (car park on right) and walk up a steep path.*
The Venus is on the right, standing over a fountain.The origins of the statue are uncertain. It has been taken for a Roman idol or an Egyptian Isis. As it was the object of almost pagan worship, it was twice thrown into the Blavet, once by order of the ecclesiastical authorities; the people fished it out. The figure which was recarved in the 18C, bears only a very remote resemblance to the Goddess of Beauty.

EXCURSIONS

○ **St-Adrien Chapel.** – *7 km - 4 miles NW. Leave Baud by the D 3 towards Guémené and after 3.2 km - 2 miles turn right into the D 327 to St-Barthélemy.* The road follows the valley of the Blavet before reaching St-Adrien hamlet with its splendid 18C granite houses. The 15C chapel stands below the road, between two fountains; the one on the right is surmounted by a Calvary. Inside there is a simple roodscreen, carved on the nave side and painted on the other, adorned with statues of Christ and the Apostles. *Pardon* on third or fourth Sunday in August.

St-Michel Chapel. – *8 km - 5 miles NE, plus 1/4 hour on foot Rtn. Leave Baud by the D 768 towards Pontivy and after 3 km - 2 miles turn into the D 197 to Guénin, then follow the signposts.* Leave the car near the 16C chapel of Maneguen which is adorned with a carved band on the west façade; note the well (1878). *Take the uphill path to the left of the close.* At the summit (165m - 541ft) is St-Michel Chapel. Wide **panorama**.

Camors Forest. – *5 km - 3 miles S.* It extends over some 650 ha - 1 606 acres.

Floranges Forest. – *10 km - 6 miles SE.* 780 ha - 1 927 acres of state-owned forest, ideal for walks.

Étang de la Forêt. – *13 km - 8 miles SE.* A fine stretch of water on the Loc with facilities for boat hire and fishing.

★★★ La BAULE Pop 14 688

Michelin map 🔢 fold 14 or 🔢 folds 51, 52 – Local map p 108 – Facilities

La Baule is one of the best known seaside resorts on the Atlantic coast and one of the most fashionable in Brittany. In 1879, the construction of La Baule was started near **Escoublac** *(p 108)*, the old town which had been buried under the dunes. In 1840, measures were taken to fix the dunes by planting 400 ha - 1 000 acres of maritime pines. The town enjoys a mild climate as it is protected from the strong winds to the east and west by the Chémoulin and Penchâteau Points and to the north by the forest.

★★ **Sea Front.** – Stretching for about 5 km - 3 miles between Pornichet and Le Pouliguen, this elegant promenade, lined with luxurious hotels, modern buildings and the Casino, looks down upon a beautiful fine sandy beach and the bay of La Baule dotted with tiny islands.

The Esplanade Benoît, reserved for pedestrians only, ends at the west at the pleasure boat harbour *(port de plaisance)* which is in a well sheltered channel *(étier)* linking the ocean to the salt marshes.

★★LA BAULE-LES-PINS

La Baule extends eastwards by this resort, which was built in 1930, in an area forested with pine trees. The attractive Allée Cavalière leads to the Escoublac Forest. Salt-water swimming pools in operation all year round are part of a thalassotherapy institute (salt-water cure).

★ **Dryades Park.** – This lovely park, near the Place des Palmiers, is landscaped with trees of many varieties and colourful flower beds.

EXCURSIONS

★ **Guérande Peninsula (Presqu'île de Guérande).** – *Round tour of 62 km - 39 miles – about 5 1/2 hours. Description p 107.*

★ **From La Baule to St-Nazaire by the coast road.** – *Round tour of 38 km - 24 miles – about 2 hours.*
The coast road provides good views of the bay of La Baule and goes through the seaside resorts of Pornichet *(p 165)*, and by the D 292, Ste-Marguerite and St-Marc.

BÉCHEREL Pop 528

Michelin map 🔢 fold 16 or 🔢 fold 25

Seignorial lands from 1123 to 1790, Bécherel perched on a hill (alt 176m - 577ft), is a former stronghold. Only a few ruins still stand.
The street names Chanvrerie *(chanvre* – hemp), Filanderie *(filandre* – fibre), etc., evoke former times when flax was cultivated and the purest linen thread was produced in the area.
There is a view as far as Dol, Dinan and Combourg.

⊙ **Caradeuc Château.** – *1 km - 1/2 mile W.* This former home of a famous Attorney-General, Louis-René, Marquess of Caradeuc de La Chalotais 1701-1785 *(p 179)*, has a very fine **park★**. This charming French garden is pleasantly shaded and landscaped with pools, basins and statues. From the terrace north of the château there is an immense view towards Dinan and the Upper Valley of the Rance.

EXCURSION

Round tour of 34 km - 21 miles. – *Time: about 1 hour. Leave Bécherel by the D 20 which passes in front of Caradeuc Château. After 4 km - 2 1/2 miles turn right.*

St-Pern. – Pop 773. The head office of the Congregation of the Little Sisters of the Poor *(p 197)* is established in the old château of the Tour St-Joseph.

After Plouasne the road continues to the lovely site of Neal Pond. At the entrance to the village of Guitté turn right to Guenroc.

Guenroc. – Its name comes from the white rocks which dominate it.

Rophémel Dam (Barrage de Rophémel). – Take the path to the small belvedere from where there is a view of the reservoir. This dam is part of the Rance hydro-electric power scheme *(p 175)*.

Return to Bécherel by Le Val and Plouasne.

BEG-MEIL

Michelin map 🔢 fold 15 or 🔢 fold 32

Beg-Meil (the Point of the Mill), scattered amidst pines and pathways, is located at the mouth of La Forêt Bay and opposite Concarneau. This resort has beaches both on its bay and oceanside. On the bay side there are small rocky wooded coves: Oiseaux Beach and La Cale Beach. On the ocean side there are dunes: the well equipped Sémaphore Beach, while from the vast Dunes Beach (or Grande Beach), the Glénan archipelago is visible in the distance.
From Beg-Meil Point there is a fine view of Concarneau and La Forêt Bay.

⊙ **Boat trips.** – *During the season there are regular services to Concarneau (p 77) across the bay, the St-Nicolas Island (Glénan p 102) and Quimper (p 168) by the Odet (p 172).*

Michelin map 🔢 folds 11, 12 or 🔢 folds 48, 49
Access: see the current Michelin Red Guide France

This, the largest of the Breton islands, is a shist plateau measuring about 84 sq km - 32 sq miles - 17 km long and 5 to 10 km wide – 11 × 3 to 6 miles. The mean altitude is 40m - 128ft (highest point: 63m - 200ft). It is crossed by many valleys which cut deeply into the high rocks and end as beaches or harbours. The east side, which is well protected, has many creeks with good bathing.

There is a marked contrast between the middle of the plateau, exposed to wind, sun and rain and covered with wheat fields alternating with patches of gorse, and the small sheltered valleys, with their lush fields and fine trees and where whitewashed houses are clustered together.

Fouquet, Marquis of Belle-Ile. – Belle-Ile belonged to the Abbey of Ste-Croix in Quimperlé *(p 173)* and the Gondi family before it was bought in 1650 by the Superintendent Fouquet.

The latter, wishing to make the island a safe retreat in case of misfortune, completed the fortifications – he added 200 cannons. His immense wealth even enabled him to keep his own fleet, of which the flagship was the *Grand Écureuil* (Great Squirrel – the Fouquet coat of arms includes a squirrel with the motto: "How high shall I not climb?").

This daring policy, added to the swindles and slights which he practised on Louis XIV, was his undoing.

The last act was played out at Nantes, which the Court was visiting in 1661. D'Artagnan and the Musketeers seized Fouquet as he came out of the castle and put him in a coach which made all speed for Vincennes. He died in 1680.

A fortified rock. – As an outlying citadel of the French coast, Belle-Ile has been attacked many times by British and Dutch fleets. The British took the island twice – in 1572 and 1761 – and occupied it until the Treaty of Paris (1763) returned it to the French.

The island has conserved its defensive system: in addition to Le Palais citadel, fortified by the military architect Vauban, there are several 18 and 19C isolated outworks (redoubts) around the coast.

Canadians, Bretons. – In 1766, 78 Canadian families came to live on the island; they brought with them the potato many years before Parmentier introduced it to France. These Canadians were descendants of the French who had lived in Acadia since the beginning of the 17C and had refused to submit to the English who had held Nova Scotia from the time of the Treaty of Utrecht, 1713. The Acadian families were moved to New England and then, after the Treaty of Paris, to France and Belle-Ile.

A refuge for artists. – Since the late 19C, numerous are the artists who have been attracted by the beauty and calm of this isle: Claude Monet, Sarah Bernhardt and the musician Albert Roussel.

LE PALAIS *Time: 2 hours*

The island's main town (Pop 2 389) is where most of the facilities are to be found. Boat services link it to Quiberon on the mainland. Arriving by boat or from the Rue des Remparts there is a good view of the port, with its fishing and pleasure craft, overlooked by the citadel.

★ **Vauban Citadel.** – *Tour of ⏱ ramparts signposted.*

Built in 1549 on the orders of Henri II, the citadel was Fouquet's stronghold. The double ramparts and powerful corner bastions show Vauban's influence. The citadel was both a prison and barracks till 1961. Note the incredible thickness of the walls and in the southwest corner a three walled round tower, the remains of the first castle, which was transformed into a powder magazine by Vauban. Numerous **views** of Le Palais and the coast from the Governor's bastion.

The **museum** housed in the vaulted rooms of the Louis XIII style military buildings contains interesting documents on the island's history and souvenirs of its illustrious hosts from Fouquet to Albert Roussel.

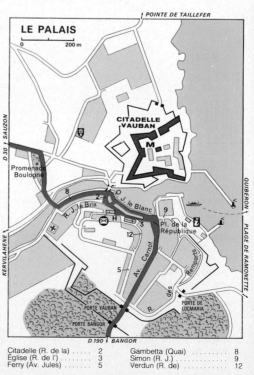

LE PALAIS

Citadelle (R. de la)	2	Gambetta (Quai)	8
Église (R. de l')	3	Simon (R. J.)	9
Ferry (Av. Jules)	5	Verdun (R. de)	12

Port-Coton Needles

★★ ① THE CÔTE SAUVAGE

Round tour of 49 km - 30 miles – about 4 hours – local map p 58

Leave Le Palais by the Quai Gambetta and the Promenade Boulogne and turn right towards the citadel. Near the coast, bear left and then right.

Taillefer Point. – Near the signal station there is a fine **view** over Le Palais roadstead, Kerdonis Point, Hoedic and Houat Islands and the Quiberon Peninsula.

Turn round and make for Sauzon.

Nearby is **Port-Fouquet,** a pretty rocky creek.

★ **Sauzon.** – Pop 563. This small port with its busy marina lies in a pretty **setting**★ on the left bank of the estuary of the Sauzon River. A pleasant excursion *(1 1/2 hours on foot Rtn)* starting from the port, takes you round **Cardinal Point** and affords views over the approach to the port, the Taillefer Point, the Quiberon Peninsula and the Poulains Point.

★ **Poulains Point.** – *1/2 hour on foot Rtn.* From the car park, on the left overlooking a creek is the Sarah Bernhardt Fort, which is near the estate where the actress spent her summers. Make your way down the slip to the sandy isthmus which connects the island with Poulains Point on which stands a lighthouse and which is completely cut off at the Spring Tide. From the point there is a **panorama**★ from left to right of the Vieux-Château Point, the great rocks of the Côte Sauvage, Groix Island, the peninsula and bay of Quiberon, the Rhuys Peninsula, the islands of Houat and Hoedic, Taillefer Point and the Dog's Rock (Rocher du Chien).

Turn back and after 2 km - 1 mile turn right.

★★ **Apothecary's Shop Grotto** (Grotte de l'Apothicairerie). – *1/2 hour on foot Rtn.* Its name is derived from the cormorants' nests which at one time were placed in rows in the rocky cavities, like the jars on the shelves of a chemist's shop. At the end of the point go down a flight of steps (on the right) cut in the rock (caution: slippery steps). The grotto forms a deep cavity into which the sea thunders. In bad weather the site is dramatic and dangerous, when the sea is calm the water takes on a fine blue-green colour.

Return to the junction and turn right.

On Kerlédan Moor, on either side of the road to Port-Donnant stand the **menhirs** Jean and Jeanne, one of schist the other of granite, said to be young fiancés punished because they wanted to meet before their wedding-day.

★★ **Port-Donnant.** – *1/2 hour on foot Rtn; car park.* The setting is superb: a fine sandy beach and a rolling sea enclosed between high cliffs. Bathing is dangerous.

⏱ **The Great Lighthouse** (Grand Phare). – The lighthouse opened near Goulphar in 1835 and itself 46m - 150ft high, stands perched on a rock so that its light is actually 84m - 275ft above sea level. The beam carries 130 km - 75 miles making it one of the most powerful in Europe. From the balcony there is a fine **view**★★ of Belle-Ile, the islands and the coast round Lorient and as far as the Rhuys Peninsula.

★ **Port-Goulphar.** – *Time: 1/4 hour on foot Rtn.* This is one of the most charming sites on the island. After the Goulphar manorhouse take a steep road downhill to the port, a long, narrow channel where the clear waters reveal richly coloured algae, at the foot of picturesque cliffs. A group of islets marks its entrance. The best **view**★ of this curious mass of rocks can be enjoyed from the cliff facing the Grand Large hotel.

★★ **The Port-Coton Needles** (Aiguilles de Port-Coton). – Port-Coton is so called because the sea there seems to boil and builds up a great mass of foam like cotton wool. At the end of the road loom the Needles *(illustration above);* some of these pyramids are pierced by grottoes. Follow the cliff edge to the right for a good view over Port-Coton Bay.

Bangor. – Pop 638. This village takes its name from the religious settlement or "bangor" founded by the first Celtic monks who settled on the island.

Port-Kérel. – *2.5 km – 1 1/2 miles from Bangor.* This sheltered beach in a rocky setting is the most popular on the island.

Return to Le Palais by the Bangor and Vauban Gates.

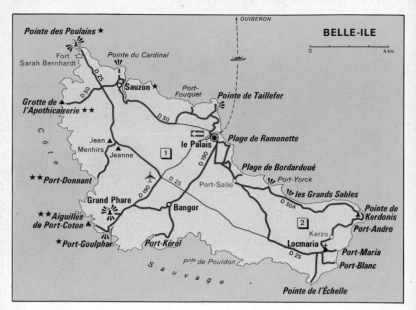

★ 2 KERDONIS POINT

Round tour of 33 km - 20 miles – about 2 hours

Leave Le Palais by Avenue Carnot and Rue Villaumez on the left.

Ramonette Beach (Plage de Ramonette). – Backing on to the point, this is the beach for Le Palais.

At the entrance to Port-Salio, turn left.

Bordardoué Beach (Plage de Bordardoué). – Go through the door in the former fortifications to discover a fine sheltered, sandy beach.

Turn round and bear left twice.

The road descends towards **Port-Yorck** with Bugul Point to the right and Gros Rocher Point to the left which is extended by an islet on which stands an old fort. The road from Port-Yorck to Kerdonis Point commands superb **views★** over Houat and Hoedic and the neighbouring islands, the Morbihan coast and Le Palais roadstead.

Les Grands Sables. – This, the largest beach on Belle-Ile, has traces of fortifications erected in 1747 as in the 17 and 18C British and Dutch forces made several attempts to land on the island.

Kerdonis Point. – At the southern tip of the island stands a lighthouse which commands the sea lane between Hoedic and Belle-Ile.

Port-Andro. – A sandy beach off a small valley where the English forces landed in 1761.

Make for Locmaria via Kerzo.

Locmaria. – Pop 602. The village is reputed among the islanders for the practice of sorcery. In the shaded square stands the church of Notre-Dame-de-Boistord (1714) to commemorate, according to legend, a splendid elm cut down by the Dutch to replace a broken mast. The trunk cracked as it fell, terrifying the crew.

Port-Maria. – A downhill road to the right of the church leads to this deep cleft in the rocks which offers a fine sandy beach at low tide.

Turn left on leaving Locmaria.

Port-Blanc. – Small cove overlooked by the cliffs of Arzic Point.

Return to the D 25 and bear left twice.

Échelle Point. – *Unsurfaced road after Skeul hamlet.* A semicircle of jagged rocks in a wild setting.

Turn back, bear left and after 2 km - 1 mile, make a right turn to return to Le Palais by the Bangor and Vauban Gates.

The Michelin Sectional Map Series (1:200 000)
covers the whole of France

When choosing your lunchtime or overnight stop use
the above maps as all towns listed
in the Red Guide are underlined in red.

When driving into or through a town use
the map as it also indicates all places
with a town plan in the Red Guide.

Common reference numbers make the transfer from map to plan easier

BELLE-ISLE-EN-TERRE

Michelin map 📖 folds 7, 8 or 📖 S of fold 7

This old township stands in a picturesque area at the meeting of two rivers, the Léguer and the Guic.

Every year, on the third Sunday in July, the Locmaria festival is held at Belle-Isle-en-Terre: the main event is a Breton wrestling match, an original and very ancient sport *(see p 226: Pardons)*.

Locmaria Chapel. – *1 km - 1/2 mile N on the D 33 towards Trégrom and an uphill road to the right.*

The chapel, which stands in the cemetery, contains a fine 16C **rood-screen** adorned with coloured wood statues of the Apostles on one side.

EXCURSIONS

★ **Menez-Bré.** – *9 km - 5 1/2 miles NE – about 3/4 hour. Leave Belle-Isle-en-Terre on the N 12, the Guingamp road. 2.5 km - 1 1/2 miles after Louargat, turn left into the Menez-Bré road which goes steeply uphill.*

The Menez-Bré, a lonely hill with an altitude of 302m - 991ft, rises out of the Trégorrois Plateau to a height of 150 m - 492 ft. The St-Hervé Chapel on the summit commands a wide **panorama**★ to the north where the plateau slopes gently towards the sea, cut by the deep valleys of the Trieux, the Jaudy, the Guindy and the Léguer, to the south over the maze of hills and valleys of Cornouaille, and to the southwest towards the Arrée Mountains.

Loc-Envel. – *Pop 105. 4 km - 2 1/2 miles S – about 3/4 hour. Leave by the Callac road, the D 33, and turn right fairly soon into the D 33B which is winding and picturesque.*

The **church** of Loc-Envel in Flamboyant Gothic style rises from the top of a mound and dominates the village. To the left of the belfry-porch, note three small semicircular openings through which the lepers followed the services. One is struck, on entering, by the Flamboyant **rood-screen**★ and the rich decoration of the wood panelled **vaulting**★. Also interesting are the carved friezes running below the vaulting, the two hanging keystones, a Christ in benediction at the entrance to the choir and a Holy Trinity with angels at the transept crossing. The four supporting ribs of the crossing have each at their base a coloured statue of an Evangelist. The 16C furnishings are in keeping with the statuary and carvings: the screens near the font, the ancient statues, the main window in the chancel and the later 17C altarpiece at the high altar.

Gurunhuel. – *Pop 440. 9 km - 5 1/2 miles SE by the D 22 – about 1/4 hour.*

Near the 16C church stands a Calvary of the same date. From the base rise three crosses: the central one bears a Crucifixion with Christ between the Virgin Mary and St John on one side and a Virgin of Pity on the other. The other two crosses show the robbers, their souls are depicted in the form of little figures leaving their bodies and being received by an angel in the case of the good robber, and a demon in the case of the bad robber. Standing on the base are a Roman soldier, St Peter, St Michael and St Paul.

★ BÉNODET

Michelin map 📖 fold 15 or 📖 fold 32 – Local map p 172 – Facilities

This charming seaside resort lies in a pretty, verdant setting at the mouth of the Odet estuary.

Bénodet with a fine beach and small harbour often used by yachts *(port de plaisance)* also has a casino.

> *Daily boat services for pedestrians and cyclists, to Ste-Marine on the opposite bank of the Odet.*

⊙ **Pyramid Lighthouse (Phare de la Pyramide) (B).** – *Take the Avenue de la Plage and then bear right onto the Rue du Phare.*

From the balcony around the lantern (192 steps) the **panorama**★ extends along the coast from the Bay of Concarneau to the Eckmühl lighthouse, and at sea to the Glénan Archipelago. To the north you overlook the wooded countryside cut by the Odet spanned by Cornouaille Bridge.

View over the Odet (E). – *Access by the Kercréven Road.* This viewpoint affords a fine view of the river, the yachting harbour between wooded shores and Cornouaille Bridge.

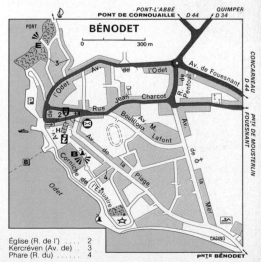

Église (R. de l') 2
Kercréven (Av. de) . . 3
Phare (R. du) 4

BÉNODET★

Bénodet Point. – *Take the Corniche de la Plage, then follow the shores along the Corniche de la Mer to reach the Lichavan Dune.*
Extensive view *(viewing-table and telescope).*

○ **Cornouaille Bridge** (Pont de Cornouaille). – *1 km - 1/2 mile NW.*
This elegant modern structure carries the D 44 across the Odet. The bridge's total length is 610m - 2 001ft and it rises to a height of 30m - 98ft above the water. There is a good **view★** of the port, Ste-Marine, the estuary and the Odet, up-river.

EXCURSION

From Bénodet to Concarneau by the coast road. – *40 miles - 25 miles – about 3 hours. Leave Bénodet E by the D 44 towards Fouesnant and after 2 km - 1 mile turn right.*

Le Letty. – A small hamlet by the Mer Blanche, a large pool sheltered by a dune and linked to the ocean by a narrow channel. Sailing school.
Return to the D 44.

Le Perguet. – Note on the right the Ste-Brigitte Chapel (16C) with an unusual stone staircase on the roof leading to the pierced belfry crowning the transept crossing. There is a ceramic workshop 50 m from the chapel.
After 2.5 km - 1 mile, take the D 154 to the right to Mousterlin Point.

Mousterlin Point. -- From the end of the point there is an extensive view of the coast from Lesconil Point to Trévignon Point, with in the distance Moutons Island and the Glénan archipelago. The Eckmühl lighthouse can be seen on the right after dark.
Turn round. After 2 km - 1 mile bear right and 4.5 km - 2 3/4 miles farther on turn right.

Beg-Meil. – *P 55.*
Turn back and after 3 km - 2 miles bear right.

Cap-Coz. – From this small resort built on a sandy spit, the view extends on one side over La Forêt Bay, Beg-Meil and Concarneau and on the other side over Port-la-Forêt and La Forêt-Fouesnant.
A pleasant excursion can be enjoyed by taking the **coastal path** *(1 hour on foot Rtn – access through a door after the pine grove at the far end of the great wall along the road leading to the beach).* This path runs along La Forêt Bay as far as La Roche-Percée, overlooking or crossing small coves and affording fine views of the coastline from Kerleven to Trévignon Point.

Fouesnant. – *P 99.*

La Forêt-Fouesnant. – Pop 2 149. Facilities. This quiet village possesses a small parish close and a 16C Calvary with four corner pilasters. The church porch, dating from 1538, is adorned with two old, rough-hewn statues of St Roch and St Mélar. Inside, at the high altar are an altarpiece and, on either side, two 17C statues. The chapels at the far end of the church contain, to the right, a wooden statue of St Alan and to the left, a font (1628) with a piscina and a basin hewn from the same block. In the chapel on the south side of the chancel stand a *Pietà* and a late 17C painting of the Rosary. Breton and Celtic music all day.
Take the coast road towards Concarneau and half-way down bear right.

Port-la-Forêt. – This port for pleasure craft has been built near La Forêt-Fouesnant. There are boat services to Glénan Islands *(p 102)* and up the Odet *(p 172).*

The road runs along Kerleven Beach at the bottom of La Forêt Bay, then after a steep descent (1 in 7), along St-Laurent cove and crosses Saint-Jean Bay to Concarneau *(p 77).* Beautiful **sites★**, especially at high tide.

BOAT TRIPS

★★ Up the Odet River. – *Time: 1 1/2 hours; departure from Bénodet. Description of the* ○ *trip down the Odet on p 172.*

Loctudy; Glénan Islands. – *Crossing time: 1/2 hour for Loctudy and 1 3/4 hours for the Glénan Islands. Descriptions of Loctudy p 130 and of the Glénan Islands p 102.*

BERVEN

Michelin map 🗺 fold 5 or 🗺 fold 4 – 1.5 km - 1 mile N of Plouzévédé

The triumphal arch through which you enter the parish close *(details on parish closes p 37)* is a fine specimen of Renaissance art with its three semicircular arches and its pilasters with capitals.

★ **Church.** – The 16C church has a façade surmounted by a square tower crowned with
○ a dome with small lanterns and ornamented by balustrades; it was the first of its kind in Brittany (1573) and served as a model for many others.
A wooden rood-screen stands before the very fine chancel **enclosure★**, ornamented on the front with small fluted granite columns and at the sides with wooden ones. In the chancel are 17C stalls with arm-rests in the form of winged caryatids. In the chapel to the left of the chancel is a 16C niche with shutters whose panels depict, in low relief, scenes from the life of the Virgin; in the centre is a statue showing the Virgin on a crescent moon. There is another niche at the far end of the nave, on the left, and on the shutters are illustrated six episodes in the life of Christ: His Childhood on the left and the Passion on the right.

BINIC

Michelin map **59** fold 3 or **230** fold 8

Binic is a delightful resort whose port sheltered fishing schooners in winter in the past. It is now used by pleasure craft and a few coastal fishing boats.

Penthièvre Pier. – The pier closing off the outer harbour is reached by Quais Jean-Bart and Surcouf. From a belvedere on the jetty there is a pleasant view of the beach with its raised huts dominated by a pine-topped knoll and the port.

⊙ **Museum.** – Mementoes and models recall the great Newfoundland fishing expeditions. There are also regional costumes, crafts and old postcards.

EXCURSION

Round tour of 18 km - 11 miles. – *Time: about 2 1/2 hours. Leave Binic by the D 786 towards Paimpol, and turn left into the D 4 to Lantic. After 3 km - 2 miles bear left in the direction of Trégomeur and 5 km - 3 miles farther on, right into an uphill road.*

⊙ **Moulin de Richard Zoo.** – At Trégomeur. The zoo set in parkland (10 ha - 25 acres) includes monkey ranges, a safari park where llamas, deer, dwarf goats, emus, Patagonian hares, gnu, wild boar etc. roam freely and an exotic enclosure on an island with chimps, gorillas, baboons and many birds.

> *Go round the zoo and at the first junction turn right, follow the road which runs down into a verdant valley, bear left once and then keep turning right to reach Notre-Dame-de-la-Cour.*

⊙ **Notre-Dame-de-la-Cour.** – At **Lantic.** The chapel is a fine 15C building with stone vaulting. Beautiful **stained glass windows★** (15C) at the back of the high altar illustrate the life of the Virgin in eighteen panels; in the south transept, the window depicting St Nicolas is also 15C. The chancel contains the 17C tomb of Guillaume de Rosmadec in Kersanton granite as well as 14 and 16C statues. A 17C Calvary stands in the small square. *Pardon on 15 August.*

> *Return to Binic via Prido and the Ic Valley.*

BLAIN

Michelin map **63** fold 16 or **230** fold 54

The Nantes to Brest canal separates this market town from its castle, whose main building is now occupied by a private school, the Institution N.-D. de la Groulaie.

⊙ **La Groulaie Castle (Château de la Groulaie).** – This fortress which originally belonged to Olivier de Clisson became Rohan family property from 1407 to 1802. Despite the fact that in 1628 Richelieu razed the ramparts impressive **ruins★** still stand. The 16C **Drawbridge Tower** (Tour du Pont-Levis) with its pepperpot roof, overlooks the now dry moats. Beyond the outbuildings stand the 15C **King's Apartments** (Logis du Roi). The main façade with its tall pinnacled dormer windows, strange gargoyles and its brick patterned chimney stacks, reveals all the charm of the Renaissance. The rather severe looking tower to the right is called the **Constable's Tower** (Tour du Connétable, 1386).

EXCURSION

★ **Round tour of 13 km - 8 miles.** – *NW by the D 15, the road to Guéméné-Penfao.*

★ **Gâvre Forest** (Forêt du Gâvre). – The road crosses the stands of oak interspersed with beeches and pines, which cover 4 400 ha - 10 900 acres to reach the Belle Étoile crossroads, the meeting point of ten converging avenues.

> *Turn right towards Le Gâvre and at La Maillardais turn left onto the track.*

La Magdeleine Chapel. – Formerly part of a leper hospital, this modest 12C chapel with a timber roof in its chancel has a charming 15C polychrome **Virgin★**.

> *Return to La Maillardais and continue straight on to Le Gâvre.*

Le Gâvre. – Pop 892. The 13-15C church (restored) has a strange 17C lateral belfry. Inside there is a timber cradle roof. The stained glass windows dating from the 1930s evoke the First World War.

> *Return to Blain on the D 42.*

★ BOURBANSAIS Château

Michelin map **59** fold 16 or **230** fold 25 – 14 km - 9 miles SE of Dinan

This impressive late 16C building, enlarged in the 18C, stands in an immense park. Three generations of the Huard family, counsellors to the Breton parliament, have contributed to the embellishment of the French-style garden.

⊙ **Zoo and Gardens.** – Situated in a lovely verdant setting (3 ha - 7 acres), the zoo contains animals from five continents: deer, wild animals, monkeys, birds, etc.

After the zoo go to the château. The main building is flanked by pinnacled turrets and saddleback roofed pavilions characteristic of the 18C. One of the façades looks onto the garden. There are 18C urns perched on small columns in the middle of the lawn.

⊙ **Château interior.** – On the ground floor the rooms are decorated and furnished in the 18C style and contain 17C Aubusson tapestries and a fine collection of porcelain from the India Company. In the peristyle, added in the 19C, are exhibited documents, archives and personal objects belonging to the past owners which evoke the château's history. The kennels, in the outbuildings, house a pack of dogs.

Michelin map **59** fold 2 or **230** fold 8
Access: see the current Michelin Red Guide France

🕐 Bréhat is a much frequented holiday resort. Its pink rocks stand out against the sea. Cars are not allowed, however tractors are used for transportation.

GEOGRAPHICAL AND HISTORICAL NOTES

A mild climate. – Bréhat, which is about 3.5 km - 2 miles long and 1.5 km - 1 mile wide, consists of two islands joined in the 18C by a bridge built by Vauban. The coast, very broken and indented, is surrounded by 86 islets and reefs. Thanks to its mild climate (winter average 6°C-43°F), mimosa, eucalyptus and fig trees grow out in the open and the façades are decked with geraniums. There is little rain, the clouds generally passing over the flat island to condense over the mainland. The island's interior is a labyrinth of paths lined with honeysuckle or flower-decked dry stone walls, low houses with masses of hydrangea bushes, villas with vast gardens, a couple of cows in a tiny field or sheep on the heath. Its southern part is more welcoming than the rugged north. This colourful island has attracted such personalities as: Prosper Merimée, Ernest Renan, Louis Pasteur, Madeleine Renaud and Jean-Louis Barrault.

A varied history. – Bréhat owes its name (Breiz Coat: Brittany of the Woods) to an Irish monk, St Budoc, who landed on Lavrec Island in 470 AD. A mediaeval fortress facing this island was destroyed by the English in 1409 and local people were put to death at the Crec'h ar Pot mill (moulin) on North Island. La Corderie Bay, on the west coast, was used as anchorage. According to local tradition, it was a sea-captain from Morlaix, Coatanlem, living in Lisbon, who revealed the existence of the New World to Christopher Columbus in 1484 – eight years before its official discovery – and showed him the course taken by the island's fishermen already familiar with Newfoundland waters. During the Wars of Religion, in 1591, Crec'h Tarek mill on South Island served as a place of execution. In 1598, Henri II ordered the castle to be razed. In the 19C the island was frequented by privateers and during the last war, it was occupied by German troops until 4 August 1944 (the lighthouses were blown up).

TOUR *allow 1/2 day*

The island is criss-crossed by concrete paths with arrows at ground level showing the way.

Le Bourg. – The houses of the island's capital, are grouped around a small square lined with plane trees. In the 12 and 18C church, which has an unusual granite wallbelfry, the high altar and the font grille are 17C and the lectern is 18C.

Bois de la Citadelle. – Planted with conifers, it overlooks the cliff. From the life-boat shelter below, there is a good **view**★ of Kerpont channel, which is impressive at low tide when the mass of rocks is visible, and Béniguet Island.

La Corderie. – Bounded by the Pont ar Prat (also known as Vauban Bridge), this vast bay between the two islands is the main harbour. Beautiful villas.

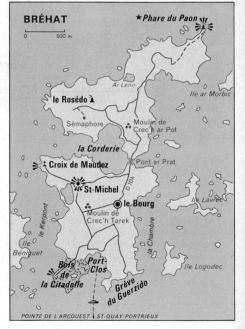

Guerzido Beach (Grève du Guerzido). – It includes the Petit and Grand Guerzido, the most popular beaches.

Maudez Cross (Croix de Maudez). – Erected in 1788 amid the heather and facing the ocean, the cross evokes the memory of a monk named Maudez who founded a monastery in the year AD 570, on a neighbouring island. There is a fine **view**★ of the islands of Béniguet to the left and Maudez to the right and the reefs.

★ **Paon Lighthouse (Phare du Paon).** – *On the tip of North Island.* The paved platform at the foot of the lighthouse affords a remarkable **view** of the rugged coastline, the chasm, the pink rocks and the shingles. This is the wildest part of the island.

🕐 **Port-Clos.** – This is a landing point for the boat services.

Rosédo Lighthouse (Le Rosédo). – Dating from 1862, it stands inland.

St-Michel Chapel. – High on a mound (26m - 85ft; 39 steps), this chapel serves as a landmark for ships. There is an extensive **view**★ over South Island, the Kerpont channel and Béniguet Island, Birlot Pool overlooked by the ruins of a once tide-operated mill *(p 175),* La Corderie Bay and North Island and in the distance, Talbert Spit (Sillon de Talbert).

BOAT TRIPS

★★ Tour of the Island. – *Time: about 1 hour.* The tour allows the visitor to admire the changing aspects of the coast: the beauty of the northern rocks and cliffs, the Mediterranean charm of the eastern shore and the ever changing colour of the sea, which is often a deep blue.

★ The Trieux Estuary. – This pleasant excursion on the Trieux river, whose banks are in turn sheer, rocky and wooded and at times low-lying and under cultivation, offers views of the pretty site of Lézardrieux with its suspension bridge. The river flows at the foot of the La Roche-Jagu Castle *(p 184)* which can be reached by a fairly steep path through woodlands.

★ BREST   Pop 160 355

Michelin map **58** fold 4 or **230** fold 17 – Local map p 44

After the war, Brest was rebuilt on a geometric plan with its main artery at the wide Rue de Siam which links the naval base to the Place de la Liberté.
The streets open onto the Penfeld or the Cours Dajot from where there are good views over the magnificent roadstead *(rade)*.
It has also developed into the second university centre of Brittany with a thriving cultural centre. Erected on the shore of Ste-Anne-du-Portzic *(p 66),* the Oceanographic Centre offers opportunities for scientific research.

HISTORICAL NOTES

The English set foot in Brest (14C). – During the War of Succession which began in 1341, Montfort, ally of the English, was rash enough to let them guard the town. When he became Duke of Brittany, Montfort tried to drive out the intruders by force of arms. He failed as did the King of France. At last, in 1397, Charles VI persuaded the King of England, Richard II, who had married his eldest daughter, Isabella, to restore Brest to the Duke.

The "Belle Cordelière". – On 10 August 1513, St Lawrence's Day, the English fleet of Henry VIII set out to attack Brest. The Breton fleet sailed to meet it, however its panic-stricken commander fled back to the channel. The *Belle Cordelière,* the gift of Anne of Brittany to her Duchy and on which 300 guests were dancing when the order came to weigh anchor, covered the commander's retreat and bore the brunt of the attack. Fire broke out on board the *Cordelière* as she was fighting gun to gun with an English ship. The commander, Hervé de Portzmoguer, or as he was known in France: Primauguet, knowing that his ship was lost, exhorted his crew and his guests to die bravely with the words: "We will now celebrate the Day of St Lawrence who died by fire!" The two ships blew up together.

The Work of Colbert (17C). – Colbert, the greatest Minister the French Navy ever had, completed the task begun by Richelieu, making Brest the maritime capital of the kingdom. To obtain good crews he set up the Inscription Maritime (marine record and administrative office) which still exists today. After completing their military service, fishermen between the ages of eighteen and forty-eight are placed on the French Naval reserve; the Inscription Maritime looks after them and their families throughout their lives.
Colbert also founded at Brest a school of gunnery, a college of marine guards, a school of hydrography and a school for marine engineers. From this enormous effort a magnificent fleet emerged. Ships reached a tonnage of 5 000 and carried up to 120 big guns; their prows and sterns were carved by such artists as Coysevox.
Duquesne improved the naval dockyard, built ramparts round the town and organized the defense of the channel (Le Goulet). Vauban, the military architect, completed the undertakings. Tourville improved mooring facilities in the roadstead laying down buoys to which ships could moor instead of dropping anchor.

The "Belle Poule". – In 1778, during the American War of Independence, the frigate *La Belle Poule* encountered the British *Arethusa* and forced her to retreat. This victory was very popular at court and all the ladies wore a new hair-style *La Belle Poule* which included, perched on their tresses, a model ship in full sail.

The "Surveillante". – In 1779 a British captain, George Farmer, waged that no French frigate could destroy his *Québec.* Du Couëdic, who commanded the *Surveillante* frigate challenged the wager – this was the beginning of one of the most furious sea duels of all time.
After a spirited battle, north of Ushant, both ships were dismasted. The sails of the *Québec* fell across its guns setting the ship on fire. Du Couëdic ordered rescue action. Later the *Québec* blew up with the wounded Farmer. Du Couëdic died from wounds received during the fight. The *Surveillante* was brought back to Brest where it was triumphantly welcomed and Du Couëdic was laid to rest in the Church of St Louis (destroyed in 1944).

Brest during the War. – As the advanced base of Europe, Brest with its port, dockyard and roadstead, was of first class strategic importance to the Germans. The naval and commercial authorities just managed to clear the port completely in June 1940 before the Germans marched in and began to use it. They also built a concrete shelter for submarines at Laninon. Brest became a considerable threat to Allied convoys sailing between America and Great Britain, and was, therefore, heavily bombed for four years. In September 1944, when the Americans entered, after a 43-day siege, they found a city in ruins.

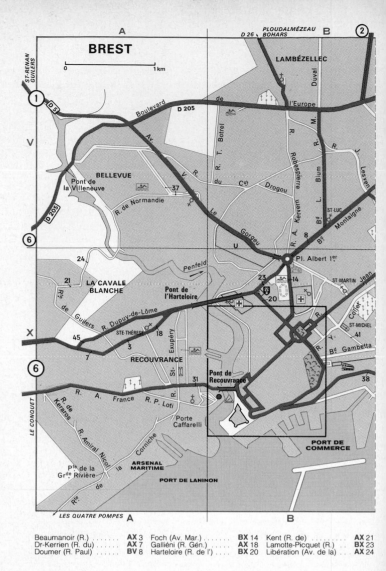

BREST

SIGHTS

Cours Dajot (EZ). – This fine promenade was laid out on the ramparts in 1769 by convicts from the naval prison. There is an excellent **view★★** from the viewing table at the east end of the promenade. You see the Brest roadstead from the mouth of the Élorn, and past the Ménez-Hom and the Roscanvel Point right over to Portzic Point. The anchorage is vast (150 km² - 58 sq miles), deep (12-20m - 6-10 fathoms – over large areas), framed between heights and connected with many big estuaries. It communicates with the Atlantic through a channel, with steep banks, 5 km - 3 miles long and about 1 800m - 1 mile wide. This information explains why Brest has had such great military importance for more than 2 000 years.

To the left the estuary of the Élorn crossed by the great Albert-Louppe Bridge, makes a safe anchorage for yachts. In the foreground is the commercial port. Beyond lies the Plougastel Peninsula, hiding the southeast of the roadstead. On the south side of the roadstead, at Lanvéoc, the Naval School is located; nearby the nuclear submarine base is situated on Ile Longue. On the horizon to the right you see the Crozon Peninsula and the opening of the sound between Portzic Fort and the Espagnols Point.

Before the castle, the inner harbour, protected by its breakwater, serves as anchorage for the fleet. The building overlooking the roadstead between Brest and Ste-Anne-du-Portzic houses the naval base and school.

The Commercial Port (Port de Commerce) (EZ). – *As viewed from Cours Dajot.* It was built in 1860 to take the overflow of military and cargo vessels from the Penfeld basin. The present trade, mainly agricultural, increases yearly and now exceeds 2 million tons a year. Imports include cereals for stock feeding, hydro-carbons, cement and exotic wood while exports are principally potatoes and frozen chickens. The Atlantic maritime servicing station includes facilities such as 3 dry docks, one for ships up to 500 000 tons, 5 wet docks, refueling and tank cleaning (degasification) plants.

The Brest Naval Base (Port de Guerre). – The base was founded in the Penfeld river valley; the estuary is enclosed and winding, 3 km - 2 miles long, 80-100m - 262-328ft wide and 10-12m - 30-38ft deep at low tide. For small ships and the simple building methods of the past, this was an ideal situation; work could be carried on in shelter from storms. It is different now with the huge modern arsenal plant, handling ships of over 35 000 tons, 250m - 800ft long. Huge works have been carried out.

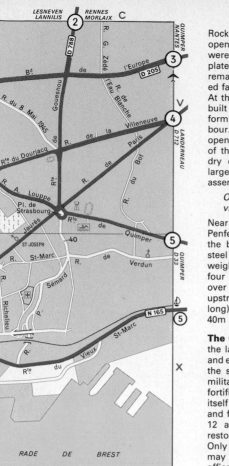

Rock was blasted and hills razed to make open spaces and erect buildings; these were built up in storeys to the level of the plateau above, yet the Penfeld dockyard remained cramped and had to be extended farther into the open.

At the end of the 19C a breakwater was built parallel with the Laninon beach to form the boundary of a great inner harbour. The port of Laninon was developed; open spaces were arranged to take some of the arsenal buildings, and two large dry docks are for the maintenance of large tonnage ships and the other for the assembling of prefabricated elements.

Only French nationals are allowed to visit the arsenal and naval base.

Near the entrance to the dockyard the Penfeld is crossed by the **Recouvrance Bridge,** the biggest drawbridge in Europe. The steel span, about 87m - 285ft long and weighing some 530 tons, swings between four concrete pylons (64m - 209ft high) over the quays of the dockyard. Farther upstream the **Harteloire Bridge** (634m - 2 080ft long) crosses the dockyard at a height of 40m - 128ft.

The Castle (Château) (DZ). – The castle is the last reminder of the history of Brest and enables one to study at close quarters the site that gave the port of Brest its military value. The Penfeld Gate has been fortified since Roman times and the castle itself had often been besieged. The towers and fortifications were built between the 12 and 17C. The perimeter wall was restored at the end of the war.

Only the naval museum and the ramparts may be visited as the castle houses the offices of the Harbour Police (Préfecture Maritime).

Cross the guard towers or Paradis Towers built in 1464. The towers were used by the Duke of Brittany's business agents, and from 17C they housed the garrison on the upper floors with a prison on the ground floor. A naval museum has now been installed there.

Maritime Museum (Musée de la Marine). – The museum, which is a branch of the Maritime Museum in Paris, presents rare models of old ships, navigational instruments and paintings depicting the heyday of sail navigation in the 18C.

A tour of the museum housed in several of the castle towers, enables the visitor to see traces of Gallo-Roman ruins (3C), the Madeleine Tower (3-15C) and the towers of the Paradis Gateway (15C). The wall-walk is devoted to the history of the castle which is seventeen centuries old. The tour also includes the first floor of the keep (14-17C), the small oratory used by Anne of Brittany in 1505; from the Azenor Tower (13C) and the keep's lower floors there are fine views over the roadstead and the Penfeld.

Tanguy Tower (Tour Tanguy) (DZ). – Standing opposite the castle on the other bank of the Penfeld, this 14C tower dominates the arsenal and houses the **museum of old Brest.** Dioramas executed by a local painter, Pierre Perou, evoke Brest's main historical events: pre-Revolution *(1st floor);* Revolution to present day *(2nd floor).*

★ **Museum** (EZ M). – The museum has 17 and 18C paintings from the Italian, French and Dutch schools (Crespi, Recco, Van Loo and Schalcken, respectively). The 19C works include the Neo-Classicism of Delorme *(Hero and Leander),* the Romanticism of Cibot and the experimentalism of the local Pont-Aven school (Lacombe and Emile Bernard). Note the luminous pastels of Levy-Dhurmer and canvases by Manet, Utrillo, and Suzanne Valadon.

St Louis (EY). – This church is a large modern building (1958) in keeping with the St-Louis Square that it overlooks. The impression of height is increased by the vertical lines of the adjoining bell-tower. The main part of the building is in rough stone.

The interior, which is very plain, again emphasizes the vertical theme. The stained glass windows are simple and let in a lot of light. Skilful design focuses the light from a window over the nave directly onto a great Crucifix above the high altar both by Kaeppelin. In the chapel of the Blessed Sacrament on the south side, hanging above a golden altar, is a modern tapestry, with a yellow background, by Olin. The chapel and the baptistry to the left of the porch are illuminated by the light of the stained glass windows by Zac.

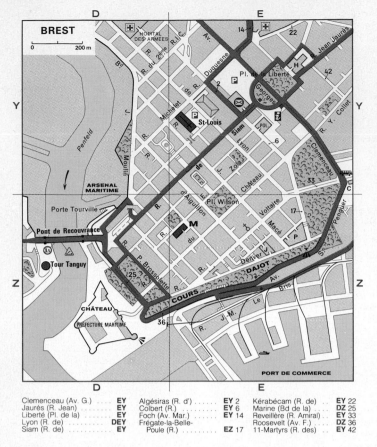

EXCURSIONS

Round tour of 61 km - 38 miles. – *Time: about 2 1/2 hours. Leave Brest W by the Rue de la Porte (***AX 31***) and turn left into the Rue St-Exupéry to reach the corniche road (Route de la Corniche). Drive straight on at the 4-Pompes.*

☉**Portzic Lighthouse** (Phare du Portzic). – *Cross the bastion at the entrance of the Military Training School (Centre militaire d'Entraînement de Sécurité) and bear left twice.* From the lighthouse the **view** extends over the naval base at Laninon, the roadstead, the Plougastel Peninsula, Espagnols Point and the Brest Channel.

Turn left at the entrance of Cosquer.

Ste-Anne-du-Portzic. – It is located along the beach in Ste-Anne Bay; walk a short distance along the coastal path to enjoy fine views.

An uphill road leads to the **Oceanographic Research Centre of Brittany** at Diable Point on the sound (Goulet). This forms part of the National Oceanographic Research Centre (Centre National pour l'Exploitation des Océans – CNEXO). Since 1968 a small village has been built to accommodate the Centre, with a port, fish farm and marine research facilities.

Make for La Trinité, turn left and after 2 km - 1 mile bear left.

☉**Petit-Minou Lighthouse.** – Nearby is a viewing-table. The lighthouse is built on the tip of the Petit Minou Point near a fort. A stairway (116 steps) opening on to the keepers' quarters gives access to a platform which affords a beautiful **view★** of the Goulet, the Crozon Peninsula and Raz Point.

Return to the D 789 and bear left; after 7 km - 5 miles turn left.

The road skirts Trez-Hir beach giving a fine view of Bertheaume Bay and crosses Plougonvelin. Before you reach St-Mathieu Point, note on the right, near a house, two Gallic steles topped by a cross which are known as the Monks' gallows (Gibet des Moines).

★★ **St-Mathieu Point.** – *P 198.*

From St-Mathieu Point to Renards Point, the *corniche* road runs along the Porsliogan shore and affords a view of the Ushant archipelago with the Four Channel and Béniguet Island to the fore.

Renards Point. – This headland to the left of Conquet beach offers lovely views of St-Mathieu Point, Ushant and Molène.

Return to Le Conquet by the Corniche du Port and Ste-Barbe Point (view of the port and Kermorvan Point).

Le Conquet. – *P 46.*

Return to Brest by the direct route on the D 789 and by ⑥ on the town plan.

Round tour of 56 km - 35 miles. – *Time: about 1/2 day. Leave Brest by ⑤ on the local map.* You pass on the left the road leading to **Kerhoun,** a resort nicely situated on the right bank of the Élorn.

Albert-Louppe Bridge. – Called after the chairman of the General Council of Finistère who promoted it, this bridge crosses the Élorn estuary. It is 880m - 2 887ft long and has three 186m - 610ft spans. Four statues by the sculptor Quillivic stand at the bridge ends – a man and a woman from the Léon region on the Brest shore and a man and a woman from Plougastel on the opposite shore. The bridge rises over 42m - 137ft high above the river and offers a very fine **view★** over the Élorn Valley and the Brest roadstead.

1 km - 1/2 mile after the bridge bear right towards Plougastel-Daoulas.

★ **Plougastel-Daoulas.** – *P 158.*

★ **Plougastel Peninsula.** – *The rest of the drive is described on p 158.*

Tour of the Abers. – *197 km - 122 miles – allow 1 day. Description p 44.*

⊘ BOAT TRIPS

★ **On the roadstead.** – The tour includes a visit of the naval port and the fortified channel (Goulet).

★ **Across the roadstead.** – The crossing links Brest to Le Fret on the Crozon Peninsula.

★★ **Ushant** (Ile d'Ouessant). – *P 210.*

The times indicated in this guide

when given with the distance allow one to enjoy the scenery
when given for sightseeing are intended to give an idea
of the possible length or brevity of a visit.

★★ BRETONNE CORNICHE

Michelin map **59** fold 1 or **230** folds 6, 7

The Bretonne Corniche is the coast road which joins Perros-Guirec and Trébeurden following the "pink granite coast", which starts at Arcouest Point. It is certainly one of the most interesting runs in north Brittany.

The strange forms of the enormous pink granite rocks which are the attraction of the Brittany Corniche are due to erosion. Granite is composed of quartz, mica and feldspar. The feldspar turns into kaolin (china clay), which is washed away by the water, and the residue of quartz grains makes sand, which is carried away by rain or waves. Little by little the stone changes shape and presents surprising forms: almost perfect spheres, chiselled and fretted masses, boldly balanced piles and swaying stones. Erosion here has been very severe because the rocks are coarse grained and are therefore easily broken up.

Local imagination has given names to some of the rocks: Napoleon's Hat, St Yves, the Gnome, the Witch, the Death's Head, the Elephant, the Whale, the Ram, the Rabbit, the Tortoise, the Horse, the Thimble, the Torpedo, the Armchair, the Umbrella, the Sentinel, the Corkscrew, etc.

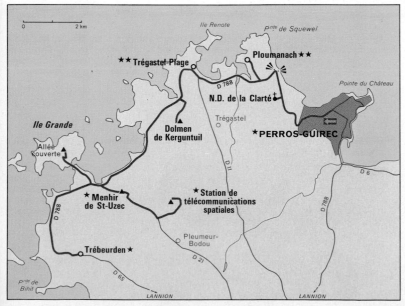

FROM PERROS-GUIREC TO TRÉBEURDEN

27 km - 17 miles – about 5 hours – Local map p 67

After the town of Perros-Guirec *(p 155),* the road skirts the small hill on which the signal station stands and a **view**★ opens up straight ahead onto the rocks of Ploumanach, seaward of the Seven Islands, looking back of the beaches of Perros-Guirec and, in the distance, of the Port-Blanc coast.

Notre-Dame-de-la-Clarté Chapel. – *P 156.*

★★ **Ploumanach.** – *P 159.*

★★ **Trégastel-Plage.** – *P 206.*

As you come out of the village, at the end of a short rise, you get a view looking backwards, of the Seven Islands.

After 1.2 km - 3/4 mile, turn left and then right.

Dolmen and covered alley of Kerguntuil (Dolmen et Allée couverte de Kerguntuil). – From the dolmen by the roadside to the left, can be seen at the end of a field the covered alley which can be reached by walking in front of the farm buildings.

Then the road runs close to the sea, at high tide the shore can become wild and picturesque. It is a strange coast, dotted with islands and reefs.

Soon after the Café Paccata, at the top of a slight rise (*about 1 km - 1/2 mile before the Penvern crossroads),* a dolmen hidden amidst the foliage looks down onto the Kerivon shore.

Turn left towards Pleumeur-Bodou. At Penvern hamlet, bear left after the Café du Menhir.

★ **St-Uzec Menhir** (Menhir de St-Uzec). – A giant menhir surmounted by a Crucifixion with roughly carved instruments of the Passion surrounding the figure of a praying woman.

Take the road below the menhir to rejoin the D 21 to Pleumeur-Boudou, then turn left and 400m - 1/4 mile farther on, left again.

★ **Space Telecommunications Station of Pleumeur-Bodou.** – *P 156.*

Grande Island. – *Cross the bridge.* The island offers a landscape of heaths bordered by blue granite shores. There are megalithic remains, in particular a covered alleyway northeast of the village.

Return to the corniche road and turn left towards Trébeurden (p 205).

BRIGNOGAN-PLAGES Pop 881

Michelin map **58** folds 4, 5 or **230** folds 3, 4 – Local map p 44

A seaside resort lying at the end of the Pontusval Bay and possessing a magnificent sandy beach. On either side of Brignogan piles of rocks, sometimes curiously shaped, separate small beaches.

Pontusval Point. – This walk crosses a countryside dotted with blocks of granite. The Men Marz, which stands halfway, is a fine example of a menhir, 8m - 25ft high, surmounted by a Cross.

EXCURSION

Goulven. – Pop 470. *7.5 km - 5 miles SE. Take the road to Lividic Beach, then the coast road along Goulven Bay. At Plounéour-Trez, turn left after the church.*
This little village has a restored 15-16C **church.** The **belfry**★ which dates from the Renaissance is one of the finest in Brittany. To the right of the porch, which opens under the belfry is a fine Gothic doorway with twin doors and a carved stoup on the pier between them.
Inside the church are a monumental Renaissance stoup, a high altar in Kersanton granite and an altar decorated with six carved and painted panels illustrating St Goulven's miracles. The 16C organ loft has been built on to a former roodscreen. Two fine 17C embroidered banners are displayed in the chancel in the summer.

BULAT-PESTIVIEN Pop 531

Michelin map **59** folds 1, 11 or **230** N of fold 21 – 17 km - 11 miles SW of Bourbriac

Bulat-Pestivien is a former pilgrimage centre. A *pardon* takes place on the Sunday after 8 September.

★ **Church.** – This fine building was put up in the 15 and 16C. The Renaissance tower, which is the oldest of this period in Brittany, had a spire added in the 19C. There are remarkable porches.
Inside is a monumental sacristy – adorned with a frieze of macabre design – with a loggia which projects into the church. There is a curious lectern representing a young peasant in the local Vannes costume. Facing the entrance stands a table, 5m - 16ft long and dating back to 1583, decorated with geometric designs, on which were placed offerings made at *pardons.*
Bulat possesses three sacred fountains: the fountain to the Virgin (1718) in the cemetery and, on either side of the Callac road out of the town, the fountain of the Seven Saints (1683) and the Cock fountain (16C).
There is a fine Calvary (1550) with a striking Entombment at **Pestivien** (*1 km - 1/2 mile N of Bulat).* Unfortunately it has been defaced.

CAMARET-SUR-MER

Michelin map **58** fold 3 or **230** folds 16, 17 – Facilities

An important spiny lobster port in France *(details p 20)*, Camaret is also a quiet and simple seaside resort.

On the shore, to the left of the *Sillon,* a natural dyke which protects the port, is a small sand and shingle beach, the Corréjou Beach.

The poet Saint-Pol-Roux *(p 29)*, who moved to Boultous Manor between Lagatjar and the ocean in 1907, is buried in the cemetery.

The landing of 1694. – The Crozon Peninsula, which forms an advanced bastion for Brest, has been attacked many times by the British, Spanish and Dutch. Vauban, the military architect, fortified it in 1689. Five years later, during the reign of William III, an Anglo-Dutch fleet tried to make a landing, but the fort and hidden batteries covering the port were very effective; several ships were put out of action, and the landing troops were decimated. A charge by dragoons scattered the attackers, and the coastguard militiamen, with their pitchforks and scythes, completed the rout. The encounter, which caused a sensation at the court of Louis XIV, ended with 1 200 killed and 450 taken prisoner from the enemy side and only 45 wounded among the French.

Submarine experiment. – It was in Camaret bay in 1801 that the American engineer **Fulton,** who had settled in France in 1797, carried out an underwater experiment. He had built a small vessel which, with a crew of five, could be propelled under water with jointed oars at a speed of two knots. It could stay under water for six hours. This rudimentary submarine was intended to affix to the hull of an enemy ship a bomb or "torpedo" containing 100 lb of powder, which was to be exploded by a time mechanism.

A British frigate, at anchor in the bay, was to serve as the target. Fulton attacked, but unfortunately for him the ship, though unaware of his approach, weighed anchor and sailed away. This failure spoilt the inventor's chances and he returned to America. It was not until the last quarter of the 19C that this bold concept became a practical project.

⊘ **Notre-Dame-de-Rocamadour.** – This chapel stands at the end of the dyke. It was built between 1610 and 1683 and restored after a fire in 1910. It was originally a pilgrimage chapel on the pilgrim route to Rocamadour in Quercy; from 11C the pilgrims from the north who came by sea used to disembark at Camaret to continue the journey by land. A *pardon* is held on the first Sunday in September: benediction of the sea.

⊘ **Vauban Castle.** – A massive tower surrounded by walls was built by the military architect Vauban at the end of the 17C on Sillon Point. It houses a small naval museum devoted to the town's history and sea-faring traditions. There are fine views of the Brest channel, Espagnols Point, the port of Camaret and the town.

EXCURSIONS

★★★ **Penhir Point.** – *3.5 km - 2 miles SW by the D 8 – about 1 hour. P 155.*

★★ **Espagnols Point.** – *Round tour of 36 km - 23 miles N – about 1/2 hour. Leave Camaret by the D 8, going towards Crozon; turn left into the D 355 at the top of a hill after passing the last houses. The rest of the drive is described on p 85.*

⊘ BOAT TRIP

Les Tas de Pois. – *P 155.*

★ CANCALE

Michelin map **59** fold 6 or **230** fold 12 – Local map p 97

The **setting**★ of this fishing port and seaside resort is picturesque. To get a good view take the tourist road (route touristique – *one-way*) which branches off the D 76 to the right 2.5 km - 1 1/2 miles after the Portes Rouges crossroad. As you drive into Cancale the **views**★ of the resort and Mont-St-Michel Bay are splendid.

The town has derived its gastronomic reputation for centuries from the oysters which flourish in the beds in the bay *(parc à huîtres)* and which oyster lovers come to eat in the hotels and bars around the port. Sales reached their highest level in the First Empire with 48 million oysters in one season.

Now only young oysters bought from Auray are cultivated in the bay, for a mysterious disease around 1920 decimated the native spat. Since then spat has begun to flourish in the immense beds in the open sea and an oyster with a particular flavour is developing due to the richness of the plankton of Mont-St-Michel Bay *(details p 20)*.

SIGHTS

★ **The Port** (Z). – A fine scene at high tide. Go to the Fenêtre jetty for a view of the bay and, at low tide, of the oyster beds. Formerly La Houle haven, the port is surrounded by a picturesque quarter where sailors and fishermen lived. A street, the Vaubaudet or Val du Baudet was the only link with the town of Cancale, the upper quarter where the landsmen and traders lived.

⊘ **St-Méen Church** (Z B). – From the tower's upper platform (189 steps), where there is a viewing table, you can enjoy a wide **panorama**★ of Mont-St-Michel Bay, Granville and some forty belfries. In clear weather you can see the Chausey Isles and Jersey.

⊘ **Museum** (Y M). – Housed in the former Church of St-Méen (1714), it is devoted to the arts and traditions of the Cancale region and to the life of Jeanne Jugan *(p 197)*. There is also a presentation relating to the sailing school which has been in existence in the city for over a hundred years.

CANCALE

*Book well in advance as
you may have difficulty
in finding
a room for the night
during the summer season.*

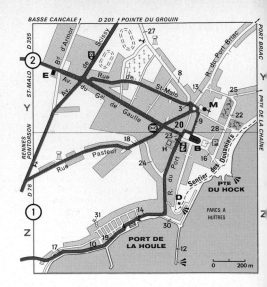

★ **Hock Point and the Sentier des Douaniers** (Z). – From the point you get a **view**★ over Cancale Rock, the Bay of Mont-St-Michel and the mount itself; below on the right, at the foot of the cliff, are the oyster beds *(parc à huîtres).* On either side of the Hock Point you may take the Sentier des Douaniers (Customs Officers path) and enjoy a walk overlooking the shore. If you follow the coastline as far as Port-Mer you will get a splendid view of the Chaîne Point opposite Cancale Rock.

War Memorial (Monument aux Morts) (Z D). – Extensive view of the Bay of Mont-St-Michel, Mont-Dol and below the port and the oyster beds.

Jeanne Jugan's House (Maison de Jeanne Jugan) (Y E). – The house is the birthplace of Jeanne Jugan (1792-1879), the founder of the order known as the Little Sisters of the Poor *(details p 197).*

Chaîne Point. – *1.5 km - 1 mile northwest towards Rimains Islands (car park) – plus 1/4 hour on foot Rtn. Leave Cancale by the Rue des Rimains* (Y 25). *Leave your car after about a mile and go on foot to a high platform facing Rimains Island and Cancale Rock.* The view extends from Landes Island to Mont-St-Michel.

EXCURSION

★★ **Grouin Point.** – *4.5 km - 2 1/2 miles N by the D 201 – about 1/2 hour – local map p 97. Leave Cancale by the Rue du Stade* (Y 27), *then turn right into the road which leads straight to the Grouin Point. At the end of the road, after the Hôtel de la Pointe du Grouin, leave your car on a vast parking area and take a path, to the right of the signal station, which leads directly to the point.*
In a fine setting, this wild, rocky headland overlooks the sea from a height of 40m - 131ft and affords a **panorama** which stretches from Cape Fréhel to Granville and the Bay of Mont-Saint-Michel with in the distance the Chausey Isles. At low tide one can take a path to a cave in the cliffside (height 10m - 32ft, depth 30m - 98ft).
The Landes Island, opposite, is a bird sanctuary and nature reserve.

★ CARANTEC   Pop 2 522

Michelin map 58 fold 6 or 230 fold 5

Carantec, which lies on a peninsula between the estuary of the Penzé and the Morlaix River, is a family seaside resort. There are several bathing beaches; the most important are the Grève Blanche and the Grève du Kélenn, the latter being the larger.
Pardons are held at Carantec, on Whit Monday and the third Sunday in July and the blessing of the sea the Sunday after 15 August.

⊙ **Church.** – This modern church contains, in the apse, a fine 17C silver **processional cross**★ and a less ornate one to the right of the chancel entrance.

The Priest's Chair (La Chaise du Curé). – From this rocky platform, the **view**★ extends from left to right over the Porspol and Blanche beaches with St-Pol-de-Léon and Roscoff in the background, as far as Pen-al-Lann.

Pen-al-Lann Point. – *1.5 km - 1 mile E, plus 1/4 hour on foot Rtn. Take the Rue de Pen-al-Lann and leave your car at a roundabout. Take the downhill path through pine trees to a rocky height.*
The **view**★ extends along the coast from the Bloscon Point crowned by Ste-Barbe Chapel, near Roscoff, to Primel Point, opposite you can see the castle on Taureau Island, which guarded the mouth of Morlaix River *(p 140).*

Callot Island. – From the Grève Blanche port you can reach the island by car *(car park)* at mid-tide. The island is excellent for fishing.
⊙ The **Chapel of Our Lady** on the island was founded in the 16C and rebuilt in the 17 and 19C. Inside is a 16C statue of the Virgin. A great many pilgrims come to the *pardon* on the Sunday after 15 August.

Michelin map **58** fold 17 or **230** fold 20 – Local map p 149 – Facilities
See the town plan in the current Michelin Red Guide France

In the Roman era Carhaix was an important town commanding seven main roads. In the middle of a cattle-rearing district, the town is a milk production centre.

La Tour d'Auvergne (1743-1800). – Carhaix's famous son is Théophile-Malo Corret, known as La Tour d'Auvergne. When still very young he became keenly interested in the Breton language but he was a soldier at heart. During the Revolution his exploits were such that he, a junior captain at 46, was offered the most exalted rank; but he refused – he wanted to remain with his troops.

Whenever this hero could pause in his campaigns, he would bring his faithful Celtic grammar out from under his shirt. At last he retired and gave all his time to his favourite study.

Then the son of his Celtic master was called up for the army. La Tour, moved by the old teacher's grief, took the young man's place and enlisted, at 54 years of age, as a private soldier in the 46th half-brigade. New exploits followed. Bonaparte offered La Tour a seat on the Legislative Council, but failed to overcome his modesty. He was awarded a sword of honour and the title of "First Grenadier of the Republic". He was killed in 1800, during the Rhine campaign. All the army mourned for him. Every year, the last Sunday in June, Carhaix celebrates the name-day of La Tour d'Auvergne.

SIGHTS

St-Trémeur Church. – A porch opens on to the bell tower (16C); the tympanum over the doorway is adorned with the statue of St Trémeur whose legend dates from the 6C *(p 174)*.

House of the Seneschal (Maison du Sénéchal). – *No 6 Rue Brizeux.* This fine Renaissance building houses the Tourist Information Centre. It has a 16C façade, the ground floor is of granite decorated with carvings and the corbelled upper storeys are faced with slate and adorned with statuettes.

Plouguer Church. – *Access via Rue de l'Église.* Rebuilt on Romanesque foundations in the 16C, the church was burnt down in 1923 and later rebuilt in red sandstone.

EXCURSION

Round tour of 80 km - 50 miles. – *Time: about 4 hours. Leave Carhaix by Rue Oberhausen and Rue des Abattoirs in the direction of Plounavézel. Turn right at Croissant Marie-Joffré. 3 km - 2 miles farther on, past the Lesquern hamlet on the left, bear right in a bend into an unsurfaced road.*

St-Gildas Chapel. – The road leads through woodlands to the 16C chapel which has a square bell-tower crowned by a stone spire and grotesques at the east end. The St-Gildas beacon (238m - 781ft) stands to the right.

Return to the main road and turn right.

After the junction for Carnoët, there is a view of the Arrée Mountains.

Bear left towards Plourac'h.

Plourac'h. – Pop 513. The Renaissance church in the form of a T was built largely in the 15 and 16C. The south face is the most ornate. The porch, which is Gothic in character, contains statues of the Apostles surmounted by canopies. A beautiful Renaissance doorway with windows on either side is crowned by three gables adorned with coats of arms. Near the font is a 18C altarpiece depicting the mysteries of the rosary. Among the many statues ornamenting the church should be noted those of St Guénolé, St Maudez, St Adrian and St Margaret. Also a *Pietà* in which the Virgin wears a Breton cloak of mourning.

Go back to the D 54 which provides fine views of the countryside, then bear right along the D 28 to Callac.

Callac. – Pop 2 957. This town is dominated by the ruins of Botmel Church. In front of the stud farm stands a bronze statue of the stallion Naous. The town is also the home of the Breton spaniel, a pointer.

Take the D 787 on the left, then the D 50, the Bulat road, on the right.

Bulat-Pestivien. – *P 68.*

You arrive at Burthulet by the D 31.

Burthulet. – The simple 16C chapel stands in melancholy surroundings; one does not doubt the truth of the legend that here "The devil died of cold".

Make for Ty-Bourg and bear right.

St-Servais. – Pop 481. The writer Anatole Le Braz *(p 29)* was born here. 16C church.

Take the road opposite the church towards St-Nicodème. After 2 km - 1 mile turn right.

★ **Corong Gorges.** – *1 hour on foot Rtn. From the roundabout at the end of the road follow the path leading to the gorges.* The path runs along the river and into the Duault Forest. The river disappears beneath a mass of rocks to reappear as a series of cascades.

Turn round and bear right and right again in the direction of Locarn.

⊘ **Locarn.** – Pop 575. Its **church** contains 17C furnishings (altarpiece, pulpit, statues), a remarkable 16C stained glass window and in the north transept, a carillon-wheel and the panels of a Flemish altarpiece, also of that period. Displayed in the presbytery is the **treasury**★. Note the following objects made of silver-gilt: St Hernin's bust and reliquary (in the form of an arm) both 15-16C, a processional cross and a 17C chalice.

Return to Carhaix-Plouguer via Trebrivan.

Michelin map **63** fold 12 or **230** folds 35, 49 – Facilities
See the town plan in current Michelin Red Guide France

Carnac was already known as a prehistoric capital. The name of Carnac is often associated with megalithic monuments *(p 34)*.

(S. Chirol)

Kermario Lines

★★ **J. Miln and Z. Le Rouzic Museum of Prehistory** (M). – Housed in a former ⊙ presbytery, this museum founded in 1881 by a Scotsman, J. Miln, and added to by Zacharie Le Rouzic, traces the evolution of man and the civilizations in the Carnac region between 450 000 BC (Lower Palaeolithic era) and 8C AD (Early Middle Ages). It contains tools fashioned by "homo erectus", polished axes made of rare flints, necklaces and pendants made of *callais* (a blue stone like turquoise), carved slabs, decorated vases, bronze and gold-leaf arms and ornaments, casts of carvings on the megalithic monuments of the Neolithic era, reconstructions of tombs, coins, statuettes, etc.

★ **Church.** – This 17C church is dedicated to **St Cornely,** the patron saint of horned cattle; his statue stands on the façade between two oxen. A massive bell-tower topped by an octagonal spire dominates the building. The saint's *pardon* is held here *(p 226)*. The porch on the north side is surmounted by a canopy in the form of a crown which is unique in Brittany. Inside, the wooden vaults are covered with curious 18C paintings depicting in the nave the life of the saint, in the aisles the life of Christ and of St John the Baptist, and scenes from the life of the Virgin. The communion table, pulpit and chancel grille (18C) are of wrought iron. The organ was built in 1775.

★ **CARNAC-PLAGE**

Carnac-Plage, with its gently shelving beach, has been developed in the shelter of the Quiberon Peninsula. View of the coast, Houat, Belle-Ile and the Quiberon Peninsula.

★★ **THE MEGALITHIC MONUMENTS**   *time: 2 1/2 hours*

A tour of the numerous megalithic monuments: lines, dolmens, tumuli, to the north of Carnac makes an interesting excursion.

★★ **Ménec Lines (Alignements du Ménec).** – The Ménec Lines, over 1 km - 3/4 mile long and 100m - 330ft wide, include 1 099 menhirs arranged in 11 lines. The tallest is 4m - 12ft high.

They begin with a semi-circle (or cromlech) of 70 menhirs partly surrounding the hamlet of Ménec.

★ **Kerlescan Lines (Alignements de Kerlescan).** – *Illustration p 34.* In this field (880 × 139 m - 962 × 153 yds), 540 menhirs are arranged in 13 lines and the whole is preceded by a semicircle of 39 menhirs.

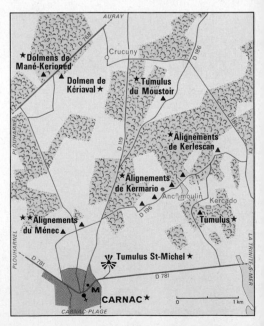

★ **Kermario Lines** (Alignements de Kermario). – 982 menhirs in 10 lines occupy a similar area to the Ménec Lines.

★ **Kériaval Dolmen.** – A dolmen with side chambers added to the main area.

★ **Mané-Kerioned Dolmens.** – A group of three dolmens; the first has eight uprights with stylised engravings: axes, spirals, coats of arms...

★ **Kercado Tumulus.** – *Leave the car at the entrance to the Castle of Kercado.*
⊘ This tumulus is 30m - 98ft across and 3.50m - 11ft high and covers a fine example of a dolmen. A menhir stands on the summit. Note the carvings on the table and four uprights.

★ **Moustoir Tumulus.** – A central chamber with several small side chambers covered by a heap of stones.

★ **St-Michel Tumulus.** – The tumulus, which is 120m long and 12m high - 395 × 38ft,
⊘ is a mound of earth and stones covering two burial chambers and some twenty stone chests. Most of the artefacts found there are now in the Carnac Museum and the archaeological museum *(p 215)* in Vannes.
The visitors' gallery was added when the excavations were carried out.
From the top of the mound, where there stand a Chapel to St Michael, a small Calvary and the Touring Club de France viewing table, there is a **view★** of this megalithic region, the coast and the islands.

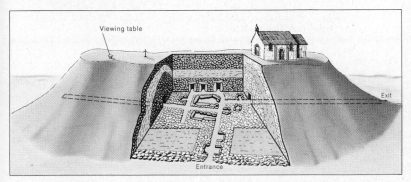

St-Michel Tumulus. – Section of internal chambers and galleries

EXCURSIONS

★ **Other Megaliths.** – *8 km - 5 miles NW. Leave Carnac by the D 789 to Lorient.*

★ **Rondossec Dolmens.** – *To the left on leaving Plouharnel.* Three underground chambers.

Vieux-Moulin Menhirs. – *After the level crossing.* These stand in a field to the right of the road.

Ste-Barbe Lines. – *Near the road on the left in the direction of Ste-Barbe.*

★ **Crucuno Dolmen.** – *Take a road to the right.* It rises against a farm in the centre of the hamlet of Crucuno. Only one chamber remains with the great table supported by eleven uprights.

Mané-Croch Dolmen. – *500m - 1/3 mile beyond Crucuno, on the left.* A typical dolmen with side chambers.

★ **Kerzerho Lines.** – *To the right of the road at the entrance to Erdeven.* 10 lines including 1 129 menhirs.

⊘ **St-Michel and Ste-Anne-de-Kergonan Abbeys.** – Gregorian chants. *Take the D 781 towards Lorient. After 2 km-1 mile bear right into a road leading to St-Michel Abbey (Benedictine nuns). The approach road to Ste-Anne Abbey (Benedictine monks) is to the right after the Plouharnel cemetery.*

Times and charges for admission to sights described in the guide are listed at the end of the guide.

The sights are listed alphabetically in this section either under the place – town, village or area – in which they are situated or under their proper name.

Every sight for which there are times and charges is indicated by the symbol ⊘ in the margin in the main part of the guide.

Michelin map **59** fold 18 or **230** folds 27, 28 – 9 km - 6 miles NW of Vitré

The **village square**★ composes a harmonious scene with its collegiate church, its small town hall with a large four-sided roof, and the few houses, former canons' residences, standing around an old well.

Collegiate Church. – This 14 and 15C church, with a single nave, has some fine Renaissance canopied **stalls**★, and an elegant door, of the same period, which opens onto the sacristy, the former chapterhouse. To the left of the high altar and in a chapel to the left of the chancel are two stone and marble mausolea (1551-1554) belonging to the d'Espinay family, who founded the church. (The d'Espinays were cousins of François II.)

The two handsome Renaissance **stained glass windows**★, made in Rennes, are noteworthy: depicted in the apse is the Passion of Christ and in the sacristy the sacrifice of Abraham *(to see this window, enter the chancel and look above the woodwork on the right).* In the nave, the south chapel contains a 17C altarpiece recounting scenes of the Passion and the north chapel is adorned with a 14C Virgin – both of these works are in polychromed wood.

⊙ South of Champeaux in a pleasant verdant setting stands the **Château d'Espinay,** an elegant 15 and 16C building.

Michelin map **63** folds 7, 8 or **230** fold 41

On the borders of Brittany and Anjou, surrounded by woods dotted with pools, stands this old fortified town with its fine castle.

At the town gates, on the road to Pouancé, at the Carrière des Fusillés there is a memorial to the twenty-seven hostages executed by the Nazis on 22 October 1941. The recesses at the base contain soil from the place of execution.

Françoise of Foix and François I (16C). – Among the ladies of Châteaubriant were two whose memory has survived the centuries. One, Sibylle, gave a rare example of conjugal fidelity; when her husband returned from a Crusade in 1250, she died of joy as she embraced him.

The story of the second, Françoise de Foix, is less edifying. At the age of eleven she was married to Jean de Laval, Count of Châteaubriant. He was terribly jealous, tried to keep his child-wife away from the dangers of the outside world and sulked in his castle. None the less, Françoise grew in beauty, wit and culture. She aroused great curiosity.

François I sent word to the Count that he would like to meet her. Laval took no notice. When the King insisted, he went to Court, but alone; his wife, he said, liked only to be alone, and moreover she was weak minded. The Count had arranged with his wife that she should join him only at a certain signal. A servant came upon the secret and sold it to the King. One fine day Laval saw Françoise alighting from her coach and being received with great honours. Mad with rage, he left the Court, leaving his wife unprotected. Dazzled by this brilliant new life, she yielded and became the King's mistress.

However royal loves are not eternal and she was superseded by the Duchess of Etampes. Laval returned, took his wife away to Châteaubriant and shut her up, with her daughter, aged seven, in a room hung with black. The child sickened and died. The mother stayed there for ten years, when, it has been said her husband hastened her end in 1537 with a thrust of his sword.

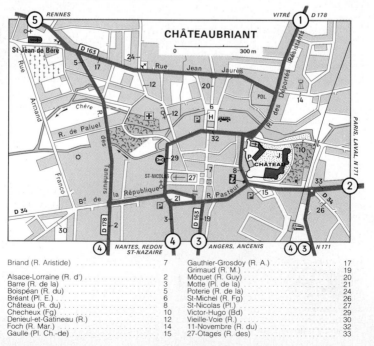

CHÂTEAUBRIANT

SIGHTS

★ **The Castle** (Château). – A ⊙ part of the castle which has been remodelled several times is feudal and another part, dating from the Renaissance, was built by Jean de Laval. You can stroll round it along the esplanade and the gardens which go right down to the Chère.

Enter through the Place Charles de Gaulle.

All that remains of the feudal castle is a large keep on a height, connected with the entrance fort and the chapel by walls against which the two wings of the main building stand. The three wings of the Seignorial Palace, opposite, are connected by elegant Renaissance pavilions. The roof is ornamented with dormer windows, which are emblazoned with the coat of arms of Châteaubriant, Laval and Montmorency.

CHÂTEAUBRIANT
(CASTLE)

Building stages
■ 11 to 15 C.
▨ 16 C.

0   50 m

The tour takes you up the central staircase (1) to a balcony from where there is a lovely view onto the courtyard, embellished with gardens and a huge chestnut tree, the keep, and the city's roof tops. Continue on to the room (2) of Françoise of Foix with its coffered ceiling and monumental early 17C carved wood chimney. Next to it is the oratory (3) with the tombstone of Françoise of Foix on which is carved an epitaph by Clément Marot.

The Magistrate's Court (Tribunal d'Instance - J) occupies a part of the Palace while the public library (B) is housed in the south wing.

There are only two sections left of the colonnade which surrounded the courtyard: the covered gallery (4) which ends at a charming staircase–pavilion and the other section (5) enclosing the main courtyard.

St-Jean-de-Béré. – The church's oldest parts comprising the chancel and the transept crossing, which are built of fine red sandstone, date from the end of the 11C, the nave is 12C.

Outside, near the picturesque south porch (16C), is a rustic altar from which services were held at the time of the plague.

Above the porch there are two low reliefs depicting the Annunciation (13C) and the Visitation (15C).

Inside you will see the ornately decorated altarpiece at the high altar (1665), in the north transept the altarpiece of the Virgin (1658) and left of the nave the altarpiece of St Blaise (1693).

A 17C panel representing the Eternal Father is placed in the nave across from the entrance; a Virgin of the 15C and a statue of St Julian (15C) and other 17C statues including a St Elizabeth representing Maria Theresa, Louis XIV's wife, are also noteworthy.

CHÂTEAUGIRON   Pop 3 265

Michelin map 🔟 fold 7 or 🔟 fold 41

This old town, which was famous for its hemp sailcloth used for rated ships in the 17C, has preserved an impressive fortified castle and picturesque half-timbered houses (mainly in the Rue de la Madeleine). In the church a fine 16C wooden Crucifix hangs above the altar.

Castle. – The moat, 13C keep which in the 14C was capped by a pepperpot roof, 15C clock tower, chapel and living quarters, rebuilt in the 18C and housing administrative offices, are all that remain of the castle. From the Boulevard du Château there is a full view of the castle and its site.

EXCURSIONS

Bois-Orcan Manorhouse (Manoir du Bois-Orcan). – *N of town 2.5 km - 1 1/2 miles on the D 101 and left on another road.*
Reflecting in the moat beside the solitary weeping willow the 16C manorhouse, with its main range flanked by two turrets and its chapel, paints a lovely picture.

Nouvoitou. – Pop 1 615. *3.5 km - 2 miles W on the D 34.*
⊙ The 15C **church** contains, in the nave and to the right, 15C polychrome and gilt alabaster panels. Outside note the 17C cemetery cross and a 16C tombstone.

CHÂTEAULIN

Pop 6 102

Michelin map 58 fold 15 or 230 fold 18 – Local map p 50

This little town stands on a bend of the Aulne, in the green and deep valley through which the canalised river flows. Two lines of shady quays are its most decorative feature. The tide does not reach Châteaulin. It dies out a little way downstream, at Port-Launay, where small seagoing ships can tie up to the quay.

Salmon fishing. – Châteaulin shares with Châteauneuf-du-Faou the distinction of being the chief salmon fishing centre in the Aulne Valley; the salmon has always appeared on the coat of arms of the town. Hundreds of these fish come up the river to spawn, trying to leap the small waterfalls formed by the overflows from the locks. Fishing is done 10 or 15m - 33 or 50ft below the lock, with fly or spinner.

⊙ **Notre-Dame.** – *Access via Rue Graveran and a road to the left.* The chapel which has been remodelled in 17 and 18C, stands against a background of trees and old 17C houses. In the former cemetery, a 15C cross evokes a rather curious scene of the Last Judgment. Inside there are 13C remains (columns, capitals) and under the organ, a 15C group of St Anne and the Virgin and Child.

EXCURSIONS

Round tour of 54 km - 34 miles. – *Time: about 3 1/2 hours. Leave Châteaulin by the D 887 towards Crozon and after 3.5 km - 2 miles, turn right into the D 60 which crosses Dinéault. You pass the massif of the Ménez-Hom on your left and come in sight of the Aulne before you reach the road to Trégarvan.*

⊙ **School Museum.** – Near Trégarvan. To the left of the crossroads is a museum created by the Armorique Regional Nature Park *(p 49)*. A traditional courtyard, shaded by lime trees, precedes the school building with a large classroom dating from the early 20C on the ground floor. On the first floor are the teacher's quarters and a room devoted to the history and development of Brittany.

Trégarvan. – Pop 192. Beautiful **site★** by the Aulne. Fine views of the river.

Return to the D 60 and turn right to reach Argol.

Argol. – Pop 707. Go into the parish close by a monumental doorway built in the Classical style in 1659. The equestrian statue of King Gradlon is part of an old calvary and is similar in style to the horsemen of Ste-Marie du Ménez-Hom *(p 204)* and St-Sébastien Chapel *(p 50)* and that on the entrance arch at Guimiliau.

Rejoin the D 887 towards Crozon and turn left. After 1.5 km - 1 mile bear right into the D 63 to St-Nic.

Glimpses of Douarnenez Bay.

⊙ **St-Nic.** – Pop 737. 16C **church** with a pierced belfry. Note a Descent from the Cross in the north chapel and an altarpiece of the Rosary in the south chapel.

Continue on the D 63 towards Plomodiern and after 1 km - 1/2 mile turn right.

⊙ **St-Côme.** – This little chapel built in homogeneous style and typically Breton character possesses a rare harmony. An elegantly decorated façade is surmounted by a well-proportioned belfry. Inside, the mid–17C **woodwork★** testifies to the skill of Breton craftsmen. The framework rests on friezes that are carved with motifs taken from flora and fauna and many inscriptions. The corbels in the aisles depict strange figures and also worthy of note are a fine wooden Christ and the elegant group formed by the altarpiece and the front of the high altar.

Return to the D 63 the road to Plomodiern and take the D 108, a restricted road, opposite, then turn right.

An overall view of Douarnenez Bay unfolds; on the way up, note a dolmen in a field 30 m away to the left.

Turn right into the D 887 towards Châteaulin and left immediately afterwards.

★★★ **Ménez-Hom.** – P 133.

Return to the D 887 and bear left.

Ste-Marie du Ménez-Hom. – P 204.

Return to Châteaulin by the D 887.

Cast. – Pop 1 578. *7 km - 4 miles SW of Châteaulin by the D 7, the road to Douarnenez.* Standing in front of the church is an attractive sculpture, known locally as St Hubert hunting. The Saint, accompanied by his squire and two basset hounds, is kneeling beside a minute horse and in front of a stag bearing a cross. Behind the town hall, in the courtyard of the presbytery is a statue of St Tugen.

CHÂTELAUDREN

Pop 973

Michelin map 59 fold 2 or 230 fold 8

The town, an important commercial centre, stands in the Leff Valley, a river known for its trout.

Notre-Dame-du-Tertre. – The chapel is perched on a mound; to reach it on foot take the Notre-Dame *venelle* (alley) or by car the Rue Aribart-Notre-Dame. The chapel was built in 1400 by St Vincent Ferrier *(p 214)* and enlarged in the 16 and 17C.

Enter by a small door in the south transept.

Ninety-six **panels★** dating from the 15C on the chancel vaulting, forming a group of unusual size in France, depict scenes from the Old and New Testaments; those in the chapel to the south of the chancel, the lives of St Margaret and St Fiacre. There is a very fine gilded wooden **altarpiece★** (1673) at the high altar; in the chapel to the north is an alabaster statue of Our Lady (15C).

★ COMBOURG

Michelin map **59** folds 16, 17 or **230** fold 26

This small old town, standing at the edge of a great pool and dominated by an imposing feudal castle, is picturesque. On the Place Albert-Parent, the 16C restored Maison de la Lanterne houses the Tourist Information Centre. Tourists who only want to take a quick look at the castle from the outside, should walk along the local road which branches off the Rennes road and goes along beside the pool facing the castle and the village.

Chateaubriand at Combourg. – The castle, which was built in the 11C, was enlarged in the 14 and 15C and restored in the 19C. It belonged first to the Du Guesclin family, and then in the 18C to the Count of Chateaubriand, father of François-René, the great Romantic writer.

In his *Memoirs,* Chateaubriand *(details of his life p 193)* recalled the two years he spent at Combourg in his youth, adding still more to their romantic nature. The Count, a sombre and moody man, lived very much in retirement; when the family met he would walk up and down for hours in the drawing-room, in silence, while no one dared to speak. The Countess, who was unwell, only kept a distant eye on the children. Months passed without a visitor. Left to themselves, the boy and his sister Lucile grew close, sharing their boredom, their dreams and their fears.

The old castle, almost deserted, was gloomy; the pool, the woods and the surrounding heath breathed sadness. The Cat Tower (Tour du Chat), in which François-René had his lonely room, was haunted; a former Lord of Combourg was said to return there at night in the form of a black cat, for which the boy watched anxiously. The owls fluttering against the window and the wind rattling the door and howling in the corridors made him shiver.

It was there that the dreamy and melancholy soul of the writer was formed, or perhaps confirmed.

★ The Castle. – The exterior of the castle appears like a powerful fortress: its four massive towers, with pepperpot roofs, its crenellated parapet walk, and its thick walls slit by narrow openings. The interior was rearranged in 1876. The tour takes you to the chapel, the drawing-room (now divided into two), the Archives, where souvenirs of the author are displayed: autographs, awards, furniture, etc., and to the Cat Tower, where young François-René's austere bedroom was located.

From the parapet walk there are nice views of the locality, the lake and the park.

EXCURSION

Lanrigan Château. – *5 km - 3 miles E. Leave Combourg by the road to Rennes and after the lake bear left onto the road that runs along the south bank of the lake to the château.*

The little château of Lanrigan with its well balanced proportions would recall the smaller châteaux of the Loire if it were not built of granite. The château has a charming Renaissance façade. In the angle formed by the main building and its flanking tower an original note is added by a gracefully constructed gallery.

★★ CONCARNEAU

Michelin map **58** fold 15 or **230** folds 32, 33 – Facilities

Concarneau, France's third largest fishing port and one of the biggest markets for tunny *(details of fishing and maritime life p 19),* possesses many fish canneries and holds a colourful **fish auction market** *(criée).*

Apart from the amusing and interesting scene of its seagoing life, the port has the picturesque attraction of a walled town enclosed in granite ramparts. It is also a popular seaside resort.

(Roux/Explorer)

Concarneau. – Fish auction market

There is an attractive **general view**★ of Concarneau, its inner harbour (arrière-port) and the bay *(below)* from road D 783 where it crosses the Moros Bridge (Pont du Moros) on entering the town by ② on the plan.

The **Filets Bleus Festival**★ (Blue Nets) *(p 226)* includes various folk events (dances and processions in local costumes). First held in 1905, it was originally organized to aid sardine fishermen and their families.

★★ WALLED TOWN (VILLE CLOSE)

time: 2 hours

Narrow alleys cover the islet of irregular shape (350 × 100m - 1 150 × 330ft) linked to the mainland by two small bridges between which stands a fortified building. Massive ramparts, built in the 14C and completed in the 17C, surround the town.

Cross the two small bridges and pass under a gateway leading to a fortified inner courtyard. There is a fine well.

🕐**Walk round the ramparts.** – *Follow the signs. For the first part of the tour, go up a few steps on the left and follow the parapet walk.*

Glimpses of the inner harbour and the fishing fleet can be caught through the loopholes. You also get an overall impression of the Gunpowder Tower (Moulin à Poudre).

Return by the same path to the starting-point and descend the steps for the second part of the tour.

After skirting the Little Castle esplanade (Esplanade du Petit Château) giving on to the marina, you overlook the channel between the two harbours.

When you reach a big tower turn sharp left and go down a ramp to a walkway beneath the ramparts.

Return to the town by the Porte du Passage. By the corner of the Hospice take the Rue St-Guénolé, which bears left towards the Place St-Guénolé.

🕐**Shellwork Display Centre (A).** – Scenes, bouquets and people are made out of shells and shell-fish. The imagination of the artist is shown throughout – note especially the landscape scene of the Walled Town with waves of mussels beating its sides, a bristling cat and an impressive Louis XV vessel with sails made of local mother-of-pearl.

From Place St-Guénolé a short alley leads to the **Porte au Vin** through the ramparts. As you go through the gate you will get a typical view of the trawlers moored in the harbour. The Rue Vauban goes in front of the fishing museum and brings you back to the way out of the walled town.

★**Fishing Museum (Musée de la Pêche) (M¹).** – This museum is located in the former arsenal 🕐which also served as barracks and a fishing school. Accompanying notices, models, photos, dioramas explain the history of Concarneau, its evolution as a port, its fishing industry (whale, cod, sardine, tuna, herring), boats, its canning industry, shipbuilding and navigational equipment.

A large hall is devoted to exhibits relating to fishing in distant waters: an Azores whaleboat and other boats, a harpoon gun, a giant Japanese crab, a coelacanth (a fish whose origins date back 300 million years). The aquarium has 40 tanks containing fish, turtles and other marine life.

ADDITIONAL SIGHTS

The Harbours. – By way of the Avenue Pierre-Guéguin and the Quai Carnot, go and take a quick look at the inner harbour, particularly the new harbour (nouveau port), where the main fishing fleet (trawlers and cargo boats) is moored; you may see the unloading of crustaceans or fish (mainly frozen tuna). Then follow the Avenue du Docteur P. Nicolas and walk round the outer harbour (avant-port), alive with pleasure craft. The embarkation point for excursions is at the end of this quay, on the left.

On the left of the Quai de la Croix is the marine laboratory (Laboratoire Maritime) of 🕐the Collège de France. Inside visit the **Marinarium (B M²)**, an exposition devoted to the sea world: aquariums, dioramas and audio-visual displays.

After passing the picturesque old fish-market where fish used to be sold by auction, the Little Chapel of Our Lady of Succour (N.-D.-de-Bon-Secours, dating from the 15C) and a small lighthouse, you may skirt the Port de la Croix (follow the Boulevard Bougainville), which is sheltered by a jetty. Looking back, there is a good view of the Cabellou Point and, farther on, of the Beg-Meil Point. Out at sea are the Glénan Islands.

The Beaches (A). – Go along the Boulevard Katherine-Wylie which runs beside the Plage du Miné and affords good views of La Forêt Bay and Beg-Meil Point, then take the Boulevard Alfred-Guillou which leads to the Plage des Petits Sables Blancs and the Plage des Grands Sables Blancs.

EXCURSIONS

From Concarneau to Pont-Aven by the coast road. – *45 km - 28 miles - about 2 hours. Leave Concarneau by ② on the town plan, the D 783 towards Quimperlé and after 2.5 km - 1 1/4 miles bear right.*

★**Cabellou Point.** – *Go round the point starting from the right.* The car park affords a fine view★ of the site of Concarneau and the walled town. The road skirts the rocky coastline amld the villas and pine trees and offers pretty views of La Forêt Bay and Glénan Islands.

Return to the main road and make for Quimperlé. Turn right at Pont-Minaouët and right again at Kermao.

The road goes through **Pouldohan** (fine beach and sailing school) and leads via Pendruc to Jument Point.

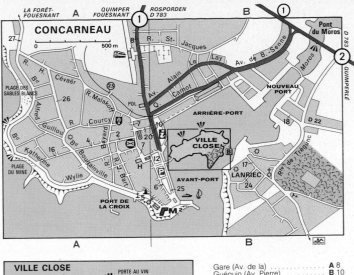

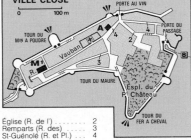

VILLE CLOSE		

Église (R. de l') 2
Remparts (R. des) 3
St-Guénolé (R. et Pl.) ... 4

Gare (Av. de la) .... **A** 8
Guéguin (Av. Pierre) .... **B** 10
Le-Lay (Av. Alain) .... **B**

Berthou (R. Joseph) .... **A** 2
Courbet (R. Amiral) .... **A** 4
Croix (Quai de la) .... **A** 5
Dr.-P.-Nicolas
(Av. du) .... **B** 6
Écoles (R. des) .... **A** 7
Jaurès (Pl. Jean) .... **B** 12
Libération (R. de la) .... **A** 16
Maudit-
Duplessis (R.) .... **B** 17
Moros (R. du) .... **B** 18
Morvan (R. Gén.) .... **A** 20
Pasteur (R.) .... **B** 24
Pénéroff (Quai) .... **B** 25
Renan (R. Ernest) .... **A** 26
Sables-Blancs (R. des) .... **A** 27

Jument Point. – *1/4 hour on foot Rtn.* Fine rocky site and view of Cabellou, the bay and Beg-Meil, and the coast of Loctudy in the distance.

Make for Trévignon Point going via Lambell where you turn right, Lanénos and Ruat.

On the way, note the vertical granite panels forming the walls of the farm buildings.

Trévignon Point. – An old fort stands at the tip of the headland; fishing boats and the life-boat are berthed in the tiny port to the west. Fine **view★** to the right of La Forêt Bay and Beg-Meil, Bénodet Bay, and on the left of the Glénan Islands and near the coast of Verte and Raguenès Islands.

Follow the road along Kersidan Beach. Bear right into the Glénan corniche road, a good viewing platform, continue along Rue de Beg-Foz and turn right.

Raguenès-Plage. – Sheltered by Raguenès Island which can be reached at half tide, the beach is hemmed in by the rocky coastline.

Continue in the direction of Port-Manech. At Trémorvézen, turn right after the chapel.

Kerascoët. – A quiet hamlet with typical thatched farms.

The road then descends to **Rospico Bay,** a small cove with a beach.

At Kerangall, turn right towards Port-Manech. The remainder of the excursion is described in reverse order starting from Pont-Aven on p 161.

From Concarneau to Bénodet by the coast road. – *40 km - 25 miles – about 3 hours. The excursion is described in reverse order on p 60.*

⊘ BOAT TRIPS

There are boat services between Concarneau and the Glénan Islands which also offer tours on the Odet.

Drive through French towns using the plan in the Michelin Guide France.

Features indicated include:

– throughroutes and by-passes

– new streets

– car parks and one-way systems

All this information is revised annually.

★★ CORNOUAILLE

Michelin map 58 folds 13, 14, 15 or 230 folds 16, 17, 18, 31, 32

Historic Cornouaille, the Kingdom and then the Duchy of mediaeval Brittany, extended far to the north and east of its capital, Quimper, reaching Landerneau, the neighbourhhood of Morlaix and Quimperlé. The area included in our tour is much smaller and is limited to the coastal districts of Cornouaille, west of Quimper and south of Douarnenez. This very extensive coastline is marked by two rocky peninsulas, Cape Sizun, "Le Cap" and the Penmarch Peninsula which are its main attractions for tourists. This is a maritime country in which fishing plays an important part; the ports of Guilvinec, Audierne and Douarnenez specialize in sardines and spiny lobster.
The interior is densely cultivated (potatoes and early vegetables), and the countryside with its tranquil horizons is covered with small hamlets of whitewashed houses.

★★ CAPE SIZUN

From Quimper to Plozévet

156 km - 97 miles - allow 1 day - Local map pp 80-81

★★ **Quimper.** – *Time : 2 1/2 hours. Description p 168.*

 Leave Quimper by the D 63 NW by the Rues de Locronan and de la Providence.

The road goes up the rural valley of the Steïr with its wooded slopes and crosses an undulating countryside.

⊘ **Plogonnec.** – Pop 2 888. The 16C **church,** remodelled in 18C, has a fine Renaissance tower; it also has 16C stained glass windows; in the chancel from left to right the windows recount the Transfiguration, the Passion, the Last Judgment, etc. At the entrance to the *placître (p 37)* at the east end of the church, there is a Gothic triumphal arch to the cemetery.

★★ **Locronan.** – *P 129.*

The D 7, with the extensive Forest of Nevet on its left, leads to the sea.

Kerlaz. – 16 and 17C church with a pierced bell tower.

There is a good view of Douarnenez, which is reached after skirting the fine Plage du Ris.

★ **Douarnenez.** – *P 92.*

 Leave Douarnenez, go through Tréboul and make for Poullan-sur-Mer where you turn left and then right and right again.

⊘ **Notre-Dame-de-Kérinec Chapel.** – The chapel, surrounded by trees, dates from the 13 and 15C; the elegant bell tower was struck by lightning in 1958 but an exact replica, as it appeared in the 17C, has been built. Note the flat east end and to the left the rounded pulpit dominated by a Calvary. Inside, look at the massive pillars of the transept crossing which suggest that a central bell tower was to be built but the project was most likely abandoned and in its place, a belfry porch was erected.

 Proceed to Confort.

⊘ **Notre-Dame-de-Confort Church.** – The 16C church with its galleried belfry dating from 1736, has old stained glass **windows** in the chancel one of which is a Tree of Jesse. Over the last arch in the nave, on the north side, hangs a carillon wheel with twelve little bells. The chimes are rung to beg the Virgin for the gift of speech for children who have difficulties in speaking and for other favours.
Alongside the chapel is a Calvary with a triangular base dating from the 16C; the 13 statues of the Apostles were redone in 1870.

 Leave Confort in the direction of Pont-Croix and turn right, then left towards Beuzec-Cap Sizun and ag⌐ın right after 2 km - 1 mile.

★ **Millier Point.** – A small lighthouse stands in this arid site. From the point *(1/4 hour on foot Rtn)* there is a beautiful **view**★ of Douarnenez Bay and Cape Chèvre.

 On leaving Beuzec-Cap Sizun bear right.

★ **Beuzec Point.** – From the car park there is a **view**★ of the approach to Douarnenez Bay, the Crozon Peninsula and in fine weather, of St-Mathieu Point.

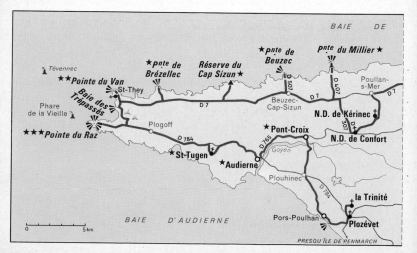

★ **Cape Sizun Bird Sanctuary** (Réserve du Cap Sizun). – The most interesting time for a visit
⏱ is at nesting time in the spring. Starting in March most birds finish nesting by mid-July.
The adults and chicks then leave the sanctuary progressively through the month of
August. In the magnificent and wild setting of the Castel-ar-Roc'h, more than 70m -230ft
above sea level, can be seen, sitting on their nests and feeding their young, such sea
birds as razorbilled auks and guillemots, crested cormorants, common herring gulls,
lesser black-headed gulls, great black-backed gulls which are the rarest of all,
tridactylous seagulls, petrels, etc.

★ **Brézellec Point.** – *Park the car by the lighthouse enclosure.* Go to the rock platforms nearby.
There is a magnificent **view**★ *(illustration p 43)* along the longest stretch of coast in
Brittany of saw-tooth rocks and sheer cliffs: the Crozon Peninsula, St-Mathieu Point,
Van Point and Tévennec Point can be seen.

Turn back and turn right towards the Van Point.

★★ **Van Point.** – *1 hour on foot Rtn.* The 15C **St-They chapel** stands on the left of the path. On
⏱ the point itself follow the half-hidden path, bearing always to the left, which goes right
round the headland. Van Point, which is too big to be seen all in one glance, is
nevertheless less spectacular than the Raz Point, but it has the advantage of being off
the tourists' beaten track. There is a **view**★★ of Castelmeur Point, Brézellec Point, the
Chèvre Headland, Penhir Point, St-Mathieu Point and the Tas de Pois rocks on the right;
Sein Island, the Vieille Lighthouse and Raz Point on the left. *It is recommended that
you do not climb down the cliffs.*
The landscape becomes ever harsher: no trees grow; stone walls and barren moss
cover the final headland.

Turn round and take immediately on the right a small road which hugs the coast leading
to Trépassés Bay and affording fine views of the jagged coastline from Raz Point to
Sein Island.

Trépassés Bay. – It was once thought that the drowned bodies of those who had been
shipwrecked, and which the currents brought to the bay, gave the bay its name of Bay
of the Dead. Another, less macabre explanation, based on the existence of a stream
that flowed in the marshes, was that the original Breton name for the bay was "boe
an aon" (bay of the stream), which became "boe an anaon" (bay of the troubled souls).
Now it is believed that the bay was the embarkation point from the mainland for Druids'
remains which were taken over to Sein Island for burial. According to local legend,
the town of Is *(details p 25)* once stood in the little valley which is now covered in
marshes.
A splendid swell runs freely and powerfully into the bay.

★★★ **Raz Point.** – *P 177.*

*Take the D 784 in the direction of Audierne and after 10 km - 6 miles, turn right
towards St-Tugen.*

★ **St-Tugen.** – The nave and the tower of the **St-Tugen Chapel** are in the Flamboyant Gothic
⏱ style of the 16C, the transept and the east end in the Renaissance style of the 17C. There
is a fine south porch surmounted by an elegant pierced tympanum and containing six
statues of Apostles in Kersanton granite and three 16C statues of Christ, the Virgin and
St Anne.
Inside may be seen interesting 17C furnishings including several altarpieces and a
curious catafalque with two statues of Adam and Eve at each end. The baptismal chapel,
surrounded with balustrades and painted panels, contains a chimney with granite fire-
dogs. The statue of St Tugen *(p 25)* stands to the right of the high altar. There is a 16C
fountain below the chapel. A *pardon* is held every year *(p 226).*

★ **Audierne.** – *P 51.*

The road follows the verdant valley of the Goyen or Audierne river.

★ **Pont-Croix.** – *P 162.*

Go to Plouhinec, the native town of the sculptor Quillivic, and after the church turn
right towards **Pors-Poulhan**, a tiny port sheltered by a pier. Before Plozévet there are fine
views of Audierne Bay and Eckmühl lighthouse.

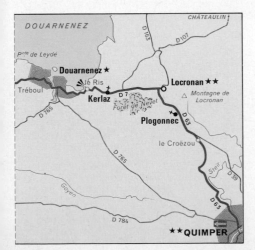

*Respect the life
of the countryside
Go carefully
on country roads
Protect wildlife,
plants and trees.*

Plozévet. – Pop 3 181. There is a 15C porch to the Gothic church. Five arches in the wooden vaulted nave are Romanesque and date from the 13C. To the right of the building flows a sacred fountain *(details on fountains p 36)*. A menhir has been placed here as a 1914-18 war memorial.

🕐 **Chapel of the Holy Trinity.** – *1 km - 1/2 mile from Plozévet.* The chapel is shaped like a T; the nave was built in the 14C and the remainder added in the 16C. This is the most interesting part outside: note the charming Louis XII decoration on the south transept face. Inside, the nave arches come down on to groups of thin columns with florally decorated capitals.

★PENMARCH PENINSULA

From Plozévet to Quimper

84 km - 52 miles – allow 1/2 day – Local map p 83

The journey is made through the *"bigouden"* country which has become known through the local costume of the women and especially the unique head-dress in the shape of a little lace menhir.

From Plozévet *(see above)* to the tip of the Penmarch Peninsula the sea breaks against a great sweep of shingle, continually rolling and knocking the stones of the 20 km - 12 mile arc. The even coastline, altogether inhospitable and desolate, does not possess a single cove where a ship could shelter. The little villages with their white houses, which lie back from the coast, turn, for their livelihood, entirely to the hinterland.

The **Penmarch Peninsula** was one of the richest regions in Brittany up to the end of the 16C: cod-fishing (the "lenten meat") brought wealth to the 15 000 inhabitants. But then the cod deserted the coastal waters, and a tidal wave brought devastation. Final disaster came with the brigand **La Fontenelle** *(p 93)* who took the locality by surprise in spite of its defences. He killed 5 000 peasants, burned down their houses and loaded 300 boats with booty which he then took back to his stronghold on Tristan Island.

Plozévet. – *Description above.*

Leave Plozévet S towards Penhors; the road then follows the coastline.

Penhors. – *For access to the chapel, make for the beach.* In September the great *pardon* of Notre-Dame-de-Penhors, one of the largest of Cornouaille *(p 226)* takes place. The night before (Saturday) there is a procession with torches. On the Sunday the procession *(illustration p 27)* walks through the countryside until it comes to the shore line and back to the chapel where the benediction of the sea takes place.

Proceed to Plovan.

Plovan. – Pop 720. Little 16C church with beautifully coloured modern stained glass windows and a fine turreted belfry. Nearby is a 16C calvary.

Languidou Chapel. – The ruined 13-15C chapel still has some interesting points, particularly the fine rose window.

Make for Plonéour-Lanvern via Tréogat.

🕐 **Languivoa Chapel.** – *1.5 km - 1 mile to the east of Plonéour-Lanvern.* This 14 and 17C chapel (restored) forms an imposing ensemble adorned by rose windows and Gothic arcading. The dismantled belfry porch still dominates the devastated nave and Classical style entrance with its engaged Doric columns. The chapel contains the Virgin of Notre-Dame-de-Languivoa suckling her child.

(Christiane Olivier, Nice)

Languidou Chapel

At Plonéour-Lanvern take the D 57 to Plomeur and after 2 km - 1 mile turn right.

★★ **Notre-Dame-de-Tronoën Calvary and Chapel.** – *P 150.*

Continue along the road bearing right and right again.

Torche Point. – The name is a corruption of the Breton "Beg an Dorchenn": flat stone point. Fine **view**★ of the St-Guénolé rocks and the Audierne Bay. There is a tumulus with a large dolmen.

Pors-Carn Beach (Plage de Pors-Carn). – This great sandy beach along La Torche Bay is the terminal point of the telephone cable linking France and the USA.

★ **Finistère Prehistorical Museum** (Musée Préhistorique). – *At the entrance to St-Guénolé.* A 🕐 series of megaliths and Gallic steles or obelisks called *lec'hs* stand around the museum. Start the visit from the left to see the exhibits in chronological order, from the Stone Age to the Gallo-Roman period. On display are, in the first gallery, a reconstruction of an Iron Age cemetery, Gallic pottery with Celtic decorations and a Gallic stele with spiral carving; in the south gallery, polished axes of rare stone, flint arrowheads, bronze weapons and chests with grooves.

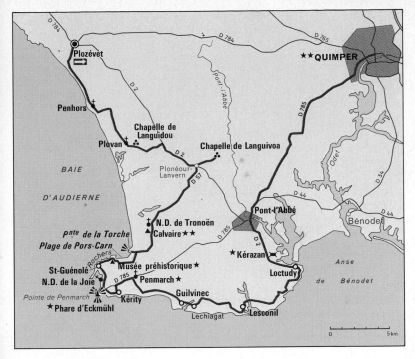

The museum contains all the prehistoric antiquities discovered in Finistère except for the rich collection displayed in the Museum of National Antiquities at St-Germain-en-Laye *(see Michelin Green Guide to Paris)*.

St-Guénolé. – Facilities. The modern church is charming although a little dark; it stands near the old square tower that is all that remains of the old 15C church. Behind the fishing port (coastal fishing: sardines, mackerel) are the famous **rocks** against which the sea breaks furiously.

Notre-Dame-de-la-Joie Chapel. – This 15C chapel with its pierced belfry is flanked by two turrets. The 16C calvary is adorned with a *Pietà*. A *pardon* is held on 15 August.

★ **Eckmühl Lighthouse** (Phare d'Eckmühl). – The Eckmühl Lighthouse stands at the very end ⊘ of the Penmarch headland.The lighthouse is 65m - 213ft tall and its light of 2 million candle-power has a range of 54 km - 33 1/2 miles. From the gallery at the top of the tower (307 steps) there is a **view**★★ of Audierne Bay, Raz Point, the lighthouse on Sein Island, the coast of Concarneau and Beg-Meil and the Glénan archipelago.

Passing to the left of the lighthouse, you will reach the very tip of the headland on which stand the old lighthouse – it now serves as a marker for ships at sea –, a little fortified chapel and a signal station. The sea is studded with reefs covered in seaweed.

Farther east, as at Penmarch the coast is a succession of rocky points and dunes.

Kérity. – Little port devoted to fishing along the coast. Ste-Thumette Church (1675) has an elegant gabled front flanked by a turret.

★ **Penmarch.** – Pop 6 466. The parish includes several villages: St-Guénolé, Kérity, Tréoultré ⊘ and St-Pierre. The **St-Nonna Church**★ was built in the 16C in the Flamboyant Gothic style. At the east end and on either side of the doorway, the buttresses are carved into high or low reliefs of ships and caravels, recalling that the church was built with moneys from shipowners. A gable tower crowns the roof. Inside there are several old statues: in the south chapel, St Michael and St Anne with the Virgin and Child; in the south aisle hangs the Wish of Louis XIII.

Proceed to Guilvinec by the coast road.

Guilvinec. – Pop 4 108. Trawler fishing port with many sardine and tunny boats as well as three fish canneries which handle the fish as it is unloaded. With **Lechiagat** where numerous pleasure boats anchor, it forms a well sheltered harbour. Beaches unfold behind the dunes as far as Lesconil.

Lesconil. – Facilities. Small trawler fishing port.

Make for Loctudy via Palue-du-Cosquer and Lodonnec.

Loctudy. – P 130.

★ **Kérazan-en-Loctudy Manor.** – The manorhouse was bequeathed to the Institut de France in ⊘ 1929 by Joseph Astor, the son of the U.S. Senator. It consists of two wings at right angles, one of which dates from the 16C, the other one from the 18C (enlarged in 1913). The furnished rooms, which are adorned with Louis XIV panelling, contain collections of pictures and drawings from the 17C to the present: Flemish, Dutch and French schools. Note especially Joseph Vernet, Maurice Denis and Auguste Goy, one of Ingres's followers, who evokes the Breton life of the past.

Pont-l'Abbé. – P 164.

Leave Pont-l'Abbé by ① on the local map and return to Quimper.

★★ **Quimper.** – Time 2 1/2 hours. Description p 168.

★ Le CROISIC

Michelin map **63** fold 14 or **230** fold 51 – Local map p 108 – Facilities

An animated port where fishing boats and pleasure craft intermingle and an important centre for the cultivation of shellfish, Le Croisic overlooks the Grand Traict lagoon and is an agreeable small seaside town which has many summer holiday visitors. The **Port-Lin** beach, facing the Atlantic, is 800 m - 1/2 mile from the centre of the town on the far side of the peninsula; that of **St-Goustan**, on the roadstead, is 1 km - 1/2 mile away.

The Port. – The port is well protected by the Tréhic jetty and is divided into several basins by three islets. It is a picturesque and busy scene in winter with the arrival of the prawn boats. The quays are flanked by 17C houses often ornamented by wrought - iron balconies.

⊙ The new **fish market** *(criée)* built on one of the islets commanding the access to the port, is a pleasant modern building. A gallery open to visitors overlooks the area where auctions are held.

★ **Côte d'Amour Aquarium.** – In addition to a collection of local marine fauna
⊙ (octopuses, conger-eels, etc.) visitors can see penguins, tropical turtles, morays and piranhas. On display on the 1st floor are fish from the coral reefs. Exhibited also is a fascinating collection of shells and coral. Note also the 38 kg - 84 lb stuffed coelacanth.

Hôtel d'Aiguillon. – The 17C building includes the town hall and a naval museum.

⊙ **Naval Museum.** – Displayed in 3 rooms on the ground floor are: manuscripts (15-19C), engravings, ship models, navigational instruments, a bust of Richelieu by Le Brun and one of Colbert by Coysevox, and a diorama of the salt marshes. Also exhibited is the map illustrating a sea battle, during the Seven Years' War (1756-1763), between the French and the English when in 1759 Admiral Hawke defeated Admiral Conflans off Le Croisic. In the garden is a **cannon** (1670), from the *Soleil Royal* a ship sunk in the battle, which was decorated after cartoons by Puget.

Notre-Dame-de-Pitié. – This 15 and 16C church, with its 17C 56m - 84ft **lantern tower**, overlooks the port. Inside it has a short nave, with a flat east end illuminated by a window with Flamboyant tracery and 3 side aisles. A Virgin, Our Lady of the Wind, decorates the central pier of the Renaissance portal, which opens onto the Rue de l'Église.

Old houses. – To admire the beautiful corbelled and half-timbered houses, walk through the little streets near the church. Note Nos 25, 20, 28 in Rue de l'Église, No 4 Place du Pilori and Nos 33, 35 in Rue St-Christophe.

Mont-Esprit. – This is a drive laid out on an artificial mound (30m - 98ft high) built from ships' ballast. From the top there is a fine **view**★ to the east of the salt marshes (marais salants) and Batz, to the west on to the town and in the distance the Atlantic.

Mont-Lénigo. – Ships at one time unloaded their ballast here and in 1761 trees were planted. The **view**★ goes over the roadstead, the Tréhic jetty (850m - 2 789ft long), and its lighthouse (1872) at the entrance to the port; the Pen Bron Dyke (1724) is across the way as is its hospital centre. A shaded walk goes down to the esplanade where is the memorial (1919) by René Paris, erected to Hervé Rielle, the coxswain, who saved 22 ships of the French fleet from disaster in 1692, by directing them to St-Malo.

EXCURSION

★ **The Côte Sauvage.** – *Round tour of 26 km - 16 miles – about 2 hours – Local map p 108. Leave Le Croisic by D 45, NW of the plan.*
After the cure centre, the road follows the coast passing St-Goustan and its salt marsh where eels are raised. The wild coastline with rocks ends at **Croisic Point** passing the beaches of Port-Lin, Valentin and its sailing school and Batz-sur-Mer. Farther on the view opens out over Pornichet, the estuary of the Loire and the coast as far as St-Gildas Point. After **Le Pouliguen**★ *(p 166)*, return to Le Croisic by the N 171, via the charming village of **Kervalet** *(p 108)* and **Batz-sur-Mer**★ *(p 54)*.

★★★ CROZON Peninsula

Michelin map **58** folds 3, 4, 13, 14 or **230** folds 16, 17

The Crozon peninsula affords many excursions typical of the Breton coast. Nowhere else, except perhaps at the Raz Point, do the sea and coast reach such heights of grim beauty, with the giddy steepness of the cliffs, the colouring of the rocks and the fury of the sea breaking on the reefs. Another attraction is the variety of views over the indentations and estuaries of the Brest roadstead, the Goulet, the broken coast of Toulinguet, Penhir, Dinan Castle, Cape Chèvre and Douarnenez Bay. From the summit of the Ménez-Hom all these features can be seen arrayed in an immense panorama.

★★★ FROM PENHIR POINT TO ESPAGNOLS POINT

Round tour starting from Crozon – 45 km - 28 miles – about 2 1/2 hours

Crozon. – Pop 7 904. The town has given its name to the peninsula in the middle of which it stands. The **church** is modern. The altar to the right of the chancel is ornamented with a large 17C **altarpiece**★ depicting the martyrdom of the Theban Legion. Below are two 17C panels: the Flagellation, on the left, and the Bearing of the Cross, on the right. Note the pulpit on which that at Locronan was modelled.

Leave Crozon by the D 8, west of the town and make for Camaret.

To the left, by Kerloch, there is a fine view of Dinan Bay, the vast beaches of Kerloch and Goulien and on a fine day, of Raz Point.

Camaret-sur-Mer. – *P 69.*

Toulinguet Point. – An isthmus bounded by Pen-Hat beach leads to the point on which stands a French Navy signal station. There is a view of Toulinguet rocks and of Penhir Point.

Return to the entrance to Camaret and bear right.

Lagatjar Lines (Alignements de Lagatjar). – They include 143 menhirs discovered since the early 20C *(details on prehistoric monuments p 34).*

★★★ **Penhir Point.** – *P 155.*

Return to the car and take the Camaret road again. Turn right after 1.5 km - 1 mile into the D 8. As you come out of Camaret leave the D 8 at the top of a climb and turn left into the D 355, once a strategic road.

The view opens out to show Camaret Bay on the left and, on the right, the Brest roadstead. The road enters the walls which enclose the Roscanvel Peninsula before Quélern. These fortifications date from the time of Vauban and the Second Empire.

This road, the D 355, running alongside the roadstead is picturesque. The curious contrast between the slopes on either side of the peninsula is striking: the western slope, facing the west wind and the sea is moorland and lacks vegetation: the eastern slope is covered with trees and meadows.

The D 355 affords views of the Atlantic, Toulinguet Point, Grand Gouin Point, Camaret Bay, the Goulet and in the far distance, St-Mathieu Point.

★★ **Espagnols Point.** – From here one can see a remarkable **panorama** which includes the town and harbour of Brest, the Elorn estuary, the Albert-Louppe bridge, the Plougastel Peninsula, and the end of the roadstead.

Then the road skirts the eastern coast of the peninsula affording a good view on the left of the Brest roadstead, the Plougastel Peninsula and, the Longue, Morts and Trébéron Islands.

Roscanvel. – Pop 803. The church was rebuilt after a fire in 1956 and now possesses fine dark stained glass windows by Labouret, and a coloured terracotta Stations of the Cross by Claude Gruher.
Note the unusual fuschia hedges in the village.

The D 355, which to the south of Roscanvel goes round the end of the roadstead, affords fine views of Longue Island (nuclear submarine base - *no entry*), and in the foreground, of the two smaller islands, Trébéron and Morts. You leave the peninsular territory once more by the ruined fortifications.

About 500m - 1/3 mile beyond St-Fiacre, turn left into D 55.

Le Fret. – A small port with regular boat service to and from Brest *(p 63)*. View of the Plougastel peninsula from the jetty.

The road runs along the jetty bordering Le Fret Bay.

When you come to a fork, take the D 155 to Crozon, leaving the Lanvéoc road on your left.

Take a last, backward look at the roadstead.

★★DINAN POINT

6 km - 4 miles – about 2 hours

Leave Crozon (p 84) by the D 308 W towards Morgat then turn right.

Windswept heathland follows after the pine groves.

★★ **Dinan Point.** – Time: 1 hour. Leave your car at the end of the road. Continue on foot, by the path on the left for about 500 m - 1/3 mile. A fine **panorama** can be seen from the edge of the cliff; on the left are Cape Chèvre, the coast of Cornouaille and the Raz Point; on the right, Penhir Point and the Tas de Pois. Skirting the cliff to the right you will see the rock or Dinan Castle, where the point ends. A natural arch joins this enormous rocky mass, **Dinan "Castle"** ("Château" de Dinan). to the mainland *(1/2 hour on foot Rtn, over rocky ground; wear non-slip soles)*. On the righthand slope of the little "castle" peninsula, take a path over the natural arch.

★CAPE CHÈVRE

11 km - 7 miles – about 2 hours

Leave Crozon (p 84) by the D 887 SW to Morgat.

★ **Morgat.** – *P 139.*

From Morgat to Cape Chèvre the road runs through an austere landscape of rocks and stunted heath, open to the ocean winds, with little hamlets of houses huddled together which seem to hide in the folds of the ground. To the left, the view gradually opens out over Douarnenez Bay, with the massive outline of the Ménez-Hom in the distance.

Turn right after 2 km - 1 mile from Morgat.

500 m - 1/3 mile past Brégoulou, leave the car in the car park from which you can enjoy a good view of the Tas de Pois and Raz Point.

La Palud Beach (Plage de la Palud). – It is not advisable to bathe here: the waves are very strong. Beautiful view of the rocky coastline.

Return to Brégoulou and turn right. Make for St-Hernot and then bear right.

★ **Cape Chèvre.** – *Time: 1/2 hour.* There is a signal station of the French Navy on the site. *Go round the signal station to the right to reach the point. Telescope.* From the former German observation point there is a fine **view** over the Atlantic and the advanced points of Finistère: Penhir Point and the Tas de Pois, Sein Island, Cape Sizun and its headlands, Van Point and Raz Point to the south of Douarnenez Bay.

Michelin map **58** folds 4, 5 or **230** fold 18

This little town lies on both banks of the Daoulas River, whose estuary forms one of the many inlets in the Brest roadstead.

★**Parish Close.** – On the left stands the abbey; ahead and slightly to the right, is a 16C porch★ adorned with statues and a multitude of carved figures and small animals. Go through the porch which serves as a belfry. The church, which has been restored, still has its 12C west door, nave and north aisle. The 17C ossuary at the east end has been turned into a sacristy. At the end of the main pathway in the cemetery stands a very old Calvary. Outside the close there is a chapel to St Anne with a 17C doorway ornamented with statues of the Virgin and St Anne.

Abbey. – Founded in the 12C by Augustinian monks, the abbey flourished until the 17C. It is now a Franciscan monastery. *Signposts at the entrance to the town lead to the west side of the abbey.*

★**Cloister.** – In the garden in front of the cloister stand statues of saints (Augustine, ⊘ Sebastian, Andrew). Only three sides of the cloister built between 1167 and 1173 remain standing. It is a very elegant specimen of Romanesque architecture with its foliage and geometric decoration. In the middle of the court is a large basin decorated with ten heads and Romanesque ornaments.

Notre-Dame-des-Fontaines Fountain and Oratory. – A path leads to a green dell where stands a fountain dated 1550 adorned with a low-relief depicting St Catherine of Sienna. Nearby is a small oratory to which remains of the abbey church were added in the 19C: door and gallery around the monks' choir, stalls, friezes. Two 13C statues are noteworthy: a Virgin and Child and St Thelo riding a stag.

EXCURSION

Dirinon. – Pop 1 838. *5.5 km - 3 1/2 miles N – about 1/2 hour. On the road to Brest about 2.5 km - 1 1/2 miles beyond Daoulas turn right to Dirinon.*
The church is crowned by a remarkable Renaissance belfry: above the square tower, two sets of bells and two storeys of balustraded balconies are surmounted by a slender, stone spire. Above the doorway with its pointed Gothic arch, stands a statue of St Nonna in a niche with pilasters. St Nonna is patroness of the parish and her tomb lies in the neighbouring 16C chapel to the right of the church. Inside, the friezes, tie and cross beams are of interest. The vaulting is adorned with 18C paintings.

Michelin map **59** folds 15, 16 or **230** fold 25 – Local map p 176 – Facilities

This historical town, with its old houses and streets, is gay with trees and gardens; it is girt by ramparts and guarded by an imposing castle, and it stands on a plateau overlooking the Rance. The port begins at the foot of a viaduct which bestrides the valley, and is used by the St-Malo and Dinard boat services and pleasure craft.

HISTORICAL NOTES

Du Guesclin against Canterbury. – In 1359 the Duke of Lancaster besieged Dinan, which was defended by Bertrand Du Guesclin *(details p 178)* and his brother Olivier. After several encounters with the superior English forces, Bertrand asked for a forty days' truce, after which, he promised, the town would surrender if it were not relieved. In violation of the truce, Olivier, who had gone out of the town unarmed, was made prisoner by an English knight, Canterbury, who demanded a ransom of 1 000 florins. Bertrand challenged the Englishman to single combat. The encounter took place at a spot now called the Place du Champ. Lancaster presided. Canterbury lost and had to pay Olivier the 1 000 florins he had demanded and surrender his arms to Bertrand. He was also discharged from the English army. This success won Du Guesclin the admiration of a pretty girl of Dinan, Tiphaine Raguenel. The union of this cultivated woman with the rough warrior, later to be Constable, was a happy one.

Du Guesclin's Tombs. – After more than twenty years' campaigning for the King of France *(p 24)* Bertrand du Guesclin died on 14 July 1380, before Châteauneuf-de-Randon, to which he had laid siege. He had asked to be buried at Dinan. The funeral convoy, therefore, set out for that town. At Le Puy the body was embalmed and the entrails buried in the Jacobins' church (now the Church of St. Lawrence). As the embalming was inadequate, the remains were boiled at Montferrand and the flesh was removed from the skeleton and buried in the Franciscans' church (destroyed in 1793). At Le Mans an officer of the King brought an order to bring the body to St-Denis; the skeleton was then handed over to him. Only the heart arrived at Dinan, where it was deposited in the Jacobins' church. It has since been transferred to St Saviour's.
So it was that while the kings of France had only three tombs (for the heart, entrails and body), Du Guesclin had four.

Royal good humour. – During the League, Dinan was surprised and taken by partisans of Henry IV. One of the attackers, a worthy burgher of St-Malo named Pépin, went off at a gallop to take the good news to the King. In Paris he hurried to the Louvre. "Sire, I've taken Dinan", he cried. As Marshal de Biron seemed incredulous, Pépin turned maliciously to Henri: "He knows better than I do, yet I was there!" But Pépin was very tired and asked boldly: "Is this the house of God, where no one eats or drinks?" The King gave him a meal. The next day he asked him if he would like a title. "No, Sire," answered the proud citizen of St-Malo, "at home I drive the nobles out of our town with a stick. But give me a horse, for mine's dropped dead!"

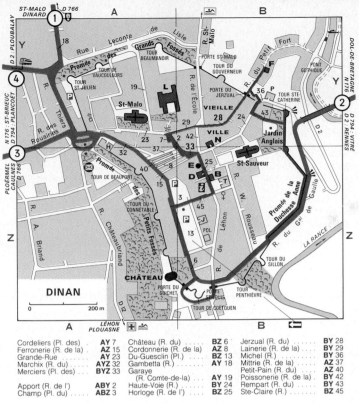

★OLD TOWN (VIEILLE VILLE) *time: 1 1/2 hours*

Leave from the Place Du-Guesclin.

On the square, surrounded by 17 and 18C town houses, is the statue of Du Guesclin by Frémiet.

Turn right into the Rue Ste-Claire and left into the Rue de l'Horloge.

Hôtel Kératry (BZ B). – This attractive 16C mansion with three granite pillars, houses the Tourist Information Centre.

House of the Recumbent Figure (Maison du Gisant) (BZ D). – In this house a sculptor of recumbent figures worked.

○ **Clock Tower (Tour de l'Horloge) (BZ E).** – In this belfry is exhibited the clock offered by the Duchess Anne. A display case is devoted to the history of Dinan's former town hall and another to the Duchess Anne. From the top (158 steps) there is a vast **panorama★★** of the town and its principal monuments and the surrounding countryside from the Bécherel region to the Channel.

Bear left into the pretty Rue de l'Apport. Under its arches merchants sold their wares.

★Place des Merciers (BZ 33). – The old well and lovely old triangular-gabled houses with wooden porches paint a pleasant scene. Glance into the rue de la Cordonnerie and Rue du Petit-Pain with its attractive houses. Nearby at no 10 Rue de la Mittrie Théodore Botrel (1868-1925) the songwriter was born *(p 29).*

Cross the Place des Cordeliers and bear right into the Rue de la Lainerie.

★Rue du Jerzual (BY 28). – This lovely cobblestoned street slopes steeply downhill. The 15 and 16C shops lining the street are now occupied by artists: glass-blowers, sculptors, weavers...

Go through the 14C Jerzual Gate and into the Rue du Petit-Fort, which is an extension of the Rue du Jerzual and looks rather like it.

Governor's House (Maison du Gouverneur) (BY F). – *At no 24.* A fine 15C house in which a weaving and highwarp tapestry workshop has been installed.

Return to the Jerzual Gate and take the staircase to the left, follow the Michel Alley, then right into the Rue Michel and left into the Rue du Rempart.

English Garden (Jardin Anglais) (BYZ). – The terraced garden on the site of the former St-Sauveur cemetery affords a **view★★** of the Ste-Catherine Tower, the Rance, crossed by a Gothic bridge (Pont gothique) – rebuilt since the war – the port and the huge viaduct 250m - 820ft long and 40m - 128ft high. St Saviour's Basilica is in the background.

Duchess Anne Promenade (BZ). – From this promenade along the ramparts there is a lovely **view★** of the Rance, the viaduct and the port.

Go back towards town, by the 17C St Louis Gate, go round the 14C Coëtquen Tower before reaching the castle (p 88) and Petits Fossés Promenade. By the Guichet Gate, flanked by two semi-cylindrical towers, you arrive at the Place Du-Guesclin.

ADDITIONAL SIGHTS

★ **The Castle (Château) (AZ).** – You may visit the Coëtquen Tower (its two floors served as a prison) and the keep. The enormous 14C tower, known as the Dungeon of Duchess Anne 34m - 100ft high has bold machicolations. There are old statues in the stairway. It contains a museum: effigies, mediaeval funerary sculpture and other exhibits.
In the chapel sacerdotal vestments and tombstones are displayed; in the guardroom are 19C Breton furnishings and old measures. The High Constable's room is devoted to the history of Dinan and local crafts. The Armoury contains head-dresses *(coiffes)* from the Dinan area.
There is a fine **panorama★** from the terrace above the parapet walk.

St Saviour's Basilica (Basilique St-Sauveur) (BZ). – A Romanesque porch surmounted by a Flamboyant Gothic gable opens the façade; all of the wall to the right is 12C, except the outside chapel which was added in the 15C and is decorated by twin bracketed arcades, partly blinded, and lovely carved capitals. The rest of the church is 15 and 16C. The dome of the tower, which was destroyed by lightning, was replaced in the 18C by a timber steeple covered with slates.
The lack of symmetry inside the building is noticeable; the south side is Romanesque, while the north side, chancel and transept are in the Flamboyant Gothic style. In the north transept a 15C cenotaph restored in the 18C, contains the heart of Du Guesclin. Note the 18C high altar, the 12C granite baptismal font (in the first chapel of the side aisle), a 15C stained glass window representing the Evangelists (in the fourth chapel of the side aisle). In the ambulatory on the right side, in the first chapel is a carved polychrome figure of Our Lady of Virtue (13C). The modern windows were made in the Barillet workshop.

As you leave the basilica, on Place St-Sauveur, there is a house (on the left) with pillars – where in 1847 Auguste Pavie explorer of Indochina and diplomat was born.

Former Beaumanoir Mansion (Ancien Hôtel Beaumanoir) (BY N). – The mansion has an attractive Renaissance doorway. In the courtyard notice the window decoration and a 16C turret containing a lovely staircase.

Former Franciscan Monastery (Ancien couvent des Cordeliers) (AY L). – The monastery is now a school. A handsome doorway, decorated by a frieze of eight small niches (which once contained statues), opens onto the path, which leads to the school. Of the former monastery, the 15C Gothic cloister and the main courtyard, with its turrets with pepperpot roofs of the same period, can still be seen. The ensemble has been restored to quite an extent. Good view of the east end of St-Malo church.

St-Malo (AY). – This church in the Flamboyant Gothic style was started in the 15C and finished in the 19C. The chancel and east end which are all that is left of the early work, are worth seeing.

Grands Fossés Promenade (ABY). – This magnificent avenue is bordered on one side by the Rue Leconte-de-Lisle and on the other by the northern ramparts. Admire the St-Julien, Vaucouleurs and Beaumanoir Towers and the St-Malo Gate.

Petits Fossés Promenade (AZ). – This promenade skirts the outside of the 13-15C ramparts. Looming above are the castle, and the Connétable and Beaufort Towers.

EXCURSIONS

Banks of the Rance. – *Time: 1 hour on foot. Go down to the Rance and cross the Gothic bridge (Pont gothique).*
On the right, take a path *(no cars allowed)* which passes under the viaduct and follows the river in a green and sheltered **setting,** where it is pleasant to stroll.

Léhon. – *2 km - 1 mile S, plus 1/2 hour sightseeing.* Pop 3 149.
The priory of St-Magloire was founded in 12C on the site of a 9C abbey sacked by the Normans in 975 AD. The church, rebuilt in 13C and restored in late 19C, has a rounded doorway adorned with small columns and surmounted by a horizontal string-course decorated with heads. The Angevin style ogive vaulted nave contains the tombs of the Beaumanoir family and a 13C stoup on which sickles were sharpened at harvest time. On the north side of the church is the ruined 17C cloister lined by two 17C buildings framing the 14C monks' refectory.
From the castle ruins perched on top of a hillock at the entrance to the village there is a good view of the Rance Valley.

★ **Tour of the Rance.** – *87 km - 54 miles – allow 1 day. P 175.*
In season you can go down the Rance by boat, but if you wish to return the same day you will have to take a bus or train back.

Corseul. – Pop 2 022. *11 km - 7 miles. Leave Dinan by ③, the N 176, bear right onto the D 794.*
Already known by the Celts and Gauls, Corseul was then conquered by the Romans, as was most of the area. A large quantity of artefacts dating back to these various periods are gathered in the town hall : in the garden of Antiquities, to the right of the building, where columns and capitals are exhibited and on the 2nd floor in a small **museum.** Housed in the museum are dressed stones, funerary urns, coins, red and black pottery, tiles and, in display cases, public and family life have been traced.
In the church on the pillar, to the right of the baptismal chapel, is the funerary stele of Silicia, a Roman officer's mother, who died in Corseul.
However, the most remarkable vestige is the **Temple of Haut-Bécherel,** said to be the Temple of Mars *(1.5 km - 1 mile on the road to Dinan and right on an uphill road).* It is a polygonal tower with masonry in small courses, dating from Emperor Augustus' reign.

Bourbansais Château. – *14 km - 9 miles SE of Dinan. P 61.*

Michelin map **59** fold 5 or **230** fold 1 – Local maps pp 97 and 176

This smart resort, which lies in a magnificent setting on the estuary of the Rance, opposite St-Malo, is frequented by the international set and especially by British and Americans. The place was "launched" about 1850 by an American named Coppinger and developed by the British. Before that it was small fishing village and an offshoot of St-Énogat.

The tourist will be interested by the extraordinary contrast between Dinard and St-Malo: the former, a luxurious resort with modern installations, intense social activity, princely villas and splendid gardens and parks; the latter an old city, surrounded by ramparts, possessing a family beach and a commercial port.

SIGHTS

★★**Moulinet Point** (BY). – *Start from the Grande Plage.*
A walk to this point offers a series of magnificent **views**★★ of the coast from Cape Fréhel, on the left, to St-Malo on the right, and, farther on, of the Rance estuary.

★**The Grande Plage or Plage de l'Écluse** (BY). – This beach of fine sand, bordered by luxurious hotels and the casino, extends to the end of the cove formed by the Moulinet and Malouine Points. Following the promenade along the beach to the left you will reach a terrace from which you can see St-Malo.

★**The Clair de Lune Promenade and the Prieuré Beach** (BYZ). – This walk
⊙ *(pedestrians only)* lies along a sea wall which follows the water's edge and offers pretty views over the Rance estuary. Lovely multicoloured flower beds and remarkable Mediterranean vegetation embellish the promenade.
The **Prieuré Beach** is at the end of the promenade. It owes its name to a priory founded here in 1324.

⊙ **Aquarium and Marine Museum** (BY M). – The **Natural History Museum** comprises an aquarium with 24 pools filled with fish and crustaceans from Breton waters; a second room is devoted to birds which nest along the coast and in the bird sanctuaries.
Next is the **Marine Museum** which presents mementoes of Commandant Charcot's polar expeditions.

DINARD

Féart (Bd) .... **BYZ**	Boutin (Pl. J.) .... **BY** 4	Lhotellier (Bd) .... **AY** 17
Leclerc (R. Mar.) .... **BYZ** 16	Clemenceau (R. G.) .. **BY** 6	Malouine (R. de la) ... **BY** 18
	Coppinger (R.) .... **BY** 7	Pichot (R.) .... **BZ** 19
Abbé-Langevin (R.) ... **AY** 2	Corbinais (R. de la) ... **AZ** 8	Près.-Wilson (Bd) .... **BY** 20
Albert-Ier (Bd) ...... **BY** 3	Croix-Guillaume (R.) ... **AZ** 10	Renan (R. E.) .... **AY** 21
	Douet-Fourchet (R. des). **AZ** 12	République (Pl. de la) . **BY** 22
	Gaulle (Pl. du Gén.-de) **BZ** 13	St-Lunaire (R. de) .... **AY** 25
	Giraud (Av. du Gén.) .. **BZ** 15	Vernet (R. Y.) .... **BY** 26

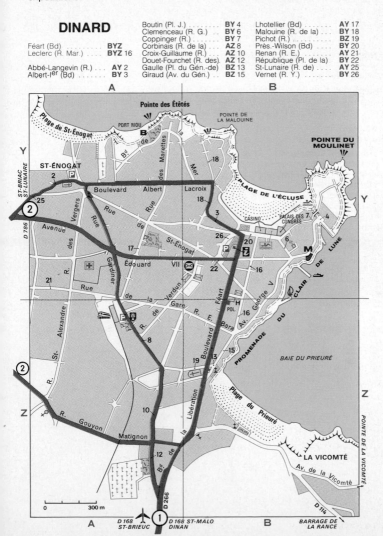

Étêtés Point (AY). – View of the islands and the coast beyond St-Malo.

Port-Riou Garden (AY B). – This terraced garden, below the Étêtés Point, offers a fine **view** as far as Cape Fréhel.

St-Énogat Beach (AY). – The beach lies in a picturesque setting under steep cliffs.

★★**Vicomté Point (BZ).** – *2 km - 1 mile – plus 1 hour on foot Rtn.*
The Vicomté, a fine estate divided into lots, is becoming one of the most fashionable quarters of Dinard.
The circular road *(chemin de ronde) (walk it),* starting at the Avenue Bruzzo offers splendid **vistas**★★ towards the roadstead, the Rance estuary and the Rance tidal power scheme.

⏱ BOAT TRIPS

★★★**St-Malo.** – *Crossing: 10 minutes. Description of St-Malo p 193.*

★★★**Cruise to Cape Fréhel.** *From St-Malo with stop-over at Dinard. Description of Cape* ⏱ *Fréhel p 102.*
On the way out the boat skirts the coast as far as Cape Fréhel, and goes round the Island of Cézembre on the way back.

★★**Dinan, by the Rance.** – *Description p 176.*

⏱**Cézembre Island.** – A fine sea trip. The island has a popular beach of fine sand.

Chausey Islands. – *See Michelin Green Guide Normandy.*
A small archipelago of granite islands, islets and reefs.

AIR TRIPS

⏱*Regular daily flights leave for the Channel Islands of Jersey and Guernsey.*

The annual Michelin Guide France gives the addresses and telephone numbers of the main car dealers, tyre specialists, general repair garages and garages offering a night breakdown service.

★ DOL-DE-BRETAGNE   Pop 4 974

Michelin map **59** fold 6 or **230** fold 12

Dol, a former bishopric and proud of its fine cathedral, is now the small capital of the "Marais", marsh, district *(p 92).* It stands on the edge of a cliff about 20m - 64ft high which was washed by the sea until the 12C.

SIGHTS

★★**St Samson's Cathedral.** – *Time : 1/2 hour.*
The cathedral is a vast structure, built of granite in the 12 and 13C and remodelled during the next three centuries. It gives an idea of the importance that the bishopric of Dol then enjoyed.
On the outside, the most interesting part is the south wall, which includes two porches: the very fine **Great Porch**★ (14C) and the "Little porch" (13C) with its fine ogive arcade. Seen from the north, the cathedral looks like a fortress, its crenellated parapet was linked to the old fortifications of the town.
The interior, 100m - 328ft long, is impressive. Notice in the chancel: the medallion-glass **window**★★ (13C restored), the eighty stalls (14C), the Bishop's throne (16C carved wood), and above the high altar the 14C wooden Statue of the Virgin, coloured in 1859. In the north arm of the transept, is the tomb of Thomas James, Bishop of Dol (16C); it is the work of two Florentine sculptors Antoine and Jean Juste. In the south aisle note the Christ Reviled; in the axial chapel there are two 18C reliquary figures of St Samson and St Magloire.

DOL-DE-BRETAGNE

Châteaubriand (Pl.)	7
Grande-Rue des Stuarts	10
Le-Jamptel (R.)	12
Briand (Av. Aristide)	2
Carmes (R. des)	3
Cathédrale (Pl. de la)	4
Ceinte (Rue)	6
Écoles (R. des)	8
Mairie (Pl. de la)	13
Normandie (Bd de)	14
Paris (R. de)	15
Saint-Malo (Rue de)	17
Touliers (Place)	19

With this guide use the Michelin Maps (scale 1:200 000) shown on p 3.

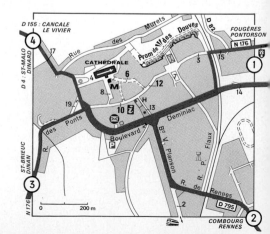

★ **Promenade des Douves.** – This public garden (also known as Promenade Jules-Revert) has been traced along the north part of the old ramparts. Fine **view**★ of the Dol Mound and Dol Marsh (Marais).

⊘ **Treasury Museum** (M). – The museum is installed in the 16C treasury *(Trésorerie)* and is devoted, for the most part, to the history of Dol: dioramas, wax figures, models and arms. The treasury contains a fine collection of polychrome wooden statues (13-19C) of old Breton saints as well as rare 17-18C faience statues from Rennes and Quimper of virgins.

Old houses. – The streets near the precincts of the cathedral have interesting old houses.

Grande-Rue-des-Stuarts (10). – No 17 (florist) dates from the 11 and 12C and has Romanesque arcading; no 27 is 13C (antique-dealer); no 33 is a 1617 dwelling with fine dormer windows; no 18, a former Templars' inn with a 12C vaulted cellar, is now transformed into a bar-*crêperie;* a charming 16C courtyard is at no 32.

Rue Le-Jamptel (12). – No 31 dates from the 12 or 13C (chemist); no 27 is a 15C house decorated with pillars.

Rue Ceinte (6). – This street was where the chapterhouse was formerly located. No 1 and no 4 are both 15C houses (the latter is a *crêperie);* no 16 dates from 1668.

EXCURSIONS

Round tour of 29 km - 18 miles. – *Time: about 1 3/4 hours. Leave Dol by ② on the town plan, the D 795. Leave the D 4 on your left, 600m – about 1/3 mile after turn left then turn right into a tarred road.*

Champ-Dolent Menhir. – The dolmen, one of the finest in Brittany, stands 9m - 30ft high. The name Champ-Dolent (Field of Pain) refers to a legendary struggle which is supposed to have taken place here.

Turn around and bear right onto the D 4.

Épiniac. – Pop 1 104. In the north aisle of the church, on the altar, is a 16C polychromed high relief representing the Dormition of the Virgin; in the chancel is a finely carved 17C wood canopy.

At La Boussac turn right then at Lépinay turn right again. Leave the car beside the lake near a lane (two white posts).

⊘ **Landal Castle.** – The approach on foot *(1/2 hour Rtn),* starting along the lake bank, past a guardhouse, along an avenue lined with great trees makes a pleasant walk. The sudden appearance of the imposing feudal castle standing in a wooded setting is striking.
The 15C ramparts flanked with round towers wall a part of the courtyard in a corner of which stands the castle. The outbuildings across the way and the pond, below the main entrance, close the courtyard.
A small chapel and a dovecote were built outside the walls.

Follow the road then bear left.

Broualan. – Pop 268. In the centre of the village near a small yet remarkable Calvary stands a 15C church, enlarged in the 16C. The east end is decorated with pinnacled buttresses and lovely Flamboyant windows. The small columned bell tower rests on the large arch which separates the nave from the chancel. Inside several small granite altars and finely worked credences (side tables) can be seen. The tabernacle of the high altar is supported by angels. Note the 16C polychrome stone *Pietà.*

Via La Boussac and the D 155 return to Dol-de-Bretagne.

Notre-Dame-du-Tronchet Abbey. – *10 km - 6 miles. Leave Dol by ③ on the town plan and bear left on the D 119 towards Le Tronchet.*
This former Benedictine abbey was built in the 17C. A large cloister and a hostel (which houses the presbytery) stand amid the ruins. The church contains beautiful 17C woodwork.

★ **DOL Mound** (MONT DOL)

Michelin map **59** fold 6 or **230** fold 12

This granite mound, though only 65m - 208ft high, overlooks a great plain and resembles a small mountain. The remains of many prehistoric animals – mammoth, elephant, rhinoceros, reindeer, etc. – and flint implements have been unearthed on its slopes.
It is possible to go round the mound by car by way of the surfaced road *(chemin de ronde).*
The summit is reached from Mont-Dol church (see below) by a road with a hairpin bend and with an average gradient of 1 in 6.
With a little imagination and the help of the plan you can reconstruct the legendary struggle which took place here between **St Michael** and Satan. Satan was thrown down so violently that he made a depression in the rock and scratched it with his claw. With one blow of his sword, the Archangel made a hole in the mountain into which he hurled his enemy. But the Devil reappeared on Mont-St-Michel and mocked St Michael. As he made one bound from Dol to Mont-St-Michel, St Michael left the imprint of his foot on the rock.
⊘ A signal tower put up in 1802 serves today as a belfry for the **Chapel of Notre-Dame-de-l'Espérance.** A gigantic chestnut tree planted in the 17C to the right of the road on the way up, is noteworthy.

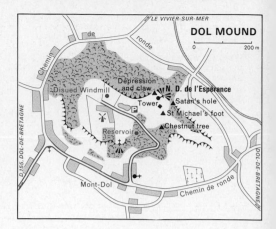

★ **Panorama.** – To the north, from the chapel's chevet, can be seen the Chausey Islands and Cancale and Grouin Points; to the northeast, Mont-St-Michel, Avranches and Granville; from the Calvary, to the south, on the edge of the Marais, Dol and its fine cathedral with the Hédé heights in the background; to the southwest, Dinan; to the west St-Malo and St-Servan; and below, the Dol Marsh fields with their bordering hedges and trees.

The Dol Marsh. – This is the name given to land reclaimed from the marshes and the sea in Mont-St-Michel Bay. Seen from the mound the countryside looks strange and monotonous; it extends for about 15 000 ha - 40 000 acres from the mouth of the Couesnon River to near Cancale. The old shore line ran through Cancale, Châteauneuf, Dol and St-Broladre and along the D 797.

Until some time between the 4 and 8C the marshland and the Bay of Mont-St-Michel were covered by a great forest; Mont-St-Michel and the Dol Mound were just hills. When the sea invaded the area they became islands. Later, the water-level fell, leaving many marshes which were still flooded by the high tides. From the 12C onwards the local people began to drain the area – a work that has gone on until the present day. The Marsh proper is today a fertile wooded district of 12 000 ha - 32 000 acres where cereals, vegetables and forage are grown. Apple trees dot the fields, and long lines of poplars or willows divide the country into a chessboard pattern.

The establishment of large-scale mussel-beds in the Vivier area has somewhat modified its appearance and given it a new impetus.

The polders. – When the marshes had been reclaimed, work was started on areas that had always been part of the sea-bed; these lay beyond the marsh and to the west of the Couesnon canal. They have been transformed by polders used in the same way as in Holland. The areas now appear as an empty plain cut across by canals and dykes with new buildings and modern farms. The main roads branch off the D 797 and are built on dykes, extending with the polders and crossing the lines of poplars that mark each new stretch of land reclaimed from the sea. Only exceptionally high tides reach the top of the banks along the bay. Grass grows on them, forming the famous salt pastures *(prés-salés)*, the sheep which graze there yield very good meat.

Church of Dol Mound. – *In the village.* In this restored church fine 12 to 14C frescoes recounting the life of Christ were found in the nave: on the north side is the Entrance into Jerusalem, the Kiss of Judas; and on the right side Hell, the Descent into Limbo and the Entombment.

DONGES
Pop 6 988

Michelin map 🔢 fold 15 or 🔢 folds 52, 53 – 17 km - 11 miles E of St-Nazaire

The oil port of Donges, which is an annexe of the port of Nantes-St-Nazaire *(p 143)*, has constructed two berths for large oil tankers. The town is also an important refining centre.

The village, at some distance from the refinery complex, was rebuilt after the Second World War.

★ **Church.** – This is built of concrete and granite. A huge Calvary set in a parabolic arc, with a stained glass window as background, dominates the west façade. Standing back and to the right is the square bell-tower crowned by a slender, copper-covered steeple. Inside there is the same feeling of simplicity and upwards sweep as when standing before the façade. Twin arches, as sharply pointed as they are pure in line, divide the side chapels. These like the nave and chancel are lit by stained glass windows by Max Ingrand.

★ DOUARNENEZ
Pop 17 813

Michelin map 🔢 fold 14 or 🔢 fold 17 – Local map p 81 – Facilities

Douarnenez, Ploaré, Pouldavid and Tréboul were amalgamated to form the community of Douarnenez. This community, lying on either side of the Pouldavid estuary, is engaged in contrasting activities. Douarnenez is the great centre for fishing and canning. Tréboul is joined to the rest of the community by a big steel bridge across the Port-Rhu estuary and is a much frequented seaside resort.

The site of the town, deep in a great bay with gracefully curving shores, the lively and colourful picture of its quays, and the streets of the old quarter, zigzagging down to the sea, are Douarnenez's chief attractions.

The port is one of the busiest on the Breton coast. It handles mackerel, sardines, tunny and crustaceans.

La Fontenelle (16C). – According to local tradition the palace of King Mark was at Douarnenez and the island at the mouth of the Pouldavid estuary was, therefore, given the name of his nephew, Tristan *(details about Tristan and Isolde p 25)*.

In the 16C this island was the lair of one La Fontenelle, the most dangerous of the guerilla leaders who devastated the country during the troubles of the League.

La Fontenelle seized Tristan Island. To obtain materials for fortifications he demolished those of Douarnenez. His cruelties are legendary *(p 82)*. In 1598 he agreed to lay down his arms on condition that he was allowed to keep this island; this was granted by Henri IV.

But in 1602 the King took his revenge: involved in a plot, La Fontenelle was sentenced to be broken on the wheel.

SIGHTS

Start from Boulevard Camille-Réaud.

This route brings the visitor to the viewpoint of the "Guet" where the Port-Rhu River runs into the bay.

Port-Rhu River and the Dames Beach (Plage des Dames) (Y). – A *corniche* road runs along the shore and affords picturesque views of Tristan Island (now the property of the J. Richepin family), Tréboul, the narrow streets clustering round the port, and the estuary, which is spanned by a viaduct 24m - 78ft high. There lies Port-Rhu, the commercial port of Douarnenez.

The path then skirts the small beach, Plage des Dames and ends on an esplanade beside the sea.

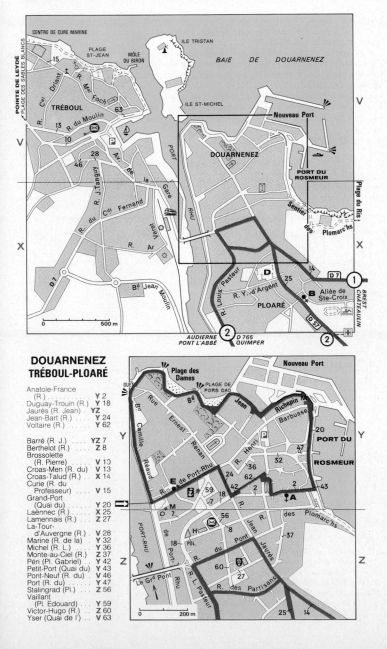

★ **Boulevard Jean-Richepin and the New Harbour** (Nouveau Port) (Y). – Follow this boulevard, which offers superb **views★** of Douarnenez Bay. You will see the new fishing port, which is developing in the shelter of a jetty some 741 m - 800 yds long. Do not fail to go on to this new jetty, from which there is a still wider view of the bay, dominated by the Ménez-Hom.

★ **Rosmeur Harbour** (Port du Rosmeur) (Y). – Here the tourist will get interesting and amusing glimpses of local life, especially when the fish is sold by auction. A walk along the Rosmeur pier also offers a good view of the harbour quarter.

Take Rue A.-France uphill to the left.

Ste-Hélène (Y A). – *Go in by the small door on the south side.*
This chapel, in the Flamboyant Gothic style, was remodelled in the 17 and 18C. Over the side altars there are some 18C pictures and at the end of the nave, two 16C stained glass windows.

Return to the Place Gabriel-Péri by way of the covered market. In the morning the open-air market presents a colourful scene.

Continue along Rue Jean-Bart and turn left into Rue de Port-Rhu.

⊙ **St-Michel** (Y E). – Built in 1663, it has a semicircular chancel and transept, and a small domed belfry. The vaulting is decorated with 17C paintings.

Return to the starting-point by Place de l'Enfer.

⊙ **Boat trips.** – Facilities for boat trips or fishing parties.

PLOARÉ

⊙ **Church** (X B). – The church dates from the 16 and 17C. It is crowned by a fine Flamboyant and Renaissance **tower★**, 55m - 180ft high, with a crocketed steeple with four pinnacles at the corners.
The façade is flanked with Gothic buttresses surmounted by pinnacles, while the buttresses of the apse and transept are crowned with small Renaissance lanterns. Inside note the high altar's carved altarpiece and a 17C painted wooden group representing the Holy Trinity.
Laënnec (1781-1826), the inventor of the stethoscope, is buried in the cemetery (X D). Kerlouarnec, the country house where this eminent physician died, can be seen at the end of a fine avenue leading to the chapel of Ste-Croix (1701).

POULDAVID

By ② of the plan, the D 765 towards Audierne, and take the first road on the left.

⊙ **Church.** – 32 steps. Built on the hillside, the church has a 15C porch, a 14C arcaded nave and a 16C chancel. The chancel vaulting is adorned with sixteen 16C painted panels illustrating scenes from the Passion.

TRÉBOUL

The much frequented resort of Tréboul lies at the foot of a wooded hill *(town plan p 93)* on the left bank of the Port-Rhu River. It is an important sailing centre with a pleasure boat harbour and a sailing school. It also has a salt-water cure centre (centre de cure marine). A pleasant path along the rocky ridge between the Biron pier (môle du Biron) and the Sables Blancs beach (Plage des Sables Blancs) affords fine **views** of Douarnenez Bay and the Ménez-Hom.

EXCURSIONS

★ **Plomarc'hs Path** (Sentier des Plomarc'hs) **and the Ris Beach** (X). – *Time : 2 1/2 hours on foot Rtn.*
The path begins at Rosmeur harbour and runs along the side of a slope affording some very picturesque **views★** of Douarnenez. It leads to the Ris Beach (Plage du Ris).

Return by the same way or by the D 7.

★ **Leydé Point.** – *Round tour of 6 km - 4 miles NW. From the Plage des Sables-Blancs follow the Pors-ar-Soner path, to the right, across woods and heath.* It overlooks the coast, giving fine views of Douarnenez Bay. *Before the village of Leydé leave the car and take the coastal path of the Roches Blanches.* **View★** *from the point.*

Go down to a road which, bearing left, brings you back to Tréboul.

Le Juch. – *Pop 751. 8 km - 5 miles. Leave Douarnenez by ② on the town plan, the D 765. 6 km - 4 miles farther on, turn left for Le Juch.*
Fine **view** of Douarnenez Bay, the Crozon Peninsula and the Ménez-Hom. Inside the 16-17C church, the old 16C stained glass window at the east end shows scenes from the Passion: to the left and right of the chancel are statues depicting the Annunciation, placed in niches with 16C painted shutters. At the beginning of the north aisle is St Michael overcoming a dragon known as the Devil of Le Juch. *Pardon on 15 August.*

Guengat. – *Pop 1 677. 14 km - 9 miles. Leave Douarnenez by ② on the town plan, the D 765. 11 km - 7 miles farther on, turn left, for Guengat.*
⊙ In the Gothic **church** at the entrance to the choir is, on the left column, a Flemish statue of St Barbara and, on the right column, a 16C Virgin and Child. In the choir itself, are 16C **stained glass windows★** depicting the Passion, the Last Judgment and the Virgin between St John the Baptist and St Michael, and a carved frieze with animals (hare, fox, wild boar), people and floral decoration. It is worth going into the cemetery to see the Calvary.

Michelin map **59** folds 4, 5, 6 or **230** folds 9, 10, 11

The name, given to this part of the coast between the Grouin Point and Le Val-André, includes some famous beaches: Dinard, St-Lunaire, Paramé, etc., and the famous city of the privateers: St-Malo. The Emerald Coast is broken, rocky and picturesque. From it a series of points, from which fine panoramas can be seen, project into the sea. The coast is bisected by the estuary of the Rance, on which an enjoyable boat excursion between Dinan and St-Malo can be made.

The scenic road along the Emerald Coast is among the major tourist attractions of Brittany's east coast. Although it does not hug the coast all the way it offers many excursions to the points enabling the visitor to enjoy spectacular sites with views and panoramas typical of this jagged coastline.

1 FROM CANCALE TO ST-MALO

23 km - 14 miles – about 5 hours – Local map p 97

★ **Cancale.** – *P 69.*

Leave Cancale by ② on the town plan, turn right towards the Grouin Point 300m - about 1/4 mile farther on.

★★ **Grouin Point.** – *P 70.*

The road, which is *a corniche* road as far as Le Verger, follows the coast and offers lovely views.

Notre-Dame-du-Verger. – *Bear right towards the beach.* This small chapel, rebuilt in the 19C, is venerated by the sailors of Cancale *(pilgrimage 15 August).*

Inside there are models of different kinds of sailing vessels: sloops, three-masted ships, schooners, etc.

After Le Verger, there is a good view of the Du Guesclin Cove and Island. A small fort stands on it.

La Guimorais. – A quiet seaside resort. Its fine beach, Plage des Chevrets, stretches between the Meinga Point and the Bénard peninsula which encloses the harbour of Rothéneuf on the east.

The road skirts the harbour of Rothéneuf. This stretch of water almost completely empties itself at low tide; the flow of the tides was once used to work a mill *(p 175).* On the right the elegant 17C **Château du Lupin,** built by a wealthy St-Malo shipowner, is of interest.

Rothéneuf and Le Minihic. – *P 198.*

From D 201 there are fine glimpses of the Bay of St-Malo.

★★ **Paramé.** – *P 198.*

★★★ **St-Malo.** – *P 193.*

St-Malo extends southwards to St-Servan-sur-Mer *(p 197).*

2 FROM ST-MALO TO DINARD

Here the tourist has a choice of excursions:

The crossing of the Rance estuary by the D 168, which goes over the crown of the Rance tidal power scheme (usine marémotrice) and affords glimpses of the estuary.

A tour★ of the Rance Valley★★ by car. *(allow one day).* – A picturesque excursion. The visit to Dinan is worth the detour. *Description p 176.*

3 FROM DINARD TO CAPE FRÉHEL

67 km - 42 miles – about 4 hours – Local map pp 96-97

★★★ **Dinard.** – *P 89.*

Unfortunately, the road does not follow all the indentations of the coast between Dinard and Cape Fréhel. However, it has interesting *corniche* sections and opens up fine panoramas and remarkable scenery. Many fashionable and family resorts lie along the coast.

★★ **St-Lunaire.** – *P 192.*

★ **La Garde Guérin Point.** – *1/4 hour on foot Rtn.* After crossing the point at its base, turn right into a road as it descends to the foot of the hill, which is honeycombed with casemates *(car park).* Climb on foot to the top of the promontory, from which a fine **panorama★★** extends from Cape Fréhel to the Varde Point.

The road traverses the Dinard golf course (60 ha - 148 acres).

St-Briac-sur-Mer. – Pop 1 748. This pleasant resort with its picturesque and varied sites, has a fishing harbour and a marina, and many good beaches. There are good views of the coast from the Emerald Balcony (Balcon d'Émeraude) and the Sailors' Cross (Croix des Marins – *access: from the Emerald Balcony by a path on the left, just before a bridge).*

As you come out of St-Briac you cross the Frémur River on a bridge 330m - 984ft long, to reach Lancieux; fine view.

Lancieux. – Pop 1 156. This village has a very extensive beach of fine sand, from which there is a lovely view of the Ébihens Island and the advanced points of the coast, St-Jacut-de-la-Mer, St-Cast and Cape Fréhel. In the centre of the village stands the old bell tower of the former church. The square tower is capped by a dome and its lantern.

In Ploubalay take the road towards Dinard and 800 m - 1/2 mile farther turn left.

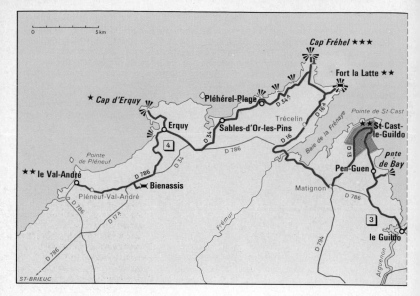

⊙ **Ploubalay Water Tower** (Château d'eau de Ploubalay). – The water tower has a circular terrace 104m - 341ft high which offers an excellent **wide view★★** of Ploubalay, the Dinan countryside, the Frémur River, St-Jacut, St-Cast Point, Cape Fréhel, St-Malo and in clear weather the Chausey Islands and Mont-St-Michel.

St-Jacut-de-la-Mer and the Chevet Point. – The road follows a long peninsula and goes through St-Jacut a small fishing port and seaside resort. After skirting the beach of Le Rougeret, you will reach the high and picturesque cliff at the **Chevet Point;** there is a fine **view★** of the Island of Ébihens, opposite, and its tower; also, to the left, of the Bay of Arguenon (note the upstanding poles – *bouchots* – where mussels mature) and St-Cast, and to the right of the Bay of Lancieux.

Le Guildo. – *P 111.*

Bay Point. – *Go towards St-Cast on the coastal road. A road on the right leads to a large car park.* The **view★** includes the Arguenon estuary with its lines of mussel poles and St-Jacut peninsula and the Island of Ébihens.

Pen-Guen. – Fashionable fine sandy beach.

★★ **St-Cast-le-Guildo.** – *P 190.*

Leaving St-Cast the road makes a big loop round the head of the Bay of La Frênaye.

After Trécelin, take the D 16^A which leads to the fort (car park).

★★ **La Latte Fort.** – *P 128.*

Go back to the Cape Fréhel road.

★★★ **Cape Fréhel.** – *P 102.*

④ FROM CAPE FRÉHEL TO LE VAL-ANDRÉ

34 km - 21 miles – about 2 1/2 hours – Local map above

★★★ **Cape Fréhel.** – *P 102.*

The tourist road D 34^A, which twists and turns on the moor, affords striking **views★★** of the sea, cliffs and golden beaches. It traverses a pine forest.

Pléhérel Beach. – The beach is on the right after a forest of conifers. A scenic view of Cape Fréhel and, in the foreground a succession of tiny coves carved into the dunes may be enjoyed.

Sables-d'Or-les-Pins. – The Channel can be seen through the pine forest. From the fine sandy beach a group of small islands can be distinguished especially that of St-Michel and its chapel.

After the Plurien intersection, the St-Quay coastline comes into view across St-Brieuc Bay.

As you enter Erquy go towards the cape.

★ **Cape Erquy.** – *1/2 hour on foot Rtn.* From the point where the road ends there is an extensive view of grey-pink shingle beaches lapped by transparent waters, opposite Caroual Beach, Vallées seashore, Pléneuf Point and Verdelet Islet and beyond St-Brieuc Bay, Arcouest Point, and Bréhat Island.

Pleasant footpaths bordered by bracken cross the heath dotted with patches of yellow and mauve and afford glimpses of the reefs.

Erquy. – Pop 3 426. Facilities. Located in a cliff-setting this busy scallop fishing port is growing rapidly. The finest of its numerous beaches, Caroual, is noted for its view of the bay and the cape.

Bienassis Château. – *P 212.*

The D 786 goes to Le Val-André.

★★ **Le Val André.** – *P 212.*

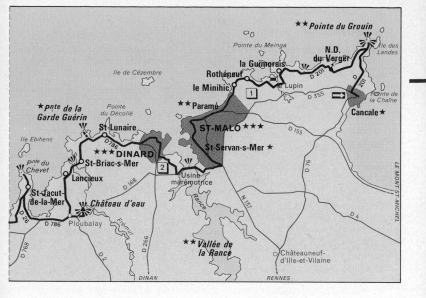

The layout diagram on page 3 shows the Michelin Maps covering the region. In the text, reference is made to the map which is the most suitable from a point of view of scale and practicality.

Le FAOU
Pop 1 574

Michelin map **58** fold 5 or **230** fold 18 – Local map p 50

The town, at the head of the Faou estuary, occupies a **site★** which has a lot of character at high tide.

Main Street. – This is flanked by old houses with overhanging upper storeys and slate-covered façades.

Church. – The 16C church stands on a terrace overlooking the river. It has an elegant 17C domed belfry, a double transept, a canted east end and an ornate sculptured south porch.

EXCURSION

Round tour of 25 km - 16 miles. – *About 1 hour. Leave Le Faou by the D 791 in the direction of Crozon.*

★ **Térénez coast road** (Corniche de Térénez). – At first the road affords views over the estuary of the Le Faou River and, in the distance, the Plougastel Peninsula *(p 158)*. Farther on, as you skirt the Aulne estuary, you will see Landévennec *(p 124)* ahead, on the right and, soon afterwards, the whole of the Landévennec Peninsula and the course of the Aulne. At the end of a short rise you will overlook the narrow part of the Aulne Valley, crossed by the Térénez Bridge.

Térénez Bridge (Pont de Térénez). – This elegant structure has a central span of 272m - 893ft.

At the top of the hill before the bridge bear left on a road which leaves the river and reaches a plateau.

Belvedere. – From the belvedere on the right of the road, there is a scenic **view** of a bend of the Aulne Valley, Trégarvan hamlet and the north face of Ménez-Hom.

Go to Ty-Jopic via Rosnoën passing by the Quimerch radio station and take the D 770 to the left.

Quimerch. – P 50.

Return to Le Faou by the D 770 running downhill.

Le FAOUËT
Pop 3 185

Michelin map **58** fold 17 or **230** fold 20

This village is the centre of a very picturesque district extending between the Stêr Laër and the Ellé, two rivers flowing from the Noires Mountains.

Market (Halles). – The covered market with its great slate roof supported at the sides on short granite columns and at the ends by massive porches, was built in 16C. Inside there are three naves under the fine timberwork. A domed lantern crowns the building.

Square (Grand Place). – in this shady square in front of the market, stands a monument to **Corentin Carré**, the youngest soldier of France. In 1915 he enlisted at the age of fifteen, and died in aerial combat in 1918. He was then a sergeant-major.

Le FAOUËT

EXCURSIONS

★ **St-Fiacre Chapel.** – *P 191.*

Round tour of 30 km - 19 miles. – *About 3 hours. Turn right on leaving Le Faouët by the D 769 towards Gourin and make for Ste-Barbe bearing right all the way.*

Ste-Barbe Chapel. – *P 204.*

Return to the D 769 and turn right and 500 m - 1/3 mile farther on make a right turn into D 790 towards Rostrenen.

The road goes up the **Ellé Valley.**

To the left in a bend two pillars mark the entrance to Langonnet Abbey.

⊘ **Langonnet Abbey.** – Rebuilt in 17-18C, the abbey, now a home for retired priests, has kept its 13C chapterhouse which has been converted into a chapel. Its graceful palm-leaf vaulting is noteworthy. There is a small **museum** devoted to African Missions to the left of the path.

Take the D 109 opposite the abbey entrance and after 3 km - 2 miles, turn right.

The road skirts **Bel-Air Lake** (Étang du Bel-Air) which has facilities for water sports (fishing, pedalos at Priziac).

Turn right into the D 132 to Le Faouët and after 1 km - 1/2 mile bear left.

⊘ **St-Nicolas Chapel.** – The little chapel stands alone in a beautiful setting of pines and fine trees. The style of the building is Gothic strongly influenced by Renaissance design. The Renaissance **rood-screen★**, which it is interesting to compare with the Gothic one to be found at St-Fiacre, is a fine piece of Breton sculpture on wood. Above an attractive screen, the legend of St Nicholas is shown in nine panels, while on the other side, caryatids separate niches containing figures of the Apostles. There are also polychrome 16C statues in stone. *Pardon on 2nd Sunday in July.*

Return to the D 132 towards Le Faouët.

By the Ellé Bridge, a pleasant walk may be enjoyed along the river to Ste-Barbe Chapel.

Each year
the Michelin Guide France
presents a multitude of up-to-date facts in a compact form.
Whether on a business trip, a weekend away from it all
or on holiday take the guide with you.

★★ **Le FOLGOËT**   Pop 2 826

Michelin map **58** fold 4 or **230** folds 3, 4 – Local map p 45

You should see this little village and its magnificent Basilica of Our Lady (Notre-Dame) during the great *pardon (p 226).* It is the best known in the Léon region and one of the biggest in Brittany. The ceremonies begin at 6pm the day before and continue the day after. The *pardon* of St Christopher with the blessing of cars is on the 4th Sunday in July.

Legend. – The name of Folgoët (Fool's Wood) recalls the legend attached to the foundation of the shrine. In the middle of the 14C a poor half-wit named Salaün lived in a hollow oak in a wood, near a spring not far from Lesneven. He knew only a few words, and he constantly repeated them: "Itron Gwerc'hez Vari" (Lady Virgin Mary). After his death a lily grew on his grave; the pistil made the words "Ave Maria" in gold letters. Men dug up the earth and found that the lily sprang from Salaün's mouth. News of the miracle spread in Brittany. The War of Succession was raging then. The Pretender Montfort vowed that if he won he would build a sumptuous chapel for the Virgin. After his victory at Auray *(details p 52)* he gave orders for the building to begin. The altar was to stand over the spring where the simpleton used to drink. The work was completed by Montfort's son in 1423.
The chapel was pillaged during the Revolution. To save it from being demolished, twelve farmers joined together to buy it. It was returned to the parish at the Restoration, and has been gradually repaired since.

★★ **Basilica.** – *Time: 1/2 hour.* A great esplanade with inns on each side leads up to the church, but is not even wide enough to hold the crowd on *pardon* days. The **north tower★** of the façade supports one of the finest belfries in Brittany.
The basilica is square, which is unusual; the Chapel of the Cross forms a branch like a transept at the end of the chancel, its east wall prolonging this part of the building. This chapel has a fine **porch★**. Salaün's fountain, where pilgrims come to drink, stands outside, against the east wall. The water comes from the spring under the altar.
Inside is a masterpiece of Breton art of the 15C, the admirably carved granite **rood-screen★★**. Five 15C Kersanton granite altars stand in the east end. The Chapel of the Cross and the apse are adorned by fine rose windows. There is a 15C statue of Our Lady of Folgoët.

South of the basilica the little 15C manorhouse of Le Doyenné, though much restored, forms an attractive group with the pilgrim's inn and the church.

⊘ In the inn, a small **museum** contains a collection of 15, 16 and 17C stone statues, archives and 15C furnishings.

FOUESNANT

Pop 5 430

Michelin map **58** fold 15 or **230** fold 32 – Facilities

This town is in the middle of one of the most fertile areas in Brittany; the villages stand among cherry and apple orchards. This is also where the best Breton cider is produced. The costumes and head-dresses of Fouesnant are a very pretty sight at the feast of the apple trees and at the *pardon* of St Anne *(p 226)*.

Church. – This 12C church was partly rebuilt in the 18C. On the square stands a small 17C Calvary; the monument to the dead, left of the porch, is the work of the Breton sculptor Quillivic, remarkable for the stately yet serious expression of the peasant woman wearing a local head-dress.

Inside the church the tall granite pillars are adorned with fine Romanesque capitals. An unusual stoup is built into an engaged pillar. A triumphal arch separates the nave from the transept where the altar stands. Naive statues are located in the chancel and entrance.

EXCURSION

From Bénodet to Concarneau by the coast road. – *40 km - 25 miles. Description p 60.*

★★ FOUGÈRES

Pop 25 131

Michelin map **59** fold 18 or **230** fold 28

This former stronghold is built in a picturesque setting on a promontory overlooking the winding valley of the Nançon. Below it, on a rocky height almost entirely encircled by the river, stands a magnificent feudal castle whose walls, with their thirteen big towers, are among the most massive in Europe.

HISTORICAL NOTES

A frontier post. – Standing on the border of Brittany and France, Fougères acquired great military importance in the early Middle Ages, when its barons were very powerful. The most famous is Raoul II. He lived in the middle of the 12C under Conan IV, known as "the Little", Duke of Brittany. This weak sovereign submitted to Henry II Plantagenet, King of England and Duke of Normandy, but the proud Raoul rebelled against the English yoke. He formed a league with some of the Breton nobles and opened the struggle against Henry II. In 1166 Henry II invested Fougères, which capitulated after three months' siege. The castle was completely demolished, Raoul immediately began to rebuild it, and part of his work still stands.

In the 13C the fief passed to some Poitou noblemen, the Lusignans. They claimed to be descendants of the fairy Mélusine and gave her name to the finest of the towers that they added to the walls.

Fougères is an example of a formidable fortress which was often taken. Among those who fought their way into it were St Louis, Du Guesclin, Surienne, a leader from Aragon in the service of the English (at night without striking a blow), La Trémoille, the Duke of Mercœur and the men of the Vendée.

After the union of Brittany and France, there were a succession of governors at Fougères; ten of its towers bear their names. The castle was then mainly used as a prison. In the 18C it became private property. The town bought it in 1892.

In the Chouan country. – Victor Hugo, in *Quatre-vingt-treize* (Ninety-three), and Balzac in *Les Chouans* have introduced Fougères and its surroundings into their stories of the royalist rebellion. They gleaned their information on the spot. In 1836 the poet, accompanied by Juliette Drouet (who was born at Fougères), gave a glowing account of the town and castle. "I should like to ask everyone," he wrote, "have you seen Fougères?" Balzac stayed with friends at Fougères, explored the neighbourhood with survivors of the rebellion and wrote his novel there in 1828.

The Breton and Vendéen revolt continued, with a few pauses, from 1793 to 1804. Its supporters were named after their call imitating the hoot of an owl *(chat-huant)*. The instigator of the movement was the Marquis of La Rouërie (1756-1793), who was born at Fougères. His life was a real adventure story. A turbulent youth resulted in a warrant for his arrest; to avoid the Bastille, he fled to Switzerland. Thinking he had a religious vocation, La Rouërie shut himself in a Trappist monastery. But he then felt the call to arms. Discarding the habit, he went to America, where the War of Independence was being fought, and became a general in the American Army. He returned to France on the eve of the Revolution. When it broke out the Marquis refused to emigrate and prepared for resistance by a war of surprise and ambuscade, well suited to the Breton country. He organized stores of hidden arms and provisions and recruited a secret army which would rise at a sign. But the plotter was betrayed and obliged to flee. He went into hiding and died, worn out, in January 1793. The following month the Convention decreed the mass levy: Brittany rebelled, and the war foreseen by La Rouërie broke out.

The shoe town. – In the 13C and for 300 years Fougères made a lot of money by manufacturing cloth first of wool then of hemp when the sailcloth of Fougères flapped on the yards of the French fleet until the triumph of steam.

In 1832 the fabrication of woollen slippers began; leather shoes followed in 1852, the workers sewing them by hand at home. 1870 saw the introduction of sewing-machines, and mechanical techniques gained ground every day. In 1890 about thirty factories were mass-producing cheap shoes, chiefly for women. After the First World War the eighty factories in the town felt the effects of foreign competition and the world crisis. The remaining ones now manufacture shoes, mostly for women.

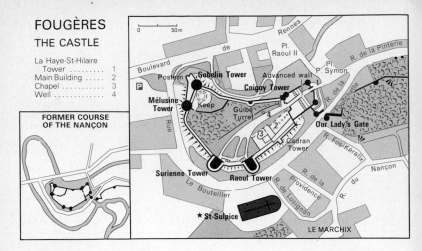

FOUGÈRES
THE CASTLE

FORMER COURSE OF THE NANÇON

★★ THE CASTLE *time: 1 1/2 hours*

The castle (château) is a fine example of military architecture of the Middle Ages. There is an interesting general view from the public garden *(p 101)*.

The site is curious. A loop in the river, washing a rocky eminence, a very narrow peninsula in shape, formed an excellent defensive position. Military architects took advantage of this site to build ramparts and towers and turn the peninsula into an island by a short diversion of the Nançon at the base of the loop. As the castle was connected with the upper town by the city ramparts, the garrison could take part in its defence; they also had the advantage of being able to retire into the fortress and hold it, should the town fall, as a frontier post for the Duchy of Brittany. The fortress as we see it has suffered much in the course of centuries. The wall is complete, with its curtains closely following the lie of the land and its thirteen towers. Unfortunately we can no longer see the high keep that commanded all the defences; it was razed in 1166 by King Henry II of England and there are now only traces which can be seen when visiting the inside of the castle. The main buildings which occupied part of the inner court were also demolished down to their foundations at the beginning of the 19C. History tells us that the defenders often succumbed and that attackers were able to seize these high walls, either by surprise attack or after long sieges. An outer tour of the castle shows the attackers' point of view; an inner tour, that of the defenders.

★ **Outer tour.** – *Park your car in the Place Raoul II, skirt the fortifications and then, left, along the Rue Le-Bouteiller.*

As you circle the walls you will see the splendid towers in all their variety of appearance and structure. At the start you will also see in the middle of the north rampart, the 14C Guibé Turret, a corbelled sentry-post built on to the wall.

Going round the spur formed by the ramparts towards the west, you will see how massively the defences are concentrated at this point. The whole forms a triangle with two towers at the base and a postern at the apex. The 15C postern today looks out on empty space, but it was once connected with a double arcade that crossed the moat to communicate with an outwork. The 13 and 14C Gobelin Tower, to the left of the postern, and the 14C Mélusine, to the right, are round and overlook the walls from a height. Stripped of their machicolations and with their upper parts probably rebuilt they have lost much of their proud aspect. The Mélusine is regarded as a masterpiece of military architecture of the period; it is over 13m - 41 1/2ft in diameter, with walls 3.50m - 11ft thick and rising 31m - 99ft above the rock.

Farther on are two squat, horseshoe-shaped towers, the Surienne and the Raoul, which mark the last stage in the building of the castle (15C). Built to serve as platforms for artillery, they contain several storeys of very strong and well-preserved gun platforms. To resist enemy artillery fire, their walls are 7m - 22ft thick. At the end of the 15C, artillery had been in use for nearly a century and a half, and siege warfare often took the form of an artillery duel at short range. The design of the machicolations shows that military art at that time was not indifferent to decoration.

Opposite the two towers stands the Church of St-Sulpice. On the right is the Place du Marchix Quarter (p 101).

Still following the walls, you will see the 13C Cadran Tower, two centuries older than the others. It is small, square and badly damaged, not nearly as strong as its neighbours and recalling the time when fire-arms had not yet taken the place of bows and arrows. Farther on, Our Lady's Gate is the only one left of the four rampart gateways preceding the four gates in the walls which encircled the town. The left-hand tower, which is the higher and is pierced with narrow loopholes, dates from the 14C; that on the right, with very ornamental machicolations, dates from the 15C, as do the Surienne and Raoul towers. In the middle, over the carriage gateway, are vertical slits to receive the arms of the drawbridge.

Go under the gate and follow the Rue de la Fourchette, then turn a sharp right into the Rue de la Pinterie.

50 m farther on cross the gardens laid out along the former parapet-walk which has been reconstructed. From there you get a good view of the Nançon Valley and the castle.

To leave the garden, go under the ruins of a beautiful chapel doorway and go once more into the Rue de la Pinterie on the left. This leads to the castle entrance.

★★ **Inner tour.** – The entrance *(plan 100)*, preceded by a moat filled from a diversion of
⏱ the Nançon, is through the square tower of La Haye-St-Hilaire. To reach it, you first
had to go through a town gate and the wall before it. The castle has three successive
walls. The *Avancée* (advanced wall) was guarded by three 13C towers with many
loopholes. When this line of resistance had been crossed, attackers would enter a small
courtyard on the island formed by a second diversion of the river, and would come
under the converging fire of defenders posted on the four sides. Thus exposed, the
attackers had to cross a second moat before reaching the main ring of fortifications,
guarded by four towers dating from 12 and 15C. When both lines had been stormed
they would burst into the main inside courtyard; but the defenders still had a chance
to rally. A third position, the redoubt, girt with a wall and two towers, and the keep
(demolished after the 12C), made a long resistance possible, and from these positions
the garrison could still seek safety in flight through the postern.

Entering the great courtyard, go round the walls on the wall walk. This enables one
to appreciate the might of such a fortress and also to enjoy some good views of
Fougères. The Raoul Tower houses a small shoe (17 to early 20C objects) and costume
(head-dresses, shawls, etc.) museum. At the end of the highest wall of the castle is
the Mélusine Tower which from the top (75 steps) commands a fine view of the castle
and the town. Farther on are the remains of the keep and north wall, and beyond the
Guibé Turret and the Coigny Tower (13 and 14C), whose second and third storeys were
turned into a chapel in the 17C. The summit was disfigured by the addition of a loggia
during its first restoration in the 19C. In the courtyard there is an open-air theatre.

ADDITIONAL SIGHTS

★ **St-Sulpice** (AY). – A Gothic building in the Flamboyant style; although it was erected
between the 15 and the 18C it has great homogeneity. It has a slim 15C slate covered
steeple. The inside is enriched with 18C woodwork, nonetheless the 15C granite
altarpieces★ in the chapels retain our attention. The Our Lady Chapel (on the left) contains
the altarpiece dedicated to Anne of Brittany, the church's donor. In the niche underneath
the Brittany coat of arms is the miraculous 12C statue of the Virgin (Notre-Dame des
Marais). Off the south aisle, in the Tanners Chapel, there is an imposing altarpiece
adorned with vine leaves, crockets, small animals and the instruments of the Passion.

Le Marchix Quarter. – This area around the Place du Marchix (AY), with its
picturesque old houses, has always been of interest to painters.

From the Rue Fos-Kéralix which skirts the Nançon, there are good views of the old
ramparts now converted into a public garden. Take a walk along the Rue du Nançon
with its 16C houses. There are other interesting houses at the corner of the Rue de
la Providence and the Rue de Lusignan as well as in the Rue de Lusignan.

On the Place du Marchix are two fine 16C houses, nos 13 and 15. Take the Rue des
Tanneurs to cross the bridge over the Nançon; looking back, you will see a picturesque
group formed by the backs of the houses of the Place du Marchix.

★ **Garden** (Jardin Public) (AY). – This lovely garden is laid out partly in terraces on the site
of the former town walls and partly on the slopes down into the Nançon River valley.
Follow the low wall prolonging the balustrade to the entrance for an extensive view
of the woodlands typical of the Fougères region. From the terrace closed off by the
balustrade, there is an interesting general **view★** of the castle.

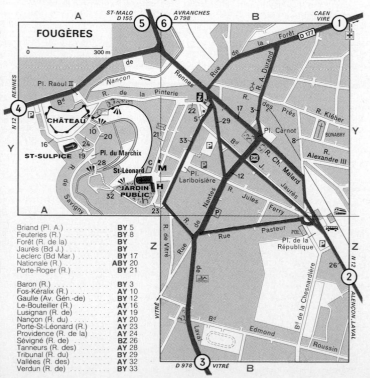

St-Léonard (AY). – The 15-16C church has a richly decorated 16C north façade and a 17C tower. It is lit by modern stained glass windows by Lorin; however in the chapel of the Cross, on the left as you go in, are two 12C scenes of the life of St Benedict, and in the baptismal chapel pieces of 16C **stained glass windows★**.

La Villéon Museum (ABY M). – The museum in a restored 16C porticoed house, displays some 40 paintings by Emmanuel de la Villéon (1858-1944), an Impressionist painter and a native of Fougères.

Town Hall (AY H). – A 16C building with a Renaissance doorway (partly walled up).

Fougères State Forest (Forêt domaniale de Fougères). – *3 km - 2 miles NE. Leave Fougères by ①, D 177.* Those who like walking in a forest will spend pleasant hours strolling in the fine beech woods, along the forest roads. They can see two dolmens in ruins and a line of megalithic stones called the Druids' Cord (Cordon des Druides) near the Chennedet crossroads. At Landéan, at the edge of the forest, near the Recouvrance crossroads are the 12C cellars once used as a secret hide-out by the lords of Fougères.

★★★ FRÉHEL Cape

Michelin map 59 fold 5 or 230 fold 10 – Local map p 96

The **site★★★** of this cape is one of the grandest on the Breton coast. Its red, grey and black cliffs rise vertically to a height of 70m - 229ft and are fringed with reefs on which the swell breaks heavily. The coastal **panorama★★★** (especially beautiful towards evening) is immense in clear weather: from the Grouin Point, on the right, to the Island of Bréhat, on the left. The Channel Islands can sometimes be seen.

The **lighthouse** (145 steps), built between 1946 and 1950, is lit by a lamp of 3 kW; the light carries only 200m - 656ft in foggy weather but it can be seen 110 km - 70 miles away when it is clear weather. From the gallery at the top of the tower there is an immense view of the horizon: on a clear day you may see Bréhat to the west, Jersey to the north, Granville, a part of the Cotentin Peninsula and the Chausey Islands to the northeast. At a point 400 m - 1/4 mile from the lighthouse a siren mounted in a shelter gives two blasts every minute in foggy weather.

Walk round the cape *(tour: 1/2 hour)*, beginning left of the lighthouse. After passing the extreme point where stands the siren, you can look down on the Fauconnière rocks, crowded with seagulls and cormorants; the contrast between the mauvish red of the rocks and the blue or green of the sea is striking. Near the Restaurant de la Fauconnière take a steep path on the right; halfway down, it reaches a platform from which there is another remarkable view of the Fauconnière rocks: the deep blue sea tones in with the pale pink granite.

Boat trips, to view Cape Fréhel from the sea, leave from St-Malo and call in at Dinard. This is by far the best way to see the cape.

★★ GAVRINIS Tumulus

Michelin map 63 fold 12 or 230 fold 50 – Local map p 138

The Gavrinis Tumulus is the most interesting megalithic monument in Brittany *(details on prehistoric monuments p 34)*. It is situated on the Island of Gavrinis, at the mouth of the Morbihan Gulf, south of Larmor-Baden, from which it can be reached.

Crossing and tour. – 6 m high and 50 m round (20ft - 164ft) the tumulus is made of stones piled on a hillock *(p 34)*. It was discovered in 1832, and it contains: (1) a covered gallery 14m - 46ft long with twenty-three supports, on which lie nine tables - the supports are covered with carvings; (2) the funeral chamber, probably a royal tomb, with a ceiling made of a single granite slab, 4 m by 3 m (12 × 9ft), resting on eight supports placed in a rectangle.

From the top of the tumulus there is a wide view of the Morbihan Gulf.

On the tiny island of **Er Lanic,** a little south of Gavrinis, are two tangent circles of menhirs *(cromlechs)* in the form of a figure eight of which half is submerged. This gives evidence of the subsidence of the soil in prehistoric times which created the gulf. At low tide the menhirs reappear.

GLÉNAN Islands

Michelin map 58 fold 15 or 230 fold 32
Access: Boat services

The archipelago consists of nine islets surrounded by reefs and lies off Concarneau.

TOUR

Boats go to **St-Nicolas** which has a few houses, a skin diving school (Centre International de Plongée) and a breeding pool for crustaceans. A footpath goes round the island affording good views of the coast from Penmarch to Le Pouldu.

To the north lies **Brunec Island** and to the south **Loch Island** pinpointed by a chimney from a former sea-weed factory. Both are privately owned.

Penfret with its lighthouse, **Cigogne** (The Stork) on which an annexe of the marine laboratory of Concarneau *(p 78)* is housed in an 18C fort, and **Drénec** are three islands from which operates the internationally famous sailing school, the Centre Nautique de Glénan. **Giautec Island** and other uninhabited islands are kept as bird sanctuaries; gulls, terns, oyster catchers and cormorants nest there.

Michelin map **63** folds 14, 15 or **230** fold 52

Also known by the name of **Grande Brière Mottière,** this region covers 6 700 ha - 16 550 acres of the total 40 000 ha - 98 840 acres belonging to the **Brière Regional Nature Park.** 15 000 ha - 37 050 acres of the park, which was designated in 1970, are marshland. Lying to the north of St-Nazaire the area is renowned for its wildfowling and fishing. The world at large was to discover this region in 1923, through the pages of Alphonse de Chateaubriant's novel, *La Brière.* Although the factory now plays a part in the livelihood of the people, their way of life remains unique.

The Brière in the past. – In early geological times the area was a forested, undulating basin which reached to the hills of Sillon de Bretagne. Neolithic man (7 500 BC) was expelled from the area when there was a momentary maritime incursion. Marshes formed behind the alluvial banks deposited by the Loire. The trees died and were submerged and vegetable matter decomposed to form **peat bogs,** often entrapping fossilised tree trunks, known as **"mortas",** over 5 000 years old.

The Brière from the 15 to 20C. – This swampy area was subdivided, water pumped and the drainage improved. In 1461, the area became the common property of all Briérons, a fact which was to be confirmed by several royal edicts. For centuries the Briérons have cut the peat, gathered the reeds and rushes for thatching, woven baskets with the buckthorn, tended their gardens and kept poultry. They have trapped leeches, harpooned eels, placed eel-pots in the open stretches of water and wickerwork traps to catch pike, tench and roach, and hunted with their dogs in a boat hidden by a clump of willow trees. For ages the Briéron has propelled with a pole his **blin,** a flat-bottomed boat, loaded with cows or sheep going to pasture. In spite of these activities the Briéron women had to work, also, to make ends meet. In the 19 and early 20C two workshops in St-Joachim *(p 104)* employed approximately 140 women to make wax orange blossoms. These flowers were used to make splendid brides' head-dresses exported throughout Europe *(see Bride's House p 104).*

The Briéron of the 20C has remained closely attached to the land, but by force of circumstance he is turning more to local industries: metallurgy in Trignac, dockyards and aeronautics at St-Nazaire. Nevertheless, he continues to fish, shoot, graze animals or cut reeds, and pay his annual fee. Change is inevitable, roads now link the islets, locks have been built, marsh has become pastureland but despite it all La Grande Brière has retained its charm and when the Briéron returns home he fishes and shoots for his own pleasure. Many who have boats are willing to take visitors on trips on the network of canals and smaller channels beautiful with yellow irises *(mid-May to mid-June)* and pearly water lilies *(mid-June to late July).*

★★ **Boat trips.** – Larger canals are linked by smaller bulrush bordered channels, great pools open up vast horizons broken only by the steeples of the surrounding villages. In winter the flooded marshes, with reeds the colour of ripe grain, are bathed in colours reflecting an ever-changing sky. The Brière has its charm in all seasons: the mass of flowers in spring; the summer cloak of green slashed by the black banks and the russet tints of autumn with the cries of wildfowl overhead.

ROUND TOUR STARTING FROM ST-NAZAIRE

83 km - 52 miles – about 1/2 day

St-Nazaire. – Time 1 1/2 hours. Description p 199.

Leave St-Nazaire by ①, the N 171.

Trignac. – Pop 7 195. This rural community has seen the implantation of new industries. A road to the left leads to the **Pont de Paille** which affords a **view** of the Trignac canal.

At **Montoir-de-Bretagne** turn left onto the D 50.

St-Malo-de-Guersac. – Pop 3 291. The largest of the islets (13 m - 43ft high), it offers a **view** from Guérande in the west to the hilly region, Sillon de Bretagne, to the east.

The road passes near the slate roofed houses and the small port of **Rosé,** a former departure point for the barges plying upstream to Nantes or Vannes.

(Jacques Guillard/Scope)

The Keeper's House. – In the house situated to the left of the road to the locks, there is an exhibition devoted to the fauna and flora to be found in the marshland. An aquarium contains the main species of fish of the Brière.

The Lock Keeper's House (Maison de l'Éclusier). – The house is located on the Rosé canal. The lock keeper operated the two locks which regulated the water level of the marsh. Slides and various documents illustrate the formation and evolution of the marsh. Docked alongside the canal is the *Théotiste* which was used to transport peat.

Nature Reserve (Parc animalier). – *Take field-glasses. Cross the bridge over the canal and take the path to the right to the reception building 800 m - 1/2 mile farther on. It can also be reached by barge (pick-up point to the right of the bridge).* A path *(about 1 km - 1/2 mile)* cuts through the park (26 ha - 168 acres), with observation posts for silent and patient vigil. There are descriptive panels to help you identify the flora and fauna.

Bear left before St-Joachim.

★ **Fédrun Islet** (Ile de Fédrun). – Linked to the St-Joachim road by two bridges, this, the most attractive of the islets is entirely surrounded by marshland. The islet has two roads: one which divides it into two and the other which runs around it. At no 130 of the circular road is the **Bride's House.** The interior of the house, arranged in the typical Briéron style, displays a collection of brides' head-dresses decorated with wax orange blossoms and an explanation of how they are made. At no 180 are the Administrative Services of the Regional Nature Park. At no 308 stands the **Briéron Thatched Cottage** (Chaumière Briéronne) which shows a typical interior of a Brière cottage. The low, flower bedecked houses retain the traditional thatched roof. The cottages on the islet's periphery are backed by a **dyke,** often planted with vegetables and fruit trees, which, itself borders the **canal** *(curée)* where the residents tie up their boats.

St-Joachim. – Pop 4 260. The former centre of wax orange blossom manufacturing, the village extends along the two islets of **Brécun** (alt 8m - 26ft) and **Pendille** dominated by the tall white spire of its 19C **church** with very low aisles. The altar is adorned by a stone Calvary and the ambulatory has fine Romanesque arcading.

The D 50 traverses the islets of **Camerun** and **Camer** where several thatched cottages stand.

La Chapelle-des-Marais. – Pop 3 037. At the entrance to the village, on the right is the **Clogmaker's House** (Maison du Sabotier) where lived the last Briéron craftsman. There is a display of tools, machinery and clogs with an audio-visual presentation. In the **church** where the granite pillars stand out against the white stone, there is a polychrome statue of St Corneille, protector of the flocks. In the town hall a 7m - 23ft fossilized **tree trunk** *(morta)* is on view.

Take the road in the direction of Herbignac, the D 33 and after 4 km - 2 1/2 miles turn left.

Ranrouët Castle. – *Leave the car in the car park and go behind the farm.* This 12-13C fortress *(under restoration)* dismantled in 1616 by Richelieu, burnt under the Revolution, is spectacular with six round towers and encircled by a moat (dried-up). Cannon balls embedded in the right tower wall, recall that the castle once belonged to the Rieux family whose coat of arms includes nine gold cannon balls.

Return to the D 33 and turn right. At Mayun, a wickerwork centre, take the D 51.

Les Fossés-Blancs. – From a landing stage on the canal to the north, there is a fine **view** of the Brière. A tour on the marsh provides an opportunity to study the flora and occasionally the fauna.

St-Lyphard. – Pop 2 364. In the **church's** belfry (135 steps) a belvedere has been set up. A **panorama★★** extends onto the Brière and from the Loire estuary to the mouth of the Vilaine encompassing Guérande and its salt marshes.

Follow the D 51 towards Guérande and at 12 km - 7 1/2 miles turn left.

★ **Kerbourg Dolmen.** – On a mound near a windmill stands this gallery grave.

Continue in the direction of Le Brunet.

Kerhinet. – This hamlet consists of 18 thatched cottages, which have been partly restored. One of the cottages with its outbuildings and its typical Briéron interior is open to visitors.

Go on to Le Brunet and from there the road continues to Bréca.

Bréca. Good view over the Brière and the Bréca canal.

Return to the D 47. At St-André-des-Eaux turn left into the D 127.

La Chaussée-Neuve. – It was from this former port that the boats loaded with peat used to leave. Stocks of cut reeds stand out to dry. From here there is a wide **view★** over the Brière.

Return to the D 47 which leads back to St-Nazaire.

GRAND-FOUGERAY
Pop 2 032

Michelin map **63** fold 6 or **230** fold 40

This small town includes a church, which is partly Romanesque and which has on its south side a 13C cemetery cross. On the Place de l'Église is a 15C edifice, the former law courts of the lords of Fougeray.

Keep. – *Follow the directions for Sion and 50m after the crossroad bear right into a pine bordered lane.* Of the old castle there remains the restored keep. During the War of Succession in 1354 Du Guesclin captured the castle by a ruse. Having learnt that firewood was to be delivered to the castle, he and his men disguised themselves as woodcutters carrying sticks. When they got into the place they brought out their weapons and slew the garrison. *Details about Du Guesclin, pp 24, 52, 86, 113, 178.*

EXCURSION

Langon. – Pop 1 214. *12 km - 7 1/2 miles. Leave Grand-Fougeray W on the D 56.* From the Port-de-Roche bridge which crosses the Vilaine River there are pleasant views.

Once over the bridge bear left.

On the village square stand the parish church and the Chapel of St Agatha.
The chapel is a small Gallo-Roman building with a single nave and lovely brick-and-stonework. Most likely devoted to Venus, as evidenced by the remains of frescoes discovered in the apse, the chapel was, in the Middle Ages, consecrated to St Agatha. The parish church was rearranged from the 13 to 17C. Inside are 17C wood altarpieces and a 15C canopied stone baptismal font. On the wall of the north apsidal chapel is a 12C fresco representing God the Father in an almond-shaped glory.
Overlooking the town, on the Moulin moor (lande du Moulin) stand the Young Women of Langon (Demoiselles de Langon) about 30 menhirs which, legend has it, represent some young women who, one day, preferred dancing on the moor to going to vespers.

★ GROIX Island

Michelin map **58** fold 12 or **230** fold 34
Access: see the current Michelin Red Guide France

Groix is smaller than its neighbour, Belle-Ile, but has the same geological form – a mass of schist rock worn away by the sea. The coast to the north and west is wild and deeply indented: there you will see cliffs and giant rocks, valleys and creeks. The east and south sides of the island are flatter and along the coast there are many sheltered sandy creeks. Small villages are dotted amid the vast expanses on which grow gorse and heather.
Groix is the birthplace of the Breton poet J. P. Calloch who wrote in Celtic and is known under the name of Bleimor.

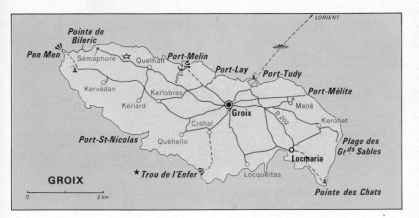

TOUR

Groix. – Pop 2 605. This is the capital with its low slate-roofed houses grouped round the church. The belfry is crowned by a tuna fish as a weather vane.

Locmaria. – Facing the open sea, this village with its winding streets has a small harbour where fishing and pleasure boats seek shelter behind a jetty.

Pen-Men. – The western tip of the island to the right of the Pen-Men lighthouse. This rocky headland offers splendid views of the Morbihan coast extending from Talut Point to Port-Manech.

Grands Sables Beach. – This is the largest beach where garnets can sometimes be found in the sand.

Bileric Point. – Near the Beg-Melen signal station *(not open to the public)*. A seagull nature reserve.

Chats Point. – This is the most low-lying part of the island on which stands a small lighthouse. Fine view of the south coast.

Port-Lay. – This safe anchorage, where trawlers used to shelter, is in a beautiful setting★.

Port-Melin. – This little creek can only be reached on foot down a steep slope. From the platform there is a good **view** of the approach to Port-Tudy and of the Lorient coast in the distance.

Port-Mélite. – A rocky cove with a beach. The view extends from the Barre d'Étel to the Talut Point.

Port-St-Nicolas. – A large bay with deep, clear waters hemmed in by cliffs.

Port-Tudy. – Sheltered by two piers, it offers a direct link with Lorient. This former tunny-fishing port is now a safe harbour for trawlers and pleasure boats.

★ **Trou de l'Enfer.** – A deep opening in the cliff face into which the sea surges with great force. It is a wild, barren site but with a beautiful **view** of St-Nicolas Point.

★ GUÉHENNO
Pop 844

Michelin map **63** fold 3 or **230** fold 37 – 11 km - 7 miles SW of Josselin

The **Calvary★** stands in the cemetery near the church *(details on Calvaries p 38)*. It dates from 1550, was destroyed in 1794 and restored in the last century. All its beauty lies in its perfect composition. Carved in the shaft of the central cross is Jesse, father of David. Before it stands a column, with the instruments of the Passion, on which a cock is perched in allusion to the denial of St Peter. Behind this monument is a small ossuary whose entrance is protected by the figures of two guards on duty. A low relief framed in the left gable depicts the Passion.

★ GUÉRANDE
Pop 9 475

Michelin map **63** fold 3 or **230** fold 51 – Local map p 108

The town, standing on a plateau overlooking the salt marshes, has kept the appearance of the Middle Ages; its ramparts are almost intact.
On a Saturday in early July and August folk dancing at the foot of the ramparts takes place. The colourful costumes of the salt-marsh workers and the more sombre ones of the farm tenants intermingle with other local Breton costumes to make a lively picture.

GUÉRANDE

Avoid visiting a church during a service.

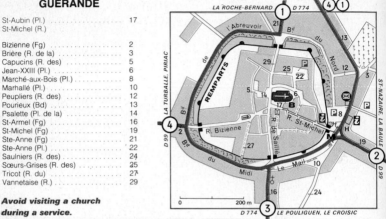

★ **Walk round the ramparts (Remparts).** – The ramparts, in which there is still no breach, were built in the 15C. They are flanked by six towers and pierced by four fortified gateways. In the 18C the Duke of Aiguillon, Governor of Brittany, had the moats filled in (although the north and west sections still contain water) and arranged the present circular promenade, which the tourist can follow by car.

The St-Michel or Castle Gate (M). – The gatehouse, was once the governor's house (15C) and is now a museum.
On the 1st floor, formerly the soldiers' living quarters, two interiors have been reconstructed: that of the Briéron inhabitant with its waxed furniture and that of the salt marsh worker with its furniture painted in a deep plum-red colour. The 2nd floor, where the governor resided, is embellished with paintings, porcelain from Le Croisic, pottery and other everyday objects typical of the area. On the 3rd floor (note the beautiful timberwork) a weaving loom (1832), and old bourgeois, salt marsh workers and farm tenants costumes, on life-size figures, are exhibited.
The relief plan of a salt pan shows how it is equipped and works.

★ **St-Aubin (B).** – This collegiate church, built from the 12 to 16C, presents a granite façade decorated with bell-turrets and crocketed pinnacles. To the right a pulpit is embedded into a buttress. The **interior** is imposing with vast pillars in the transept. The Romanesque columns of the nave support Gothic arches whose **capitals** portray grotesque and floral decoration. The 15C chancel with aisles opening onto four 16C chapels is lit by a magnificent 18C **stained glass window** showing the Coronation of the Virgin. On the left the small 14C window, shows the Martyrdom of St Peter. The **crypt** to the right contains a Merovingian sarcophagus (6C) discovered under the chancel, a 16C recumbent figure and a tombstone also of the 16C. In the nave, opposite the pulpit, is a 16C wood carved Christ.

The Michelin Green Tourist Guide Portugal

Picturesque scenery, buildings

Scenic routes

Geography, Economy

History, Art

Touring programmes

Plans of towns and buildings

A guide for your holidays

★ GUÉRANDE Peninsula

Michelin map **63** folds 13, 14 or **230** folds 51, 52

This is a very interesting district in which you may see, besides the curious landscape of the salt marsh country, several beaches of which La Baule is the finest; the picturesque Côte Sauvage; busy fishing ports; Guérande and its ramparts; and Batz and its church.

The former gulf. – Between the rocky Batz Island and the Guérande ridge a great sea gulf stretched in the Roman era. According to some writers this was the scene of the naval battle in which the fleet of the Veneti was destroyed *(details p 137)*. A change of level of approximately 15m - 50ft turned the gulf into marshes.

Sand brought down by the currents linked Batz Island with the mainland through the strip on which La Baule and Le Pouliguen stand. To the west the sandy Pen Bron Point has not quite reached the island; a channel remains open opposite Le Croisic through which the sea flows at high tide into the Grand and Petit Trait, vestiges of the former gulf. At low tide it retreats, exposing mud-flats on which the coast dwellers raise oysters and mussels, clams and periwinkles. The rest of the marsh is used for salt-pans.

Salt-pans. – Extending over some 2 000 ha - 4 940 acres, these form a great chessboard bounded by low banks of clay soil. The sea water, brought in by the high tides through canals or *étiers*, spreads and is caught in a series of tidal reservoirs which get shallower and shallower; in the *œillets*, which it reaches last, the depth is only two inches. It is here that the salt crystallizes as the water evaporates.

From late June to mid-September men collect the grey salt formed at the bottom with large rakes, while women skim the white salt off the surface with flat spades. The salt is put to dry on little platforms built on the banks, then piled in large heaps or *mulons* at the edge of the salt-pans before being stored in sheds or just covered up.

Though some have been abandoned there are now about 10 000 *œillets* on the peninsula, including Guérande and Mesquer. Each *œillet* measures 70-80sq m - 853-861sq ft and gives 1 300 to 1 500 kg - 2 860 to 3 300 lb of grey salt and 80 kg - 176 lb of white salt, each year. In a very dry summer it may amount to 3 000 kg - 6 600 lb *per œillet*.

(Hug/Explorer)

A salt marsh worker

A hard struggle. – The salt pans of Guérande were very prosperous until the Revolution, for, thanks to a relic of the former rights of the province, the salt could be sent all over Brittany without paying the *gabelle* or salt tax. Dealers or salt makers could exchange it in neighbouring provinces for cereals. Trafficking by "false salt makers" or smugglers often occurred.

Today the competition of salt marshes in the south, favoured by hotter sunshine and of the salt mines in the east is getting severe. The drying, refining and testing of locally gathered salt is now being undertaken in a modern factory at Batz.

(Jacques Guillard/Scope)

Guérande Peninsula. – Salt marshes

Cliffs and Dunes. – The cliffs and rocks of the Côte Sauvage, between Penchâteau Point and Le Croisic, offer a striking contrast to the immense sandy beach at La Baule. In 1527 a violent wind spread the sand accumulated in the Loire estuary over the village of **Escoublac** *(p 55)*. After this gale, which lasted for several days, sand continued to accumulate, and in the 18C the last inhabitants finally left the place. The village was rebuilt several miles farther back. The pines planted to fix the dunes form the Bois d'Amour of La Baule. The coast which became very popular in the 19C, took the name of **Côte d'Amour**.

ROUND TOUR STARTING FROM LA BAULE
62 km - 39 miles – about 1/2 day

★★★ **La Baule.** – *P 55.*

> *Leave La Baule by the N 171. On reaching Le Pouliguen turn left immediately after the bridge.*

★ **Le Pouliguen.** – *P 166.*

The road hugs the coast and there is soon a fine view of the shore south of the Loire as far as the St Gildas Headland and the Banche Lighthouse.

★ **The Côte Sauvage.** – *The road is described in the opposite direction p 84.*

★ **Le Croisic.** – *P 84.*

★ **Batz-sur-Mer.** – *P 54.*

Kervalet. – A small village of salt marsh workers with a chapel dedicated to St Mark.

Saillé. – Built on an island amidst the salt marshes, this town is the salt capital. A former chapel ⊙ contains the **salt marsh workers' house** *(Maison des Paludiers)*. Engravings, tools, furnishings and costumes illustrate the life of the salt marsh worker; slide shows explain how they work.

> *Turn left into D 92, the road to Turballe through the salt flats.*

La Turballe. – Pop 3276. The modern buildings of the town stretch along the seafront. The busy artificial port receives both pleasure craft and sardine boats. The modern granite Church of St-Anne has a low belfry adjoining the apse. The chancel is lit by small stained glass windows (1907).
The **view** is beautiful along the coast after Lerat.

> *After Penhareng, turn left twice.*

★ **Castelli Point.** – *From the car park a path along the cliffs ridge takes you to the point from where there is a nice view of the rocky creeks.* On the right the Dumet Island and the low shore of the Rhuys Peninsula are visible. On the left are the roadstead and peninsula of Le Croisic with the church towers of Batz and Le Croisic.

Piriac-sur-Mer. – Pop 1263. A small resort and fishing village. In the square, before the church, there is a fine group of 17C houses.

> *To get out of Piriac take the road that runs beside the harbour towards Mesquer, turn right towards Guérande. Go through St-Sébastien.*

⊙ **Trescallan.** – The main square is dominated by a small Calvary. The **church** with buttresses has fine columns with capitals and inside, in the south aisle, is a statue of St Bridget.

From the D 99, as it runs along the Guérande ridge there is a fine view of the salt marshes and the harbour of Le Croisic. In the evening the light effects on the marshes are remarkable.

★ **Guérande.** – *P 106.*

⊙ **Careil Château.** – Still inhabited, this former 14C stronghold was altered in the 15 and 16C. Of the two wings one is Renaissance with gracious dormer windows, the second is plainer; its dormer windows have armorial decorated pediments. The stone flagged guardroom and the adjoining salon have fine beams. Take a spiral staircase which goes up to the soldiers' living quarters; note the timbered ceiling. The captain's room has a chimney which bears a Maltese cross.

> *Return to La Baule by the D 92.*

If you are puzzled by an abbreviation or a symbol in the text or on the maps, look at the key on p 42.

La GUERCHE-DE-BRETAGNE

Pop 4075
Michelin map ⬚ fold 8 or ⬚ folds 41, 42

This little town, once a manorial estate with Du Guesclin as its overlord, still retains some old houses besides an interesting church. The local cider is famous.

Church. – Only the chancel remains of the original building erected in 1206. The nave and the south aisle were rebuilt in the 16C; the north aisle and the belfry are modern (end of the 19C). The riches of this church lie in its 16C stalls with their amusing Gothic misericords – the carved decoration of the woodwork is clearly of the time of Henri II (1547-59), a more advanced period – and the remains of the 15 and 16C stained glass windows. The fine Annunciation should also be noted. Remarkable raising pieces ornament the wooden vaulting of the nave.

Old houses. – Houses with porches may be seen in the Place de la Mairie, near the church and in the neighbouring streets.

EXCURSIONS

★ **Round tour of 43 km - 27 miles.** – *Time: about 2 1/2 hours. Leave La Guerche by the Rennes road, D 463. At Visseiche turn left into the D 48 which soon reaches an arm of the Marcillé Lake (Étang de Marcillé) formed by the junction of the Seiche and Ardenne Valleys; hence its curved shape. On leaving Marcillé-Robert, cross the Seiche and bear left towards Retiers which follows the bank of the other arm of the lake. Turn right after 800 m - 1/2 mile to Theil and then right again 3 km - 2 miles farther on. On the right, 800 m - 1/2 mile from the road, stands the Fairies' Rock.*

★ **The Fairies' Rock** (La Roche aux ⊙ Fées). – This is one of the finest megalithic monuments in Brittany. To judge from its appearance it was not intended as a funeral monument, it is, therefore, neither a dolmen nor a covered alleyway. Built in purple palaeozoic schist, it consists of 42 stones, of which half a dozen weigh between 40 and 45 tons each. There is a massive portico entrance and then a low ceilinged corridor leading to a large, very high room which is divided. Since, according to legend, it was built by the fairies, young couples wishing to get married came there to get the fairies' counsel on the night of the new moon. The man walked round the rock in a clockwise direction, the girl anticlockwise; if, by the time they had returned to their starting

(J. Bars/Azimut)

La Roche-aux-Fées

point, each had counted the same number of stones all was well; if the difference in number was not more than two, they might still find happiness, but if the number varied by more than two it was best to separate immediately.

Turn round and go to Le Theil then turn left into the D 94 for Ste-Colombe.

⊙ **Les Mottes Lake.** – Charming artifical lake towered over by magnificent trees.

When within sight of Ste-Colombe, turn left into the D 47.

⊙ **Retiers.** – Pop 3 444. Proud little town where the church contains paintings and three 17 and 18C altarpieces in carved wood.

Cross Arbrissel, the birthplace of Robert d'Arbrissel who founded the famous abbey of Fontevraud (near Saumur) where he was buried.

From Rannée, the D 178 takes you to La Guerche.

Round tour of 36 km - 22 miles. – *Time: 2 1/2 hours. Take the D 95 NW from La Guerche. After Carcraon, which is at the end of a lake – with its shaded shores arranged for fishermen (shelters, landing-stages) – you come to Bais.*

Bais. – Pop 1 913. The town is built on the side of a hill and overlooks the little valley of the Quincampoix. The porch of the Gothic church stands over a fine Renaissance doorway consisting of twin doors beneath a triangular pediment; the doors also have individual pediments. The rich and fantastic decoration of the doorway juxtaposes skulls, salamanders, the bust of François I and Aphrodite triumphant.

Louvigné-de-Bais. – Pop 1 124. The chapel with barrel vaulting south of the chancel is the only remnant of an earlier **church** (11C). The 16C building has Gothic arcades with short pillars. The reredos of the high altar is 17C. There are superb **stained glass windows★**: in the south aisle windows of the Resurrection and the Transfiguration designed by a painter from Vitré in 1542 and 1544; in the north aisle Christ's descent to Hell made in 1567 and very well repaired in 1607; a window of 1578 of the life of St John and, the nearest to the chancel a window of the life of the Virgin (1543 or 1548).

Leave Louvigné-de-Bais towards Janzé, at La Gaudinais turn left towards Moulins.

⊙ **Monbouan Château.** – In a lovely verdant setting stands Monbouan (1771). It is surrounded by a moat and vast outbuildings. Inside several rooms can be visited: the old kitchen, the salon, and the entrance hall with its great staircase and graceful wrought-iron balustrade. The hall is decorated with paintings after cartoons by Boucher.

Drive to Moulins and from there bear left to La Guerche-de-Bretagne.

★★ GUERLÉDAN Lake

Michelin map **59** fold 12 or **230** folds 21, 22

In the midst of the Argoat, a highly picturesque region, the waters of the Blavet River form a winding reservoir known as Lake Guerlédan – a magnificent stretch of water surrounded by trees. It is one of the finest sights of inland Brittany and a lovely place for water sports.

★★**Boat Trips.** – Boats starting from Beau Rivage and Sordan Bay offer tours of the ⊘ beautiful lake.

TOUR OF THE LAKE

Round tour of 44 km - 27 miles starting from Mur-de-Bretagne – about 3 1/2 hours

Mur-de-Bretagne. – Pop 2 165. This is one of the liveliest towns in the interior of Brittany. The 17C St Suzanne Chapel with its graceful belfry-porch (1670), stands on the north side of the town as you enter it. It is set in picturesque green surroundings; the great oaks often inspired the painter Corot (1796-1875).

Rond-Point du lac. – In Mur-de-Bretagne, a road to the right *(signpost)* leads to a round-about which affords a lovely **view★** of the lake and dam.

> *Return to Mur-de-Bretagne and take the D 35 in the direction of Guémené-sur-Scorff and after crossing two bridges over the canal and the Blavet, turn right.*

⊘ **St-Aignan.** – Pop 651. In the charming little 12C **church** are fine woodcarvings of the Tree of Jesse to the left of the chancel and a Trinity with the Evangelists to the right. Note also a statue of St Mark and a *Pietà*.

> *Make for the dam.*

Guerlédan Dam (Barrage de Guerlédan). – A belvedere overlooks this gravity-type dam (45m - 147ft high, 206m - 240yds long along the top and 33.50m - 109ft thick at the base) with a capacity of 55 million cubic metres and extending over 12 km - 7 miles in the Blavet Gorges. The power station at the foot of the dam generates an average of 23 million kWh per year. Below the dam is the former port of the Nantes-Brest canal, now fallen into disuse between Guerlédan and Pontivy.

> *Come back by the same road for 1 km - 1/2 mile and bear right.*

The road runs through a countryside of fields and pastureland until you come to the Quénécan Forest.

> *Then bear right.*

Sordan Bay (Anse de Sordan). – Pleasant site on the edge of the Guerlédan Lake.

Quénécan Forest. – The forest of 2 500 ha - 6 175 acres stands on an uneven plateau overlooking the Blavet Valley. Apart from beech and spruce around Lake Fourneau and Les Forges des Salles the forest, abounding in game (deer, wild boar), consists of pine, scrubland and heath.

Les Forges des Salles. – This is a charming place. To the right nestling in a small verdant valley and below a fine group of trees lie the hamlet of Les Forges and its castle. Until the beginning of 19C, the hamlet had several furnaces where Breton ore was smelted with wood fuel.

> *Continue in the direction of Ste-Brigitte on the D 15ᴬ.*

There are fine views on the right of Lake Fourneau.

> *At 1.7 km - 1 mile in a bend bear right into an unsurfaced road running through the forest. After 800 m - 1/2 mile leave the car in a parking area and take a path to the left.*

Les Salles Lake and Castle. – *1/2 hour on foot Rtn.* Of Les Salles Castle there remain only a few ruins and the main building, which has become a farmhouse. From nearby there is a pretty view over the lake.

> *Return to Les Forges and back to the main crossroads, then bear left.*

The road runs down the valley of the Forges stream, then enters the Blavet Valley, which it crosses.

> *Leave the car in the car park before the bridge to the left.*

Bon-Repos Lock. – The lock on the Blavet River, the old corbelled bridge, the former lock-keeper's house and the overflow form a pretty picture.

> *Go over the bridge and take the towpath to the right.*

Bon-Repos Abbey. – This 12C Cistercian abbey, a dependent of Boquen Abbey *(p 120)*, rebuilt in 14C and embellished in early 18C, was sacked and destroyed during the Revolution. Partly hidden by the vegetation, the fine façade of the abbey house, the sober architecture of the monastic buildings and the vast size of the church may still be admired.

> *Make for the N 164 and turn left towards Gouarec, immediately after the bridge bear left to the Daoulas Gorges.*

⊘ **Bothoa Mill.** – *Entrance to the right under the bridge spanning the road.* In this former mill is exhibited a large **collection of minerals★** (great blocks of amethyst, agate, rock crystal, rose quartz, etc.) mostly from Europe.

★ **Daoulas Gorges.** – *Go up the gorges by the D 44.* The fast flowing waters of the Daoulas run in a narrow, winding valley with steep sides covered with gorse, broom and heather. To join the Blavet which has become the canal between Nantes and Brest, the river has made a deep cut through a belt of schist and quartzite. The slabs of rock rise almost vertically; some end in curious needles, with sharp edges.

> *2 km - 1 mile farther on reverse into a lane before two houses at the place known as Toulrodez and turn back.*

The N 164 towards Loudéac which you take to the left, crosses undulating country and provides views of the lake.

After 5 km - 3 miles turn into the little road towards the lake.

After dropping down into a small pine wood it provides a beautiful **view**★ of Lake Guerlédan as it follows the lakeside banks before rejoining the N 164 at Caurel.

Beau-Rivage. – Leisure and sailing centre.

Proceed to Caurel and turn right towards Loudéac on the N 164. After 3.5 km - 2 miles turn right into the D 767 to return to Mur-de-Bretagne.

Poulancre Valley. – *6.5 km - 4 miles N of Mur-de-Bretagne by the D 63 in the direction of St-Gilles-Vieux-Marché.* The valley is deeply sunk between rocky or wooded slopes and forms narrow and very picturesque gorges. It leads to St-Gilles-Vieux-Marché, a pretty flower-decked village.

Le GUILDO

Michelin map 59 fold 5 or 230 folds 10, 11 – 10 km - 6 miles S of St-Cast – Local map p 96

This village lies in a picturesque setting on the shore of the Arguenon estuary. From the bridge across it you will see, on the right bank, the ruins of the Castle of Le Guildo. In the 15C this was the seat of Gilles de Bretagne, a carefree and gallant poet, who led a gay life at Le Guildo and among his friends in the neighbourhood. But Gilles was suspected of plotting by his brother, the reigning duke, and thrown into prison. As he did not die fast enough he was smothered. Before he died he summoned his brother to the judgement of God. A short time later the Duke, prostrated with remorse, expired.

The Ringing Stones (Les Pierres Sonnantes). – *3 km - 2 miles W by the D 786, the road to Erquy. After the bridge, bear right on the road which goes to the harbour, leave your car on the quay and take a lane along the Arguenon (15 min Rtn).*
Opposite the ruins of the castle *(to the right, on the far bank)* you will find a pile of rocks which emit a metallic note when you strike them with a stone of the same type. This resonance is due to the perfectly even grain of the rocks.

★★ GUIMILIAU   Pop 760

Michelin map 58 folds 5, 6 or 230 folds 4, 5 – Local map p 153

The fame of the little village of Guimiliau is due to its very remarkable parish close *(details of closes p 37)* and to the magnificently ornamented furniture of its church.

★★PARISH CLOSE *time: 3/4 hour*

★★**Calvary.** – The Calvary, the most curious and one of the largest in the region, dates from 1581 to 1588 and includes over 200 figures. On the upper part stands a large cross with a thorny shaft bearing four statues grouped in pairs: the Virgin and St John, St Peter and St Yves. On the platform are 17 scenes from the Passion and a composition representing the story of Catell-Gollet *(details p 38)* above the Last Supper. The figures on the frieze are numerous and depict, in no chronological order, 15 scenes from the life of Jesus. The four Evangelists stand at the corners of the buttresses.

★**Church.** – This 16C building was rebuilt in the Flamboyant Renaissance style at the beginning of the 17C.
Go round the south side of the church to see the triple-panelled apse, which is charming. Continue round the building, to the façade where the bell tower (1530) stands, all that remains of the original church.
The **south porch**★★ is remarkable. The arching adorned with statuettes gives an interesting picture of the Bible and the Gospels. Above the triangular pediment over the porch is the statue of St Miliau, King of Cornouaille and patron saint of the area. To the left of the porch is a small ossuary with low reliefs depicting scenes from the life of Christ. The inside of the porch is a fine example of a form of decoration frequent in Brittany *(details p 35)*. Under the usual statues of the Apostles is a frieze ornamented with rose medallions, tresses and scenes from the Old Testament. Note on the left side, near the date 1606, the Creation of Woman. In the end wall two round arched doorways, surmounted by a statue of Christ, frame a Kersanton granite stoup.
Inside, the church with its two naves and 5 side chapels, is roofed with panelled vaulting. At the end of the north aisle is a fine carved oak **baptistry**★★ dating from 1675. Eight spiral columns support an elaborately carved canopy, surmounted by a dome which shelters a group representing the baptism of Our Lord.
In the **organ loft** are three 17C **low reliefs**★; on the nave side, David playing the harp, and St Cecilia at the organ; opposite the baptistry, the Triumph of Alexander.
The **pulpit**★, dating from 1677, is ornamented at the corners with statues of the four Sibyls. The panels carry medallions representing the Cardinal Virtues.
The chancel with its central stained glass window (1599) is closed by a 17C altar rail adorned with embroidered banners (1658) and a gold cross. Note from right to left: the **altarpiece of St Joseph**, on which can be seen, St Yves, the patron saint of barristers between a rich man and a poor one, and the blind St Hervé with his wolf; the **altarpiece of St Miliau**, representing scenes from the Saint's life *(p 123)*; the **altarpiece of the Rosary,** with 15 mysteries in medallions, is surmounted by a Trinity.

Funerary chapel. – The chapel in the Renaissance style, dating from 1648, has an outdoor pulpit set in one of the windows.

Sacristy. – Built in 1683 it carries a statue of St Miliau on its conical roof.

GUINGAMP

Pop 9519

Michelin map 59 fold 2 or 230 folds 7, 8

This quiet little town is an important agricultural market which is rapidly expanding industrially. Of the original feudal city parts of the ramparts and a ruined castle remain.

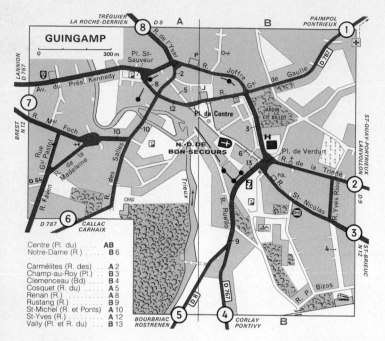

SIGHTS

★ **Basilica of Notre-Dame-de-Bon-Secours** (B). – This church was built in the Gothic style in the 14C (a Romanesque part remains at the transept crossing); but two centuries later the south tower collapsed, demolishing the south side of the nave. The town asked several architects to plan its reconstruction. One old master presented a purely traditional Gothic design; but a young man named Le Moal submitted plans in which the Renaissance style, almost unknown in Brittany at that time, appeared. Quite unexpectedly the people of Guingamp awarded the prize to the "revolutionary". Since then the church has had the unusual feature of being Gothic on the left and Renaissance on the right.

At the west end, two tall towers, the 13C Clock Tower to the left and the Renaissance tower to the right, frame a very fine round arched doorway with delicate decorations, half sacred and half profane.

Enter by the Notre-Dame-de-Bon-Secours doorway which opens into the Rue Notre-Dame. In a chapel formed by the doorway stands a Black Virgin, the church's patroness. A great *pardon (p 226)* draws thousands of pilgrims. The procession is held by candlelight. After the procession three bonfires are lit on the Place du Centre by the bishop who presides over the ceremony.

Inside, the church is unusual with its numerous pillars and graceful flying-buttresses in the chancel. The triforium is adorned with trilobed arches with a quadrilobed balustrade while lower down the nave has striking Renaissance decoration.

Place du Centre (AB). – Here are a few old houses – nos 31, 33, 35, 39, 48 and corner of Rues St-Yves and du Cosquet, and the fountain called **"la Plomée"**, with three lead and stone basins dating from the Renaissance.

⊙ **Town Hall (1699)** (B H). – It is housed in the old hospital (Hôtel-Dieu), formerly a monastery of the Hospitallers Order. The cloisters, great staircase and fine Italian-style chapel (1709) may be visited.

Ramparts (AB). – All that remains of the town's fortifications which were dismantled on Richelieu's orders can be seen on Place du Vally.

EXCURSIONS

★ **Menez-Bré.** – *13 km - 8 miles W – about 1 1/4 hours. Leave Guingamp by ⑦, N 12 to Brest. 11.5 km - 7 miles from Guingamp, after a house on the right, turn right (signposted) into a steep uphill road (max. 1 in 5 1/2) which leads to the summit of the Menez-Bré. Description p 59.*

Grâces. – *Pop 2 308. 3.5 km - 2 miles. Leave Guingamp by the D 54, W on the town plan. Turn right after 2 km - 1 mile; shortly after you will see the large church standing beside the road in the centre of the village.*

⊙ Originally the **Church of Our Lady** would appear to have been a pilgrims' chapel, probably founded by Queen Anne. Built in the 16C, it was slightly altered in the 17C and restored in the 19C. The four gables of the single aisle give it a saw-tooth silhouette from the south.

Inside, the barrel roof timbers of the nave and aisles rest on a magnificently carved frieze. A satirical picture of drunkenness is the main theme; but there are also hunting scenes, monsters, and a poignant Holy Face surrounded by little angels. Note also the tie-beams of the nave. A wooden shrine contains the relics of Charles of Blois, killed at the Battle of Auray *(p 52)*.

Round tour of 39 km - 24 miles. – *Time: about 2 hours. Leave Guingamp by ⑤ on the town plan.* The D 8 follows the Trieux Valley and then, for a short while, goes into the Kerauffret Wood which lies over on the left. The countryside is almost flat.

⊙ **Bourbriac.** – Pop 2 567. Rising in the centre of the town and surrounded by gardens, is the church with its towering belfry 64m - 210ft high. There have been several buildings erected on the site: of the first there remains a crypt probably of the 10 or 11C; of the Romanesque church which followed, there is the very high transept crossing – the tower above it was burnt down in the fire of 1765 and has been replaced by a pinnacle turret. In 1535 building on the west tower began; it is a remarkable example of the style that was to come: while the big ogival arched porch and all the lower floor are in the Flamboyant style, the remainder of the tower is definitely Renaissance. The spire was added in 1869.

Inside the tomb of St Briac is invoked as a cure for epilepsy. Behind the tomb is the sarcophagus of St Briac dating from Merovingian times.

Take the D 22 towards Plésidy and then D 5 in the direction of St-Péver.

After 2 km - 1 mile, note on the left below the road the small **Toul-an-Gollet Manor,** a pleasant 15C granite building with a pepperpot turret and mullioned windows.

Turn left at the crossroads and before the bridge over the Trieux, take a small road to the right.

⊙ **Notre-Dame-de-Restudo.** – This 14-15C chapel retains traces of 14C frescoes depicting the Last Supper and chivalry scenes, in the nave and chancel which are separated by a great ogival arch. *Pardon on 30 June.*

Turn back and take the D 767 back to Guingamp.

The Trieux Valley offers varied scenery.

After 2 km - 1 mile bear right to Avaugour.

⊙ **Avaugour Chapel.** – The chapel stands in an attractive setting and contains a finely carved wood sacrarium (shrine) of the 16C and interesting statues of the Apostles.

Make your way up the Trieux Valley back to Guingamp by the D 767.

HÉDÉ
Pop 470

Michelin map **59** fold 16 or **230** fold 26

The village stands on a hill between the Ille-et-Rance Canal, and a pond. Houses and hanging gardens, the ruins of a feudal castle on a rocky promontory all create a picturesque scene.

⊙ In the Romanesque **church** there are an alabaster Virgin and a high altar in wood; both date from the 17C.

The Eleven Locks. – *1.5 km - 3/4 mile NE by the D 795 to Combourg at La Madeleine. After the bridge over the canal, bear left to the carpark by the lock-keeper's house.* There are eleven locks, three before and eight after the bridge, to negotiate a drop of 27m - 89ft on the Ille-et-Rance canal. Pleasant walk in a pretty setting along the towpath.

EXCURSION

Round tour of 17 km - 10 miles. – *W – time: about 1 1/2 hours.*

★ **Church of Les Iffs.** – *Time: 1/4 hour.* The church is an attractive Gothic building with an entrance porch and belfry, as well as fine Flamboyant style windows in the south wall. Inside are nine lovely 16C **stained glass windows**★ inspired by the Dutch and Italian schools (16C): scenes of the Passion (in the chancel), Christ's childhood (in the north chapel), the Story of Susannah and the Two Elders (in the south chapel). Found in the nave are two low reliefs representing the Apostles and a font carved with a hare playing a musical instrument (1458), a double 15C baptismal font, and a Stations of the Cross carved in wood by Colette Rodenfuser (1965). Discovered underneath the wood reredos was an odd looking triangular high altar.

★ **Montmuran Castle.** – *800 m - 1/2 mile N of Les Iffs, at the end of a fine avenue lined with*
⊙ *oak and beech trees.*

The 17C main building, the façade of which was remodelled in the 18C, is ensconced between 12C towers and a 14C entrance fort. A drawbridge across the moat leads to the narrow portcullised gateway framed by two massive round machicolated towers. One of these towers houses the guardroom and a small museum evoking the past history of the castle. Behind the entrance fort an external staircase goes to the chapel where Du Guesclin *(details p 178)* was knighted in 1354 after a skirmish with the English in the neighbourhood. He later married, as his second wife, Jeanne de Laval.

From the towers (84 steps) there is a panorama of the Hédé and Dinan countryside.

Turn around and bear right.

Tinténiac. – Pop 2 598. The town is in a pretty spot by a lock on the Ille-et-Rance canal.
⊙ The **church** rebuilt in 1908 has preserved parts of the former church: on the north wall a small Renaissance door, a gift of Admiral Coligny, is decorated with Ionic columns and a frieze with angels' heads; to the right of the chancel is an odd-looking polygonal 14C stoup, known as the Devil of Tinténiac with grimacing faces carved on it.

The N 137 returns to Hédé.

Hennebont is a former fortified town on the steep banks of the Blavet. A *pardon* takes place at Hennebont on the last Sunday in September *(p 225)*.

The siege of 1342. – During the War of Succession *(p 20)* one of the Pretenders, Jean de Montfort, was held prisoner in the Louvre. In 1342 his wife, Jeanne of Flanders, was besieged in Hennebont by Charles of Blois and the French. The Countess fought like a true knight, but the attackers opened a breach in the walls. The garrison, demoralized, compelled her to negotiate. She obtained permission to march out with the honours of war if her reinforcements did not arrive within three days. Before the set date, the English fleet sailed up the Blavet and saved the town.

SIGHTS

⊘ **Notre-Dame-du-Paradis.** – On the huge Place Maréchal-Foch stands the 16C Gothic church of Our Lady of Paradise. Its very big **belfry★** is surmounted by a steeple 65m - 213ft high. At the base of the tower a fine Flamboyant porch ornamented with niches leads into the nave which is lit by stained glass windows by Max Ingrand. A Renaissance gallery houses the organ (1652).

Iron well. – Old well (1623), with fine wrought iron work.

Broërec Gate and ramparts. – This gateway, a vestige of the 13C fortifications, was ⊘ once used as a prison. The **gatehouse towers** are used for exhibitions. *Go through the door and take a stairway on the left up to the wall walk.* The 15C ramparts of the old fortified town afford a lovely view of the Blavet Valley spanned by the railway viaduct. Gardens are laid out along the walls.

⊘ **Stud (Haras).** – The Hennebont stud farm numbers about 140 stallions. It supplies breeding animals (draught horses, Breton post-horses and some bloodstock) to stations in South Finistère, Morbihan and Ille-et-Vilaine. The stud houses the premises of a national riding club.
You may visit the ruins of the Abbaye de la Joie within the grounds. The 17C gateway is interesting.

Kerbihan Park (Parc de Kerbihan). – *Access by the Rue Nationale and Rue Léo-Lagrange (the latter reserved for pedestrians).*
The park, bordered by the St-Gilles stream, is planted with species (all labelled) from the five continents.

EXCURSION

Round tour of 70 km - 43 miles. – *Time: about 3 1/2 hours. Leave Hennebont by the D 781. After 1 km - 1/2 mile turn left into the D 9 in the direction of Carnac.*

Kervignac. – The new houses stand on the left of the road. Skilfully reconstructed the little city encircles a charming modern church.
The plan of the Church of Our Lady of Pity (Notre-Dame-de-Pitié) is that of a Greek cross. The four sides consist of a lower part in granite which supports the clerestory containing stained glass windows; above rises a triangular gable. In one of the re-entrant angles is a square tower surmounted by a small belfry with a pierced spire.
Inside, the lovely polished pinewood panelling goes well with the glowing stained glass windows depicting the life of the Virgin Mary and with the sober wooden Stations of the Cross outlined in charcoal and chalk.

Continue on the D 9 then bear right into D 33 to Merlevenez.

★ **Merlevenez.** – Pop 1 773. This little town also suffered during the war, but its **church★** escaped total destruction. It is one of the few Romanesque churches in Brittany which has kept intact its elegant doorways with chevron and saw-tooth archivolts, its tiers-point arches in the nave, its storiated capitals and dome on squinches rising above the transept crossing. Modern stained glass windows by Grüber illustrate scenes from the Life of the Virgin.

Return to the D 9 and farther on take a small road on the left to Ste-Hélène.

Ste-Hélène. – In this village stands a fountain to which sailors from Etel came in pilgrimage before embarking on the fishing boats. If breadcrumb thrown in the fountain floated to the surface the sailor would return safely from the fishing expedition.

Take the road to the right of the town hall (mairie) and make for Mané Hellec Point.

The route gives access to the pretty **Etel River★**, a small bay dotted with islands that specialise in oyster farming.

Mané Hellec Point. – *By a small transformer station, turn left into a surfaced road.* Lovely view of St-Cado and its chapel, Pont-Lorois, the Etel River and the Locoal-Mendon Forest.

Return to Ste-Hélène and take the road to Plouhinec; after 2 km - 1 mile bear left. At the entrance to Pont-Lorois, turn right to the Barre d'Etel.

Barre d'Etel. – Huge waves crashing into the narrow channel, obstructed by sand banks, from the Etel River, and making navigation difficult and sometimes impossible, are a spectacular sight. The view extends as far as Groix Island, Belle-Ile and the Quiberon Peninsula. The small fishing port of **Etel** is on the left bank.

Turn back.

Pont-Lorois. – This short and pretty run gives a glimpse of the wide estuary which on the left opens out into a bay and on the right narrows into a deep channel which winds down to the sea.

After the bridge, bear left in the direction of Belz and left again to St-Cado.

St-Cado Chapel. – *1/4 hour on foot Rtn.* This is a former Templars' chapel and, like the church at Merlevenez, is one of the few Romanesque buildings in the Morbihan. Its general simplicity, with unornamented rounded arches, capitals with very plain decoration and dim lighting, contrasts with the fine Flamboyant style gallery running on the inside of the 16C façade. It is in this chapel that the deaf sought help from St Cado whose stone bed and pillow can still be seen. The chapel, the Calvary and the little fishermen's houses make a charming Breton **scene**★ especially at high tide. The St-Cado fountain stands below the east end.

At St-Cado, bear left after the transformer station.

The road runs along the Etel river passing the Kerhuen dolmen.

Make for Belz bearing right; at Belz turn left and take the D 16 in the direction of Pluvigner. After Locoal-Mendon, turn left towards Verdon Point.

Verdon Point. – As with all the points of the bay, the far end of Verdon Point is devoted to oyster farming; after crossing the isthmus and before taking the uphill road through the pines, bear right to reach a platform from which there is a fine view over the oyster farming area. At low tide it is possible to walk round the point.

Take the direction of Langombrac'h which you pass on the left and make for Landevant. At the town entrance, turn left into the D 33 towards Merlevenez.

This road passes the extreme point of the Etel River which is best seen at high tide.

At Nostang, the D 164 leads straight back to Hennebont.

HOËDIC Island

Michelin map **63** fold 12 or **230** fold 50
⊙ Access: boat services from Quiberon and Vannes

Separated from Houat Island by the Sœurs Channel, the smaller Hoëdic Island (2.5 km by 1 km) has the same granite formation with beaches and rocky headlands. Two lagoons extend east of the town while the island is covered in sparse heathland where grow wild carnations, a few cypresses, fine fig trees and tamarisks. Fresh water is supplied from an underground water bearing bed.
The boats dock at Argol Harbour. There are two other harbours – Port de la Croix and Port Neuf – which attract pleasure craft to the island whose mainstay is tourism. A gently sloping road leads to the town with a small chapel on the right and a menhir on the left.

Town. – The south-facing houses stand in groups of three or four. Near the former beacon is the church of St-Goustan named after a Cornish hermit who came to the island for a few years. It has fine 19C furnishings; note the two angels in white marble by the high altar.

Old Fort. – The fort, built in 1859 and partly hidden by the dunes, can be seen on the road to Port de la Croix. There is also a ruined 17C English fort at Beg-Lagatte.
Footpaths by the sea take you round the island to discover the beaches and admire the lovely **views** of the mainland, Houat Island, Belle-Ile and of the reefs.

HOUAT Island   Pop 390

Michelin map **63** fold 12 or **230** folds 49, 50
Access: see the current Michelin Red Guide France

This island (5 km by 1.3 km) of the Ponant archipelago, situated 15 km - 9 miles off the Morbihan coast, is a granite ridge fringed by cliffs. Because of its location commanding the access to Quiberon Bay, it was occupied three times by the English in 17 and 18C. The boats dock in the new harbour on the north coast where the fishing fleet is moored. A road leads uphill to the town.

Town. – Pretty houses, whitewashed and flower-decked, line the winding streets and alleyways leading to a square in the centre of the town in which stands the communal well, and to another square next to the church.
The church built in 19C, commemorates St Gildas, an English monk and patron of the island, who visited Houat prior to founding the monastery of St-Gildas-de-Rhuys *(p 191).*

Go round the church and follow the path skirting the cemetery.

From the belvedere, there is a fine **view**★ of the harbour and of the Rhuys peninsula.

Beaches. – There are numerous beaches nestling in small creeks but the loveliest extends to the west, facing Hoëdic Island, near the old harbour which was damaged in a violent storm in 1951.

⊙ **Lobster Farm.** – *800m - 1/2 mile. Take the road past the St-Gildas cooperative, along the tennis courts and round the fort and follow the downhill road on the right.*
Nestling in a small valley, the farm was created in 1972 to restock the island's waters. The tour shows the different breeding stages.
To the left of the farm, in another valley near Salus beach is the desalination plant which supplies fresh water to the island.

For hotels with private tennis courts, gardens,
swimming pool, or equipped beach
look in the current Michelin Guide France.

Michelin map **58** fold 6 or **230** fold 19 – Local map p 50

The forest, the pond, the running water and the rocks make Huelgoat one of the finest **sites★★** in inner Brittany which come under the aegis of the Armorique Regional Nature Park *(p 49)*. Huelgoat is not only a good excursion centre but a favourite place for anglers (especially for carp and perch in the lake and trout in the river).

★★ THE ROCKS *time: 1 1/2 hours on foot*

Access. – *Take a small alleyway to the left of a house in Rue de Berrien past the lake and follow the signposted path.*

Mill Rocks (Chaos du Moulin). – The path cuts through the rocks dominating the course of the Argent River. This pile of rounded granite rocks, surrounded by greenery, is very picturesque.

Devil's Grotto (Grotte du Diable). – *To reach this, climb down an iron ladder.* A brook babbles under the rocks.

Amphitheatre (Théâtre de Verdure). – Beautiful setting.

Logan-stone (Roche Tremblante). – *Left bank.* By leaning against this 100-ton block at a precise point, you can make it rock on its base.
Nearby, is a **clog-maker's hut (B)**, faithfully recreated to recall the huts in which lived these artisans and their families during the time spent felling trees for the wood required for their work.

The Virgin's Kitchen Pots (Ménage de la Vierge). – An enormous pile of rocks shaped rather like kitchen utensils.

An uphill path, known as Lovers' Walk (Sentier des Amoureux), leads directly through the woods to Artus' Cave and to the Boars' Pool (p 117).

Violette Alley (Allée Violette). – A pleasant path in the woods along the left bank of the Argent River.

To return to the centre of Huelgoat, at Pont-Rouge, turn right into the D 769^A and then take the Rue du Docteur-Jacq.

★ THE FOREST

The beauty of Huelgoat is in its hilly forest (alt 180-210m - 590-688ft), cut by deeply sunken watercourses and scattered with great blocks of granite. Extending over some 600 ha - 1 482 acres, it has some fine specimens of beech, oak, spruce and pine. It is criss-crossed by paths leading to fine sites *(signposts)*. There are car parks along the D 769^A.

★ **Horseshoe Walk (Promenade du Fer à Cheval) and the Chasm (Le Gouffre).** – *1/2 hour on foot.* After Pont-Rouge, take the Horseshoe Walk. A pleasant walk through the woods along the Argent River. *Then return to the D 769^A for 300 m - about 1/4 mile.* A stairway (39 steps) leads down to the chasm. The Argent River flowing from the Huelgoat lake, falls into a deep cavity to reappear 150 m farther on. A path leads to a belvedere *(1/4 hour Rtn - difficult and no security ramp)* commanding a view of the chasm. You can continue this walk through the woods by the river passing near the Fairies Pool (Mare aux Fées) and combining it with the Canal Walk.
Follow the signposts to the Mine (La Mine), turn right at the bridge into an unsurfaced road and at the former mine, continue along an uphill path to the right to the power station (usine électrique). A footbridge spans the canal and leads to the opposite bank.

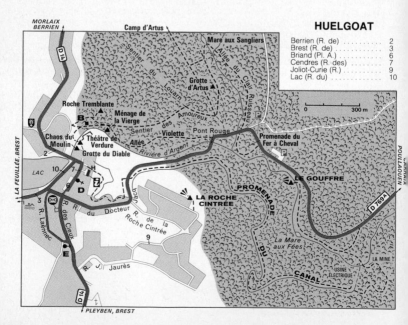

HUELGOAT

(R.J. Pratz/Azimut)

Huelgoat. – The forest

★ **Canal Walk (Promenade du Canal).** – *2 hours on foot Rtn by the Rue du Docteur-Jacq.* This follows the bank of the upper canal. A pond and two canals were dug in the 19C to work the silver-bearing lead mines, already known to the Romans. The waters were used to wash the ore and drive a crusher. The upper canal now serves a hydro-electric power station, which produces 400 kWh. From the far end of the canal walk you may continue on to the chasm; this walk is described in reverse order above.

Walk. – *1 1/2 hours on foot Rtn. From the car park after the Pont-Rouge, take the Allée du Clair-Ruisseau.*
This path half-way up the slope affords fine views of the rock-strewn stream bed.
A stairway (25 steps) on the left leads down to the **Boars' Pool** (Mare aux Sangliers) in a pretty setting of rocks shaped rather like boars' heads, hence the name. Cross over the rustic bridge to the Allée de la Mare on the left.
After the great stairway (218 steps) which provides the quickest access to **Artus' Camp** (Camp d'Artus), you can see up above, on the right, the entrance to **Artus' Cave** (Grotte d'Artus).
Continue up the path which after 800 m - 1/2 mile takes you to the camp. Boulders mark the entrance which was dominated by an artificial mound.
It was an important example of a Gallic fortified site, bordered by two enclosures. In spite of the encroaching vegetation it is possible to go round the camp by a path *(1 km - 1/2 mile)* following the remaining second elliptical enclosure which is fairly well preserved.

ADDITIONAL SIGHTS

★ **The Cintrée Rock (La Roche Cintrée).** – From the top of the rock *(1/4 hour on foot Rtn)* there is a **view★** of Huelgoat; to the north are the Arrée Mountains and to the south the Noires Mountains.

Church (D). – A 16C church with a modern belfry stands near the main square in the town centre. Inside there are sculptured cornices and to the left of the chancel is a statue of St Yves, the patron of the parish, between a rich man and a pauper.

Notre-Dame-des-Cieux (E). – Overlooking Huelgoat, this Renaissance chapel with its 18C belfry, has curious painted low-reliefs depicting scenes from the life of the Virgin and the Passion around the chancel and the side altars. A *pardon* takes place on the first Sunday in August.

The current Michelin Guide France
offers a selection of pleasant quiet and well situated
hotels. Each entry includes the facilities provided
(gardens, tennis courts, swimming pool and equipped beach)
and annual closure dates.

Also included is a selection of establishments recommended for their cuisine:
– well prepared meals at a moderate price, stars for good cooking.

The current Michelin Guide Camping Caravaning France
indicates the facilities and recreational amenities offered
by each individual site.
Shops, bars, laundries, games room, tennis courts,
miniature golf, children's play area, paddling pool,
swimming pool...

★ HUNAUDAIE Castle

Michelin map **59** N of folds 14, 15 or **230** N of fold 24

ⓥ The castle ruins of La Hunaudaie rise in a lonely, wooded spot. Still impressive and severe, they reflect the power of the great barons, equals of the Rohans, who built the castle.

The castle, built in 1220 by Olivier de Tournemine, was partly destroyed during the War of Sucession *(p 22)*. Rebuilt and enlarged by Pierre de Tournemine in the 14C, enriched in the 17C by Sébastien de Rosmadec, husband of one of the Tournemine heiresses, it was dismantled and then burnt by the Republicans at the time of the Revolution. The pillage of the castle stones was only stopped when the castle was bought by the French government in 1930.

The shape is that of an irregular pentagon with a tower at each corner. The two smallest derive from the first building, the other three were built in the 14-15C. The moat was once fed by two lakes. A bridge replacing the original drawbridge gives access to a large rounded doorway surmounted by a coat of arms. This leads to the courtyard.

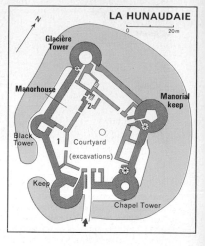

Pass along the 14-15C keep on the left, the 13-15C Black Tower at the foot of which traces of the kitchens (1) can still be seen, to reach the Glacière Tower.

Glacière Tower. – This 15C tower is north facing hence its name *(glacière* = ice-house). Go up the spiral staircase (40 steps) to admire the elegant structure and chimneys, and the view of the moat.

Manorhouse. – 15-16C. The ruined walls and the splendid Renaissance stairway (2) give some idea of the lay-out of this great building.

Manorial Keep. – This 15C tower with its spiral staircase (73 steps) is the best preserved. The monumental chimneypieces and loopholes in the walls are noteworthy. View of the courtyard and moat.

A fifth tower closing off the pentagon is the 13-14C Chapel Tower.

★★ JOSSELIN

Pop 2740

Michelin map **63** fold 4 or **230** fold 37 – Facilities

This little town stands in a picturesque setting. Its river, the Oust, reflects the famous castle of the Rohan family. Behind the fortress-castle, on the sides and the summit of a steep ridge, old houses with slate roofs are scattered around the basilica of Our Lady of the Brambles (Notre-Dame-du-Roncier).

The prosperity of the region depends on tourism and local industries such as meat canning and cardboard manufacturing.

HISTORICAL NOTES

The Battle of the Thirty (14C). – By the middle of the 14C the Castle of Josselin had already been razed and rebuilt. It belonged to the Royal House of France; Beaumanoir was its Captain; the War of Sucession was raging *(p 22)*. Josselin supported the cause of Blois; the Montfort party held Ploërmel, where an Englishman, Bemborough, was in command. At first the two garrisons had frequent encounters as they ravaged the countryside; then the two leaders arranged a fight between thirty knights from each camp: they would fight on foot, using sword, dagger, battle-axe and pike.

(S. Chirol)

Josselin. – The Castle

After taking Communion and praying all night at Our Lady of the Brambles, Beaumanoir's men repaired, on 27 March 1351, to the rendezvous on the heath at Mi-Voie, between Josselin and Ploërmel (5 km - 3 miles from Josselin at a place called Pyramide; a stone column marks the spot today). In the opposite camp were twenty Englishmen, six Germans and four Bretons. The day was spent in fierce hand-to-hand fighting until the combatants were completely exhausted. Josselin won; the English captain was killed with eight of his men, and the rest were made prisoners. During the struggle, which has remained famous as the Battle of the Thirty, the Breton leader, wounded, asked for a drink. "Drink your blood, Beaumanoir, your thirst will pass!" replied one of his rough companions.

Constable de Clisson (14C). – Among the owners of Josselin the greatest figure is that of Olivier de Clisson who married Marguerite de Rohan, the widow of Beaumanoir. He acquired the castle in 1370. He had a tragic childhood; for when he was only seven his father was accused of betraying the French party in the War of Succession and beheaded in Paris. The widow, Jeanne de Belleville, who had been quiet and inconspicuous hitherto, became a fury. She hurried to Nantes with her children and, on the bloody head of their father nailed to the ramparts, made them swear to avenge him. Then she took the field with 400 men and put to the sword the garrisons of six castles which favoured the French cause. When the royal troops forced her to flee, she put to sea and sank every ship of the opposite party that she met.
In this school Olivier became a hardened warrior and his career, first with the English and then in the army of Charles V, was particularly brilliant. He was a comrade in arms of Du Guesclin and succeeded him as Constable. All-powerful under Charles VI, he was banished when the King went mad, and he died in 1407 at Josselin. At this time the castle, entirely rebuilt and guarded by nine towers, was a very important stronghold. It then passed to the Rohan family, who still own it.

The de Rohans at Josselin (15 and 17C). – In 1488, to punish Jean II de Rohan for having sided with the King of France, the Duke of Brittany, François II, seized Josselin and had it dismantled. When his daughter Anne became Queen of France she compensated Jean II, who was able in the rebuilding of the castle, to create a masterpiece worthy of the proud motto of his family: "Roi ne puis, Prince ne daigne, Rohan suis" (I cannot be king, I scorn to be a prince, I am a Rohan). The owner of Josselin showed his gratitude to the Queen in the decoration of the palace; in many places, carved in the stone is the letter A, crowned and surmounted by the girdle which was Anne's emblem, and accompanied by the royal *fleur-de-lys*. In 1629 Henri de Rohan, the leader of the Huguenots, the sworn enemies of Richelieu, met the Cardinal in the King's ante-room where the cleric, who had just had the keep and five of the nine towers of Josselin razed, announced with cruel irony: "I have just thrown a fine ball among your skittles, Monsieur."

★★THE CASTLE (CHÂTEAU) *time: 3/4 hour*

To get a good **view★** of the castle stand on the Pont Ste-Croix, which spans the Oust River. From this point the building has the appearance of a fortress, with high towers, curtain walls and battlements. The windows and dormer windows appearing above the walls belong to the palace built by Jean II in the 16C.
The castle is built on a terrace of irregular shape, surrounded by walls of which only the bases remain, except on the side which is seen from the bridge. The isolated "prison tower" marked the northeast corner of the enclosure.
Looking out onto the park, which is where the courtyard once was, the delightful **façade★★** of the main building (restored in the 19C) makes an extraordinary contrast with the fortifications of the outer façade. Nowhere else in Brittany has the art of the sculptor been carried further in that hard material, granite: brackets, florets, pinnacles, gables, crowns and curled leaves adorn the dormer windows and balustrades.
Only the ground floor is open. In the panelled dining room stands a statue of Olivier de Clisson by Frémiet. Beyond the hall in which are hung portraits of the de Rohan family, is the richly furnished main saloon with its delicately carved chimney which bears the de Rohan motto. There are over 3 000 books and some portraits in the library.

Dolls Museum. – Housed in the stables, it contains some 500 antique dolls from the **Rohan collection**, complete with accessories.

JOSSELIN

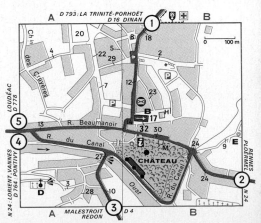

ADDITIONAL SIGHTS

★ **Basilica of Notre-Dame-du-Roncier** (B B). – Founded in the 11C and several times restored and remodelled the basilica is, generally speaking, in the Flamboyant style; note the wonderful gargoyles which adorn its three sides. It is famous for its great *pardon (p 226).* This has been called the "barker's pardon" since 1728, when three children were cured of epilepsy at the festival.

The name, Notre-Dame-du-Roncier, which dates only from the 15C, is based on a very old legend. About the year 800 a peasant, cutting brambles in his field, discovered a statue of the Virgin. He picked it up and carried it home, but the statue returned to its place. The man understood that the Virgin wanted a sanctuary, which became Our Lady of the Brambles, to be built on the spot. The miraculous statue was burnt in 1793. Only a fragment of it remains which is kept in a reliquary and displayed in the basilica, against the pillar to the left of the chancel.

Inside, in the south chapel divided from the chancel by a window decorated with rosettes, is the **mausoleum★** of Olivier de Clisson and his wife Marguerite de Rohan (15C). The chapel of the Virgin of the Brambles is on the left of the chancel (modern statue). In the nave is a fine wrought iron pulpit of the 18C. The organ case is 16C. The modern stained glass window in the north transept was designed by Grüber.

⊙ **Ascent of the tower.** – *Access by the Place A. de Rohan.* The tower commands a lovely view of the northeast façade and inner court of the castle, and far over the whole countryside.

Ste-Croix (A D). – The chapel has an 11C nave. From the surrounding cemetery, which is ornamented with a Calvary, there is a pretty view of the Oust and the castle.

After a visit to the chapel, stroll in the picturesque Ste-Croix quarter with its narrow streets and old houses some of which are corbelled.

Fountain of Notre-Dame-du-Roncier (B E). – Built in the 17C. A place of pilgrimage.

Old houses. – The old houses are found in the basilica's precinct especially on Rue des Vierges and Place Notre-Dame. Nevertheless, the most picturesque is at no 7 Rue des Trente dating from 1624; beside it is a house built in 1663.

JUGON-LES-LACS   Pop 1 351

Michelin map **59** folds 14, 15 or **230** fold 24

The town of Jugon adjoins the pool into which flow the Rosette and the Rieule rivers thus forming the great Jugon lake (67 ha - 0.26 sq miles) popular for boating and fishing. The church which was partly rebuilt in 19C retains its 13C porch, a saddle-back roofed belfry (15C) and the south transept doorway adorned with stylised carvings. In Rue du Château stands the former Savoy mansion (1634) built on the rock.

EXCURSIONS

★ **Hunaudaie Castle.** – *9 km - 5 miles N. Leave Jugon W by the N 176 towards St-Brieuc and after 2 km - 1 mile bear right. At St-Igneuc turn right after the church in the direction of Pléven, and by Le Clos du Puits Café, turn left.*

⊙ **St-Esprit-des-Bois Old Farm.** – Go into the courtyard surrounded by the traditional buildings on a small holding with their usual implements: outhouses, cart and wood sheds, stables, cellar and bread oven. The communal living room with its great chimneypiece is furnished in typical Breton style.

Go round the farm and bear right to rejoin the D16 to Pléven where you turn left and 600 m - about 1/3 mile farther on, left again towards Hunaudaie Castle.

★ **Hunaudaie Castle.** – *P 118.*

⊙ **Boquen Abbey.** – *15 km - 9 miles SW in the direction of Collinée. At Plénée-Jugon take the signposted road which runs through the Arguenon Valley.*

The abbey was founded by the Cistercian Order in 1137 and grew considerably. But it began to decline under the *commendam* system and during the Revolution and the building was later sacked; in 1936 the first monk returned to a ruin.

Leave the car in the car park opposite the reception area.

On the left are the monastery buildings where silence is observed. The church in the sober Cistercian style has a 12C nave and transept, a 15C chancel with a flat chevet lit by fine grisaille windows. Note in the chancel a statue of Our Lady of Boquen (15C) and an old statue of Christ in simple style. A stairway in the north transept leads to the former monks' dormitory.

★ KERJEAN Castle

Michelin map **58** fold 5 or **230** fold 4 – 5 km - 3 miles SW of Plouzévédé

⊙ Kerjean Castle, half fortress, half Renaissance mansion, rises in the midst of a huge park. Towards the middle of the 16C Louis Barbier inherited a fortune from his uncle, a rich abbot of St-Mathieu, and decided to devote his money to building a castle which would be the finest residence in Léon. In 1710 part of the building burned down, later the castle was sacked.

However the castle which has belonged to the State since 1911, has since been restored except for the right wing. The buildings are guarded by a moat and a rampart with walls up to 12m - 40ft thick. A dwelling house with two wings and a large portico enclose the main courtyard, which is adorned with a fine Renaissance **well.**

The chapel has a wooden vault with carved beams and cornices. The kitchens have monumental chimneys; part of the house forms a small museum of Breton art containing very fine old **furniture** (box beds, chests, etc.). The tour takes you to the room where the virtuous Françoise de Quélen locked up four gentlemen who tried to seduce her in her husband's absence, and the hiding place of Suzanne de Coastanscour, the last lady of Kerjean, (1794).
At the end of the north park, a Renaissance fountain overlooks a pool.

★ KERMARIA

Michelin map **59** folds 2, 3 or **230** fold 8 – 3.5 km - 2 miles NW of Plouha

The **Chapel of Kermaria-an-Iskuit**★ (House of Mary who preserves and restores health) is a popular scene of pilgrimage (3rd Sunday in September). This former baronial chapel, in which a few of the bays of the nave are 13C, was enlarged in the 15 and 18C. Above the south porch is the former 16C court room, with a small balcony. The inside of the porch is adorned with statues of the Apostles *(details of porches p 35)*.
Kermaria has some 15C **frescoes**★ which decorate the walls over the arcades. The best preserved, in the nave, depict a striking dance of death. Death, in the shape of jumping and dancing skeletons and corpses, drags the living into a dance; those depicted include pope, emperor, cardinal, king, constable, *bourgeois,* usurer, lover, lord, ploughman, monk, etc. Above the high altar is a great 14C Christ. In the south transept are five alabaster **low reliefs**★ of scenes from the life of the Virgin. There are numerous wooden statues, including in the transept a curious 16C figure of the Virgin suckling her unwilling Child and a Virgin in Majesty (13C).

EXCURSION

★**Lanleff.** – Pop 87. *5.5 km - 3 miles. Leave Kermaria by the D 21 to the left and after Pléhédel, bear left.* In the village, away from the road, stands the **temple**★, a circular building, a former chapel or baptistry built by the Templars in the 12C on the model of the Holy Sepulchre in Jerusalem. Twelve round arched arcades connect the rotunda with an aisle set at an angle with three apsidal chapels to the east. Note the simple decoration of the capitals: small figures, animals, geometrical figures, foliage.

★★ KERNASCLÉDEN   Pop 434

Michelin map **58** fold 18 or **230** folds 21, 35

This small village possesses a beautiful church built by the de Rohan family.

★★**Church.** – *Time: 1/2 hour.* Though the church at Kernascléden was consecrated in 1453, thirty years before the chapel of St-Fiacre *(p 191),* there is a legend that they were built at the same time and by the same workmen. Every day, angels carried the men and their tools from one site to the other.
A characteristic feature of this church is the striving for perfection that appears in every detail. The very slender tower, the foliated pinnacles, rose carvings and delicate tracery help to adorn the church without overloading it. Two porches open on the south side. The left **porch**★, which is the larger, is ornamented with statues (restored) of the twelve Apostles *(details of porches p 35).*
Inside, the church has ogival stone vaulting. The vaults and walls surmounting the main arches are decorated with 15C **frescoes**★★ representing episodes in the lives of the Virgin and Christ. The finest are the Virgin's Marriage, Annunciation (left of chancel) and Burial (right of chancel). In the north transept are eight angel-musicians; over the triumphal arch (on the chancel side), the Resurrection of Christ. On the walls of the south arm are fragments of a dance of death and a picture of Hell (facing the altar) which is remarkable for the variety of tortures it depicts.
There are many 15C statues in wood and stone: Our Lady of Kernascleden to the left of the high altar, St Sebastian and a *Pietà* in the nave.

EXCURSION

Castle and **Forest of Pont-Calleck.** – *4 km - 2 miles S. Take the D 782 in the direction of Le Faouët and at Kerchopine, turn left.* The road skirts the site of Notre-Dame-de-Joie, a children's home housed in **Pont-Calleck Castle** which was rebuilt in 1880. The tiny chapel of Notre-Dame-des-Bois stands at the entrance to the park.
Continue towards Plouay. The road runs through the **forest of Pont-Calleck.** A small road to the left descends steeply towards Manepile and leads to a lake which affords a lovely view of the site of the castle. Return to the Plouay road for a pleasant drive through the narrow Valley of the Scorff.

LAMBADER

Michelin map **58** fold 5 or **230** fold 4 – 8 km - 5 miles NE of Landivisiau

The 15C **Chapel of Notre-Dame,** ruined after the Revolution and rebuilt on the same plan at the end of the 19C, is crowned by a belfry-porch 58m - 190ft high.
Enter by the north door. Inside is a very fine carved wood **rood-screen**★ in the Flamboyant style (1481), bearing statues of the Virgin and the Apostles and an ornate staircase leads to the gallery. The altars on either side of the rood-screen and at the end of the nave are adorned with granite statues from a former 16C Calvary.
A sacred fountain with a *Pietà* stands below on the south side of the chapel.

Michelin map **59** folds 4, 14 or **230** folds 23, 24

Lamballe is a picturesque commercial town built on the slope of a hill crowned by the church of Notre-Dame-de-Grande-Puissance. It is an important market centre.

Bras-de-Fer before Lamballe (1591). – The town, which was the capital of the County of Penthièvre from 1134 to 1420, suffered a great deal in the War of Succession (p 22). During the League it was one of the strongholds of Mercœur, Duke of Penthièvre (Charles IX made the County a Duchy). In 1591 Lamballe was besieged by the famous Calvinist captain, La Nouë, nicknamed "Bras-de-Fer", because he wore a metal hook in place of the arm he had lost. He was killed during the siege of the town. Henri IV keenly felt his loss. "What a pity," he exclaimed, "that such a little fortress destroyed so great a man; he alone was worth an army!" In 1626 César of Vendôme, Lord of Penthièvre, the son of Henri IV and Gabrielle d'Estrées, conspired against Richelieu and the castle was razed by order of the Cardinal. Only the chapel remains.

The Princess of Lamballe (Revolution). – In 1767, at the age of twenty, the Prince of Lamballe (the heir to the Duchy of Penthièvre) led such a dissolute life that his father, the Duke, in an effort to reform him, married him to a Piedmontese princess; but the heir did not mend his ways, and he died, worn out with debauchery, three months later.
In 1770, when Marie-Antoinette married the future Louis XVI, she made friends with the young widow, who remained faithfully attached to her for twenty years. When the tragedy of the Revolution took place, the Princess of Lamballe bravely stood by the Queen. She died a year before her: in the massacres of September 1792, the rioters cut off her head and paraded it on a pike.

LAMBALLE

		Beloir (Pl. du)	4	Hurel (R. du Bg)	25
		Boucouets (R. des)	7	Jeu de Paume (R. du)	26
Bario (R.)	3	Caunelaye (R. de la)	9	Leclerc (R. Gén.)	29
Cartel (R. Ch.)	8	Champ-de-Foire (Pl. du)	12	Marché (Pl. du)	30
Dr-A.-Calmette (R. du)	15	Charpentier (R. Y.)	14	N.-Dame (R.)	33
Martray (Pl. du)	32	Dr-Lavergne (R. du)	16	Poincaré (R.)	34
Val (R. du)	43	Foch (R. Mar.)	19	St-Jean (R.)	37
		Gesle (Ch. de la)	23	St-Lazare (R.)	38
Augustins (R. des)	2	Grand-Boulevard (R. du)	24	Villedeneu (R.)	45

SIGHTS

★ **Stud (Haras national).** – Founded in 1828, the stud contains 125 stallions (mostly post-horses and Breton draught horses). From the beginning of March to mid-July, all the stallions are sent out to breeding stands in the Côtes-du-Nord and the north of Finistère. The stud houses the premises of a school of dressage (40 horses) and a riding club (20 horses). A horse show is held the weekend after 15 August with a special display by ten teams to round off the events on the Sunday. The visit includes the stables, blacksmith's shop, carriage house, saddle room, riding school and main court.

Collegiate Church of Notre-Dame. – The Gothic church has Romanesque features, in particular the remarkable north doorway with slender columns and carved capitals supporting the covings, a bay in the nave and the north transept. At the entrance to the south aisle in the chancel is a fine carved wood rood-screen in the Flamboyant style. On the south side of the church with its buttressed gables, there is a terrace built in 19C which affords a fine view of the town and the Gouessant Valley.
To the left of the church, a shady esplanade has been created on the site of the castle.

Place du Martray (32). – Old houses. The most remarkable is the former **Executioner's house** (15C – M) which contains the Tourist Information Centre and two museums.

Local Museum (Musée du Vieux Lamballe et du Penthièvre). – Ground floor. Pottery from Lamballe, etchings of the old town, head-dresses and costumes of the region.

Mathurin-Meheut Museum. – First floor. Works by the local painter M. Meheut (1882-1958).

St-Martin. – This former priory was remodelled many times in the 15-18C. On the right is an unusual little porch (11-12C) with a wooden canopy (1519).

★ LAMPAUL-GUIMILIAU

Michelin map **58** fold 15 or **230** fold 4 – 4 km - 2 miles SE of Landivisiau – Local map p 153

This place has a complete parish close *(details on closes p 37)*. The church is especially noteworthy for its rich decoration and furnishings.

★ PARISH CLOSE *time: 1/2 hour*

Triumphal arch. – The round arched gateway to the cemetery is surmounted by three crosses (1669).

Funerary chapel. – The former ossuary (1667) abuts on the arch and has grooved buttresses crowned with small lantern turrets. Inside is the altar of the Trinity, with statues of St Rock, St Sebastian and St Paul and his dragon.

Calvary. – Very plain (early 16C) but damaged.

★ Church.

– The church is dominated by a 16C bell tower whose steeple was struck by lightning. The apse, with a sacristy added in 1679, forms a harmonious whole in which the Gothic and Classical styles are blended. The porch on the south side dates from 1533 *(details of porches p 35)*. Under it are statues of the twelve Apostles and, between the two doors, a statue of the Virgin and Child and a graceful Kersanton stoup.

Inside★★, a 16C **rood-beam** *(illustration p 36)* spans the nave, bearing a Crucifix between statues of the Virgin and St John. Both its faces are adorned with sculptures representing, on the nave side, scenes from the Passion and, on the chancel side, the twelve Sibyls separated by a group of the Annunciation. The pulpit dates from 1759. At the end of the south aisle is a **font** surmounted by a canopy dating from 1651. Higher up, on the right of the St Lawrence altarpiece, is a curious stoup (17C) representing two devils writhing in the holy water; above, the Baptism of Christ.

In the chancel are 17C stalls, and on each side of the high altar, carved woodwork: on the left, St Paul on the road to Damascus and his escape; on the right, St Peter's martyrdom and the divine virtues. The side altars have 17C altarpieces.

The altar of St John the Baptist, on the right of the chancel, is adorned with low reliefs of which the most interesting (left) represents the Fall of the Angels after Rubens. The altar of the Passion, on the left of the chancel, has an altarpiece in eight sections in high relief with lifelike figures and, on the top, the Resurrection. On either side are two panels showing the Birth of the Virgin (left), a rare theme in Brittany, and the Martyrdom of St Miliau (right), a King of Cornouaille beheaded by his jealous brother.

In the north side aisle is a 16C *Pietà* with six figures carved out of a single piece of wood and also two 17C banners, embroidered in silver on a velvet ground (in a cupboard). The impressive **Entombment** was carved by the naval sculptor, Anthoine. Note Christ's head which is in white stone whereas all the other figures are coloured (1676). The organ case is 17C. The sacristy contains a 17C chest.

LANDERNEAU

Michelin map **58** fold 5 or **230** fold 4 – Local map p 153

The ancient town of Landerneau, once the capital of Léon, is built in a pretty setting. It is an excellent centre from which to make excursions including the tour of the parish closes *(p 153)*.

Landerneau is the port of the Élorn estuary where salmon and trout are fished. The town is also the market for the locally grown spring vegetables and later market garden produce and fruit.

The saying "That'll make a din in Landerneau" (il y aura du bruit dans Landerneau) arose from the practice of the local inhabitants of serenading and mocking any widow should she decide to marry again.

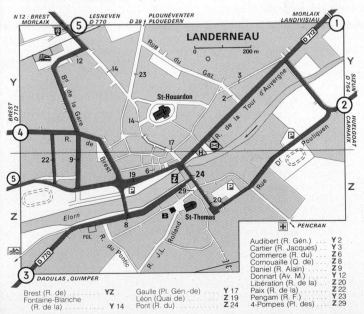

Brest (R. de) . . . . **YZ**
Fontaine-Blanche
(R. de la) . . . . **Y** 14

Gaulle (Pl. Gén.-de) . . . . **Y** 17
Léon (Quai de) . . . . **Z** 19
Pont (R. du) . . . . **Z** 24

Audibert (R. Gén.) . . . . **Y** 2
Cartier (R. Jacques) . . . **Y** 3
Commerce (R. du) . . . . **Z** 6
Cornouaille (Q. de) . . . **Z** 8
Daniel (R. Alain) . . . . . **Y** 12
Donnart (Av. M.) . . . . . **Z** 9
Libération (R. de la) . . . **Z** 20
Paix (R. de la) . . . . **Z** 22
Pengam (R. F.) . . . . . . **Y** 23
4-Pompes (Pl. des) . . . **Z** 29

Old Bridge over the Élorn (Z 24). – Picturesque, with old, overhanging houses. Go to the Hôtel de Ville (Town Hall) for a good view of the bridge.

St-Houardon (Y). – The Renaissance domed tower and the porch (1604) on the south side of this church remain.

⊙ **Church of St Thomas of Canterbury** (Z). – This 16C church has a belfry-porch (1607) with three superimposed balconies. Inside, note the charming decoration of the cornice in the north aisle and the great 18C altarpiece at the high altar.

Former ossuary (Z B). – Erected as an annexe to the church of St Thomas in 1635.

Old houses. – These are to be found mainly on the right bank of the Élorn River: No 9 Place du Général-de-Gaulle (Y 17); the turretted house (1664) known as the house of the Duchess Anne; the façade at No 4 Rue Fontaine-Blanche; at No 5 Rue du Commerce, house with decorated turret and dormer windows (1667) and at the corner, a house dating from 1648.

EXCURSIONS

★★**Parish Closes.** – *Round tour of 130 km - 81 miles. Description p 153.*

★**Pencran.** – *P 155.*

★ LANDÉVENNEC
Pop 377

Michelin map 58 folds 4, 5 or 230 fold 18

Situated on the Landévennec peninsula which is part of the Armorique Regional Nature Park *(p 49),* the village of Landévennec stands in a pretty **site**★ at the mouth of the Aulne river, which is best seen by taking the steep road to the right from Gorréquer. A belvedere to the right offers a fine **view**★ of Landévennec. Below is the course of the Aulne River, with the Island of Térénez; beyond, the Landévennec Peninsula and the Faou River.

A steep descent leads to the settlement, a little summer resort surrounded by woods and water and Mediterranean vegetation.

The Abbey. – The Benedictine Abbey, rebuilt in 1958, and the ruins of the former abbey to the right are approached from different roads.

Benedictine Abbey (Abbaye Benedictine). – *To get to the abbey turn right halfway downhill into a tree-lined alleyway and follow the road signs.* Only the church is open to visitors who may attend the services.

⊙ **Ruins of the former abbey** (Ancienne Abbaye). – *Entrance 200 m below to the right of the village centre.* The monastery founded by the Welsh St Guénolé (Winwaloe) in the 5C and remodelled several times, ceased to exist in 18C and only the ruins of the Romanesque church remain. The plan can be deduced from the column bases, wall remains and doorway: a nave and aisles with six bays, transept, chancel and ambulatory with three radiating chapels. At the entrance to the south transept, there
⊙ is a monument thought to be the tomb of King Gradlon *(p 25).* In an **exhibition room,** a diorama illustrates the outstanding events of the monastery's history.

LANDIVISIAU
Pop 8 057

Michelin map 58 fold 5 or 230 fold 4 – Local map p 153

Landivisiau is a busy town. Its cattle fairs are among the biggest in France.

St-Thivisiau. – A modern church in the Gothic style. It still has the belfry and the fine granite **porch**★ of a former 16C church. Note the elegant canopies above the statues of the Apostles and the delicate ornamentation round the door.

St-Thivisiau Fountain. – *Take the narrow Rue St-Thivisiau.* This 15C fountain is decorated with eight granite low-reliefs.

St-Anne. – The chapel was an ossuary in the 17C. The façade is adorned with caryatids. Death is represented to the left of the west doorway.

LANMEUR
Pop 2 133

Michelin map 58 fold 6 or 230 folds 5, 6 – Local map p 48

The small town of Lanmeur is situated in a market gardening area on the Trégorrois Plateau.

⊙ **Church.** – Only the crypt and the belfry of the original church have been retained in the edifice put up in 1904. Inside, panels with photographic blow-ups retrace the life of St Melard; each picture is taken from a chapel dedicated to this Saint who had his right hand and left foot amputated. An angel is shown bringing him a new silver hand and foot. There is also a curious statue of the saint.

The pre-Romanesque **crypt**★ *(access to the left of the main altar, light switch at the foot of the stairway)* is ascribed to the 8C and is one of the oldest religious buildings in Brittany. The vaulting rests on eight massive pillars, two of which are decorated. A fountain stands to the left of the west door.

Archaeological excavations have brought to light two rare and very old (6C?) carved gold figurines.

Kernitron Chapel. – *In the cemetery close*. This large building has a 12C nave and transept and 15C chancel. Look at the outside of the Romanesque doorway of the south transept; the tympanum depicts Christ in Majesty surrounded by the symbols of the evangelists.

Inside, at the entrance to the south aisle, there is a fine carved wooden balustrade; in the nave, a rood-beam carries Christ on the Cross between the Virgin and St John; to the right of the high altar stands a statue of Christ in Fetters and in the chapel facing the entrance a statue of Our Lady of Kernitron (*pardon* on 15 August) with to the right in a small chapel a charming statue of St Anne and the Virgin.

★ LANNION   Pop 17 228

Michelin map 59 fold 1 or 230 fold 6

Lannion, a port on the Léguer River, spread out on both banks of the river will attract the tourist by its typical "Old Brittany" character. It is the birthplace of the novelist Charles Le Goffic (1863-1932) (*p 29*), whose statue by Jean Boucher stands at the corner of Avenue E.-Renan and Rue de la Mairie.

The Centre de Recherches de Lannion and the Centre National d'Études des Communications where research is undertaken in telecommunications and electronics have been built 3 km - 2 miles north of Lannion at the crossroads of the D 11 and the D 788.

LANNION

Augustins (R. des) . . . . . **Z** 3	Buzulzo (R. de) . . . . **Z** 4	Letaillandier (R. E.) . . . . . **Z** 20
Centre (Pl. du) . . . . **Y** 5	Chapeliers (R. des) . . . . **Y** 6	Mairie (R. de la) . . . . **Y** 21
Pont-Blanc	Cie-Roger-Barbé (R.) . . . **Y** 7	Palais-de-Justice
(R. Geoffroy-de) . . . **Z** 25	Coudraie (R. de la) . . . . **Y** 8	(Allée du) . . . . **Z** 24
	Du-Guesclin (R.) . . . . . . **Z** 9	Pors an Prat (R. de) . . . . **Y** 26
Aiguillon (R. d') . . . . **Z** 2	Frères-Lagadec (R. des) **Z** 12	Roud Ar Roc'h (R. de) . . **Z** 28
	Keriavily (R. de) . . . . . . **Z** 14	St-Malo (R. de) . . . . **Z** 29
	Kermaria (R. et Pont) . . **Z** 16	St-Nicolas (R.) . . . . **Z** 30
	Le-Dantec (R. F.) . . . . . **Y** 18	Trinité (R. de la) . . . . . . **Y** 32

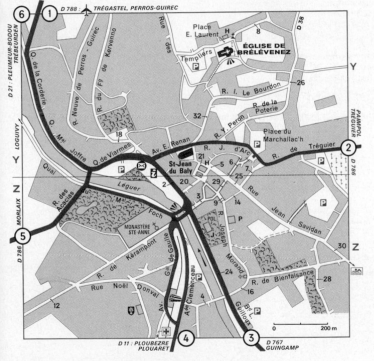

SIGHTS

★ **Old houses** (YZ). – The beautiful façades of 15 and 16C houses, half-timbered, corbelled and with slate roofs, may be admired especially at Place du Général-Leclerc (Nos 23, 29, 31, 33), Rue des Chapeliers (Nos 1-9), Rue Geoffroy-de-Pont-Blanc (Nos 1, 3) and Rue Cie-Roger-de-Barbe (Nos 1, 7). At the corner of the latter, on the left, a granite cross has been sealed in the wall at the spot where the Chevalier de Pont-Blanc distinguished himself in the heroic defence of the town during the War of Succession (*p 22*).

★ **Brélévenez Church** (Y). – The church was built on a hill by the Templars in the 12C and remodelled in the Gothic period. The bell tower is crowned by a granite spire and dates from the 15C.

Access: *on foot by a staircase (142 steps); by car, via Rues Le-Dantec, du Faubourg-de-Kervenno and des Templiers to the right.*

When you reach the terrace, there is an attractive view of Lannion and the Léguer Valley. Before entering by the Romanesque doorway on the south side, look at the curious Romanesque apse which is decorated with engaged round pillars, carved capitals and modillions.

Inside, on the left, is a stoup which was used to measure tithe wheat. In the chapels to the right and left of the chancel are 17C altarpieces. Under the chancel and ambulatory the Romanesque crypt, which was remodelled in 18C, contains an 18C Entombment.

○ **St-Jean-du-Baly** (Y). – 16-17C. Over the door of the sacristy to the left of the high altar is a fine 18C portrait of St John the Evangelist.

The Bridge (Z). – From the bridge there is a good view of the port and of the vast Ste-Anne monastery.

EXCURSIONS *local map below*

☐ **Round tour of 50 km - 31 miles.** – *Time : about 3 hours.*

Leave Lannion by ④ on the town plan, the D 11 the road to Plouaret. 1.5 km - 1 mile after Ploubezre, bear left at a fork where stand five granite crosses and 1.2 km - 3/4 mile farther on, turn left.

★ **Kerfons Chapel.** – In a lovely setting, the chapel in front of which is an old Calvary, is ○ surrounded by chestnut trees. Built in the 15 and 16C, it has a flat east end, a modillioned cornice along the south wall and a pinnacle turret decorated with telamones crowning the gabled south transept. It contains a late 15C carved **rood-screen**★ and fragments of old stained glass remain in the windows of the chancel and north transept.

Turn back and take the road to Tonquédec on the left.

Soon the road starts to wind downhill providing good views over the ruins of Tonquédec in the Léguer Valley. After crossing the swiftly flowing river you will see the castle on the left *(car park).*

★ **Tonquédec Castle.** – P 205.

Turn back and at the first crossroads bear left to rejoin the D 11. Continue in the direction of Plouaret and after 1 km - 1/2 mile turn left.

○ **Kergrist Château.** – One of the principal attractions of the castle lies in the variety of its façades. The north façade is Gothic with dormer windows set in tall Flamboyant gables; the main building which belongs to the 14 and 15C, nevertheless presents an 18C façade on the opposite side, while the wings running at right angles, which were built at an earlier date, have Classical fronts overlooking the gardens. The formal French gardens extend as far as the terrace which overlooks a landscaped English garden and the woods.

Return to the D 11 and take it bearing left. After 2.2 km - 1 1/2 miles, turn left.

○ **Les Sept-Saints Chapel.** – In a verdant setting, this 18C chapel is unusual in that it is built in part on top of an imposing dolmen. From the outside, a small door in the south arm of the transept leads under the dolmen which has been turned into a crypt for the cult of the Seven Sleepers of Ephesus. According to legend, seven young Christians walled up in a cave in 3C woke up two hundred years later. Every year, an Islamic-Christian pilgrimage *(p 225)* is held in this Breton chapel.

Continue on the D 74 to Pluzunet and Bardérou and turn left into the D 767 to Lannion.

○ **Caouënnec.** – The church contains an ornate altarpiece which is nevertheless very beautiful.

Proceed towards Lannion and at Buhulien bear left in the direction of Ploubezre and 100 m - 109 yds after a farm at Pont-Keriel, turn left into an unsurfaced path through the woods.

Coatfrec Castle. – There are fine ruins of this large 16C mansion.

Make for Ploubezre and turn right into the D 11 which takes you back to Lannion.

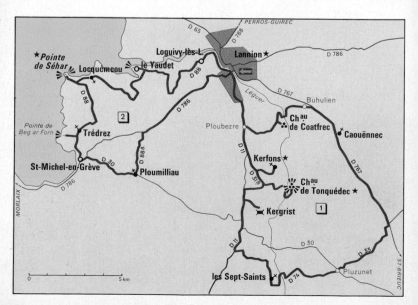

2 Round tour of 32 km - 20 miles. – *Time: about 2 hours.*

Leave Lannion by the Quai du Maréchal-Foch.

The drive, especially at high tide, along the left bank of the Léguer River is very picturesque.

Louvigny-lès-Lannion. – This town on the outskirts of Lannion clings to the hillside in a pleasant setting. The church is 15C. A curious outdoor stairway leads to the wall-belfry which was built in 1570.

Inside the church, in the chapel to the left of the chancel, there is a 17C wooden panel depicting the Adoration of the Three Wise Men with shepherds in Breton costume playing the bagpipes and the bombardon. The fine wooden balustrade in the chancel dates from the same period.

In the parish close there are three yew trees and two fountains, a Renaissance one with a granite basin and the other dating from the 15C set in the wall under an ogee arch adorned with a statue.

The road climbs in the direction of Le Yaudet.

Le Yaudet. – This hamlet in its beautiful setting was the episcopal seat in the early centuries of our era and was destroyed by the Danes (*c* 848 AD); it has remains of Roman walls and an interesting chapel overlooking the bay. Inside, above the altar, is a curious sculptured panel depicting the Trinity: a recumbent figure of the Virgin with the Infant Jesus at her side; God the Father is sitting in an alcove at the foot of the bed over which hovers a dove symbolizing the Holy Spirit. A *pardon* is held on the 3rd Sunday in May and on 15 August.

From the car park, the Corps de Garde footpath leads to a belvedere which affords a lovely **view** of the Léguer.

Return to the centre of Le Yaudet and turn right.

The road descends to Pont-Roux and climbs up again to reveal a fine **view** of the Léguer estuary and of the coast as far as Trébeurden.

At Christ, bear right towards Locquémeau.

Locquémeau. – The town overlooks the beach and the fishing harbour which are reached by a *corniche* road to the left at the entrance to the town: good views of the coast on either side of Locquémeau. The 15C **church** which has a wall-belfry flanked by a turret, contains interesting 18C altarpieces and fine sculptured tie beams, cornices and hammerbeams *(p 35).*

★ **Séhar Point.** – Leave your car near the port of Locquémeau and make for the point, from which the **view★** extends westwards as far as the Primel Point and eastwards to the resort of Trébeurden.

Take the D 88 in the direction of Plestin-les-Grèves and after 2.5 km - 1 1/2 miles, turn right into the D 88.

Trédrez. – Pop 1 069. St Yves *(p 25)* was Rector of Trédrez from 1285 to 1292. The church completed in 1500 is particularly remarkable for its 14C granite font crowned with a beautifully carved wood canopy (1540); 17C panels belonging to the altar in the south aisle depicting scenes from the life of Christ; an altarpiece in the south chapel of a beautiful Virgin and Child in a Tree of Jesse (1520); at the end of every hammerbeam angels in flight have been carved. Note also the sculptured decoration of the cornices and tie beams with animal carvings. Facing the pulpit is a fine Crucifix dating from 13C.

Leave Trédrez by the road going towards Kerbiriou and follow the road that leads to the Beg-ar-Forn headland.

Shortly before the car park there is a magnificent view of the bay and the Lieue de Grève.

Turn round and at the second junction turn right towards St-Michel-en-Grève.

The road runs beside the sea to the town and affords a good view.

St-Michel-en-Grève. – P 47.

On leaving St-Michel-en-Grève, take the D 30 to the right.

Ploumilliau. – The 17C church contains in the south transept thirteen wooden **panels,** carved and painted in many colours which illustrate scenes from the Life of Christ (Meal at the house of Simon, the Passion, the Ascension). There is also on the wall opposite the sacristy a curious portrayal of Ankou (Death), so often mentioned in Breton legend.

Return to the D 786 N and turn right towards Lannion.

LANRIVAIN   Pop 638

Michelin map 58 fold 8 or 230 fold 21 – 7 km - NW of St-Nicolas-du-Pélem

In the cemetery stands a 15C ossuary with trefoil arches. To the right of the church is a 16C Calvary, which was damaged at the Revolution and restored in the 19C, adorned with granite figures of great size.

Notre-Dame-du-Guiaudet Chapel. – *1.5 km - 1 mile N by the D 8 towards Bourbriac. At the entrance to the hamlet of Guiaudet take an alleyway marked by two granite pillars on the right.*

The chapel which dates from the late 17C, has over the high altar a curious sculptured scene representing a recumbent Virgin holding the Infant Jesus in her arms.

★ LARGOËT Castle

Michelin map **63** fold 3 or **230** fold 37 – 15 km - 9 miles NE of Vannes

⊘ These imposing feudal ruins, also known as **Elven Towers,** stand in the middle of a park. The road to the towers branches off from N 166 between two pillars.

The Castle of Largoët belonged to Marshal de Rieux, who was first a councillor of Duke François II and then tutor to his daughter, Anne of Brittany. When the troops of the King of France, Charles VIII, invaded Brittany in 1488, all the Marshal's strongholds, including Largoët, were burnt down or razed to the ground.

Pass through the 15C entrance fort built against the first entrance gate (13C). Of the castle there remains an impressive 14C keep, 44m - 144ft high, with walls 6 to 9m - 19 to 29ft thick. Near the keep is a smaller tower flanked by a lantern tower, which was remodelled as a hunting lodge.

★★ La LATTE Fort

Michelin map **59** fold 5 or **230** fold 10 – SE of Cape Fréhel – Local map p 96

⊘ A gate marks the entrance to the park. Follow the lane to the stronghold; you will pass a menhir, known as Gargantua's Finger.

This castle, which was built by the Goyon-Matignons in the 13 and 14C and restored in the 17C and early 20C, has kept its feudal appearance. It stands on a picturesque **site★★**, separated from the mainland by two gullies which are crossed on drawbridges. You will visit in succession: the two fortified enclosures, the inner courtyard, around which are located the guard room, the Governor's living quarters, the cistern and the chapel. Cross the thick walls made to shield the defender from cannon balls and go to the Échauguette tower and the cannon ball foundry. A look-out post takes you to the keep. From the parapet walk (26 steps but it is possible to walk up 21 difficult steps to the watch tower) there is a **panorama★★** of the Bay of La Frênaye, St-Cast Point, the Hébihens archipelago, the resorts of St-Briac and St-Lunaire, Décollé Point, St-Malo, Paramé and Rothéneuf, the Island of Cézembre and Meinga Point, the walls of the fort, the Sévignés Cove and Cape Fréhel.

★★ LOCMARIAQUER

Pop 1 279

Michelin map **63** fold 12 or **230** fold 50 – Local map p 138

The village commands the channel into Morbihan Bay.

Church. – It retains its 11C half-domed chancel and transept. The nave and aisles have been rebuilt in 18C. There are remarkable **capitals** adorned with geometrical designs or foliage at the transept crossing and in the chancel, and a fine stoup.

★ **Dolmen of Mané-Lud.** – It stands surrounded by houses on the right at the entrance to the village. The stones which remain standing inside the chamber are carved.

★ **Dolmen of Mané-Rethual.** – *In the centre of the village and to the right of the former town hall, take a path which passes by a group of houses and gardens.* A long covered alleyway leading to a vast chamber, the supports of which are carved.

★★ **Great Menhir** (Grand Menhir). – *Take the signposted path near the cemetery.*
The Great Menhir is broken into five pieces. Four of them remain lying on the spot; they are over 20.30m - 64ft long and their weight is estimated at about 347 tons. This is the biggest menhir known.

★★ **Merchants' Table** (Table des Marchands). – *Behind the menhir, to the right.* This dolmen, planted in the remains of a tumulus 36m - 118ft across, consists of three flat tables with seventeen pointed supports. A gallery leads under the great table which rests at one end on an ornamented support (ears of wheat ripened by the sun). Under the table is a plough in the form of an axe, connected by a shaft bearing traces of harness with an animal of which the two hind legs can be distinguished.

Before the car park, at the foot of a tree, is a small dolmen, the flat top of which is level with the ground.

EXCURSIONS

Round tour of 5 km - 3 miles. – *On the Place Évariste-Frick, take Rue Wilson.*
On leaving the village take the road on the right leading to **Kerlud** village, a group of small farms built in granite. Opposite the last house is the **Kerlud Dolmen,** partly hidden.

Return to the main road and bear right; beside the beach turn right again.

★ **Dolmen of Flat Stones** (Dolmen des Pierres Plates). – A menhir indicates the entrance to this dolmen. Two chambers are linked by a long alleyway. Remarkable engravings decorate the supports. A terrace affords a fine view of Port-Navalo and Grand-Mont Points, Houat Island with Belle-Ile in the distance, and the Crozon Peninsula.

Turn round and follow the shoreline as far as the Kerpenhir Point.

★ **Kerpenhir Point.** – *Continue past the blockhaus.* The point where stands a granite statue of a sailor's wife looking out to sea, affords a **view★** onto the Morbihan channel.

Take a road to the left. Fine glimpse of the bay.

★ **Mané-er-Hroech Tumulus.** – *At Kerpenhir take a path to the left of the road which climbs up to the tumulus.* A stairway (23 steps) gives access to the funerary chamber and to the dry stone structure forming the tumulus.

Return to Locmariaquer.

★★ **Morbihan Bay by boat.** – A motor-boat service from Locmariaquer makes it possible
⊘ to tour Morbihan Bay and the **Auray River★**.

LOCMINÉ

Michelin map 🔢 fold 3 or 🔢 fold 36

Locminé (*lieu des moines* = place where the monks are) owes its name to an abbey which was founded here in 6C. Only the façades of the twin Church of St-Sauveur (16C) and Chapel of St-Colomban remain; behind is a modern church (1975) built on the site of the nave and aisles.
In the square are two corbelled houses; one is adorned with two wooden statues.

Notre-Dame-du-Plasker. – *To the left of the east end of the modern church.* This 16C rectangular chapel is decorated in the Flamboyant style. Note inside a 16C altarpiece with a Virgin and Child and a 17C altar.

LOCQUIREC

Michelin map 🔢 fold 7 or 🔢 fold 6

Built on a rocky peninsula of the *"Ceinture dorée" (p 21),* Locquirec is a small fishing port and marina as well as a seaside resort.

★ **Church.** – Formerly the property of the Knights of Malta, this charming church has a Renaissance belfry turret. The *placître* – small square *(p 37)* – is covered with early 19C tombstones surrounded by a low-lying hedge of boxwood. The central alley is paved with memorial plaques made of Locquirec stone.
Inside, the panelled vaults of the chancel and transept are covered with 18C paintings. At the high altar is a 16C **altarpiece★** illustrating scenes of the Passion in high relief in a simple style. On the left of the chancel is a niche containing the statue of Our Lady of Succour, flanked by a Tree of Jesse and six low-reliefs depicting the life of the Virgin. At the south transept there is a 15C Trinity. In the nave, spanned by a handsome rood beam, and to the left against the pillar nearest to the chancel, is an alabaster *Pietà.*

★ **Locquirec Point.** – *1/2 hour on foot Rtn.* A walk starting near the church's east end round Locquirec Point offers fine views of Lannion Bay and coastline.

★★ LOCRONAN

Michelin map 🔢 folds 14, 15 or 🔢 fold 18 – Local map p 80 – Facilities

The little town once prospered from the manufacture of sailcloth. Traces of its golden age are to be found in its fine **square★★**, with its granite houses built during the Renaissance, old well, large church and pretty chapel. There are fine houses in the side streets (Lann, Moal, St-Maurice).

The Troménies. – The hill or Mountain of Locronan, which overlooks the town, presents a very original spectacle on days devoted to *pardons,* which are known here as *Troménies.* There are the **Petites Troménies** *(p 226)* when the procession makes its way to the top of the hill, repeating the walk that St Ronan, a 5C Irish saint, according to tradition, took every day, fasting and barefooted.
The **Grande Troménie★★** takes place every sixth year. The next will be in 1989 (2nd and 3rd Sundays in July). This *pardon,* goes round the hill, halting at twelve stations. The circuit follows the boundary of the former Benedictine priory – built on the site of the sacred forest, the "Nemeton", which served as a natural shrine –, founded in the 11C, which was a place of retreat. Hence the name of the *pardon:* Tro Minihy or Tour of the Retreat, gallicized as Troménie.

SIGHTS

★★ **St-Ronan Church and Le Pénity Chapel.** – The accoladed and inter-communicating church and chapel form a harmonious ensemble. *Enter by the main porch.* The 15C church is remarkable for its unity of style and stone vaulting. The decoration of the **pulpit★** relates the life of St Ronan and the 15C **stained glass window★** depicts scenes of the Passion. Among the old statues note that of St Roch (1509). The 16C chapel contains the tomb of St Ronan – its early 15C recumbent statue is one of the first works in Kersanton granite, a 16C Entombment with six figures and on the base two fine **low reliefs★**, and statues of Christ in Fetters and St Michael weighing Souls (15C). From the cemetery behind the church there is a good view of the church's east end.

Notre-Dame-de-Bonne-Nouvelle. – The 16C church is reached by the Rue Moal, which starts from the square and leads down the slope of the ridge. With the Calvary and the fountain (1698) it forms a typically Breton scene. Inside is an Entombment; note also the supporting arch between the nave and chancel and the stained glass windows by Manessier.

St-Ronan Workshop (Atelier St-Ronan). – *At the intersection of the Douarnenez and Quimper roads.* It includes looms, warp beams and a spinning table for hand weaving flax, linen or wool. There are also an exhibition room and a shop.

Craft workshop (Maison des Artisans). – *Place de l'Église.* In the workshop are three hand looms for the weaving of linen. Sculptures on wood and other crafts are also displayed.

Ménez Workshop (Atelier du Ménez). – *On the Châteaulin road.* The different stages of the weaving of wool, linen and silk are demonstrated in this workshop.

Museum. – *On the Châteaulin road.* The ground floor is devoted to the 19C: Quimper faience, sandstone objects, local costumes and recreation of a typical interior. On the first floor the exhibits relate to the *Troménies (see above)* and to ancient crafts. There are also pictures and engravings of Locronan and the surrounding area.

⊙ **Glass works (Verrerie du Ponant).** – *On the Châteaulin road.* A large exhibition hall and a workshop equipped with two ovens where three glass blowers work.

★ **Locronan Mountain**. – *2 km - 1 mile E. Leave Locronan by the Châteaulin road D 7; after 700 m - about 1/2 mile go straight along an uphill road (max. gradient 1 in 9).* This goes along the side of the hill providing views of the bay, Ménez-Hom and the Porzay hollow.

⊙ From the top (289m - 948ft) crowned by a **chapel** (note the stained glass windows by Bazaine) you will see a fine **panorama★** of Douarnenez Bay. On the left are Douarnenez and the Leydé Point; on the right Cape Chèvre, the Crozon Peninsula, the Ménez-Hom and the Arrée Mountains. To the right of the entrance is a granite pulpit.

Kergoat Chapel. – *3.5 km - 2 miles E on the D 7.* The Gothic chapel is dominated by its domed belfry; it has a fine 17C east end. The **stained glass windows★** are old and one shows the Last Judgment (1555).

EXCURSION

⊙ **Ste-Anne-la-Palud.** – *8 km - 4 miles NW. Leave Locronan by D 63 to Crozon. After Plonévez-Porzay, turn left.* The 19C chapel contains a much venerated painted granite statue of St Anne dating from 1548 *(legend p 26).* The *pardon* on the last Sunday in August is one of the finest and most picturesque in Brittany.

LOCTUDY   Pop 3 560

Michelin map **58** fold 15 or **230** fold 32 – Local map p 83

Loctudy is a quiet little seaport at the mouth of the Pont-l'Abbé River and a resort.

Port. – A pretty view of the wooded Island of Garo and, in the distance, the Chevalier Island in the Pont-l'Abbé estuary and Tudy Island and its beach.

Church. – Dating from the beginning of the 12C (except the porch added in 15C, its façade and belfry built in the 18C), this is the best preserved Romanesque building in Brittany. The **interior★** is elegant and well proportioned with its nave, chancel and ambulatory, radiating chapels in pure Romanesque style. Admire the capitals and column bases carved with small figures, animals, scrolls, foliage and crosses.
In the cemetery to the left of the church, near the road, is the 15C Chapel of Pors-Bihan. In front of the church is a Gallic stele 2m - 6ft high surmounted by a cross.

BOAT TRIPS

★★ **Quimper along the River Odet.** – *Description of the tour p 172. Description of* ⊙ *Quimper p 168.*

⊙ **Ile-Tudy.** – Pop 552. *12 km - 8 miles from Pont-L'Abbé.* A pretty fishing port accessible from Loctudy by boat *(passengers and two-wheeled vehicles only).*

Glénan Islands. – *P 102.*

LORIENT   Pop 64 675

Michelin map **63** fold 1 or **230** folds 34, 35

Lorient is at the same time a naval base and a dockyard, a commercial port and one of the few Breton fishing ports to be organized on an industrial basis. The new city bears no comparison with the old one of which 85% was destroyed by wartime bombing and shelling. The fishing harbour is a constant source of entertainment to strollers. The town hosts a yearly Interceltic Festival (Festival Interceltique *p 226*).

HISTORICAL NOTES

The India Company. – After the first India Company, founded by Richelieu at Port-Louis, failed, Colbert revived the project in 1664 at Le Havre. But as the Company's ships were too easily captured in the Channel by the British, it was decided to move its headquarters to the Atlantic coast. The choice fell on an extensive tract of free land on the right bank of the Scorff. The port, warehouses and dwellings erected on this site, took the name of "l'Orient", for the Company's activities were confined to India and China.
In the 18C, under the stimulus of the well known Scots financier Law, business grew rapidly; sixty years after its foundation the town already had 14 000 inhabitants. The loss of India caused the ruin of the Company, and in 1770 the State took over the port and its equipment. Under the Empire it became a naval base.
Despite the loss of monopoly, the company resumed trading in 1785 as the New India Company but ceased its activities in 1794.

The war years. – Lorient was occupied by the Germans on 25 June 1940. As of 27 September 1940 the city was subject to bombardments which intensified, as the war raged on, only to be destroyed in August 1944. The fighting between the entrenched German garrison and the Americans and locally based Free French Forces which encircled the Lorient "pocket" devastated the surrounding area so that when the townspeople returned on 8 May 1945, all that greeted them was desolation.
Today it is a fine modern town, bustling with life and activity due to the naval dockyards, the commercial port and, especially, the fishing port which, after Boulogne-sur-Mer is the largest in France.

SIGHTS

⊙ The Ingénieur-Général Stos-
skopf Submarine Base (Base
des sous-marins) and the
⊙ Dockyard (Arsenal) are not
open to foreigners.

**Keroman fishing port (Port
de pêche de Keroman) (Z).** – Best
seen in the morning at its
busiest. Partly reclaimed from
the sea, the port of Keroman
is the only French harbour
designed and equipped for
fishing from its inception in
1927. It has two basins set at
right angles: the Grand
Bassin and the Bassin Long.
The Grand Bassin is sheltered by a jetty 250m - 265yds
long which is used as a loading and unloading quay for
cargo steamers and trawlers.
The basin has two other
quays, one with a refrigera-
ting and cold-storage plant
for the trawlers and fish
dealers; and the other, as
well as the quay at the east
end of the Bassin Long, where the trawlers unload their
catch. In front of the quays is
the 600m - 650yds long market hall where auctions are
held, and, close behind it, the
fish dealers' warehouses
which open on a railway
platform and lorry loading
bay.
In six bays of the slipway,
trawlers can be dry-docked or
repaired. A large area round
the basins, available for the
industries and commerce
connected with fishing,
completes the zone.
The port of Keroman sends
out ships all the year round
for all kinds of fishing. The
largest vessels go to sea for
a fortnight and carry their
own ice-making equipment
to the fishing grounds.

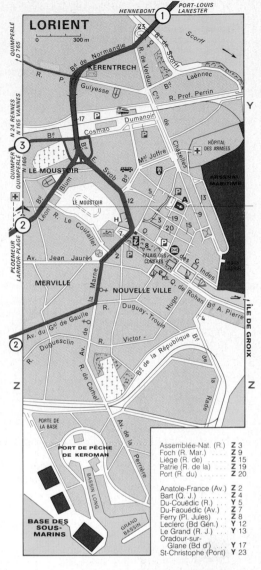

Assemblée-Nat. (R.)	**Z**	3
Foch (R. Mar.)	**Z**	9
Liège (R. de)	**Z**	15
Patrie (R. de la)	**Z**	19
Port (R. du)	**Z**	20
Anatole-France (Av.)	**Z**	2
Bart (Q. J.)	**Z**	4
Du-Couëdic (R.)	**Y**	5
Du-Faouédic (Av.)	**Z**	7
Ferry (Pl. Jules)	**Z**	8
Leclerc (Bd Gén.)	**Y**	12
Le Grand (R. J.)	**Y**	13
Oradour-sur-Glane (Bd d')	**Y**	17
St-Christophe (Pont)	**Y**	23

Notre-Dame-de-Victoire (YZ A). – Better known to the locals as the church of
St-Louis, it stands in the Place Alsace-Lorraine which is itself a successful example
of modern town planning. The church is built in reinforced concrete and has very
plain lines. It is square with a flattened cupola roof and a square tower flanking the
façade.
The whole beauty of the church lies in its **interior★**. Little panes of glass, yellow and
clear, reflect the outside light into the building from the top of the rotunda. Covering
the wall at the back of the high altar is a mural in pastel tones, while in the nave a
striking Entombment in monochrome faces a delicate Annunciation. The Stations of
the Cross drawn in outline only, show each at its most dramatic moment.

EXCURSION

The coast between Scorff and Laïta. – Round tour of 47 km - 29 miles – about
2 1/2 hours. Leave Lorient by ② on the town plan, D 29, passing the Kernével road on
the left.

Larmor-Plage. – Pop 6 381. A popular seaside resort for the people of Lorient.
The church, remodelled between 12 and 17C, contains interesting furnishings: a 17C
altarpiece at the high altar and in the north aisle, at the Jews' altar a Flemish style 16C
altarpiece which vividly portrays forty small figures on the slopes of Calvary; to the
right is a 16C polychrome statue of the Virgin and in the north aisle a 16C *Pietà* in stone.
There are other 16C statues in the chancel and under the porch (the Apostles and Christ
in Fetters).
Every year, on the Sunday before or after 24 June, there is a blessing of the Coureaux
(the channel between the Groix Island and the coast).
By tradition, warships leaving Lorient salute the Church of Our Lady of Larmor with
three guns, while the priest blesses the ship, has the church bells rung and hoists the
flag.

The D 152 from Larmor follows the coast fairly closely, passing many little seaside resorts. Note the kaolin quarries on the right. After Kerpape the drive affords extensive views of the coast of Finistère, beyond the cove of Le Pouldu and over the Groix Island. In the foreground are the coastal inlets in which lie the little ports of Lomener, Perello, Kerroch and Le Couregant and the large beach of **Fort-Bloqué** dominated by a fort. Go through Guidel-Plages on the Laïta estuary. From Guidel make for the St-Maurice Bridge *(6 km - 4 miles Rtn)* over the Laïta. The **view★** up the enclosed valley is magnificent.

From Guidel take the D 306 via Coatermalo and Gestel to Pont-Scorff. At Pont-Scorff take the D 6 towards Quéven and after 2.5 km - 1 1/2 miles turn left.

⊘ **Pont-Scorff Zoo.** – In a woodland setting on the steep banks of the Scarve, a small tributary of the Scorff, the zoo contains many species: lions, tigers, bears, wolves, emus... etc., and several kinds of birds.

Return to Lorient passing through Quéven.

⊘ BOAT TRIPS

★★ **Belle-Ile.** – *P 56.*

Port-Louis. – *Crossing time: 1/2 hour. Description p 165.*

★ **Groix-Island.** – *P 105.*

LOUDÉAC   Pop 10 756

Michelin map 59 fold 13 or 230 folds 22, 23

This little town in the heart of Brittany still holds some large fairs and markets. The region specialises in intensive farming, mainly chicken and pigs, and the countryside is dotted with large hangars flanked with tall silos. Loudéac is also well known for its ⊘ race meetings.

EXCURSION

La Ferrière. – Pop 498. *16 km - 10 miles SW. Leave Loudéac by the N 164, the road to Rennes and after 12 km - 7 miles bear right towards La Trinité-Porhoët and right again 2 km - 1 mile farther on.* In the village stands a vast 14C church with a belfry-porch. Inside, in the chancel is a stained glass window depicting the Virgin (1551); in the north transept a window of the Tree of Jesse of the same date and a granite statue of the Annunciation; in the nave a 16C Crucifixion.
The square opposite the church is adorned with a 15C calvary-cross with four unusual small figures carved on the base.

MALESTROIT   Pop 2 502

Michelin map 63 fold 4 or 230 fold 38

Near the Lanvaux moors, this picturesque town, built along the Oust canal contains interesting Gothic and Renaissance houses.

Old houses. – Half-timbered or in stone these houses are located mostly in the St Gilles' precincts. On Bouffay Square one of the residences has humorous carvings on its façade, another has preserved a pelican in wood. Stroll along Rue au Froment, Rue aux Anglais, Rue des Ponts and the Rue du Général-de-Gaulle.

St-Gilles. – This 12 and 16C church is curious for the juxtaposition of styles and the double nave. Notice the south doorway, with its two doors with 17C carved panels, flanked by massive buttresses adorned with the symbolic attributes of the four Evangelists. The lion of St Mark is mounted by the youth of St Matthew, and St Luke's ox rests on a pedestal adorned with the eagle of St John. About 3pm the shadows of the ox and the eagle between them suggest the well known profile of Voltaire. Left of the high altar is a 16C stained glass window dedicated to St Giles and in the south chapel a 16C *Pietà*.

EXCURSION

St-Marcel. – *3 km - 2 miles W.* A hall next door to the town hall has been turned into ⊘ a **museum of the Resistance** which contains moving mementos of the war in the Morbihan region: documents, equipment, reconstruction of a street in 1944, exhibits evoking the daily life of the Bretons during the Occupation, in the underground movement, etc.

Times and charges for admission to sights described in the guide are listed at the end of the guide.

The sights are listed alphabetically in this section either under the place – town, village or area – in which they are situated or under their proper name.

Every sight for which there are times and charges is indicated by the symbol ⊘ in the margin in the main part of the guide.

La MEILLERAYE-DE-BRETAGNE
Pop 1 074

Michelin map 🔢 fold 17 or 🔢 fold 55

The presence of a nearby abbey did much to stimulate the growth of this town which stands on an eminence near the **Vioreau Forest** (800 ha - 1 977 acres).

⊘ **Melleray Abbey.** – *2.5 km - 2 miles by the D 18.*
Founded in 1142 near a great pool surrounded by trees, that one can admire from the road, this Cistercian abbey has buildings which date from the 18C. The **Church of Notre-Dame-de-Melleray,** completed in 1183, has been restored to its Cistercian severity, including a series of grisaille windows. Note the pointed white stone arches resting on pink granite square pillars. In the flat chevet, the high altar is dominated by a gracious 17C wood polychrome **statue of a Virgin.**
Opposite the entrance avenue there is a curious 15C granite calvary.

Vioreau Reservoir (Grand Réservoir de Vioreau). – *5 km - 3 miles S by the D 178.* This vast reservoir with its verdant banks and sandy beaches attracts sailing enthusiasts. It is linked with several pools and feeds the Nantes to Brest canal.

★★★ MÉNEZ-HOM

Michelin map 🔢 fold 15 or 🔢 fold 18

The Ménez-Hom (alt 330m - 1 082ft), a detached peak at the west end of the Noires Mountains, is one of the great Breton viewpoints and a key position commanding the approach to the Crozon Peninsula. On 15 August a folklore festival is held at the summit.
It is reached after 2 km - 1 mile by D 83, which branches off D 887 between Châteaulin and Crozon, 1.5 km - 3/4 mile after the Chapel of Ste-Marie (p 204), going towards Crozon. Leave your car in the car park.

★★★ **Panorama.** – *Viewing table.* In clear weather there is a vast panorama. You will see Douarnenez Bay, bounded on the left by the Cornouaille coast as far as Van Point, and on the right by the coast of the Crozon Peninsula as far as Cape Chèvre. To the right the view extends to St-Mathieu Point, the Tas de Pois Islands, Penhir Point, Brest and its roadstead, in front of which you will see the Longue Island on the left, the Ronde Island and the Armorican Point on the right, with the estuary common to both the Faou and Aulne Rivers yet which separate as they flow inland. The nearer valley – that of the Aulne – follows a fine, winding course, spanned by the suspension bridge at Térénez. In the distance are the Arrée Mountains, the Mountain of St-Michel crowned by its little chapel, the Châteaulin Basin, the Noires Mountains, the Mountain of Locronan and its chapel, Douarnenez and Tréboul.
Go as far as the mark of the Geographical Institute to get a view of the horizon on all sides. You will then see, in the Doufine Valley, the village of Pont-de-Buis.

MONCONTOUR
Pop 1 015

Michelin map 🔢 fold 13 or 🔢 fold 23

Built in the 11C on a spur where two valleys meet, Moncontour is an old fortified town which retains its imposing ramparts, partly destroyed by Richelieu in 1626. Narrow alleys and picturesque stairways lead to the gateways in the curtain walls.
The Granges Castle, which was rebuilt in the 18C, stands on the top of a hill to the north of the town.

Church of St-Mathurin. – The church, built in the 16C and extensively remodelled in the 18C, has six 16C **stained glass windows★**: those in the north aisle relate in succession scenes from the life of St Yves, St Barbara and St John the Baptist, and in the south aisle, the Tree of Jesse and St Mathurin. Behind the marble high altar (1768), the restored window depicts scenes from the Childhood of Christ.

EXCURSIONS

Notre-Dame-du-Haut Chapel. – *3 km - 2 miles. Leave Moncontour by the D 768 going towards Lamballe. At the crossroads, after the filtering plant, turn right into the D 6 towards Collinée, then right again into the D 6ᴬ, cross Trédaniel and continue straight ahead (calvary on the left) until you reach the chapel at 600m - about 1/3 mile.*
You will see the wooden statues of seven healer-saints: St Mamertus, who is invoked against colic, St Livertin and St Eugenia for headaches, St Leobinus for eye ailments, St Méen for madness, St Hubert for sores and dog bites and St Houarniaule for fear. A *pardon* is held on 15 August.

⊘ **La Touche-Trébry Castle.** – *6 km - 4 miles E. Leave Moncontour by the D 6 the road to Collinée and at Trédaniel, bear left into the D 25.*
Although built at the end of the 16C La Touche-Trébry looks like a mediaeval castle. It stands protected by its defensive walls forming a homogeneous whole, unaltered in character by the restorations that have taken place. Two lodges, standing up against two huge towers, watch over the entrance which consists of a great gate and a postern with wall above.
The courtyard is regular in shape with the main building, with its symmetrical façade, at the far end. On either side, at right angles, are the two wings with pointed roofs; next to them are the outhouses, not so tall but extending all the way to the two lodges at the entrance. In the corners between the main building and the side wings stand four turrets. The towers and turrets all have domed roofs.
Inside the castle, there are some fine chimneypieces.

Michelin map **59** fold 7 or **230** fold 13

Mont-St-Michel, that "wonder of the western world", leaves an indelible memory on every visitor, so individual is its setting, so rich its history and so perfect is its architecture.

Visitors able to do so should try to attend the Feast of the Archangel Michael, which is both religious and popular, held in early autumn *(p 226)*.

Mont-St-Michel is a granite outcrop about 900m - 2 953ft round and 80m - 263ft high. As the bay is already partly filled up *(see Dol Marsh p 92)*, the mount usually stands in the midst of immense sandbanks, many of which are quicksand *(lises).*Under the action of the waves these sands often shift the estuaries along the coast. The Couesnon River which threathened the dykes and polders has been canalized and now runs to the west of the mount. Its original course was to the northwest and initially it formed the boundary between the Duchies of Normandy and

(Christiane Olivier, Nice)

Mont-St-Michel

Brittany. The tides are tremendous, they hold the record for France. There is as much as 14m - 46ft difference in level between high and low tide. As the sea-bed is flat, great tracts of sand are laid bare at low tide stretching for 15 km - 10 miles at the spring tides. The sea comes up very quickly and may be dangerous to careless tourists.

During the very high tides, twice a month and especially at the spring tides, the rising tide is a wonderful sight.

HISTORICAL NOTES

A Masterpiece. – The abbey's origin goes back to the beginning of the 8C when the Archangel Michael appeared before Aubert, Bishop of Avranches, who founded an oratory on the island, then known as Mount Tombe. This was replaced, on what had been renamed Mont-St-Michel, first by a Carolingian abbey and then, until the 16C, by a series of Romanesque and Gothic churches, each more splendid than its predecessor. The abbey was fortified but never captured.

The construction is a masterpiece of skill: granite blocks had to be brought from either the Chausey Islands or Brittany and hauled up to the site which at its crest was so narrow that supports had to be built up from the rocks below.

Pilgrimages. – Pilgrims flocked to the mount even during the Hundred Years War, the English, who held the surrounding region, granted safe conduct, on payment, to the faithful. Nobles, rich merchants and beggars were given shelter by the monks. Hoteliers and souvenir craftsmen prospered even then: pilgrims bought emblems bearing the effigy of St Michael and lead phials which they filled with sand from the beach.

Crossing the bay has its perils and there were deaths among the pilgrims by drowning and sinking into the quicksands so that the mound became known as St Michael in Peril from the Sea.

Decadence. – The abbey declined into a commandery and discipline among the monks became lax – under this system abbots were not necessarily churchmen and did not always supervise the abbey although they took the stipends. In the 17C, the Maurists were charged with reforming the monastery but in fact only made superficial architectural changes.

The conversion of the abbey into a prison in the late 18 and early 19C brought it even lower.

In 1874 the abbey and ramparts passed into the care of the State, which has restored them. Since 1966, religious life has been restored to the abbey.

Stages in the abbey's construction. – The abbey was built in several stages from the 11 to the 16C.

The Romanesque Abbey. – 11-12C. Between 1017 and 1144 a church was built on the mount's summit utilizing the earlier Carolingian building as a crypt (Our Lady Below Ground – Notre-Dame-sous-Terre) and as support for the platform on which stand the three final bays of the Romanesque nave. Additional crypts were built to support the transept arms and the chancel which extended beyond the rock crest. The conventual buildings were constructed on the mount's west slope and on either side of the nave. The entrance to the abbey is on the west side.

The Gothic Abbey. – 13-16C. In these four centuries there were constructed:
– the magnificent Merveille buildings (1211-28), to the north, for the monks, pilgrims and the reception of notable guests;
– the abbey buildings (13-15C), to the south, including administrative offices, the abbot's lodging, and the garrison's quarters;
– the entrance fort and the advanced defences to the east defending the entrance (14C);
– the church's Romanesque chancel which had collapsed was rebuilt (1446-1521) even more magnificently in Flamboyant Gothic style over a new crypt.

Alterations. – 18-19C. In 1780 the final three bays of the nave were demolished together with the Romanesque façade. The present belfry, surmounted by a beautiful spire crowned with a statue of St Michael, dates from 1897 (height: 157m - 516ft).

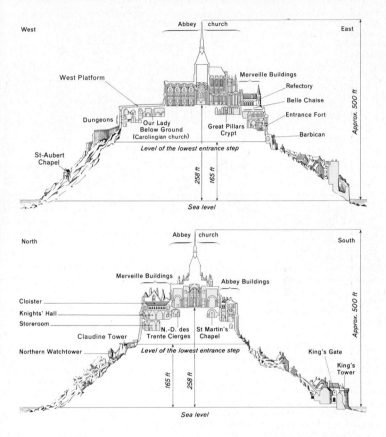

★★★ THE ABBEY

The tour takes you floor by floor through a maze of passages and stairways and not by building or period.

The Abbey's Outer Defences. – The Grande-Rue leads to the Grand Degré, a stairway to the abbey which formerly could be obstructed by a swing door. To the right is the entrance to the gardens and from there a stairway to the ramparts. Go beneath an old doorway arch to a fortified court overlooked by the entrance fort. This consists of two high towers, each shaped like a mortar standing on its breech and linked by battlements – even this military fortification shows the builders' desire for artistry with alternating courses in the wall of rose and grey granite. A staircase called the Escalier du Gouffre (the Pit) because it is steep, dark and roofed by a low cradle vault, starts from this point to the fine Guardroom or Porterie.

The Guardroom or Porterie. – This hall was the focal point of the abbey: indigent pilgrims were directed there before being passed on by way of the Merveille Court to the Almonry; visitors to the abbot and worshippers on their way to the church used the abbey staircase.

The Abbey Steps. – This great stairway (90 steps), which was defended by a 15C fortified bridge, leads from the abbey buildings on the left *(not open)* and the church (on the right) to a terrace in front of the south wall of the church, known as Gautier's Leap (**E**) after a prisoner is said to have hurled himself over its edge. The tour starts here.

The West Platform. – The view from this vast terrace formed by demolishing the last three bays of the church extends over Mont-St-Michel Bay.

★★ The Church. – The east end with its buttresses, flying buttresses, turrets and balustrades is a masterpiece of delicacy and grace. Inside there is a contrast between the simplicity of the Romanesque nave and the elegance and light of the Gothic chancel. The church is built on three crypts which are visited during the tour.

★★★ **The Merveille.** – The name, literally the Marvel, has been given to the superb Gothic buildings on the north side of the mount. The east side of the group, the first to be built from 1211 to 1218, consists from bottom to top of the Almonry, Guests' Hall and refectory; the west side, dating from 1218 to 1228, of the storeroom, Knights' Hall and cloister.

From outside the Merveille is a fortress although its pure and noble lines also give it a religious appearance. Inside, the evolution of the Gothic style is obvious from a simplicity which is almost Romanesque in the lower halls to the total mastery of grace and lightness in the cloister. Intermediary stages can be seen in the elegance of the Guests' Hall, the majesty of the Knights' Hall and the mysterious luminosity of the refectory.

The 3rd floor consists of the cloister and refectory.

★★★ **Cloister.** – The cloister appears as though suspended between the sky and the sea. The colours of the stone add variety to the overall harmony of the intricately carved gallery arcades, each supported on a cluster of five, perfect, small columns. To the right of the entrance is the lavabo (washing-trough) which was used by the monks before meals.

★ **Refectory.** – The first impression is one of disbelief for there is a diffused light throughout although light appears to come only from the two end windows. On entering farther you discover that the architect, without lessening the strength of the walls cut narrow windows at the top of the embrasures, so adding an upper, secondary light.

Old Romanesque Abbey. – The Monks' Walk and part of the dormitory are visited.

Crypt. – Of the three crypts supporting the arms of the transept and the chancel the **Great Pillars Crypt★** (15C) with its ten columns each 5m - 16ft in diameter, is the most impressive.

The 2nd floor consists of the Guests' and Knights' Halls.

★ **Guests' Hall** (Salle des Hôtes). – It was in this elegant and graceful hall 35m - 115ft long divided by slender columns into two aisles and roofed with Gothic style vaulting, that abbots received the kings St Louis, Louis XI and François I, and other important visitors.

★ **Knights' Hall** (Salle des Chevaliers). – The hall's name certainly goes back to the chivalric Order of St Michael founded in 1469 by Louis XI with the abbey as its seat. This vast and even majestic hall, 26 × 18m - 85 × 58ft, divided into four by three rows of stout columns was the monks' workroom. The lower chambers include the Storeroom and the Almonry.

Storeroom (Cellier). – It has two lines of square pillars supporting groined vaulting.

Almonry (Aumônerie). – This Gothic hall is divided into two by a line of pillars which still support the Romanesque vaulting.

Abbey buildings. – Only the guardroom is open.

★★ THE VILLAGE

The Town's Outer Defences. – The outer gate, which is the only breach in the ramparts, opens onto a fortified courtyard. On the left is the 16C burgesses' guardroom, on the right the Michelettes, English mortars captured in a sortie during the Hundred Years War. A second door leads to a second fortified court and a third door dating from the 15C, complete with machicolations and portcullis and known as the King's Gate, since above it was lodged the token contingent maintained on the mount by the King in assertion of his rights. You come out finally into the Grande-Rue. The pretty Arcade House (on the right) was where the abbot's soldiers lived.

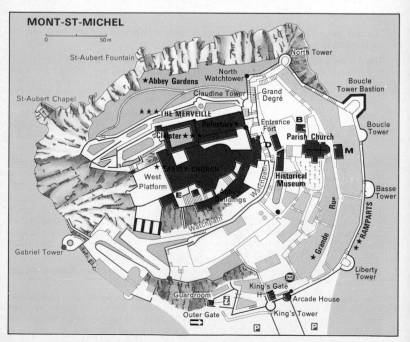

★ **Grande-Rue.** – This narrow uphill main street, lined with 15 and 16C houses and ending in steps, is picturesque and, in the summer, bustling with visitors crowding past the souvenir shops even as it was in the Middle Ages.

★★ **The Ramparts.** – 13-15C. The watchpath commands good views of the bay, particularly from the North Tower.

★ **Abbey Gardens.** –A pleasant and restful walk with a view onto the west face of the ☉ mount and the St Aubert Chapel.

☉ **Historical Museum** (Musée Historique). – On display are wax figures of people who were involved in the history of the mount; a remarkable collection of 25 000 French, English and Dutch **cover plates★**; 15 and 16C alabaster low reliefs and about a hundred copper-plate paintings (15 to 18C). In the garden, a periscope allows you to see the bay up to 30 km - 19 miles.

☉ **Mont-St-Michel Historical Museum** (Musée Historial du Mont) **(M)**. – Photographs, wax figures and dioramas recount the mount's past. A collection of cover plates is exhibited. Periscope.

Parish Church. – This 11C church, the apse of which spans the alleyway, has been greatly restored. Inside are furnishings and a Christ from the abbey. In the south side chapel is a silverplated statue of St Michael. In the chapel to the right of the altar is a 15C statue of the Virgin and in the gallery above are pilgrims' banners.

☉ **Tiphaine's House (B)**. – Du Guesclin, who was commander of the mount, is said to have lodged his wife, Tiphaine (p 86), in this house while he went off to the wars in Spain (see table p 24 giving the Principal Campaigns of Du Guesclin). Fine furniture some of which dates from the 14C.

The Truie-qui-File House (D). – Literally, the House of the Spinning Sow, where the ground floor consists only of a series of arcades.

★★ MORBIHAN Gulf

Michelin map **63** folds 2, 3, 12, 13 or **230** folds 36, 37, 50, 51

The Morbihan Gulf, an inland sea dotted with islands, offers some of the most unusual scenery in Brittany. It has the most delicate light effects, and its sunsets are unforgettable. A visit, especially by boat, is essential for the tourist who appreciates natural beauty.

HISTORICAL NOTES

In 1C BC the Veneti – after whom Vannes is named – lived around the Gulf of Morbihan. They were the most powerful tribe in Armor and when Caesar decided to conquer the peninsula he aimed his main effort at them. It was a stiff task, for the Veneti were fine sailors and had a fleet which made it useless to attack them by land. The decisive struggle, therefore, had to be waged afloat. The Roman leader had a large number of galleys, built and assembled at the mouth of the Loire which were under the command of his lieutenant, Brutus.

The encounter, which took place before Port-Navalo, is said to have been watched by Caesar from the top of the Tumiac hill (p 139). On the other hand, geologists declare that the gulf did not exist at the time of the Gallic War. At all events, it is certain that the battle took place off the southeast coast of Brittany.

The Gauls put to sea with 220 large sailing ships, with high, strong hulls. The Romans opposed them with their large flat barges, propelled by oarsmen. The total and unexpected victory of Brutus was due to several causes: the sea was smooth and this favoured the galleys, which could not face bad weather; moreover, the wind dropped completely during the battle, becalming the Veneti in their sailing ships. Finally the Romans had sickles tied to ropes. When a galley drew alongside an enemy sailing ship, a smart sailor heaved the sickle into its rigging. The galley rowed on at full speed, the rope drew taut and the blade cut the rigging; mast and sails came tumbling down. Two or three galleys then attacked the ship and boarded it.

After this victory Caesar occupied the country of the Veneti and made them pay dearly for their resistance. All the members of their Senate were put to death, and the people were sold into slavery.

GEOGRAPHICAL NOTES

Mor-bihan means "little sea", while Mor-braz means "great sea" or ocean. This gulf, which is about 20 km - 12 miles wide and 15 km - 9 miles deep from the sea to the inner shore, was made by a comparatively recent settling of the land. The sea spread widely over land already despoiled by river erosion leaving, however, inlets and estuaries which run far into the interior, and innumerable islands which give the Morbihan its special character. The Rivers of Vannes and Auray form the two largest estuaries. About forty islands are inhabited; the largest are Arz and Moines Island. The gulf is tidal; at high tide the sea sparkles everywhere around the low, flat and often wooded islands; at low tide, great mud-banks lie between the remaining channels. A narrow channel, before Port-Navalo gives passage both at high and at low tide. A current of up to 8 or 10 knots prevents the gulf from being blocked by silt from the Loire and the Vilaine.

Morbihan is thronged with boats fishing between the islands, as well as with pleasure boats and trading pinnaces using Auray and the port of Vannes. There are many oyster-beds in the rivers and along the islands (p 20).

★★ THE GULF BY BOAT

⊘ The best way to see the gulf is by boat. There are excursions starting from Vannes, Locmariaquer, Port-Navalo or Auray.

Arz Island. – Pop 277. The island 3.5 km - 2 miles long has several megalithic monuments.

★ **Moines Island.** – Pop 588. This former monastic fief is the largest of the Morbihan Islands ⊘ 5.5 km - 3 1/2 miles and the most populous. It is a particularly quiet and restful seaside resort where mimosas and camellias grow among palm trees, lemon and orange trees. Its woods have poetic names; Bois des Soupirs (Wood of Sighs), Bois d'Amour (Wood of Love), Bois des Regrets (Wood of Regrets). The beauty of the island women, often sung by Breton poets, is no doubt responsible for these gallantries.

There are several sights worth visiting: the town with its picturesque alleyways; from Trech Point, north of the island, there is a good view of Arradon Point and Gulf – note the odd-looking Calvary, its base composed of different levels and with stairs on its right side; southwards are the Kergonan semicircle *(cromlech)*, and the Boglieux and Penhap dolmens; and the Brouël Point, east of the Island, affords a view of Arz Island.

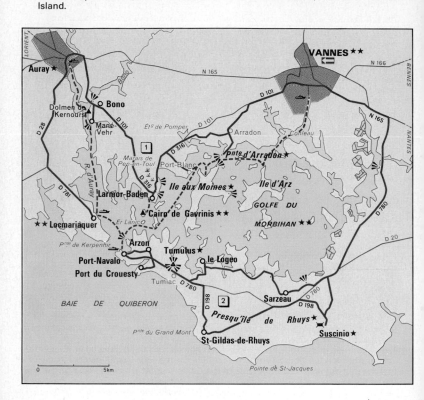

★ THE SHORES OF THE GULF

① From Vannes to Locmariaquer

49 km - 30 miles – about 3 1/2 hours

★★ **Vannes.** – *Time: 2 1/2 hours. Description p 213.*

Leave Vannes by D 101. After 5 km - 3 miles bear left towards Arradon Point. The road skirts Arradon (Pop 2 911 – Facilities).

★ **Arradon Point.** – *Turn left towards the Quarry dock (Cale de la Carrière). From here there is a very typical* **view★** *of the Morbihan Gulf in which you can distinguish, from left to right: the Logoden Islands; in the distance, Arz Island; then Holavre Island, which is rocky and Moines Island. To reach the point take the path bordering the rocks, behind the hotel.*

Turn round and go to Le Moustoir.

After the village of Le Moustoir the D 101 becomes the D 316. At the place called Moulin de Pomper note on the left the old tidal power mill *(p 175).*

Turn left on D 316ᴬ towards Port-Blanc (car parks) where you will embark for Moines Island.

★ **Moines Island.** – *2.5 km - 1 1/2 mile – plus 1/4 hour by boat. Description above.*

The road next skirts the Kerdelan creek (on the left there is a good view of the gulf and, in the distance, of Moines Island), then passes by the Pen-en-Toul marshes on its right.

Larmor-Baden. – Pop 811. A little fishing port and large oyster farming centre. From the port there is a fine view of the other islands and the entrance to the gulf.

★★ **Gavrinis Tumulus.** – *Excursion of 1/4 hour by boat from Larmor-Baden. Description p 102.*

On the left are lovely vistas of the Auray River.

Bono. – Pop 1633. From the new bridge is a picturesque **view★** of Bono, its river and harbour and the old suspension bridge. You will notice piles of whitewashed tiles used to collect oyster spat *(p 69)*. The **church** contains modern stained glass **windows★**

Before taking the new bridge towards Auray, bear left onto a downhill road.

As you leave Kernours, on the right in a small pine forest is a right angled dolmen. On this same road continue to **Mané-Verh** which offers glimpses of the Auray River.

★ **Auray.** – P 52

Leave Auray by ② on the town plan, D 28, then after 8 km - 5 miles take the D 781 on the left. The road skirts megalithic monuments.

★★ **Locmariaquer.** – P 128.

② From Vannes to Port-Navalo and back

79 km – 49 miles Rtn – about 4 hours – Local map p 138

★★ **Vannes.** – *Time: 2 1/2 hours. Description p 213.*

Leave Vannes by ③ on the local map. After St-Léonard, turn right into the D 780. The road runs along the east bank of the bay; there are several viewpoints.

★ **Rhuys Peninsula** (Presqu'île de Rhuys). – At St-Colombier you enter the peninsula, which encloses the Morbihan Gulf to the south. Its flora is reminiscent of that of the south of France.

Sarzeau. – Pop 4443. Facilities. Birthplace of the author Lesage (1668-1747), the satirical dramatist and author of *Turcaret* and *Gil Blas (p 29)*. On the small square, to the right of the church, stand two lovely Renaissance houses.

In Sarzeau go towards Brillac, the road follows the coast for some distance.

Le Logeo. – A pretty little port sheltered by the Gouihan and Stibiden Islands.

Go as far as Le Net and bear right.

★ **Tumiac Tumulus** (or Caesar's Mound). – *1/4 hour on foot Rtn. Leave your car in the car park beside the D 780 and take a dirt track to the right.* From the top of the tumulus there is an extensive **view★** of the gulf, Quiberon Bay and the islands. This was the observatory from which Caesar is supposed to have watched the naval battle against the Veneti *(p 137)*.

Arzon. – Pop 1476. In obedience to a vow made to St Anne in 1673, during the war with Holland, the sailors of Arzon march in the procession of Ste-Anne-d'Auray every year on Whit Monday. Two stained glass windows (1884) in the chancel of the church recount this story of the vow.

Port-Navalo. – A small port and seaside resort. The roadstead is enclosed to the south by a promontory on which stands a lighthouse, and to the north by Bilgroix Point which offers a good **view★** of the Morbihan Gulf *(car park)*. The beach faces the open sea.

Port du Crouesty. – Located on the bay of the same name and southeast of Port-Navalo is this pleasure boat harbour. Alongside it is a large residential complex. The 4 docks are well sheltered and can hold over 1 100 boats. From the tourist car park there is a good view of the site. Fine walk along the quay side.

St-Gildas-de-Rhuys. – P 191.

★ **Suscinio Castle.** – The grandiose ruins of Suscinio stand by the seashore on a very wild site swept by the winds from the sea; at one time the high tide used to fill the moat. The castle was built in the 13C and became the summer residence of the Dukes of Brittany. It was confiscated by François I and used as a grace and favour residence. It was greatly damaged during the Revolution so that now only six of its eight towers remain; the large buildings on the inner court have lost their roofs and their floors and only enormous chimneys are left.

Go over the moat and into the courtyard; you will see the manor house, the bakery and the west wing, reserved for guests. Cross the court diagonally to reach a staircase at the far end, on the right, leading to the north tower (131 steps), from where there is a panorama of the peninsula and Gulf. You can walk along the curtain wall and down a spiral staircase (94 steps) to the manor house.

From St-Colombier return to Vannes by the road by which you came.

★ MORGAT

Michelin map **58** fold 14 or **230** fold 17 – Facilities

Morgat is a seaside resort. The great sandy beach is enclosed to the south by a point covered with pine woods, the Beg-ar-Gador. On the north side, a rocky spur separates the Morgat beach from that of Le Portzic.

The Harbour. – Fishing boats go out from the harbour, sheltering behind a jetty where 400 pleasure craft can also anchor. Morgat offers all types of fishing to the keen sportsman. From the new jetty, there is a good **view** over the cliff, the natural arch or Gador Gate, Douarnenez Bay and the Ménez-Hom.

★ **Big caves.** – The first group of big caves, situated beyond Beg-ar-Gador, includes Ste-Marine and the Devil's Chamber (Chambre du Diable) which communicates through a chimney with the top of the cliff. The second group is at the other end of the bay. The finest grotto is that of the Altar (l'Autel). One of its attractions is the colouring of the roofs and walls.

Small caves. – Small caves at the foot of the spur between Morgat and Le Portzic beaches can be reached at low tide.

Michelin map 🏴 fold 6 or 🏴 fold 5 – Local map p 153

The first thing the tourist will notice at Morlaix is its colossal viaduct. This structure bestrides the deep valley in which lies the estuary of the Dossen, commonly called the Morlaix River. The town is busy but the port, though it is used mostly by yachts, has only limited commercial activity (sand, wood, fertilizers).

Queen Anne's Visit. – In 1505, on King Louis XII's recovery from a serious illness, Queen Anne of Brittany decided to make a pilgrimage to the saints of her duchy. She stayed at Morlaix; as the city then drew great riches from its port, its shipyards and its trade, it received the Queen sumptuously. She was presented with a little golden ship studded with jewels and a tame ermine wearing a diamond-studded collar (the ermine is the emblem of Anne of Brittany). The showpiece of the festival was a live Tree of Jesse representing all the sovereign's ancestors.

If they bite you, bite them! – In 1522 an English fleet of sixty sail came up the river on the tide. The dignitaries of Morlaix were away that day. Pillage followed. But the English troops lingered in the cellars and the citizens had time to come back. They fell on the intoxicated intruders and a hard fight ensued. It was then that the town added to its coat of arms a lion facing the English leopard with the motto: "S'ils te mordent, mords-les!"

To guard against another attack the people of Morlaix built, in 1542, the Bull's Castle at the entrance to their harbour. Louis XIV took it over and made it a state prison in 1660.

Cornic, the "blue" officer. – Cornic was the great Morlaix seaman of the 18C. He began as a privateer; his exploits were such that the King made him commander of a vessel in his Grand Corps. But Cornic was never more than a "blue" officer. Among the officers, those who had been through the Marine Guard school, nearly all noblemen, wore a red and blue uniform: they were the "red" officers. Those who had risen from the ranks wore a blue coat; they were the "blue" officers. He never rose above the rank of lieutenant.

The Revolution did him justice, but too late for him to resume active service.

The Tobacco farm (18C). – There was a tobacco factory founded by the India Company and also a "farm" which had a monopoly of sales. Prices were exorbitant and smuggling thrived. Ships loaded in England with smoking and chewing tobacco and snuff landed on the coast at night. Battles were fought between the smugglers and the farm men.

Morlaix is still a tobacco market. It has a large factory where cigars, cigarillos and snuff are made. Annually it produces approximately 300 million cigars and cigarillos, 50 tons of chewing tobacco and 15 tons of snuff.

SIGHTS

Leave your car in the Place Cornic.

★**Viaduct** (ABY). – From the Place des Otages there is a good view of the viaduct, an imposing two-storeyed structure, 58m - 190ft high and 285m - 935ft long.

Go up the stairs to the right of the viaduct.

On the left is the 16C Hôtel du Parc, an impressive horse-shoe shaped building.

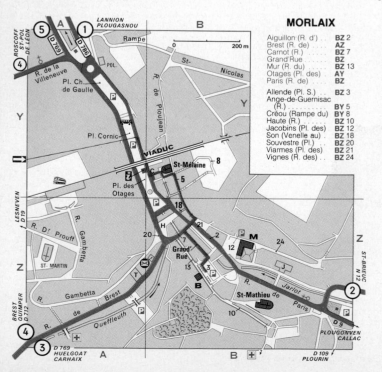

MORLAIX

Aiguillon (R. d')	BZ 2
Brest (R. de)	AZ
Carnot (R.)	BZ 7
Grand'Rue	BZ
Mur (R. du)	BZ 13
Otages (Pl. des)	AY
Paris (R. de)	BZ
Allende (Pl. S.)	BZ 3
Ange-de-Guernisac (R.)	BY 5
Créou (Rampe du)	BY 8
Haute (R.)	BZ 10
Jacobins (Pl. des)	BZ 12
Son (Venelle au)	BZ 18
Souvestre (Pl.)	BZ 20
Viarmes (Pl. des)	BZ 21
Vignes (R. des)	BZ 24

⊘ Ste-Mélaine (BY). – The church is in the Flamboyant Gothic style with an interesting porch on the south side.

Inside, the modern stained glass windows designed by Labouret and the vaulting adorned with carved friezes and tie-beams are noteworthy. A coloured wood panel in the south aisle depicts the Annunciation, the Nativity and the Flight into Egypt while in the north aisle stand the font crowned with a carved wood canopy and a Descent from the Cross.

Rue Ange-de-Guernisac (BY 5). – This street is lined with fine corbelled and half-timbered houses: the Hôtel du Relais de France at No 13 and the houses at Nos 9, 6 and 5 are of interest. Take a look in the picturesque alleyways, Venelles du Créou (BY 8) and au Son (BZ 18).

Bear right into the Rue Carnot (BZ 7).

★ Grand'Rue (BZ). – *Reserved for pedestrians.* Here you will see picturesque 15C houses adorned with statues of saints and grotesques, and low-fronted shops with wide windows *(étal)* especially at Nos 8 and 10. Originally these **old houses** comprised one large central room with skylights on to which opened the other rooms linked by a spiral staircase supported by a fine carved newel post. The museum *(below)* has a fine collection and many illustrations of these houses.

Go round the Place S.-Allende and walk up a few steps leading to the Rue du Mur.

★ Duchess Anne's House (Maison de la Duchesse Anne) (BZ B). – This corbelled mansion is three storeys tall and dates from the 16C. The façade is adorned with statues of saints and grotesques.

★ Museum (BZ M). – The museum is housed in the former church of the Jacobins, which ⊘ has a fine early 15C **rose window★** at the east end. The exhibits include the finds from archaeological digs in the region, mementoes of Morlaix's famous citizens and of Old Morlaix with its houses with skylights.

Also on display are a large collection of 13-17C religious statues, typical furniture of the Léon region (17C), household objects, farming and craft implements, and a collection of **modern paintings★**.

⊘ St-Mathieu (BZ). – The church was rebuilt in 1824 but the tower is 16C. Inside, Doric columns support a flattened vault.

To the left of the high altar is an unusual 16C wood statue of the **Virgin★** which opens. When closed it represents the Virgin suckling the Infant Jesus and open it contains a group of the Holy Trinity. On the shutters are illustrated six scenes from the life of Christ: the Annunciation, the Nativity, the Presentation at the Temple, The Flagellation and the Descent into Hell.

In the north aisle stands a fine 16C wooden statue of Christ with the Virgin Mary and St John the Evangelist.

EXCURSIONS

★ Plougonven. – Pop 3 335. *12 km - 7 miles SE by D 9 towards Callac.*

This village nestling at the foot of the Arrée Mountains has an interesting parish close *(details on closes p 37)*.

The **Calvary★★**, built in 1554, is one of the oldest in Brittany. The cross in two tiers, carries, above, the statues of the Virgin and St John, and, below, two guards; the thieves' crosses stand on either side. At the foot of the main cross there is a Descent from the Cross. On the platform and around the base are scenes depicting various episodes in the life of Christ: the Temptation in the Desert, Christ's Arrest, the Entombment, etc.

The **church,** built in 1523 and badly damaged by fire in early 20C, is dominated by a graceful belfry with a balcony, a turret staircase and striking gargoyles. In front is an ossuary with a trefoil window and a basket-arched doorway.

Ploujean. – *3 km - 2 miles N by ① on the town plan.*

This town situated in the suburb of Morlaix is famous as the birthplace of the poet, Tristan Corbière (1845-1875), and of the first French astronaut, J.-L. Chrétien (24 June 1982).

In the 11C church, remodelled in the 15C, note a fine 15C statue of the Virgin on a pillar in the Romanesque nave.

In the chapel to the right of the chancel stands Marshal Foch's pew which he used whenever he stayed at his nearby estate. There is a monument dedicated to him at the church's east end.

You'll be lost without the Michelin Maps

The Michelin Regional Map Series (1:200 000) covers the whole of France, showing:

- *the road network*
- *the width, alignment, profile and surface of all roads from motorways to footpaths*
- *emergency telephones.*

These maps are a must for your car.

Michelin maps **67** fold 3 or **230** folds 54, 55
See map of the built-up area in the current Michelin Red Guide France

Nantes is the biggest town in Brittany, but it is not purely Breton, for the Loire has always brought French influence with it. It is a city of art, a great industrial centre, a university city and a busy port. Each year, a carnival enlivens the town (p 226).

HISTORICAL NOTES

Nantes, Capital of Brittany. – Nantes was first Gallic and then Roman and was involved in the bloody struggle between the Frankish kings and the Breton counts and dukes. But it was the Normans who did the most damage. In 843 the pirates landed, rushed into the cathedral, where the Bishop was saying Mass, and put the prelate, the clergy and the congregation to death.

In 939 young Alain Barbe-Torte (Crookbeard), a descendant of great Breton chiefs, who had taken refuge in England, returned to the country and drove them out of Brittany. Having become duke, he chose Nantes as his capital and rebuilt it. Nantes was the capital of the Duchy of Brittany several times during the Middle Ages, in rivalry with Rennes. The dukes of the House of Montfort (p 22), especially **François II** governed as undisputed sovereigns and restored the prestige of the town and its title of capital.

Edict of Nantes (13 August 1598). – In 1957, Brittany, tired of disorder and suffering caused by the League and also of the separatist ambitions of its Governor, Philip of Lorraine, Duke of Mercœur, sent a pressing appeal to Henri IV, asking him to come and restore order. Before the castle he whistled with admiration. "God's teeth," he exclaimed, "the Dukes of Brittany were no small beer!" The royal visit was marked by a great historic event: on 13 August 1598, Henry IV signed the Edict of Nantes, which, in ninety-two articles, settled the religious question – or so he thought.

Sugar and "ebony". – From the 16 to the 18C, Nantes had two main sources of revenue: sugar and the slave trade, known discreetly as the "ebony trade". In the Antilles, the slaver would sell the slaves bought on the Guinea coast and buy cane sugar, to be refined at Nantes and sent up the Loire. The "ebony" made an average profit of 200 %. Philosophers inveighed against this inhuman traffic, but Voltaire, whose business acumen is well known, had a 5 000 *livres* share in a slave ship from Nantes. At the end of the 18C the prosperity of Nantes was at its height: it was the first port of France; its fleet included 2 500 ships and barques. The big ship-owners and traders founded dynasties and built the fine mansions on the Quai de la Fosse and the former Ile Feydeau.

It was said of the Nantais **Cassard** (1672-1740) that he was France's "greatest seaman". The daring, skill and luck with which he passed convoys of supplies through the strictest blockade have remained legendary.

All Drowned. – In June 1793, Nantes numbered many royalists. The Convention sent Carrier, the Deputy of the Cantal, there as its representative at the beginning of October. Carrier had already spent some time at Rennes (p 179). His mission was "to purge the body politic of all the rotten matter it contained".

The revolutionary tribunal had filled the prisons with Vendéens, priests and suspects, and a problem arose: how to make room for new arrivals. Carrier chose drowning. Condemned people were put into barges which were scuttled in the Loire, opposite Chantenay. The Convention when informed, immediately recalled its delegate. He was put on trial and was sent before the Nantes Revolutionary court, sentenced to death and guillotined in December.

In 1832 tragedy gave way to farce. The **Duchesse de Berry**, a mortal enemy of Louis-Philippe, was convinced that Brittany was still legitimist and scoured the Nantes countryside. Her failure was complete. She took refuge at Nantes but was betrayed. The police invaded the house and found it empty, but remained on watch. Feeling cold, they lit a fire in one room. Their surprise was great when the chimney-shutter fell open and out on all fours came the duchess and three of her followers, black as sweeps and half suffocated. They had spent sixteen hours in the thickness of the wall.

Development. – The abolition of the slave trade by the Revolution, the substitution of French beet for Antilles sugar cane under the Empire, and finally the increase in tonnage and draught of ships making them unable to reach Nantes were great blows to the town. Nantes abandoned its maritime ambitions and turned to metallurgy and the making of foodstuffs. A manufacturer named Collin developed a method of preserving food which was patented by Appert in 1809.

In 1856 Nantes, again with an eye to the sea, founded an outer port at St-Nazaire; the city then dug a lateral canal in 1892. As of 1911, when dredging techniques had improved, the canal was abandoned and shipping returned to the estuary. Merchant ships of 8.25m - 27ft draught can now come up to Nantes when tides are high.

Nantes today. – Nantes has been completely reconstructed and transformed since the war. An effort was made to preserve the 18C character of its old quarters and the many new buildings have been well incorporated into the town as exemplified by Le Corbusier's living unit (*unité d'habitation*, 1955) at **Rezé**. The east of **Beaulieu Islet** forms a striking contrast with the western section of the harbour populated with cranes, warehouses and popular quarters.

Located on the former **Gloriette Islet (BZ)** are the Faculty of Medicine and Pharmacy. Built on the former **Feydeau Islet (BZ)**, which has preserved its 18C houses, is the large complex *Centre Neptune* with its conference rooms, stores and post office.

The **Place de Bretagne (BY)** in the centre of town, is witness to this change: a twenty-four storey building rises opposite the 1954 Social Security and 1961 Post-Office buildings. To the north of Nantes, on the right bank of the Erdre, is the University campus.

A pedestrian zone, in the Change quarter, includes the Place du Change, Rue des Halles, Rue des Carmes, Rue du Moulin, Rue Ste-Croix and Rue de la Juiverie.

The port. – The port installations in Nantes are managed by the Autonomous Port Authority of Nantes-St-Nazaire. The equipment of the port of Nantes and its subsidiaries – Basse-Indre, Couëron and Paimbœuf – includes 90 electric cranes, 100 000 m² - 24.7 acres of covered area which includes: refrigerated depots, wine warehouses, grain silos, three floating docks and 5 km - 3 miles of public quays.

Imports consist chiefly of hydrocarbons, metallurgical products, phosphates, chemicals, sugar, timber, soya, oilcakes, citrus fruits, early vegetables and wine. Exports include cereals, fertilizers, tinplate and manufactured goods.

You will get a good overall impression of the port's main activities from the quai Wilson at the meeting of the Bras de Pirmil and Bras de la Madeleine.

Beaulieu Islet (AZ). – Arrive on the island by the bridge, Pont Anne-de-Bretagne, an integral part of the port this is the domain of great cranes and dredging companies. Boulevard Léon-Bureau leads to the État railway station and the street, Prairie-au-Duc to the Antilles quay where the banana cargoes are unloaded. At the western end of the island there are great piles of wood – whole tree trunks and planks – heaps of coal and sand, great reservoirs, the fruit and vegetable market, the refrigerated depots and attendant lorries of the firm, Loire-Atlantique, the premises of the General Maritime Company and finally to the south of the station, the great market hall of national importance.

Industrial activity. – The industry of Nantes is considerable: foundries, boiler making and mechanical engineering. There are sugar refineries, canneries and biscuit factories. The local wines, *Muscadet* and *Gros Plant (p 26)* are produced on a commercial basis. The Nantes shipyards specialize in the construction of dredgers, ore-carrying ships, ferry boats, factory ships for the fishing industry and submarines.

The metallurgical industry produces machinery and equipment for oil drilling and refining, for industrial refrigeration, for aeronautics, telephone and electronics.

On the left bank. – Located in the new industrial area, is a power station as well as a paper mill and timber manufacturing.

In the industrial corridor of the Basse-Loire, the Indret workshops specialize in the production of ships' boilers. Paimbœuf turns out chemical products and structural steel.

On the right bank. – The **Basse-Indre** works make tinplate for the canneries; the **Couëron** works handle lead and copper ore. At **Cordemais,** another oil-fired power station can be found. Crude oil is treated at Elf's refinery in **Donges** *(p 92)*.

★★ DUCAL CASTLE (CHÂTEAU DES DUCS DE BRETAGNE) (CY) *time: 1 hour*

The golden age of the castle was the time of Duke François II, when life at the castle was truly royal; five ministers, seventeen chamberlains and a host of retainers attended the Duke. Life was brilliant and very free as to morals. It was thought great fun to rush through all the rooms just after waking time: sleepers were hauled out of bed and thrown into the moat. The Duke himself had to pay a fine to avoid ducking.

The present building was begun by Duke François II in 1466 and continued by his daughter, Anne of Brittany. Defence works were added during the League by the Duke of Mercœur. From the 18C onwards the military took possession, destroyed some buildings and erected others lacking in style. The Spaniards' Tower (1), which had been used as a magazine, blew up in 1800. The north part of the castle was destroyed – *the sites of the destroyed buildings are indicated by a dotted line on the plan on p 144.* From Charles VII to Louis XIV, nearly all the Kings of France spent some time at the castle: in its chapel Louis XII married Anne of Brittany (1499); it was here that Henri IV, in 1598, signed the Edict of Nantes. Chalais, Cardinal de Retz, Gilles de Rais (Bluebeard) and the Duchesse de Berry were imprisoned in its towers.

An arm of the Loire washed the south, east and northeast walls until the building of a quay in the 19C and the filling up in the 20C of a branch of the Loire.

(Madec/Azimut)

Nantes. – Ducal Castle

The Fortress. – Today the moat has been re-established; the ditches which guarded the north and west sides have been turned into gardens and the old ditches have been restored on the other sides. An 18C bridge leads to the former drawbridge which is flanked by two massive round towers dating from the time of Duke François.

The Palace. – Behind the massive defensive wells, the court was used for jousting and tournaments, also for the performance of mystery plays and farces.

The **Golden Crown Tower★★**, a tower with fine Italian style loggias links two windowed buildings.

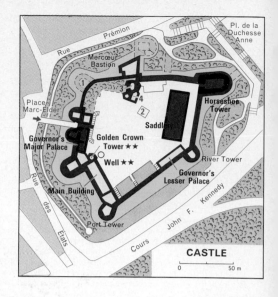

CASTLE
0   50 m

The **Main Building** built by Anne of Brittany, has a bare façade surmounted by five Gothic carved dormer windows. It was used as a dwelling house for men-at-arms.

The **Governor's Major Palace** dating from the late Gothic-Renaissance period is the ducal palace proper. It was rebuilt after the fire of 1684. The basement contained the prisons; on the ground floor are the guardrooms and kitchens; on the first and second floors, the apartments; and in the attics the servants' dormitories.

Over the **well★★** there is a wrought iron framework, once gilded, which represents the ducal crown. The curb of the well has seven pulleys and seven gargoyles for the overflow.

The Renaissance **Governor's Lesser Palace** was built under François I, the military **Saddlery** dates back to 1784.

In the courtyard, near Roman excavations, are traces of the 13-14C castle (2.); the Old Keep (3) is part of an 18C mansion which houses the porter's lodge (4).

The **Horseshoe Tower** is 16C. In the restored rooms, a special lighting enhances the vaulting with armorial decorated keystones. One of the rooms contains contemporary woven works of art (Baran, Buic, Graffin, Sheila Hicks, Claire Ziesler, etc.).

★**Museum of Local Popular Art.** – The museum is located on the 1st floor of the Governor's Major Palace. The collections include a traditional Breton house, with map and models; head-dresses and costumes of all the Breton districts, since the end of the 19C; reconstructions of interiors from Vendée and Guérande. There is also furniture from the Morbihan and Quimper regions (a 1731 wardrobe, box beds, chests, cradles, spinning-wheels).

★**Maritime Museum (Musée des Salorges).** – You will find this museum in the Saddlery building, on the 1st floor, in a large room with fine timberwork. Among the varied exhibits are three 18-19C figureheads; models of 17 and 18C vessels, in particular slave trade boats; fishing boats of many varieties; and 17-19C navigational instruments, as well as relief plans of Nantes through the ages. Documents and small-scale boats recall navigation on the Loire. The traditional trades and industries of Nantes are evoked: posters and labels represent canning and biscuit making alongside examples of printed materials and 16C Croisic pottery.

ST PETER AND PAUL CATHEDRAL
(CATHÉDRALE ST-PIERRE ET ST-PAUL) (CY) *time: 1/2 hour*

This imposing building, begun in 1434 and completed in 1893, is remarkable for its austere façade restored in 1930: two plain towers frame a Flamboyant window; note the 15C canopied niches which decorate the pillars supporting the towers. The three portals reveal finely sculpted recessed arches and on the central portal stands a statue of St Peter. From the north side one can see the chevet with its ring of fine apsidal chapels crowned by graceful pinnacles.

★★**Interior.** – Here, at Nantes, white stone replaces the granite used in purely Breton cathedrals. Being heavy, this stone has made it possible to build vaults 37.50m - 123ft high (the vaulting of Westminster Abbey is 30.50m - 100ft high).

As you enter you will be struck by the nave's pure, soaring lines, a fine example of Flamboyant work. Stand under the organ loft to appreciate the effect; you will see a double row of vertical lines springing from the ground and shooting without a break up to the keystones of the vaults, where they cross; not a single discordant note will check your eye.

Everything is based on elevation and the dimension of 37.50m - 123ft loses significance. Seen from this angle, the slender ribs of the pillars, mask not only the flat wall surfaces that separate them but all the lines, curved or horizontal, of the arcades, the triforium or the upper windows which could break the harmony of this vista, composed entirely of parallel elements.

Go round the building to the right.

In the south transept is the decorative masterpiece of the cathedral and a very great Renaissance work: the **tomb of François II★★**. This tomb was carved between 1502 and 1507 by Michel Colombe, a sculptor who was born in Brittany but settled in the Touraine. It was commissioned by Anne of Brittany to receive the remains of her father, François II, and her mother, Marguerite of Foix, and it was placed in the Church of the Carmelites. The Revolutionary Tribunal ordered it to be demolished, but the courageous town architect of the time, instead of obeying the order, hid various pieces of the tomb in the homes of his friends. It was reconstructed after the Revolution and transferred to the cathedral in 1817.

The Duke and Duchess recline on a black marble slab placed on a rectangular one in white marble. The statues grouped round them are symbolic: the angels supporting their heads represent their welcome to Heaven; the lion couching at the feet of François stands for power, and Marguerite's greyhound for fidelity. The four large angle statues personify the four Cardinal Virtues: for the Duke, Justice (crowned and holding a sword) and Strength (helmed and armed and expelling a dragon from a tower); Prudence and Temperance guard the Duchess. Prudence has two faces: in front, a young girl with a looking glass, symbolizing the future, and behind, an old man representing the past. Temperance holds a bridle to signify control over passions, and a clock representing steadiness.

Below the recumbent figures are sixteen niches containing the statues of saints interceding for the deceased, notably St Francis of Assisi and St Margaret, their patrons. Below these again, sixteen mourners, partly damaged, represent the sorrow of their people.

This magnificent group is lit by a superb modern **stained glass window**, 25m - 80ft tall and 5.30m - 14ft wide devoted to Breton and Nantes saints, the work of Chapuis. The nave and north transept also have modern stained glass windows by Anne Le Chevallier. You should pause at the transept crossing, where the impression of height is astonishing.

In the north arm of the transept is the **Cenotaph of Lamoricière★**, the work of the sculptor Paul Dubois (1879). The General is shown reclining, under a shroud. Four bronze statues represent Meditation and Charity (at his head) and Military Courage and Faith (at his feet). Lamoricière (1806-65), a great African campaigner who came from Nantes, captured the Arabian Emir Abd-el-Kader in 1847 during the wars in Algeria. He later fell into disgrace and when exiled by Napoleon III commanded Papal troops against the Italians. It is the Catholic paladin who is honoured here.

THE TOWN CENTRE   *time 1 1/2 hours*

Follow the itinerary marked on the plan pp 146-147.

Place Maréchal-Foch (CY 68). – Two fine 18C hotels flank the Louis XVI Column which was erected in 1790. From the square, which is prolonged by Cours St-André and St-Pierre, you can readily appreciate the dimensions of the cathedral, in particular its soaring height.

Porte St-Pierre (CY B). – This 15C gateway stands on the remains of a 3C Gallo-Roman wall. The gateway is built into an elegant turreted building which was formerly part of the episcopal residence.

Skirt the façade of the cathedral; go through the portal on the left.

La Psalette. – This 15C building with a polygonal turret formerly contained the chapterhouse but is now part of the sacristy.

Take the vaulted passageway on the right.

From the little square you can see the other side of La Psalette.

Bear right on the Impasse St-Laurent then left into Rue Mathelin-Rodier (the name of which recalls the architect of the cathedral and part of the castle).

It was in the house at no 3 that the Duchess of Berry was arrested *(p 142).*

Pass the Ducal Castle (p 143) on the left.

Ste-Croix Quarter. – It is an area where 15 and 16C half-timbered houses still stand: no 7 Rue de la Juiverie, no 7 Rue Ste-Croix, at nos 8 and 10 Rue de la Boucherie, at no 5 Rue Bossuet and at the Tourist Information Centre of Place du Change.

Ste-Croix (BY). – This 17C church is surmounted by the former town belfry crowned by trumpeting angels. The palm tree decoration of the chancel vaulting contrasts with the round vaulting of the nave. Large Flamboyant windows open onto the aisles. The furnishings are 18C.

★ **The 19C Town.** – It was the financier **Graslin,** Receiver General for Farmlands at Nantes, who was responsible for the creation of this area. By way of the Place du Pilori, surrounded by 18C houses, make for the **Place Royale (BZ 144)**, which was built by Crucy, the architect of the Palais de la Bourse. This is adorned by a fountain representing Nantes (1865).

The **Rue Crébillon (BZ 53)** is narrow, commercial and very busy: the people who stroll along it are said to *crébillonner.*

Opening onto the Rue Santeuil on the left, is a curious stepped shopping arcade, the **Passage Pommeraye★** (BZ 135), built in 1843, which goes down to the Palais de la Bourse. Great fluted columns support a terrace, giving access to the upper level shops and statue adorned pedestals serve as bases for lamps. A humorous note is added by the succession of faces, mice and snails carved on the stair risers.

Return to the Rue Crébillon, passing on your right the **Place Graslin (AZ)** dominated by the Corinthian-style Grand Théâtre (1783). The café on the corner, La Cigale, still has a turn of the century air and fine mosaics. Leading off from the same corner is the **Cours Cambronne★** (AZ) lined with late 18C and early 19C pillared houses.

ADDITIONAL SIGHTS

★★ **Fine Arts Museum** (CY M[1]). – This museum has particularly rich collections of ⊙ Renaissance and 20C paintings.

Of the many paintings on display throughout the patio and the other galleries the most notable works are by the Italian artist Perugino, *Saint Sebastian* portrayed as a page holding an arrow and *Saint Bernard* in the coarse brown tunic of a monk; by Tintoretto a striking *Portrait of a Man;* by Georges de la Tour *Saint Peter's Denial, the Angel appearing to Joseph in his dream, the Hurdygurdy Player;* by Lancret *La Camargo;* by Greuze *Bird Catcher* and Charles *Etienne de Saint-Morges* as a Child wearing a glistening white silk suit; by Ingres *Madame de Senonnes;* and by Courbet *The Winnowers.* In addition the museum also has several Impressionist canvases on display.

The contemporary art galleries include sculptures by the Cubist sculptor Julio Gonzalez *(Dancer),* Esther Gentle Rattner *(Totem 1964)* and Abstract works by Kandinsky, Poliakoff, Georgio di Giorgi.

Other galleries contain works by Maurice Denis, Manessier and Vasarely as well as a variety of 20C works.

★ **Botanical Gardens (Jardin des Plantes)** (CY). – Opposite the mosaic decorated station is this very fine garden which was created in 1805. This well landscaped garden includes, In addition to the masses of white, pink, purple, yellow camellias, magnolias, rhododendrons and splendid trees, several fine ponds and wooden sculpture. A statue of Jules Verne is a reminder that Nantes was the writer's native town.

Immaculée-Conception (CY E). – The former chapter of the Minimes is in an older area of Nantes where 17C porches adorn the houses, and streets narrow to alleys.

It was built in the 15C Flamboyant style by Duke François II. The façade and aisles are 17C and the 19C pulpit has small columns intertwined with a vine and snake. Modern stained glass windows light up the interior.

St-Nicolas (BY F). – The church was built in 1854 in the Gothic style. There are fine views of the church and its tall spire (85m - 279ft tall) from Place Royale and of the east end from Rue Cacault.

★★ **Natural History Museum** (AZ M[2]). – ⊙ Formerly the Mint, this building houses important natural history collections. One section deals with all aspects of shell-fish (variety, beauty of the shells and interesting cross sections), a second has a rich variety of skeletons. On the 1st floor are mostly zoological displays. A vivarium presents numerous reptiles and amphibians from all parts of the world.

★ **Palais Dobrée** (AZ K). – This Roman- ⊙ esque mansion was built in the 19C by the shipowner and collector Thomas Dobrée.

On the ground floor Romanesque and Gothic sculptures and *objets d'art* are presented in a modern setting: with 4 large statues from the cathedral belfry, carved friezes and beams, 13C champlevé enamels from Limoges, reliquary containing the heart of Anne of Brittany and an armoury. On the 1st floor a gallery shows by rotation selections of 16 to 19C engravings and watercolours. Some miniatures and jewels are exhibited in the library; there is a view of Nantes by Parott (1864) in the gallery. In addition there are numerous 15-17C Flemish, Dutch, Italian and 19C French paintings, 16C Flemish tapestries and Breton pottery. The second floor evokes the Vendéen War (1793-5) between the Royalists (Whites) and the Republicans (Blues). Letters, arms, etc., recall this bitter civil war as well as souvenirs of the Duchess of Berry *(p 142),* who attempted to rally the insurrection in its dying stages.

An underground passage housing temporary exhibitions, gives access to the Archaeological Museum *(see p 147).*

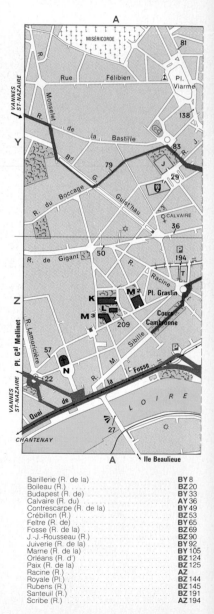

Manoir de la Touche (AZ L). – This the manor of Jean de la Touche or Jean V, a member of the Montfort family, stands alongside the Palais Dobrée. He died here in 1442 in the house which served as a country house for the bishops of Nantes.

Built in the early 15C the manor houses a small museum which contains sections on the ethnography of Oceania, South America (jewels, statuettes and vases) and Egypt (sculptures, sarcophagi, Coptic materials). There is also a display of Greek and Etruscan pottery.

★ Regional Archaeological Museum (AZ M³). – *Enter from the Rue Voltaire.*

A modern building in the Palais Dobrée gardens houses a local prehistory collection. On the first floor the Palaeolithic, Neolithic, Bronze and Iron Ages are described while an exhibition of tools, axes, jewellery and arms demonstrates the relatively slow technical evolution of those times.

The second floor presents an exhibition on art in the Gallo-Roman period, illustrated by sculptures both funerary and mythological, everyday utensils (dishes, glass and ceramic ware) and the typical decorative themes of the times.

Several display cases are devoted to the Merovingian civilization (5-8C AD). The exhibits include bricks from the earliest local Christian basilicas, jewellery and swords.

Notre-Dame-de-Bon-Port (AZ N). – Also known as the Church of **St Louis,** this unusual building overlooks the Place Sanitat. This great cubic mass is adorned by a fresco and a triangular pediment and topped by a majestic dome. Built in 1846, massive hexagonal pillars support the dome decorated alternatively with panels of stained glass and frescoes.

Place Général-Mellinet (AZ). – Eight Charles X (1924-30) mansions border this splendid square.

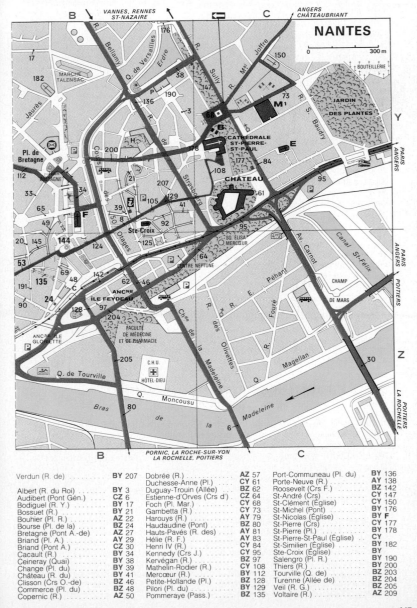

★ **Former Feydeau Islet** (BZ). – Between 1925 and 1938 the islet was linked to the mainland and a second island, Ile Glori-ette, by infilling several arms of the Loire. The islet has retained its 18C aspect, especially between Place de la Petite Hollande and the Cours Olivier-de-Clisson (no 4 was the birthplace of Jules Verne). It was here that rich shipowners used to build their vast mansions which stretch from the central street, Rue Kervégan right back to one of the outer avenues, Allées Turenne or Duguay-Trouin. Curved wrought iron balconies and grotesque masks, probably the work of seafaring craftsmen, adorn the façades. The inner courtyards have staircases with remar-kable vaulting.

Opposite on the northern bank, there are also some fine 18C houses (nos 7 and 11) on **Place de la Bourse** (BZ 24) and its continu-ation, **Quai de la Fosse** (AZ) (nos 17, 54, and 70); no 86 is the Durbe Hôtel, its outbuild-ings served as a warehouse for the India Company.

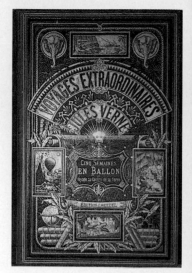

(Jules Verne Museum, Nantes)
Book cover of an original Hetzel edition

★ **Jules Verne Museum.** – *3 Rue de l'Hermitage; access via Quai de la Fosse* (AZ). A 19C mansion houses the museum devoted to Jules Verne (1828-1905), one of the first to write science fiction novels such as *Five Weeks in a Balloon; A Journey to the Centre of the Earth* and *Around the World in Eighty Days.* His life is retraced with the help of memorabilia: autographs, furniture, personal objects, portraits, busts and a collection of his works.

Ste-Anne Belvedere. – *Access is via Quai de la Fosse* (AZ) *and Rue de l'Hermitage.* From the terraced belvedere there is a good view★ of the port installations with cranes in the foreground and shipyards and Beaulieu Islet in the distance. A viewing table helps the visitor to pinpoint Nantes' main sights.

At the end of the Rue de l'Hermitage, after the Jules Verne Museum *(see above)* stands the **statue of Ste-Anne,** blessing the port, which is in a small garden.

Cross the shaded Place des Garennes which is overlooked by the west front of the Church of Ste-Anne and take the Rue des Garennes to reach the Square Marcel-Schwob.

Square Marcel-Schwob. – This garden is dominated by an expressive statue of a Breton woman cursing the sea. One can make out part of the port, the tip of Beaulieu Islet and Rezé.

★ **Erdre Valley.** – By car one can drive along the right bank of the Erdre as far as La Tortière Bridge.

★ **Boat trip.** – *Landing stage: 24 Quai de Versailles (access via St-Michel Bridge)* (BY 176). This is a favourite trip for the Nantais in a pleasantly green countryside dotted with manor houses; the 16C château de la Gacherie with its ornate windows is worth noticing. The Erdre widens beyond Sucé to form a lake, Lac de Mazerolles.

Walkers, campers, smokers
please take care

Fire is the scourge of forests everywhere

★★ NOIRES MOUNTAINS (MONTAGNES NOIRES)

Michelin map 58 folds 16, 17 or 230 folds 19, 20

With the Arrée Mountains *(p 49),* the Noires Mountains form what Bretons call the spine of the peninsula. These two little mountain chains, mainly of hard sandstone and quartzite, are not quite alike. The Noires Mountains are lower (326m - 1 043ft as against 384m - 1 229ft); their crest is narrower; their slopes are less steep and their heaths are less extensive.

The name of the chain suggests that it was once covered with forest. As in all inner Brittany, the ground became bare with time. Since the end of the last century reafforestation has been going on, and the fir woods, now numerous, once more justify the name of Black Mountains.

Quarrying of Breton slate carried out on a large scale in the past, is now concentrated on the eastern end of the chain, in the district of Motreff and Maël-Carhaix. The beds of slate bearing schist are worked by means of shafts sunk to a depth of about 100m - 325ft. The blocks are extracted by modern machinery and brought to the surface. They are cut up by electric saws into approximately the size of slating tiles and stacked in sheds where the "splitters" work with their long steel blades. Machines then cut these leaves into roofing tiles. The Breton slate quarries supply about 5% of French production (those of Anjou 45%).

ROUND TOUR STARTING FROM CARHAIX-PLOUGUER

85 km - 53 miles - allow 1/2 day - local map below

Carhaix-Plouguer. – P 71.

Leave Carhaix-Plouguer W by the N 164 towards Pleyben and after 2.5 km - 1 1/2 miles turn left into the D 769.

The road then enters the picturesque Valley of the Hyères.

At Port-de-Carhaix, after crossing the Nantes-Brest canal, bear right.

1.5 km - 1 mile farther on, note the **Kerbreudeur Calvary** on the left, parts of which are thought to date from the 15C.

St-Hernin. – Pop 765. In this place, where the Irish St Hernin is said to have settled, is a 16C parish close. The church and charnel house were remodelled in the 17C. On the beautiful slender Calvary note St Michael slaying the Dragon.

Return to the D 769 towards Gourin at Moulin-Neuf and bear right.

Slate quarries can be seen to the right and left.

St-Hervé Chapel. – *Access is by a road to the left of the D 769.* This small 16C building with a pierced pinnacle is decorated in the Flamboyant Gothic style. A *pardon* is held on the last Sunday in September.

After crossing the crest of Noires Mountains, the road runs down to Gourin.

Gourin. – Pop 5 186. Once a centre of slate production, Gourin also has white stone quarries and raises horses, cattle and poultry. The 16C church, topped by a pinnacled and domed bell-tower, contains in the south aisle, to the left of the entrance, a 16C *Pietà* in coloured wood.

At Gourin, take the Quimper road, the D 15, and at the bottom of the road bear right into the D 301 towards Châteauneuf-du-Faou.

The road climbs towards the crest of the Noires Mountains.

★ **Toullaëron Rock** (Roc de Toullaëron). – *1/2 hour on foot Rtn; 5 km - 3 miles from Gourin, leave your car and take a stony lane (private property, no picnicking) to the right bordered with oak trees. At the end of the lane, climb up the rock.*

From the top, which is the highest point in the Noires Mountains (326m - 1 043ft), a wide **panorama**★ may be enjoyed in clear weather: to the west is the densely wooded Valley of Châteaulin; to the north, the Arrée Mountains; to the south, in the distance, the Breton plateau slopes gently down to the Atlantic.

Make for Spézet and turn left off the D 117, the Châteauneuf-du-Faou road.

★ **Notre-Dame-du-Crann.** – P 150.

Turn round and bear left on to the D 117 and after 2 km - 1 mile, left again. At the entrance to St-Goazec, turn right.

Gwaker Lock (Écluse de Gwaker). – This is one of the many locks on the Nantes to Brest Canal. There is a pretty waterfall at the end of the large pool, forming a pleasant setting.

After St-Goazec, take the D 36 to the right towards Laz.

The road climbs into the lovely forest of Laz, which is mostly coniferous.

⊙ **Trévarez Forest Park** (Domaine départemental de Trévarez). – This 75 ha - 185 acre forest park surrounding a ruined 19C château, has signposted paths through the woods and a large variety of camellias, azaleas and rhododendrons which are especially beautiful in May and June.

★ **Laz Viewpoint.** – From the car park, there is a splendid view of the Aulne Valley and the Ménez-Hom.

At Laz, turn right towards Kerohan.

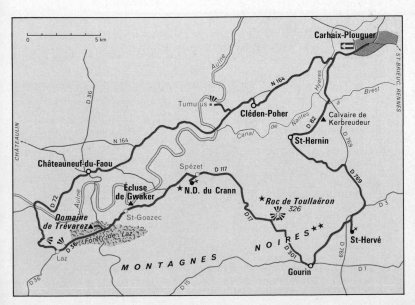

The picturesque downhill road, hemmed in by rocky ridges, affords a fine view over the Aulne Valley.

After Pont-Pol-Ty-Glas, bear right into the D 72 towards Châteauneuf-du-Faou.

The road crosses and then follows the Aulne.

Châteauneuf-du-Faou. – Pop 4 048. This village is built in very pretty surroundings on the slope of a hill overlooking the Aulne. It is an angler's delight with salmon swimming up the Aulne from the sea and also pike. In the church, the baptismal chapel decorated with scenes from the life of Christ in 1919 by Paul Sérusier (1865-1927), a painter of the Nabis group, is of interest. A *pardon* is held on the third Sunday in August at the Chapel of Notre-Dame-des-Portes.

The road from Châteauneuf to Carhaix is charming for the short distance that it follows the Aulne.

After 1.5 km - 1 mile beyond the confluence with the Nantes-Brest Canal, bear left towards La Roche and then right after some 500 m - 1/3 mile.

The road runs past farmyards to a hillock. From the top of the tumulus, there is a fine **view** of a loop of the Aulne.

Return to the road to Carhaix, the N 164.

⊙ **Cléden-Poher.** – Pop 1 118. The village has a **parish close**★ *(details p 37)* dating mainly from the 16C. The 15-16C church contains interesting altarpieces: three Flemish-style 16C panels at the high altar and 17C panelling in the chancel; the altarpiece of the Rosary (1694) in the south aisle; the retable of the Pentecost (17C) in the north aisle. In the cemetery are an ossuary turned into a chapel with an ornamental wooden roof, a Calvary (1575) and two curious sacristies with keel-shaped roofs.

Return to Carhaix-Plouguer by the N 164.

★★ NOTRE-DAME-DE-TRONOËN (Calvary)

Michelin map 🔢 fold 14 or 🔢 fold 31 – Local map p 83

The calvary and chapel of Notre-Dame-de-Tronoën stand beside the Audierne Bay, in the bare and wild landscape of the dunes.

★★ **Calvary.** – *Illustration p 38.* The calvary is the oldest in Brittany. The childhood and Passion of Christ are recounted on two friezes. The intensity and originality of the 100 figures are remarkable. Details of the sculpted figures although worn by exposure, can be justly appreciated. The scenes are depicted in the round or in high relief in a coarse granite from Scaer, which is friable and tends to attract lichen (The Last Supper and the Last Judgement on the south face are greatly damaged). Three scenes, on the north face, are in Kersanton granite: the Visitation, an unusual Nativity and the Magi in 15C vestment. Christ and the thieves are also carved in hard granite.

⊙ **Chapel.** – The 15C chapel has a pierced belfry, flanked by turrets. Beneath the vaulted roof are old statues. The ornate south door opens on to the Calvary. A *pardon* takes place annually *(p 226)*.

★ NOTRE-DAME-DU-CRANN Chapel

Michelin map 🔢 fold 16 or 🔢 fold 19 – 8.5 km - 5 miles E of Châteauneuf-du-Faou – Local map p 149

⊙ The Chapel of Our Lady of Crann known also as Our Lady of the Woods, built in 1532 stands on the side of the road in a verdant setting. There are some remarkable 16C **stained glass windows**★★ in the chapel which has a flat east end.

In the south aisle you will see the window of St Eligius illustrating the legend of the Saint, who is the patron of farriers. In the south transept are the Death and Coronation of the Virgin. Above the south aisle, is the stained glass window of St James Major, in three bays. The window in the chancel depicts scenes of the Passion in twelve bays. Above are the Last Judgment and the Triumph of Christ. The upper part of a window in the north transept shows the Adoration of the Shepherds, and the lower part, the Adoration of the Magi; another, on the right, shows the Martyrdom of St Lawrence in three panels. The window in the north aisle represents the Baptism of Jesus Christ.

The high altar is framed between two niches with **shutters**★ decorated with carvings; that on the left contains a statue of the Virgin Mother; the niche on the right contains a group of the Trinity. A *pardon* is held on Trinity Sunday *(p 226)*.

(Y. Caoudal/Azimut)

Notre-Dame-du-Crann. – Stained glass window

PAIMPOL
Pop 8 367

Michelin map 59 fold 2 or 230 fold 8 – Facilities
See the town plan in the current Michelin Red Guide France

Pierre Loti's novel *Pêcheur d'Islande* (1886 – Fisherman of Iceland) and Botrel's (*p 29*) song the *Paimpolaise* (the cliff mentioned in the song is located near the town, towards Guilben Point) brought to Paimpol both literary fame and popularity. Life has changed a great deal, however, since those days when deep-sea fishing was done off the banks of Iceland. The fishermen now tend to fish along the coast; and the port, large and impersonal, contains mostly pleasure boats. The town retains a certain prosperity as a market for early vegetables. Oyster farming has brought wealth to the region. The *pardon* of Notre-Dame-de-Bonne-Nouvelle takes place on the second Sunday in December.

A **Merchant Service College** (École Nationale de la Marine Marchande) is located in Rue Pierre-Loti.

Place du Martray. – In the centre of the town, the square retains fine 16C houses; note at the corner of Rue de l'Église the house with a square corner turret where Loti used to stay and where Gaud, the heroine of *Pêcheur d'Islande,* lived.

Théodore-Botrel Square. – In the square stand an isolated 18C bell-tower, all that remains of a former church, and a monument to the popular singer Botrel.

⊙**Maritime Museum (Musée de la Mer).** – *Quai Loti.* Paimpol's seafaring activity, from the time of the Icelandic fishing expeditions to the present day, is recalled by models, photographs and navigational instruments.

EXCURSIONS

★★ **Arcouest Point.** – *9 km - 5 miles. Leave Paimpol N by the D 789.*

Kerroc'h Tower. – It stands in a pretty wooded setting. From the first platform there is a fine **view**★ of Paimpol Bay.

Return to the road to Arcouest Point.

Ploubazlanec. – Pop 3 797. In the cemetery is a wall on which the names of men lost at sea are recorded.

At Ploubazlanec, take the road E to Pors-Even.

Perros-Hamon. – Note the small chapel dating from 1770; the west façade is adorned with statues from the former Trinity Chapel and under the south porch is a list of those lost at sea.

Continue in the direction of Pors-Even and bear left at the first junction.

Widows' Cross (Croix des Veuves). – From this spot where sailors' wives awaited the return of boats from fishing expeditions, there is a good **view** of the approach to Paimpol Bay and Bréhat.

Turn back and bear left twice to go down to the harbour.

Pors-Even. – In this small fishing village facing Paimpol lived the fisherman who was Loti's model for Yann in *Pêcheur d'Islande.*

Return to Ploubazlanec and turn right.

★★ **Arcouest Point.** – On the way down to the creek of Arcouest there are remarkable **views** of the bay and of Bréhat at high tide. Each summer the place is invaded by a colony of artists and men of science and letters. A monument – two identical pink blocks of granite set side by side – has been erected to the memory of Frédéric and Irène Joliot-Curie, who were frequent visitors to Arcouest (below the car park, before the Point's larger car park).

★★ **Bréhat Island.** – *From Arcouest Point allow 2 to 4 hours to cross and visit Bréhat. Description p 62.*

★ **The Goëlo Coast.** – *Round tour of 47 km - 24 miles – about 3 hours. Take the D 786, the St-Quay-Portrieux road and on leaving Paimpol, turn left.*

Guilben Point. – This is the cliff mentioned in the song by Botrel (*p 29*). From the point which ends in a long spur cutting the cove of Paimpol in two, there is a lovely view of the coast.

After Kérity, a road to the left leads to Beauport Abbey.

★ **Beauport Abbey.** – The large-scale ruins of the Beauport Abbey, which was founded in
⊙the 13C by the Premonstratensians, stand in an attractive green setting. The abbey passed *in commendam* in the 16C and was sold in 1790 after the last monks left.
Of the 13 and 14C church only the façade, the nave, the north aisle and the north arm of the transept remain. The long chapterhouse with its polygonal apse, lying to the east of the cloister, is an excellent example of the Norman Gothic style. In the northwest corner of the cloister, to the right of the three fine tiers-point arches which stood above the lavabo, is the elegant entrance to the large refectory which looked out over the sea. Pass into the lower court overlooked by the Duc building where lived the monks before the abbey was built, and the cellar underneath the refectory whose pointed vaulting rests on eight massive granite columns.

Return to the D 786 to St-Quay, turn left and past the pool, turn left again into an uphill road.

Ste-Barbe. – The sea can be seen from the small square (*p 37*) of the chapel the porch of which is decorated with a statue of St Barbara. A path, 250m - 820yds farther on takes you to a viewing table from where one can see beyond the meadow, Paimpol Bay and its nearby islands, the oysterbeds, Port-Lazo and Mez du Goëlo Lighthouse.

Leave Ste-Barbe and return to the D 786. At Plouézec, turn left onto the D 77 and left again to Port-Lazo.

Port-Lazo. – At the end of the road *(car park)* there is a view of Paimpol Bay and Lémenez Island.

Return to the D 77, bear left towards Bilfot Point.

★ **Bilfot Point.** – From the viewing table, the **view**★ extends westwards to Bréhat Island and eastwards to Cape Fréhel. Between the small lighthouse at Mez du Goëlo nearby and the Paon lighthouse at Bréhat in the distance the bay is studded with rocks.

Turn back and at the entrance to Plouézec, bear left.

★★ **Minard Point.** – Make for this rocky platform which affords a wide **view** over St-Brieuc bay and Erquy Cape, the Paimpol cove and Bréhat Island.

After a picturesque run along the coast to Le Questel, bear left twice after the hamlet.

Pors-Pin. – A small creek with rocks curiously shaped by erosion.

Return to the first junction and make a left turn.

The road runs along the edge of the bare cliff offering glimpses of St-Brieuc bay and leads to a **belvedere** *(car park)*. The **view**★ extends over the site of Bréhec-en-Plouha, La Tour Point, the St-Quay rocks and the coast from Erquy to Le Val-André.

Bréhec-en-Plouha. – A small harbour sheltered by a dyke and a modest seaside resort at the bottom of a cove bounded by La Tour Point on the right and Berjule Point to the left. St Brieuc and the first emigrants from Britain landed at Bréhec in the 5C *(p 22)*.

Go up the green valley of the Kergolo stream.

Lanloup. – Pop 209. The 15-16C church has an interesting south porch *(details p 35)* flanked by buttresses with niches and with St Lupus and St Giles standing on the pediment. The twelve Apostles, carved in granite, on ornate corbels precede the doorway topped by a 14C Virgin. In the cemetery are a cross (1758) and the tomb of the composer Guy Ropartz (1864-1955) in an alcove to the right of the porch.

Return to Paimpol via Plouézec.

Loguivy-de-la-Mer. – *5 km - 3 miles N. Leave Paimpol by the D 789, then take the D 15 to the left.* This little crustacean fishing port, which has a certain distinction, is simply a creek in which boats are grounded at low tide.
Climb the promontory that encloses the creek on the left to get a view of the mouth of the Trieux River, Bréhat and the many islands.

★ PAIMPONT Forest

Michelin map **59** fold 15 and **63** fold 5 or **230** folds 38, 39

The Forest of Paimpont – the ancient "Brocéliande" where, according to the songs of the Middle Ages, the sorcerer Merlin and the fairy Viviane lived *(details about Merlin and Viviane, p 25)* – is all that remains in the east of the great forest which, in the early centuries of our era, still covered a large part of inner Brittany extending from Rennes to Carhaix, almost 140 km - 85 miles distant. The cutting and clearing that went on for centuries have reduced the forest so that it now only covers an area of 7 067 ha - 27 sq miles where 500 ha - 2 sq miles belong to the state. Recently great areas have been replanted with conifers which will increase the industry of the massif.
A few charming corners remain, especially in the vicinity of the many ponds, where the trees have been left untouched. Such places give us some idea of the forest's former glory.

TOUR

Barenton Fountain. – Water from the Barenton fountain spilling over "Merlin's step" (Perron de Merlin – a stone at the edge of the fountain) was said to unleash wild storms.

Beignon. – Pop 820. The church contains lovely 16C stained glass windows: St Peter crucified (in the chancel behind the altar), Tree of Jesse (north arm of the transept).

Coëtquidan-St-Cyr-Camp. – The camp is located in the south part of the forest; and based in it are: the National Military Academy, the Military Officer's Training School for all services (founded in 1945) and the Cadets Training School: Technical and Administrative Corps (founded in 1977). A wide avenue leads to the school.
⊘ To the right of the Cour de Rivoli, the **Academy Museum**★ (Musée du Souvenir) traces the history of the Military Academy and Officers' Training School: documents and memorabilia.

⊘ **Comper Castle.** – Formerly the property of the Montfort-Lavals' and the Colignys', the castle was said to be the birthplace of fairy Viviane. Twice destroyed, in the 14 and 18C, all that remains of the castle are two curtain walls, the postern gate and a large tower; the main building was restored in the 19C.

Les Forges de Paimpont. – This picturesque village beside a pool gets its name from the forges which were located here from the 16 to late 19C. With the iron ore and wood collected in the area, the forges made a metal of quality.

Fountain of Youth (Fontaine de Jouvence). – This ordinary looking waterhole is said to be a magic fountain.

Merlin's Tomb (Tombeau de Merlin). – Two schist slabs and holly indicate that this is the tomb of the sorcerer.

Paimpont. – Pop 1 449. This market village deep in the forest, near a pond surrounded by great trees, dates from the time of the Revolution. It owes its origin to the foundation of a monastery on the site in the 7C. This became an abbey at the end of the 12C and continued until the Revolution. The 17C north wing of the abbey houses the town hall
⊘ and the presbytery. The abbey **church,** built in the 13C, was altered in the 17C. Inside you will see fine woodwork and a 16C high altar, 15 and 16C statues, in particular

St Judicaël in stone and St Méen in wood. The treasury in the sacristy displays a statue dating from the 15C, of St Anne bearing the Virgin Mary and the Infant Jesus, and a 15C silver reliquary of the arm of Saint Judicaël. There is also a remarkable 18C ivory Crucifix.

Pas-du-Houx Pool (Étang du Pas-du-Houx). – This pool situated in a pleasant spot is the largest of the forest (86 ha - 212 acres). Two châteaux were built on its shores in 1912, that of Brocéliande, in the Norman style and Pas-du-Houx.

⊘ **St-Léry.** – Pop 99. On the south side of the 14C **church** is a Renaissance porch with two elegant basket arched doors surmounted by finely carved ogee moulding. Sculpted figures frame the door on the right: the Virgin, the angel Gabriel, St Michael killing the dragon and a damned person. The door leaves are finely carved. Inside, in the nave, you will find the tomb of St Léry (16C). Across from it is a small low relief carved in wood which describes the Saint's Life. The exquisite Flamboyant chapel in the south aisle is illuminated by a stained glass window (1493) recounting the Virgin's life. A clock may be seen through a glass door under the gallery.

Near the church a 17C house *(now a school)* is ornamented with 3 lovely gables.

⊘ **Trécesson Castle.** – Surrounded by a pool, the castle built at the end of the 14C in a reddish schist has kept its mediaeval aspect. A small gatehouse flanked with corbelled turrets commands the entrance.

Tréhorenteuc. – In the church and sacristy mosaics and paintings illustrate the legend of the Valley of No Return and Barenton fountain. In the chancel there is a stained glass window of the Grail and a painting of the Knights of the Round Table *(p 25)*.

Valley of No Return (Val sans Retour). – A picturesque site. Take the unsurfaced path *(for pedestrians only)* to the Rock of False Lovers (Rocher des Faux Amants – alt 170m - 558ft). It is here that the witch Morgana is said to have entrapped wicked youths.

★★ PARISH CLOSES (ENCLOS PAROISSIAUX)

Michelin map **58** folds 5, 6 or **230** folds 4, 5, 18, 19

Parish closes *(p 37)*, which are a special feature of Breton art, are to be found mostly in Lower Brittany. The route runs through the picturesque Élorn Valley and the foothills of the Arrée Mountains *(p 49)* and includes only a few of the more interesting ones. There are many others, especially that of Pleyben *(p 157)*, further to the south.

ROUND TOUR STARTING FROM MORLAIX

130 km - 81 miles – allow 1 day

★ **Morlaix.** – *P 140.*

    Leave Morlaix by ④ of the local map on the D 712.

★★ **St-Thégonnec.** – *P 203.*

    Go round the east end of the church and bear left.

★★ **Guimiliau.** – *P 111.*

On the outskirts of Guimiliau, before the bridge under the railway, note lower down on your left a fountain decorated with three figures.

★ **Lampaul-Guimiliau.** – *P 123.*

Landivisiau. – *P 124.*

    Take the direction of Landerneau, then turn right to take the intersection at La-Croix-des-Maltotiers.

Bodilis. – Pop 1 504. *Time: 1/4 hour.* The **church**★ (16C) is preceded by a Flamboyant bell tower pierced with three openings at the base. The large sacristy, jutting out from the north aisle, is a 17C addition. It is very handsome, with a roof in the shape of an inverted hull, a richly decorated cornice and buttresses ornamented with niches.

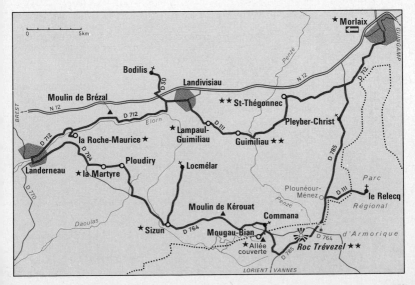

A porch opens on the south side. Inside, the chief **decorations**★ are the carved friezes and gilded altarpieces. The font canopy is carved from Kersanton granite. There is also a colourful Entombment in high relief on the porch wall.

Return to the D 712 and bear right.

Brézal Mill (Moulin de Brézal). – The mill, which has an interesting façade with a Flamboyant doorway, stands in a pleasant setting, near a pool. On the opposite side of the road is the ruined Chapel of Pont-Christ (1533).

After 3.5 km - 2 miles, bear left for La Roche-Maurice.

★ **La Roche-Maurice.** – *P 185.*

Landerneau. – *P 123.*

Leave Landerneau by ② on the town plan, the D 764 towards Sizun.

The road follows a pleasant wooded valley studded with fine rocks.

After 7 km - 4 miles, turn left.

★ **La Martyre.** – Pop 575. *Time: 1/4 hour.* This parish **close**★, the oldest in the Léon region, opens on to a triumphal arch with a Flamboyant balustrade. The ossuary (1619) is adorned with a curious caryatid and macabre motifs. The 14-16C church has a fine historiated **porch**★ (*c* 1450) on its south side. Inside, note the carved friezes, tie-beams, altarpieces and 15C chancel screen. The chancel is lit by 16C **stained glass windows**★. A *pardon* is held on the second Sunday in May and the second Sunday in July.

Ploudiry. – Pop 736. The village, which was formerly the largest parish of the Léon region, has an interesting close. On the façade of the ossuary (1635), Death is depicted striking down men of all social classes. The church, rebuilt in the 19C, retains a fine south **porch**★ dating from 1665. The high altar, behind which should be noted the window of the Passion (17C), and the side altars are good specimens of 17C Breton art.

Return to the D 764 passing through Le Traon, and turn left towards Sizun.

★ **Sizun.** – Pop 1 811. The most interesting features of the **close**★ are the **triumphal arch**★ with Corinthian capitals and the twin-arcaded **ossuary-chapel**★, both dating from the 16C. The 16C church, remodelled in the 17 and 18C, is joined by a passage to the sacristy (late 17C) which stands isolated. Inside, the decoration of the panelled vaulting is remarkable: a sculptured frieze with in the transept and chancel, angels presenting the instruments of the Passion, crocodile-headed tie-beams, keystones and fluting. The organ loft, high altar, altarpieces and font canopy are all 17C.

⊘ **Locmélar.** – *5 km - 3 miles N of Sizun.* The 16-17C **church** has imposing altarpieces and two 16-17C **banners**★. The vaulting is adorned with a frieze and sculptured beams. In the cemetery are an interesting Calvary (1560) and the sacristy with its keel-shaped roof.

Return to the D 764 and continue in the direction of Huelgoat.

⊘ **Kerouat Mill** (Moulin de Kerouat). – *Below the road, to the left.* As part of the Armorique Regional Nature Park scheme *(p 49),* a 19C mill with its house and outbuildings has been restored. In the two water-mills are presented the work done by the miller, his life style, everyday objects and furniture.

Proceed towards Huelgoat and turn left at Ty Douar.

Commana. – Pop 1 174. *Time: 1/4 hour.* The village stands on an isolated foothill of the Arrée Mountains. Within the close is a 16-17C **church**★ with a fine south porch. Inside, there are three interesting altarpieces. Note the **altar**★ to St Anne (1682) in the north aisle and an *Ecce Homo* in wood on a pillar in the transept, to the right. The font is ornamented with five statues: Faith, Hope, Charity, Justice and Temperance.

Mougau-Bian. – Beyond the hamlet, to the right, is a **covered alleyway**★, 14 m long; some of the uprights are carved on the inside with lances and daggers.

Return to the D 764 and bear right; 1 km - 1/2 mile farther on, take an uphill road to the right to join the D 765, the Morlaix road, and turn left.

★★ **Trévezel Rock** (Roc Trévezel). – This rocky escarpment, which juts up on the skyline (365m - 1 197ft), is in a remarkably picturesque spot *(photo p 17)* in a truly mountainous setting. Take the path (1/2 hour on foot Rtn) near a signpost. Go towards the left, cross a small heath, bearing to the right, and make for the most distant rocky point. From here the **panorama**★★ is immense. To the north, the Léon plateau appears, bristling with spires; in clear weather you can see the Kreisker spire at St-Pol-de-Léon and to the east Lannion Bay; to the west, the end of the Brest roadstead; to the south, the St-Michel mountain, and beyond it, the dark line of trees on the Noires Mountains.

Proceed in the direction of Morlaix.

The road passes near the Roc-Trédudon relay tower and offers lovely **views** of the Léon region as it descends.

Near Plounéour-Ménez, turn right.

Le Relecq. – Nestling in the valley, a 12-13C church and the ruins of the monastery buildings are all that remain of the former Cistercian abbey. It is a simple, austere building although the façade was restored in the 18C; note the staircase leading up to the monks' dormitory. To the right of the chancel are statues of St Benedict, ⊘ St Bernard and Our Lady of Le Relecq (15C). Two **pardons** are held every year, Ste-Anne's with a Celtic music concert and that of Notre-Dame-du-Relecq.

Turn back and bear right towards Morlaix.

⊘ **Pleyber-Christ.** – Pop 2 851. It has a small parish close. The Gothic-Renaissance **church** is preceded by a triumphal arch (1921) dedicated to the dead of the First World War. Inside the building, which has fine carved friezes and remarkable beams, are some old pews and a large low-relief of the Last Supper at the high altar. There is a small ossuary to the left of the church.

Continue towards Ste-Sève; after 3.5 km - 2 miles, take the D 712 on the right to return to Morlaix.

★ PENCRAN
Pop 1 062

Michelin map **58** fold 5 or **230** fold 4 – 3.5 km - 2 miles SE of Landerneau

This small village has a fine 16C parish close.

★ PARISH CLOSE *time: 1/2 hour*

Triumphal Arch. – The arch which was added in the 17C is crowned by three lantern-turrets.

★ **Calvary.** – A great cross with two cross-bars framed by the thieves' crosses, set in the wall to the right.

Church. – This rectangular church has an elegant belfry with a double balcony. On the south side of the church is an interesting though weather-beaten **porch★** (1553) with covings adorned with angels and musicians; on the pillars statuettes illustrating scenes from the Old Testament – Noah's Ark is on the right; under the ornate carved canopies, statues of the Apostles.
Inside the church, old statues include a *Pietà* and an Annunciation against the pillars of the nave and St Apollonia in the south aisle. In the chancel, to the left of the high altar is a fine **Descent from the Cross** (1517) in relief and painted wood in the Flemish style.

Ossuary. – It dates from 1594.

★★ PENHIR Point

Michelin map **58** fold 3 or **230** fold 16

Penhir Point is the finest of the four headlands of the Crozon Peninsula *(p 84)*. A memorial to the Bretons of the Free French forces has been erected on the cliff.
Leave the car at the end of the surfaced road. Go on to the platform at the end of the promontory for a view of the sea 70m - 229ft down below. Telescopes. Time: 3/4 hour.
The setting is magnificent as is the **panorama**: below are the great isolated rocks called the **Tas de Pois**; on the left is Dinan Point; on the right the St-Mathieu and Toulinguet Points, the second with its little lighthouse, and at the back the Ménez-Hom. In the distance can be seen on clear days, the Raz Point and Sein Island to the left and Ushant over to the right.
Tourists who enjoy scrambling over rocks should take a path going down to the left of the platform and monument. Halfway down the sheer drop of the cliff there is a view of a little cove. Here take the path on the left which climbs towards a cavity covered with a rock beyond which is the **Chambre Verte**, a grassy strip. From here there is an unusual view of the Tas de Pois and Penhir Point.

★ PERROS-GUIREC
Pop 7 497

Michelin map **59** fold 1 or **230** folds 6, 7 – Local map p 67 – Facilities

This much frequented seaside resort built in the form of an amphitheatre overlooks the fishing and pleasure boat harbour, the anchorage and the two well sheltered beaches of Trestraou and Trestignel. There are gently sloping, fine sand beaches.

⊙**Church (BB).** – A porch with delicate trilobed arches abuts on to the massive 14C belfry topped by a spire. Go into the **Romanesque nave★**, all that remains of the first chapel built on the spot. Massive pillars, cylindrical on the left and with engaged columns on the right, support capitals which are either historiated or adorned with geometrical designs.

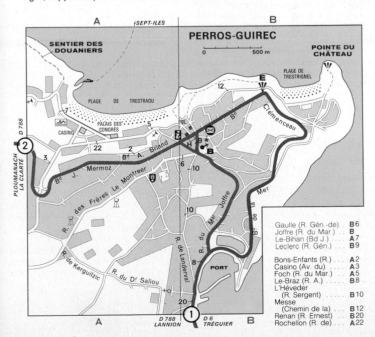

Gaulle (R. Gén.-de) . **B** 6
Joffre (R. du Mar.) . . **B**
Le-Bihan (Bd J.) . . . . **A** 7
Leclerc (R. Gén.) . . . **B** 9

Bons-Enfants (R.) . . . . **A** 2
Casino (Av. du) . . . . **A** 3
Foch (R. du Mar.) . . . **A** 5
Le-Braz (R. A.) . . . . . **B** 8
L'Héveder
  (R. Sergent) . . . . . **B** 10
Messe
  (Chemin de la) . . . **B** 12
Renan (R. Ernest) . . **B** 20
Rochellon (R. de) . . . **A** 22

It is separated by an arch from the Gothic nave built in the 14C at the same time as the chancel. The church has a 12C granite stoup decorated with small figures and several old statues: an *Ecce Homo* and the Christ above the high altar are 15C; St Lawrence and St Catherine, 16C; St James, patron of the parish, 17C. The round-arched south porch is richly ornamented.

Château Point (Pointe du Château). – From this steep little viewpoint, there is a lovely **view★** over the site of Perros-Guirec, the Sept-Iles, Tomé Island and the coast as far as Port L'Épine.

Viewing Table (B E). – A splendid **view★** of the Château Point, the Trestrignel beach, Port-Blanc, Trélevern, Trévou, Tomé Island, the Seven Islands and of the rocks below.

★★ **Ploumanach by the Sentier des Douaniers.** – *3 hours on foot Rtn. Go preferably in the morning at high tide.* Follow, on foot, the edge of the cliff, as far as Pors-Rolland to reach the lighthouse via the Squewel point. *Description of Ploumanach p 159.*

La Clarté. – *3 km - 2 miles W. Leave Perros by ②, D 788.* The pretty rose granite **Chapel of Notre-Dame-de-la-Clarté★** stands 200m back from the D 788. In the 16C the lord of Barac'h, whose ship was in danger in a fog off the coast, vowed to build a chapel to Our Lady at whatever spot on the coast that first emerged from the fog. The promised chapel was built on the height which enabled him to take his bearings; to commemorate the circumstances, it was called Our Lady of Light (Notre-Dame-de-la-Clarté). The south doorway is adorned with sculptures in low-relief: on the lintel, an Annunciation and, *Pietà;* two coats of arms and a Virgin and Child frame the mullioned window in the registry; under the porch are two 17C wood statues and 16C door panels. The tall nave includes three bays decorated with carved roses and foliage; the 15C stoup ornamented with three Moorish heads and the Stations of the Cross by Maurice Denis (1931) are also noteworthy. A *pardon* is held every year *(p 226).*

Take Rue du Tertre which starts on the south side of the chapel, leads to the top of a rocky knoll which affords a good **view★** over Pleumeur and the radar dome, Ploumanach, the Sept-Iles, Perros-Guirec and Château Point.

EXCURSIONS

★ **Signal Station (Sémaphore).** – *3.5 km - 2 1/2 miles W. Leave Perros-Guirec by ②, D 788.* From the roadside belvedere the **view★** extends to the rocks of Plouma-nach, seawards to the Seven Islands and behind to the beaches of Perros-Guirec, and in the distance along the Port-Blanc coastline.

⊘ **Louannec.** – Pop 2 191. *5 km - 3 miles E.* In the church, where St Yves once was the parish priest, to the right of the altar, there is a 15C carved wood group of St Yves. In a glass cabinet is an ancient chasuble (13C) said to have belonged to St Yves.

⊘ **The Seven Islands (Sept-Iles – Réserve Chappelier).** – *Launches leave from Trestraou beach to tour the islands.* The islands became a sea bird sanctuary in 1912.

Rouzic. – *Landing forbidden.* The boat goes near the island, also known as Bird Island where a large **colony★** of gannets, some 4 000 pairs, settle from February to September. One can see guillemots, penguins, brown, herring and great black-backed gulls, puffins, crested cormorants, oyster catchers and petrels which repro-duce in March and leave at the end of July.

(After Baranger/Jacana photo)
Seven Islands. – A puffin

The boat then skirts Malban and Bono Islands.

Monks' Island (Ile aux Moines). – The boat stops at the island *(1 hour)* where you may
⊘ visit the old gunpowder factory, the **lighthouse** (83 steps; range 40 km - 25 miles) which offers a fine panorama of the islands and the coast, the ruined fort erected by Vauban on the far tip and below the former monastery with its tiny chapel and well.

On the return journey, the curious rocks at Ploumanach Point come into view.

PLEUMEUR-BODOU
Pop 3 453

Michelin map 🗐 fold 1 or 🗐 fold 6 – Local map p 67

This village between Lannion and Penvern has given its name to an important earth station for satellite communication, which is situated 2 km - 1 mile to the north.

★ **Space Telecommunications Station of Pleumeur-Bodou (Station de Télécommuni-**
⊘ **cations Spatiales).** – Built at the request of the National Telecommunications Research Organisation (CNET) the station was to play an important role in the first demonstrations of intercontinental television transmission. The first programmes were received via the satellite *Telstar* on the 11 June 1962. A monument in the form of a menhir commemorates the occasion. Isolated on the Breton heath, the equipment is highly impressive: the great white radar dome as high as the Arc de Triomphe of Paris, transmits the necessary waves and houses a 340 ton antenna.

Since 1962 the Centre has expanded and now has five antennae for intercontinental telephone, telegraph and television links through communications satellites 36 000 km - 22 356 miles above the Equator. Inside the radar dome, an exhibition recalls the highlights of telephone communications, of Chappe's telegraph (1792) etc.

★★ PLEYBEN

Michelin map **58** folds 15, 16 or **230** folds 18, 19 – Local map p 50

The great feature of Pleyben is its magnificent parish close *(details of closes p 37)*, built from the 15 to the 17C. *Pardon* on the first Sunday in August.

★★ PARISH CLOSE *time: 1/2 hour*

Enter by a monumental door rebuilt in 1725.

★★ **Calvary.** – Built in 1555 near the side entrance to the church, it was displaced in 1738 and given its present form in 1743. Since then new motifs and scenes have been added to the monument: the Last Supper and Washing of the Disciples' Feet date from 1650. The huge pedestal with triumphal arches enhances the figures on the platform.
To follow the life of Christ start at the corner with the Visitation and move in an anticlockwise direction to discover the Nativity, the Adoration of the Shepherds, etc.

★ **Church.** – The church, dedicated to St Germanus of Auxerre, is dominated by two belfries, of which that on the right is the more remarkable. It is a Renaissance **tower★★** crowned with a dome with small lantern turrets. The other tower has a Gothic spire linked to the corner turret at the balustrade level. Beyond the arm of the south transept is a curious quatrefoil sacristy, dating from 1719, with cupolas and lanterns.
Inside, the nave is roofed with 16C carved and painted **panelling★**, just below it is a remarkable **frieze** *(illustration p 33)* decorated with mythological and religious scenes. At the high altar is an altarpiece with turrets and a two storey tabernacle (17C). At the centre of the east end is a 16C **stained glass window★** depicting the Passion. Note the pulpit, the organ case (1698), the Baptism of Christ over the font and the many coloured statues including St Yves between the rich man and the pauper.

⊘ **Funerary Chapel.** – A former 16C ossuary where exhibitions are held. The façade is adorned with basked-handled twin arches.

PLOËRDUT

Michelin map **59** fold 11 or **230** fold 21 – 7 km - 4 miles NW of Guéméné-sur-Scorff.

⊘ The **church,** (13-17C) has a fine Romanesque nave and side aisles. The rounded arches rest on solid square **capitals★** adorned with geometrical designs. Note the charnel-house abutting the south side of the church, which has a granite enclosure.

EXCURSION

⊘ **Notre-Dame-de-Crénenan.** – *5 km - 3 miles SE towards Guéméné-sur-Scorff.* It has 15-16C features and the tall square belfry dates from the 19C. Inside, the painted vaulting relates scenes from the life of the Virgin and the **friezes** especially show great originality. To the left of the altar is a Tree of Jesse with a statue of Notre-Dame-de-Crénenan, and to the right stand St Anne and the Virgin and Child.

PLOËRMEL

Michelin map **63** fold 4 or **230** fold 38

This little town in the centre of an agricultural area at the limit of Upper Brittany, was once the seat of the Dukes of Brittany and it was from Ploërmel that the Englishman, Bemborough, set out for the Battle of the Thirty (1351) *(p 118)*.

SIGHTS

★ **St-Armel** (Y B). – St Armel, who founded the town in the 6C, is shown taming a dragon which he leads away with his stole.
The church dates from the 16C. The Flamboyant Gothic and Renaissance north **portal★** presents two finely carved doors. Among the scenes depicted are religious (Christ's Childhood, Virtue Trampling on Vice) and comic ones. The Apostles have been sculpted on the door panels.

PLOËRMEL

*If you are puzzled
by an abbreviation or
a symbol in the text
or on the maps,*
look at the key on p 42.

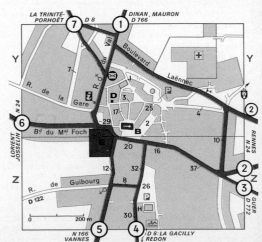

The magnificent 16 and 17C **stained glass windows★** were restored: Tree of Jesse (in the side aisle), life of St Arthmael (in the north transept); there are also modern windows by Jean Bony.

In the chapel to the north of the chancel are white marble statues of Dukes John II and John III of Brittany (14C). In the south transept, behind the Kersanton granite tomb of Philip of Montauban and his wife, is a fine 14C recumbent figure in white marble. Below the wood vaulting and at the top of the wall the frieze is worth noticing *(light switch)*.

Old houses. – In the Rue Beaumanoir, so-called in memory of the hero of the Battle of the Thirty *(p 118)* are to be found (at no 7) the 16C **Marmousets Mansion★** (**Y D**) adorned with woodcarvings, and opposite the 16C former house of the Dukes of Brittany. Other old houses may be seen in the Rue des Francs-Bourgeois.

Ploërmel Religious Order (**Y Z E**). – The order was founded in 1817 by the abbot Jean-Marie de La Mennais (1780-1860), brother of the famous author Lamennais *(p 193)*.

Astronomical Clock (**Y Z E**). – Placed in the inner courtyard of the abbey, it was created between 1852 and 1855 and was intended for the instruction of the future teachers of the coastal schools.

⊙**La Mennais Museum.** – It is housed in one of the community buildings. Note the astronomical clock. The tomb of Father La Mennais is in the chapel.

Duc Pool (Étang au Duc). – *2.5 km - 1 1/2 miles N. Leave Ploërmel by ⑥, on the N 24.* Locally known as "the lake" it is a popular excursion place (with an area of 250 ha - 718 acres). There is an artificial beach and a water sports centre.

PLOUESCAT   Pop 3 957

Michelin map 58 fold 5 or 230 fold 4

In the centre of this little town of the Leon region is a fine 17C **covered market** whose vast roof is supported on splendid beams held up on oak supports.
The indented coastline offers fine sandy beaches: Poulfoën, Frouden, Pors Meur and Pors Guen, and Kernic Bay.

EXCURSIONS

⊙**Maillé Château.** – *4 km - 2 1/2 miles from Plouescat by the D 30 towards Landivisiau.* An alley lined with chestnut and beech trees leads to this larger 17C manor house built in granite and flanked by a square Renaissance wing. The west front has an elegant mansard roof with pediments in the form of a pagoda or scroll.

Kergornadeac'h Castle. – *7 km - 5 miles from Plouescat by the D 10, the St-Pol-de-Léon road, then right towards Moulin-du-Chatel. Turn right by a calvary.* Built in 1630, it is the last fortified castle to have been erected in France. Though it is now in ruins the original square plan with the round machicolated towers at each corner is still evident. The tall chimneys are still standing. There is a small manor house in a verdant setting to the right.

⊙**Tronjoly Manor.** – *7.5 km - 5 miles from Plouescat by the D 10 towards Roscoff and left at Cléder. Beyond the town, an alley marked by two granite pillars leads to the castle.* Go round a farm and into the park. This gracious manor house was built in the 16 and 17C and was made even more attractive by the addition of the tall Renaissance dormer windows. A massive square tower stands in one corner of the main court which is enclosed by the living quarters and a terrace with a stone balustrade.

PLOUGASTEL-DAOULAS   Pop 9 611

Michelin map 58 fold 4 or 230 fold 17

Plougastel is the centre of a strawberry growing district; part of the crop is sent to Great Britain.

★★ **Calvary.** – *Illustration p 38.* Built in 1602-4 to commemorate the end of the Plague of 1598, the Calvary is made of dark Kersanton granite and ochre stone from Logonna. It is more harmonious than the Guimiliau Calvary but the attitude of the 180 figures seems more stiff, less lifelike. On either side of the Cross, the two thieves (do not appear at Guimiliau) are surmounted by an angel and a devil respectively. On the Calvary base an altar is carved; above is a large statue of Christ leaving the tomb.

⊙The **church** is built of granite and reinforced concrete; inside it is brilliant with blue, green, orange and violet all used in its decoration. The furnishings include altars and wooden altarpieces.

EXCURSIONS

St-Jean. – *4.5 km - 3 miles NE by D 29 and 500m - 1/3 mile from the crossroads, a road leading off to the left, then turn right.* The 15C chapel, remodelled in 17C, stands in a **setting★** of greenery on the banks of the Élorn.

★ **Plougastel Peninsula.** – *Round tour of 35 km - 22 miles – about 3 hours.* Lying away from main roads, the Plougastel Peninsula is a corner of the Breton countryside which may still be seen in its traditional guise.
Narrow, winding roads run between hedges through farming country, characteristically cut up into squares. There are few houses apart from occasional hamlets grouped round their little chapels. Here everything seems hidden away; you are deep in the strawberry country, but you will not see the strawberries, which grow in open fields, unless you get out of your car and look through the gaps in the hedges. Vast glassed-in areas shelter vegetables and flowers.

In May and June, however, when the strawberries are picked, there is plenty of life on the roads; often you will come upon lorries fitted with open racks in which the little baskets of strawberries are carefully packed.

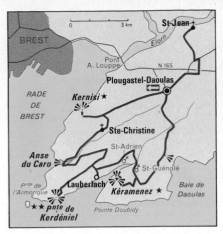

Leave Plougastel-Daoulas by a road to the right of the church; follow the signposts to Kernisi.

★ **Kernisi panorama.** – At the entrance to the hamlet of Kernisi, leave the car and make for a knoll from which you will see a panorama of the Brest roadstead, the outer harbour and town of Brest, the Élorn estuary and the Albert Louppe Bridge.

Turn round and at the second main junction, bear right towards Langristin.

⊙ **Ste-Christine.** – This 16C chapel possesses old statues in the north transept. There is a small Calvary dating from 1587.

Caro Cove (Anse du Caro). – From this pleasant setting, there is a view of Brest and the Espagnols Point, which forms the south shore of the Brest Sound.

Go back in the direction of Plougastel-Daoulas and after 3 km - 2 miles, turn right.

★★ **Kerdéniel Point.** – *1/4 hour on foot Rtn. Leave the car at the bottom of Kerdéniel and after the houses turn right and take the lane on the left (signposts) to the blockhouse.* The view extends from left to right over the Le Faou estuary, the Ménez-Hom, Longue Island, Espagnols Point, Brest and the Élorn estuary, and below, the Armorique Point and Ronde Island.

Continue by car towards Armorique Point to a tiny fishing port in a pleasant setting.

Turn back and after 3 km - 2 miles, bear right.

Lauberlach. – A small fishing port and sailing centre in a pretty cove.

Take the road on the right towards St-Adrien.

From the hillside, the road gives fine glimpses of the Lauberlach cove and passes on the right the St-Adrien Chapel (1549).

Then turn right towards St-Guénolé.

At Pennaster, go round Lauberlach cove. The Chapel of St-Guénolé (1514) stands in a wooded setting on the left side of the road.

At the first junction beyond St-Guenolé, take an uphill road on the right; turn right, then left into a stony lane.

★ **Keramenez Panorama.** – *Viewing-table.* An extensive panorama over the Plougastel Peninsula and the southern section of Brest roadstead.

Return to Plougastel-Daoulas via Lanriwaz.

★★ PLOUMANACH

Michelin map **59** fold 1 or **230** fold 6 – Local map p 67 – Facilities

This little fishing port, well situated at the mouths of the two picturesque Traouiéros Valleys, has become a well known seaside resort, famous for its piles of rose **rocks**★★ *(details p 160).* You will get a good view of them by going to the lighthouse.

(M. Fouorou/Azimut)

Ploumanach. – Municipal park

SIGHTS

Bastille Promenade. – *Entrance opposite the Chapel of St-Guirec.*
This promenade leads to another part of the rocks and gives a better view of the harbour's entrance. On a small island stands Costaeres' modern manor where Sienkiewicz, the author of *Quo Vadis,* used to live.

Beach (Plage). – The beach lies in the Bay of St-Guirec. At the far end on the left, on a rock washed by the sea at high tide, stands the oratory dedicated to St Guirec, who landed here in the 6C *(p 22).* A granite statue of the Saint has taken the place of the original wooden effigy which had suffered from a disrespectful tradition: girls who wanted to get married stuck a pin into his nose.

⊙ **The Lighthouse.** – Go down to the beach, pass in front of

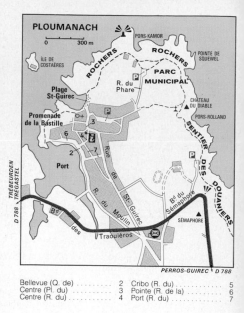

the Hôtel St-Guirec and follow the uphill path to the lighthouse, passing among splendid **rocks★★**. Note the unusual shapes: a skull, a clog turned upside down, a foot. From the platform the view extends from Trégastel to the beach at Trestel and beyond it to the coast towards Port-Blanc, taking in the Seven Islands and the Perros-Guirec Peninsula.

> *Continue past the lighthouse and pass in front of the lifeboat shelter, go round the fence of a villa to reach the municipal park.*

★★ **Municipal Park.** – This park extends from Pors-Kamor, where the lifeboat is kept, to Pors-Rolland. It is a sort of reserve where the rocky site is kept in its original state. The most interesting feature is the Squewel Point, formed of innumerable rocks separated by coves. The Devil's Castle (Château du Diable) also makes a fine picture. The park is studded with curiously-shaped rocks *(illustration p 159):* note a turtle by the sea, and inland, a mushroom, a rabbit etc.

EXCURSION

★★ **Perros-Guirec by the Sentier des Douaniers.** – *3 hours on foot Rtn. Go preferably in the afternoon at high tide.*
A path along the edge of the cliff leads from Pors-Rolland to Trestraou, the main beach of Perros-Guirec *(p 155).*

★ PONT-AVEN   Pop 3 295

Michelin map 58 fold 11 or 230 fold 33

The town lies in a very pleasant setting at the point where the River Aven, after flowing between rocks, opens out into a tidal estuary. The Aven used to drive numerous mills; hence the saying: "Pont-Aven, a famous town; fourteen mills, fifteen houses".
The place has been a favourite resort of painters; the Pont-Aven school, headed by Gauguin, was formed in about 1888. The poet and song writer Théodore Botrel *(p 151)* spent a great part of his life in Pont Aven and is buried here. Botrel started the Gorse-Bloom Festival (Fête des Fleurs d'Ajoncs) *(p 226).*

★ **Bois d'Amour.** – *Access by the Rue de Penanros to the Trémalo Chapel (car-park) or by the Rue de Villemarque.*
All along the way signposts indicate places which inspired painters of the Pont-Aven school. The Bois d'Amour borders the Aven and covers a hill.

The banks of the Aven. – *1/2 hour on foot Rtn. Walk to the right of the bridge towards the harbour.*
Follow the bank of the Aven lined with rocks and ruined water-mills. In the square beside the harbour is a statue of Botrel and on the opposite bank amid the greenery stands the red-tiled house where he lived. About 800 m - 1/2 mile farther on, there is a view of the fine stretch of water.

Trémalo Chapel. – *Leave Pont-Aven by the Rue de Penanros and take an uphill road to the right.*
This characteristic early 16C Breton country chapel is set amid fine trees. It has a lop-sided roof, with one of the eaves nearly touching the ground. Inside is a 16C wooden figure of Christ which was the model for Gauguin's *Yellow Christ.*

⊙ **Museum (Musée de la ville de Pont-Aven).** – *Go through the town hall courtyard.*
Temporary exhibitions are shown in the four galleries (paintings by the Pont-Aven school and sometimes by Gauguin).

(National Museums block)

Breton women by Gauguin

EXCURSIONS

Nizon. – *3 km - 2 miles W. Leave Pont-Aven by the D 24 towards Rosporden.*
The little Nizon church (restored) with its squat pillars dates from the 15 and 16C and contains many old statues. The colours of the stained glass windows by the master glazier Guével are remarkable. The Romanesque Calvary was also used as a model by Gauguin for his *Green Christ*.

From Pont-Aven to Concarneau by the coast road. – *45 km - 28 miles – about 1 1/2 hours. Leave Pont-Aven by the D 783, the Concarneau road and after 2.5 km - 1 1/2 miles, turn left into the D 77.*

⊙ **Névez.** – In the **Ste-Barbe Chapel** there are some old wooden statues, in particular the great statue of St Barbara and her tower.

Beyond Névez, in the direction of Port-Manech, take a road on the left leading to Kerdruc.

Kerdruc. – In a pretty **setting**★ overlooking the Aven, this small port still has some old thatched cottages.

Return to the D 77 and turn left for Port-Manech.

Port-Manech. – A charming resort with a well-sited beach on the Aven-Belon estuary. A path cut on the hillside links the port to the beach and offers fine views of the coast and islands.

Make for Rospico Cove via Kerangall. The rest of the excursion is described in the opposite direction on p 78.

PONTCHÂTEAU   Pop 7 304

Michelin map 🟥 fold 15 or 🟥 folds 52, 53

The church of Pontchâteau, which is perched on a hill in a region of windmills, now no longer in use, overlooks the little town with its houses built in terraces on the banks of the Brivet River.

EXCURSIONS

The Magdalene Calvary. – *4 km - 2 1/2 miles W. Leave Pontchâteau on the D 33 towards Herbignac. Leave the car in the car park on the left side of the road (across from the pilgrimage chapel).*
St Louis-Marie Grignion de Montfort (1673-1716), a famous preacher, had the Calvary built in 1709 on the heath of the same name. Destroyed under Louis XIV it was rebuilt in 1821.
Below the Calvary, a small chapel *(pilgrimages Sundays in summer)* contains the original wooden statue of Christ (1707).
From the Temple of Jerusalem, an alley crosses the park and leads to Pilate's Court or Scala Sancta. It is the first station in the Stations of the Cross which, farther on (on the left) are continued by large white statues derived from the local folklore. From above the Calvary the view extends to the Brière, St-Nazaire and Donges.

The Magdalene Menhir (Fuseau de la Madeleine). – *800m - 1/2 mile. Take the road to the left of the statue of the Sacred Heart, cross the park and bear left at the first crossroads.*
This menhir, 7m - 23ft tall and 5m - 16ft in circumference, stands in the middle of a field.

St-Gildas-des-Bois. – *Pop 3 112. 10 km - 6 miles NE on the D 773.*
The church, formerly a Benedictine Abbey, dates from the 12 and 13C and was remodelled in the 19C. Inside this reddish sandstone edifice are elegant 18C furnishings: choir stalls, 2 stone altarpieces, an interior porch in painted wood and a wrought iron grille which was originally at the chancel. Modern stained glass windows are by Maurice Rocher.

★ PONT-CROIX

Pop 1 842

Michelin map **58** fold 14 or **230** fold 17 – Local map p 80

A small town built up in terraces on the right bank of the Goyen, also known as the Audierne River. Its narrow streets, hemmed in between old houses, slope picturesquely down to the bridge. A great procession take place there on 15 August. Take the Petite and Grande Chère.

★ **Notre-Dame-de-Roscudon.** – The church is interesting with its Romanesque nave dating from the early 13C. The chancel was enlarged in 1290 and the transept was built in 1450 and crowned by the very fine **belfry**★ with a steeple 67m - 223ft high which served as a model for those of Quimper Cathedral. The polygonal apse was rebuilt in 1540. There is an elegant south **porch** (late 14C) with three tall decorated gables.

Inside, the church contains fine furnishings: in the apsidal chapel is a **Last Supper** carved in high relief in wood (17C); on the right of the chancel, the Chapel of the Rosary has fine **stained glass** (c 1540); and In the adjacent Chapel of the Holy Family and the Chapel of the Dead in the north transept are stained glass windows by Grüber (1977-78). The organ loft dates from the 16C.

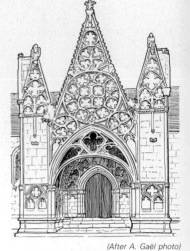

(After A. Gaël photo)

Pont-Croix. – Notre-Dame-de-Roscudon

PONTIVY

Pop 14 224

Michelin map **59** fold 12 or **230** fold 22

This little town stands on the Blavet in a green, pleasant and picturesque area.
The old town, with its narrow, winding streets, contrasts with the geometrical town plan laid out by Napoleon.

Napoléonville. – Pontivy was a prosperous town and in 1790 declared wholeheartedly for the Republic. Napoleon, who was Consul at the time, knew the local feeling and was interested in the position of this city in the centre of the province; he had a barracks, a town hall, a court and a school built and, to ensure communication with the sea, he had the Blavet canalized.

During the wars of the First Empire coastal navigation between Brest and Nantes was very dangerous because of British cruisers in the Channel. Napoleon, therefore, decided to build a canal between the two ports. As Pontivy was about halfway between them, the Emperor also decided to develop it into a town that would be the military and strategic centre of Brittany.

From 1806 the straight roads of the new town could be seen as they were dug out of the ground. The grateful townspeople called the city "Napoléonville". By the fall of the Empire Napoléonville became Pontivy once more. It changed again under the Second Empire to Napoléonville but in due course reverted again.

SIGHTS

★ **Old houses** (Y). – To admire the old half-timbered and corbelled houses of the 16 and 17C, walk along the Rue du Fil, Place du Martray, the centre of old Pontivy, Rue du Pont, Rue du Docteur-Guérin. At the corner of the Rues Lorois and Général-de-Gaulle, note the turreted house (1578), which is presumed to be the hunting pavilion of the de Rohan family, and at Place Anne-de-Bretagne, the elegant 18C buildings.

⊙ **Castle (Château)** (Y). – The castle was built in the 15C. The façade is flanked by two large machicolated towers with pepperpot roofs, all that remains of the four towers of the perimeter wall. The ramparts with walls 20m - 64ft high, are surrounded by a moat, which has always remained dry. The main building, remodelled in the 18C, is adorned with cusped gables and a spiral staircase. The visit includes the guardroom, rooms on the first floor giving on to the wall-walk, the Duke's room with its ornate ceiling and the chapel.

⊙ **Notre-Dame-de-la-Joie** (Y). – The 16C church, built in the Flamboyant style, has in the north chapel, a statue of Notre-Dame-de-la-Joie, venerated by the local people since 1696 when an epidemic decimated the town. There is a 17C altarpiece in the south chapel.

EXCURSIONS

Stival. – *3.5 km - 2 miles NW. Leave Pontivy by ⑥ on the town plan, the D 764 to Guémené-sur-Scorff.*
⊙ The former St Meriadoc Chapel, now the parish **church,** dates from the 16C. The fine **stained glass windows**★ (1552) by Jehan Le Flamant depict a Tree of Jesse at the east end, scenes from the Passion in the south transept, the Baptism of Christ near the font. Note also a 16C Virgin Nursing in the north transept and St Isidore in the south transept. An 18C ciborium crowns the high altar.

PONTIVY

The Michelin Sectional Map Series
is revised regularly.
These maps make
the perfect travelling companion.

★★ **Guerlédan Lake.** – *67 km - 42 miles – about 3 1/2 hours.* Take the D 156 to Guerlédan by the church in Stival (p 162).
The road follows the Blavet Valley. *At Le Corboulo, turn right and 500 m - 1/3 mile farther on, left towards St-Aignan. The rest of the excursion to Guerlédan Lake is described on p 110.*

Blavet Valley. – *Round tour of 40 km - 25 miles – about 3 hours.* Leave Pontivy by ④ on the town plan, the D 768 in the direction of Auray and turn right at Talvern-Nenez.

⊙ **St-Nicodème.** – The 16C **chapel** is preceded by a massive tower with a granite steeple. A Renaissance doorway leading to a 16C staircase opens at the base of the tower which can be climbed. Inside, a frieze carved with angels and musicians runs round the base of the panelled vault.
To the left of the chapel a Gothic fountain discharges into three basins in front of three niches surmounted by richly carved gables. There is a less ornate fountain in front. The presbytery, at the chapel's east end, has dormer windows and chimneys decorated with carvings. *Pardon on the first Sunday in August.*

Turn right after the chapel.

St-Nicolas-des-Eaux. – The little town is built on the side of a hill. With its chapel above the town, surrounded by the thatched roofs of the houses, St-Nicolas-des-Eaux is certainly unusual.
The road crosses the Blavet, and following the tongue of land encircled by the river bends back on itself before crossing to the narrow isthmus which overlooks the inner banks of the loop.

★ **Castennec Site.** – From the turret-belvedere to the left of the uphill road, there is a magnificent view downstream of the valley and from the car park of St-Nicolas-des-Eaux and of the valley upstream.

Turn left after Castennec.

⊙ **Bieuzy.** – Pop 842. The **church** with its high, modern tower looks even taller since it stands on an islet. The tall 16C chevet, marred by a war memorial, has Renaissance Gothic ornament. The stained glass windows form an attractive series and the woodwork and beams are also worth looking at.

To the left of the church, note two Renaissance houses with bread ovens and well. Below, to the right of the road stands a gabled fountain.

Many farms in the area have graceful 17-18C wells which are of interest.

Go to Melrand passing through La Paule.

Melrand. – Pop 1 771. Take the D 142 towards Guémené in order to cross this typically Breton town and reach the Calvary. At the top is the Holy Trinity; the shaft is ornamented with the heads of the Apostles; the base depicts the Entombment and Christ bearing the Cross. The whole stands on another base which bears two more recent statues of the Virgin and St John.

Return to Melrand and follow the D 2 towards Pontivy for 6.5 km - 4 miles then turn left.

⊙ **Quelven.** – The **chapel** was built at the end of the 15C and stands surrounded by old granite houses. The exterior is richly decorated in the Flamboyant style. The stark interior presents a gallery built of stone in the nave, a 16C alabaster low-relief in the south transept, two stained glass windows (16C), including a Tree of Jesse, in the chancel, to the left, and in the south transept.

To the left of the chancel is an opening statue of Our Lady of Quelven showing the Virgin Seated with the Infant Jesus in her lap; it has within twelve low-reliefs relating the life of Christ. A very popular *pardon* is held every year *(p 226)*. Below, 500 m - 1/3 mile to the left of the chapel stands the 16C fountain of Notre-Dame-de-Quelven surmounted by a gabled niche.

To return to Pontivy, take the direction of Gueltas and turn right and after 3 km - 2 miles left into the D 2.

Notre-Dame-de-Timadeuc Abbey. – *22 km - 14 miles – about 1 1/2 hours. Leave Pontivy by the Rues Lorois and Leperdit.*

Ⓥ**Ste-Noyale.** – Standing in the midst of lawns and trees is an elegant 15C ensemble dedicated to St Noyale and a granite cross. The chapel long and narrow, has a finely ornamented south porch and a belfry porch (finished in the 17C). The paintings on the panels inside depict the life of St Noyale.

Ⓥ**Noyal-Pontivy.** – Pop 3 066. The large **church** was built in the 15C and has Flamboyant decoration. The massive square tower set on the south transept is surmounted by a tall polygonal stone spire.

Continue towards Rohan on the D 2.

Rohan. – Pop 518. Formerly a viscounty and later a duchy, the town retains hardly any trace of the rule of the de Rohan family. The Nantes-Brest Canal, the wooded banks, the lock and the Notre-Dame-de-Bonne-Encontre Chapel (1510) make a pretty picture.

2 km - 1 mile beyond Rohan, bear right into the road leading to the abbey.

Ⓥ**Notre-Dame-de-Timadeuc Abbey.** – A Cistercian abbey founded in 1841 in a wooded setting. Slides shown with commentary at the gatehouse.

PONT-L'ABBÉ
Pop 7 729

Michelin map 🗺️58 folds 14, 15 or 🗺️230 folds 31, 32 – Local map p 83

This town, which stands at the head of an estuary, owes its name to the first bridge built by the monks of Loctudy between the harbour and the pond (étang). It is the capital of the Bigouden district which is bounded by the estuary of the Odet, the coast of Penmarch and Audierne Bay. Bigouden costume is most original *(p 26)*, and lends a picturesque note to ceremonies, markets and fairs. The head-dress is frequently worn on weekdays. A local speciality is embroidery on tulle. Dolls in costumes of all the different provinces of France are made here.

Market gardening is the basis of the region's prosperity.

The "Stamped Paper" Revolt (1675). – The glory that Louis XIV won for France cost a lot of money. In 1675 Colbert decreed that all legal acts must be recorded on stamped paper. He also reimposed taxes on tobacco and pewter vessels which Brittany had taken over, a few years before, at a cost of 2 million livres. Anger was great but repression, in the guise of the wheel and the hangman's noose, was powerful; the Parliament that protested was exiled to Vannes. Pont-l'Abbé, in particular, suffered at the suppression of the rebellion; its castle was pillaged.

SIGHTS

Notre-Dame-des-Carmes (B). – Former 14-17C chapel of the Carmelite monastery. On the right going in, at the back of the façade, stands an 18C font. Above the high altar is a 15C stained glass window with a rose 7.7m - 25ft in diameter. To the left is a modern processional banner; in the nave a statue of the Virgin and St John, both of the 16C. As you come out, turn right to go round the church and look at the flat chevet crowned by an unusual domed belfry. *Pardon* on the Sunday after 15 July.

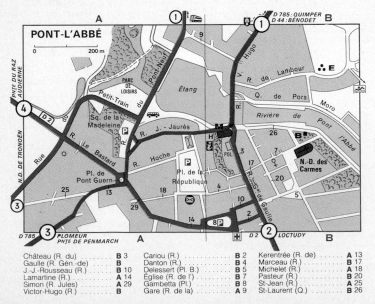

Château (R. du)	**B** 3	Cariou (R.)	**B** 2	Kerentrée (R. de)	**A** 13
Gaulle (R. Gén.-de)	**B**	Danton (R.)	**B** 4	Marceau (R.)	**B** 17
J.-J.-Rousseau (R.)	**B** 10	Delessert (Pl. B.)	**B** 5	Michelet (R.)	**A** 18
Lamartine (R.)	**A** 14	Église (R. de l')	**B** 7	Pasteur (R.)	**B** 20
Simon (R. Jules)	**A** 29	Gambetta (Pl.)	**B** 8	St-Jean (R.)	**A** 25
Victor-Hugo (R.)	**B**	Gare (R. de la)	**A** 9	St-Laurent (Q.)	**B** 26

Castle (B M). – This 14-18C fortress has a large oval tower or keep with a building attached. Go round the tower to see the turret overlooking the Rue du Château. Inside ⊙ the keep you may visit the **Bigouden Museum** housed on three floors (79 steps), which has collections of Bigouden costumes and 19C furniture, models of boats, sailing ⊙ equipment... The tour ends with a visit to a **Bigouden House.**

Bigoudens' Memorial (Monument aux Bigoudens) (B B). – This monument by the sculptor F. Bazin stands in a verdant setting by the quayside.

Lambour Church (B E). – The ruined church retains a fine 16C façade and some bays of the 13C nave. The bell-tower was razed during a peasant revolt *(below).*

⊙ **Notre-Dame-de-Tréminou.** – *2 km - 1 mile W by the Rue St-Jean* (**A 25**). Standing in a shaded close this 14 and 16C chapel (restored) has a belfry which is set above the nave.
Near this chapel, in 1675, the Cornouaille peasants in revolt adopted the "peasant code". Closely linked with the "stamped paper revolt", this mass uprising was severely crushed and many bell-towers in the vicinity were razed to the ground in reprisal. A *pardon* takes place on the first Sunday in August and the fourth Sunday in September.

EXCURSION

Plomeur. – Pop 2 852. *5.5 km - 3 1/2 miles SW. Leave Pont-L'Abbé by* ③, *the D 785.* The Church of Ste-Thumette dates from 1760 and its massive façade is flanked by low turrets. Inside are several 15C statues in the chancel and transept, and a pregnant Virgin in the south transept. At the far end of the nave is a Romanesque capital.

★ **PORNICHET**   Pop 7 284

Michelin map **63** fold 14 or **230** fold 52 – Facilities

Originally a salt marsh workers' village, Pornichet became a much frequented seaside resort in 1860. The town was known as a place of rendezvous for Parisian editors. The beach is the continuation of the 8 km - 5 mile long stretch of fine sand which encircles the Bay of Amour. The town is composed of two distinct quarters: Old Pornichet, to the southeast, which is a busy administrative centre all the year round, and Pornichet-les-Pins to the northwest, with its large villas surrounded by greenery.

Océanides Boulevard. – It runs along the beach, affording good views of La Baule, Le Pouliguen and Penchâteau Point, and leads to the small fishing port and to the pleasure boat harbour, shared also by La Baule, which can take over 1 000 boats. Pornichet also boasts a casino, a thermal treatment centre and the well known racecourse of the Côte d'Amour region created on reclaimed marshland.

PORT-LOUIS   Pop 3 327

Michelin map **63** fold 1 or **230** fold 34 – Facilities

Port-Louis is a small fishing port (tuna) and seaside resort where many of the inhabitants of Lorient may be found. It still has its 16C citadel and 17C ramparts.
Port-Louis was originally called Blavet. During the League the Duke of Mercœur captured it with the help of the Spaniards. Some young girls fled in a ship, but the Spaniards saw them and gave chase. Rather than be taken by them, the "forty virgins of Port-Louis" joined hands and jumped into the sea.
It was under Louis XIII that Blavet took the name of Port-Louis in honour of the King. Richelieu made it a fortified port and the headquarters of the first India Company *(p 130),* which failed. When Colbert founded the second Company, Lorient was built to receive it. From that time on, Port-Louis declined. Under Louis-Philippe the town found new life in sardine fishing and canning.

★ **Citadel.** – The citadel is at the entrance to the Lorient roadstead. Its construction ⊙ occured in different stages: in 1591, during the Spanish occupation by Juan del Aguila; continued in 1616-1622 by Marshal Brissac and completed in 1636 under Richelieu. Built on a rectangular plan the citadel is bastioned at the corners and sides; 2 bridges and a demilune protect the entrance. The citadel has always been a prison – among its "occupants" was Louis Napoleon, the son of Emperor Napoleon III.
A signposted path directs you to the parapet walk (note the cannons facing Groix Island) which looks onto two courtyards and the different parts of the edifice of which some contain museums.

Museum of Port-Louis. – In the entrance pavilion or keep. Exhibits trace the town's maritime past and the citadel's history.

★ **Arsenal Museum.** – Housed in the Arsenal, in a room which has fine woodwork, ship's ⊙ models (corvettes, frigates, merchant ships, cruisers, etc.), portraits of seamen, paintings and documents pertaining to navigation on the Atlantic are on display.

Powder Factory. – The former Powder Factory contains 17 to 20C arms (torpedoes, mines, mortars, etc.) and documents on naval artillery.

Sea Rescue Centre. – *In the ramparts, to the right of the Powder Factory.*
This display area devoted to sea rescue presents old and modern equipment, as well as the lifeboat used between 1897 and 1939 at Roscoff.

★★ **India Company Museum.** – Housed in the northwest wing of the Lourmel barracks, the museum traces the history of this prestigious company *(p 130)* by means of documents relating to the crews and cargoes, models of the principal ships, porcelain, silks, and mementoes of the trading posts. In the basement, there is an audio-visual presentation.

Museum of Coastal Fishing. – In a large room in the southwest wing of the Lourmel barracks are exhibited coastal fishing (the Channel, Atlantic Ocean) vessels as well as sailing boats used in regattas in the first half of the 20C.

Ramparts. – Built between 1649 and 1653 by Marshal Meilleraye, these ramparts envelop the town on two sides. On the Promenade des Pâtis a door in the wall leads to a fine sandy beach from where there is a pleasant view onto Gâvres Point, Groix Island, Larmor-Plage beach and the citadel's Groix bastion, named as such because it is across from Groix Island.

Ports. – The town has two ports: La Pointe, across from Lorient and Locmalo in the Gâvres cove.

★ Le POULIGUEN   Pop 4 488

Michelin map **63** fold 14 or **230** fold 51 – Local map p 108

Lying to the west of La Baule, it is separated from the latter by a channel (étier), spanned by two bridges, linking the ocean to the salt marshes behind the town. This former fisher village with narrow streets became a fashionable resort in 1854. The beach is sheltered by a pleasant 6 ha - 15 acre wood and the pleasure boat harbour is upstream from La Baule's.

⊙ **Ste-Anne-et-St-Julien.** – Place Mgr-Freppel. Standing near a Calvary, this Gothic chapel has a 16C **statue of St Anne** with the Virgin and the Infant Jesus in the south aisle, and a stained glass window representing St Julien (in the chancel). At the west end, on either side of the porch are two fine **alabaster panels** depicting the Coronation of Christ and the Presentation in the Temple.

★ **The Côte Sauvage.** – This stretch of coast goes from the Points of Penchâteau to Le Croisic. Skirted by boulevards and footpaths, the coastline alternates rocky parts with great sandy bays and has numerous caves which are accessible only at low tide.

QUESTEMBERT   Pop 5 213

Michelin map **63** fold 4 or **230** folds 37, 38

A small friendly town located in a verdant countryside. Around the marketplace (halles) stand elegant granite town houses (16-17C) with carved pediments. In the Rue St-Michel, in a garden, is an odd-looking turret, the roof of which is held up by two carved busts of Questembert and his wife (see House of Vannes p 214).

Marketplace (Halles). – Built in 1552 and restored in 1675. The remarkable timberwork covers the three alleys.

St-Michel. – This small 16C chapel stands in the cemetery. On the north side is a Calvary: at its base several scenes of Christ's Life; at its summit a Crucifix and a Pietà. This monument as well as the one built on the Place du Monument recalls the victory of Alain-le-Grand over the Normans in 888 at Coët-Bihan (6.5 km - 4 miles southeast of Questembert).

EXCURSION

Notre-Dame-des-Vertus. – 6.5 km - 4 miles SW on the D 7. This 15-16C chapel dedicated to Our Lady of Virtue is located beside the road near a farm. Note the portal with double basket arched windows, on the south side brackets carved in the shape of animals or figures support the ogee shaped mouldings of the door and windows. The Flamboyant bay is at the chevet. A pardon is held the Sunday after 15 August.

★ QUIBERON Peninsula

Michelin map **63** folds 11, 12 or **230** folds 35, 49

This former island is now attached to the mainland by a narrow isthmus. This natural jetty acts as a breakwater for a great bay which is often used by warships for exercises and firing practice (Polygone de Gâvres).
The landscape of the peninsula varies; the sand dunes of the isthmus are fixed by maritime pines. The ocean coast, known as the "Wild Coast" (Côte Sauvage), is an impressive jumble of cliffs, rocks, caves and reefs; to the east and south are wide beaches and two lively fishing ports.

Hoche repels the Exiles (July 1795). – Quiberon saw the rout of the Royalists in 1795. The French exiles in England and Germany had made great plans; 100 000 men, led by the princes, were to land in Brittany, join hands with the Chouans and drive out the "Blues". In fact, the British fleet which anchored in the Quiberon roadstead carried only 10 000 men, commanded by Puisaye, Hervilly and Sombreuil. The princes did not come.
The landing began on the beach at Carnac on 27 June and continued for several days. Cadoudal's Chouans (p 52) joined them. But the effect of surprise was lost; long preparations and talk among the exiles had warned the Convention; **General Hoche** was ready, and he drove the invaders back into the peninsula. Driven to the beach at Port-Haliguen, the exiles tried to re-embark. Unfortunately the British ships were prevented by a heavy swell from getting near enough to land and the royalists were captured. The Convention refused to pardon them. Some were shot at Quiberon and others were taken to Auray and Vannes and shot there (p 215).

TOUR

Quiberon. – Pop 4812. Facilities. At the far end of the peninsula, Quiberon is a popular resort with its fine south-facing sandy beach and for its proximity to the Côte Sauvage *(below)*. **Port-Maria,** which is the departure point for boat services to Belle-Ile, Houat and Hoëdic, is a busy harbour and a fishing port where a few sardine boats can still be seen. Some of the catch is marketed to be eaten fresh while the rest is canned in the local factories.

★★ **1 Round tour of the Côte Sauvage.** – *18 km - 11 miles – about 2 hours*

> *Go to Port-Maria and bear right into the coast road (signposted "route côtière").*

This wild coast is a succession of jagged cliffs where caves, crevasses and inlets alternate with little sandy beaches with crashing rolling waves *(bathing prohibited; ground-swell)*. Rocks of all shapes and sizes edge the coast, forming passages and labyrinths in which the sea boils and roars.

Small granite steles line the road on the left and mark the main sights: Port Pilote, Trou du Souffleur, Pointe du Scouro, Grotte de Kerniscob, etc., which should be seen on foot.

Beg er Goalennec. – Go around the Café Le Vivier and over the rocks to reach the tip of the promontory from where there is a pretty view over the whole length of the Côte Sauvage.

> *After the Kroh-Kollé, bear left.*

The road runs downhill towards **Port-Bara,** a cove prickling with rocks, before going inland. Surfaced roads lead to Port-Rhu and Port-Blanc; the latter has a nice white sandy beach.

★ **Percho Point.** – *Go on foot to the tip of the point.* A lovely **view**★ opens out, on the left, to the Côte Sauvage, on the right, to the Penthièvre isthmus, its fort and beach, and beyond the islands of Belle-Ile and Groix.

The last stele indicates Beg en Aud, the furthest point on this coastline.

> *Cross Portivy and drive to St-Pierre-Quiberon.*

St-Pierre-Quiberon. – Pop 2083. Facilities. This resort has two beaches on either side of the small port of Orange. Take the Rue des Menhirs to see the St-Pierre lines made up of 22 menhirs on the right.

> *The road runs along the south beach before reaching Beg-Rohu.*

🕒 **Beg-Rohu. – The National Sailing School** (École nationale de Voile) is located on this rocky tip.

> *Return to the D 768 and turn left for Quiberon.*

2 Round tour of Conguel Point. – *6 km - 4 miles – about 1 1/2 hours*

> *Leave Quiberon to the east by the Boulevard Chanard.*

Drive round the **Thalassotherapy Institute** (Institut de Thalassothérapie) where arthrosis, rheumatism, over-exertion and the after effects of injuries are treated by sea water cures.

Conguel Point. – *1/2 hour on foot Rtn.* From the tip of the point *(viewing table)* there is a view of Belle-Ile, Houat, Hoëdic, the Morbihan coast and the Quiberon bay. The Teignouse Lighthouse, near which the battleship *France* sank in 1922 after striking a reef, can also be seen.

> *Go to Port-Haliguen.*

On the left there is an aerodrome with a runway for light aircraft. Beyond Fort-Neuf, note the bustle created on the beach by the various sailing clubs and schools. The view opens out over the bay and the Morbihan coastline. Pass, on your right, an obelisk commemorating the surrender of the exiles in 1795 (p 23).

Port-Haliguen. – A small fishing and pleasure boat harbour where regattas are held in the summer.

> *Return to Quiberon by the Rue de Port-Haliguen.*

③ Penthièvre Isthmus

It provides road and rail links between the former island and the mainland.

Penthièvre Fort (Fort de Penthièvre). – Rebuilt in the 19C, it commands the access to the peninsula. *Go inside the enclosure (car park).* A monument and a crypt commemorate 59 members of the Resistance shot here in 1944.

Penthièvre. – This small resort has two fine sandy beaches on either side of the isthmus.

⊙ **Plouharnel Galleon.** – Located at the edge of Bego Cove, this modern replica of an 18C galleon displays a collection of shells and shell pictures including the Piazza San Marco in Venice, a Japanese pagoda etc.

BOAT TRIPS

★★ **Belle-Ile.** – *P 56.*

Hoëdic Island. – *P 115.*

Houat Island. – *P 115.*

★★ QUIMPER   Pop 60 162

Michelin map 🔠 fold 15 or 🔠 fold 18 – Local map p 83

The town lies in a pretty little valley at the junction (*kemper* in Breton) of the Steir and Odet Rivers. This used to be the capital of Cornouaille, and It Is here, perhaps, that the traditional atmosphere of the province can best be felt. On market days and at church services you will still find a good number of local costumes. The **Festival of Cornouaille★** *(p 226)* is an important folk festival.

HISTORICAL NOTES

St Corentine's fish. – For centuries the town was called Quimper-Corentin, after its first bishop. According to legend, Corentine lived on the flesh of a single, miraculous fish. Every morning he took half the fish to eat and threw the other half back into the river. When he came back the next day the fish was whole once more and offered itself again to be eaten. Corentine was the adviser and supporter of King Gradlon *(p 25)*.

Four men of Quimper. – The statue of **Laënnec** (1781-1826) commemorates the most illustrious son of Quimper – the man who discovered auscultation (sounding – *see Ploaré, p 94: other memories of Laënnec*).
Streets are named after Kerguelen, Fréron and Madec, three other famous men of Quimper. **Kerguelen** (1734-97) was a South Seas explorer; a group of islands bears his name. **Fréron** (1718-76) was a critic, bitterly opposed to Voltaire and other philosophers. **René Madec** (1738-84) was a hero of adventure. As a cabin boy in a ship of the India Company he jumped overboard and landed at Pondicherry. He served a rajah and became a successful man. The British found a relentless enemy in him. When he returned to France, enormously rich, the King gave him a title and the Cross of St-Louis, with a colonel's commission.

★★ CATHEDRAL (BZ)

time: 1 1/2 hours

⊙ This fine Gothic structure was built from the 13C (chancel) to the 15C (transept and nave). The two steeples were erected only in 1856, being modelled on the Breton steeple of Pont-Croix. To pay for their building the Bishop asked the 600 000 faithful of the diocese each to subscribe one *sou* a year for five years. The salt sea air quickly toned down the new stone, and it is difficult to believe that the upper part of the façade is four centuries later than the lower part.
After seeing the north side of the building make for the façade. Between the spires stands the statue of a man on horseback: this is King Gradlon *(p 25).* Until the 18C, on 26 July each year, a great festival was held in his honour. A man would climb up behind him, tie a napkin round his neck and offer him a glass of wine. Then he drank up the wine himself, carefully wiped the King's mouth with the napkin and threw the empty glass down on the square.

(Claquin/Explorer)

Quimper. – The Cathedral

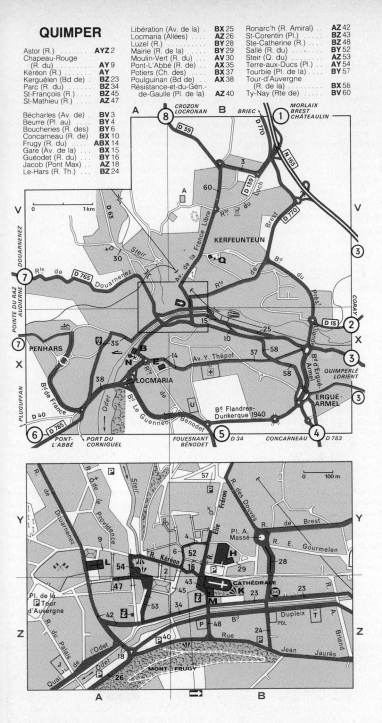

QUIMPER

Any spectator who could catch the glass as it fell received a prize of 100 gold *écus,* if the glass was not broken. It used to be said that to save money the Town Council had a few sawcuts made in the stem of the glass.

Enter by the main door.

During the League troubles in the 16C, the nave was used as a place of refuge by the inhabitants of the district. Mass was said there among palliasses, boxes and hanging linen. Plague broke out and 1 500 people died.

The first thing that strikes you on entering the church is the fact that the choir is quite out of line with the nave. It is believed that this results from unexpected difficulty encountered during building as the architect had to take into account the previous constructions.

The cathedral has a remarkable set of 15C **stained glass**★★ in the upper windows mainly in the nave and transept, depicting canons, lords and ladies surrounded by their patron saints.

The tourist, going round the fine 92m - 302ft long building, will see in the side chapels, tombs (15C), altars, frescoes, altarpieces, statues, old and modern works of art, a 17C pulpit adorned with low reliefs relating the life of St Corentin, and in the chapel beneath the south tower an Entombment copied from that in Bourges Cathedral and dating from the 18C.

★OLD QUIMPER *time: 1 hour*

The old quarter extends in front of the cathedral between the Odet and the Steir. The Rue du Parc along the Odet leads to the Quai du Steir. Note on the right, the elegant covered market, rebuilt in 1979 after a fire. From the bridge there is a lovely view upstream of the Steir lined with flower-decked houses.

Place Terre-au-Duc (AY 54). – A picturesque square lined with old half-timbered houses. This was the lay town opposite the episcopal city and included the Law Courts, the prison and the Duc de Bretagne market. Take Rue St-Mathieu (**AZ 47**) which has some fine houses, then cross the square diagonally, bearing to the right to cross the Steir by the bridge from which there is a lovely view with Mount Frugy in the distance.

★ **Rue Kéréon (ABY).** – A busy shopping street. The cathedral and its spires between the two rows of old corbelled houses make a delightful picture.

Turn left into the Rue des Boucheries then right into the Rue du Sallé.

Rue du Sallé (BY 52). – Note the beautiful old house of the Mahault de Minuellou family which has been restored and is now an antique shop.

Cross the tiny Place au Beurre to reach the **Rue Élie-Fréron**; walk up to No 22 to admire a corbelled house with a slate roof, and a Renaissance porch at No 20.

Go down to the cathedral.

At the entrance to the square, on the right, opens the **Rue du Guéodet (BY 16)** where stands a house with caryatids and figures of men and women in 16C costumes. There are traces of the old ramparts in the Rue des Douves (**BY**) and Boulevard de Kerguélen (**BZ 33**).

ADDITIONAL SIGHTS

★★ **Fine Arts Museum (Musée des Beaux-Arts) (BY H).** – Housed on the first floor of the town ⊘ hall, the museum contains an interesting collection of French and foreign paintings from the 16 to the beginning of the 20C. From the school of Bologna, note a *St Sebastian* by A. Carraci and a *Mary Magdalene* by Reni; of the Flemish school, a striking painting of the *Martyrdom of St Lucia* by Rubens; *The Evangelists* by the German Loth; from the Dutch school, an unusual *Kitchen Scene* by Kalf; and among the French, a *Still-Life* by Oudry and *Pierrefonds Castle* by Corot.

The Pont-Aven school is well represented by Bernard with his painting of *Breton Women* showing the influence he was to have on Gauguin; Sérusier *(Old Woman at Le Pouldu);* Maufra *(Pont-Aven landscape)* and Haan *(Jug and Onions).*

There are also works by artists who drew their inspiration from Brittany: P. de Belay *(Young Breton Woman),* Lemordant, Meheut, Simon. One room is devoted to the poet, Max Jacob, a native of Quimper: portraits by Picasso, de Belay, drawings, manuscripts. A remarkable 17-18C collection of drawings and engravings is exhibited in rotation.

★ **Local Museum (Musée départemental breton) (BZ M).** – This museum is devoted to Finistère ⊘ history, archaeology and folklore and is installed in the former bishop's palace. The most interesting parts of the palace were built by Bishop Claude de Rohan at the start of the 16C. There are Breton furniture, everyday objects, sculpted wood artefacts from local chapels, recumbent figures, Gallo-Roman remains and remarkable 16C wooden statues. In the Rohan tower, you will see a great **spiral staircase★** ending under a magnificent carved oak canopy and leading to the galleries displaying Quimper pottery dating from the 18C to the present time and Cornouaille costume and accessories.

Garden (Jardin de l'évêché) (BZ K). – Situated between the cathedral and ramparts. It offers a good **view★** of the cathedral chevet and spires, the Odet lined by the Préfecture with its ornate dormer windows, the former Ste-Catherine hospital and Mount Frugy.

Mount Frugy (Mont Frugy) (AB Z). – From the Place de la Résistance, a path *(1/2 hour on foot Rtn)* leads up to Mount Frugy, a wooded hill 70m - 224ft high. From the belvedere, there is a lovely **view★** of the city.

St-Mathieu (AY L). – Rebuilt in 1898, the church retains a fine 16C stained glass window of the Passion half way up the chancel.

Notre-Dame-de-Locmaria (AX N). – The Romanesque church, remodelled in the 15C and later restored, stands beside the Odet. The simple interior contains, in the north aisle, three tombstones of the 14, 15 and 17C, with a robed Christ on the roodbeam. A door in the south aisle opens on to the garden of a former Benedictine priory (16-17C) where a cloistral gallery (1669) and two 12C arches may still be seen.

Pottery workshops (Faïenceries). – The first Quimper pottery workshop was founded at the end of the 17C by a southerner who settled at Locmaria, on the outskirts of Quimper. Afterwards, his son went into partnership with a man from Nevers, and later with another from Rouen. These various employers brought workers from their respective provinces. The result was a form of decoration inspired by the pottery of Moustiers, Nevers, Rouen and even the Far East. It was about 1880, when labour was recruited at Quimper itself, that pottery with Breton themes appeared and the industry developed.

(Breton Local Museum)

Nowadays, the traditional blue ground with figures has given way to modern designs of marine flora and fauna.

The pottery is produced from Breton clay and kaolin fashioned by turning, casting and pressing, then dried at temperatures of 1040° to 1280°. The pieces are hand painted in bright colours applied on the glaze before or after firing; the next stage is tempering and finally firing at temperatures of 920° to 950°.

⊙ **Quimper Workshops** (Faïenceries de Quimper) (**AX B**). – An interesting **museum**★ presents pottery, mainly of the 19C, statuettes, vases, plates adorned with typical Breton scenes, landscapes and small figures.

⊙ **Keraluc Workshops** (Faïenceries de Keraluc) (**AX E**). – These workshops specialize in ceramics, either plain or with a typical floral decoration in shades of ochre and malachite.

EXCURSIONS

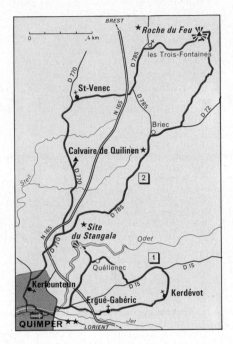

1 **Round tour of 27 km - 17 miles.** – *Time: about 2 1/2 hours*

*Leave Quimper by the Avenue de la Libération (**BX**), at the first major roundabout, turn left and take the second road to the right. 700m -about 1/2 mile farther on, take the D 115 towards Elliant.*

The road runs beside the Jet River and offers views of the wooded countryside and pastureland. *After 2 km - 1 mile, bear left.*

Ergué-Gabéric. – Pop 5 711. The early 16C church possesses in the chancel, a stained glass window depicting the Passion (1571) and a 17C group of the Trinity. The organ loft dates from 1680.

Bear right after the church towards Kerdévot Chapel.

Kerdévot Chapel. – The 15C chapel stands in an attractive setting near a Calvary, which is of a later date and unfortunately somewhat damaged. Inside, a late 15C Flemish **altarpiece**★ standing on the high altar, depicts six scenes from the life of the Virgin. There is a 17C statue of Our Lady of Kerdévot in painted wood in the nave.

Leave Kerdévot by the road on the left of the chapel, then turn left into the D 15 towards Quimper. After 3 km - 2 miles turn right towards the hamlet of Lestonan. Go through Quéllénec, turn right into a partly surfaced road 600 m - 1/3 mile to the Griffonès car park. Take the path which crosses a copse and bear left through woodland to get to two rocky platforms (1/4 hour Rtn).

★ **Stangala Site.** – The site is a remarkable one: the rocky ridge overlooks the Odet from a height of 70m - 230 ft as the river winds between wooded slopes. Opposite and slightly to the right, the hamlet of Tréouzon clings to the slopes. Ahead, in the distance, to the left of the television tower, the mountain of Locronan, with its characteristic outline and the chapel perched on its summit, can be picked out easily. On the way back, a road to the left leads down to the bank of the Odet *(1/2 hour Rtn).*

To return to Quimper, bear right as you leave the narrow road.

2 **Round tour of 57 km - 35 miles.** – *Time: about 3 hours.*

*Leave Quimper by the Rue des Douves (**BY**). Shortly after a cemetery at the entrance of Kerfeunteun, turn right.*

Kerfeunteun Church (**BV Q**). – A small square belfry with a stone spire surmounts the west façade.

The church was built in the 16 and 17C but the transept and chancel were rebuilt in 1953. It has kept a beautiful (16C) stained glass window above the high altar, depicting a Tree of Jesse with a Crucifixion above.

800 m - 1/2 mile farther on, turn right towards Brest, then left in the direction of Briec and at Ty-Sanquer, left again on the D 770.

★ **Quilinen Calvary.** – Near the main road, hidden by the trees, stands the chapel of Notre-Dame-de-Quilinen with its unusual Calvary. Built c 1550 on two superposed triangular bases, the points opposite one another, the Calvary reveals a rough and naive style. As the Cross rises to the figure of Christ above the two thieves placed close together, the statues become more and more slender. The other side of the Cross presents Christ resurrected. The south portal of the 15C chapel is decorated by a graceful Virgin between two angels.

Return to the D 770 and bear right; after 5 km - 3 miles, turn right towards the nearby St-Venec Chapel.

⊙ **St-Venec.** – The Gothic chapel contains the group in stone of St Gwen (St Blanche) and her triplets: St Guénolé, St Jacut and St Venec. The saint was endowed with three breasts. In front of the chapel is a Calvary (1556) on a triangular base similar to that of Quilinen and on the other side of the road stands a charming 16C fountain.

Take the chapel road, pass under the Quimper-Brest motorway (N165) and turn left into the D 785 towards the Notre-Dame-des-Trois-Fontaines Chapel.

This large chapel was built in the 15-16C; the calvary is badly damaged.

Proceed to the Gouézec road and turn right.

★ **La Roche du Feu.** – *1/2 hour on foot Rtn.* From the car park, take a path to the summit (281m - 899ft) which affords an extensive **panorama**★ over the Noires Mountains, the Ménez-Hom and the Aulne Valley.

Return to Quimper via Edern and Briec.

③ **Tour of the Odet.** – *Round tour of 48 km - 30 miles – about 2 1/2 hours*

Leave Quimper by ⑤ on the town plan, the D 785 to Pont-l'Abbé. After the roundabout, uphill, bear left.

Corniguel Port (Port du Corniguel). – This is the port of Quimper from which wines, timber and sand are exported. Fine view of the Odet and Kérogan Bay.

Return to the Pont-l'Abbé road, and then turn left towards Plomelin on to the D 20. At the next junction, bear left towards the Rosulien Dock.

Rosulien Dock (Cale de Rosulien). – A ruined mill stands on the right. From the dock there is a good view of the **Vire-Court**★★*(below).*

Return to the junction, turn left and after the entrance to Perennou Castle, bear left towards the Odet (signposts). From the car park, take a path (1/4 hour on foot Rtn) to the banks of the Odet with good views of the river.

Before the Croissant junction where you bear left for Combrit, the road crosses the deep Combrit cove, which presents a fine sight at high tide.

Combrit. – Pop 2 495. The 16C church has a square domed belfry flanked by two turrets. Inside, note the carved friezes and beams; in the chapel to the right of the chancel, there is a fine alabaster group of the Trinity in an alcove. An ossuary (17C) stands next to the south porch.

Proceed in the direction of Bénodet, then bear right for Ste-Marine.

Ste-Marine. – This small resort on the right bank of the Odet has a good sandy beach with a fine view over Loctudy and Lesconil Point, Moutons Island and the Glénan Islands, and a small pleasure boat harbour, from which you can enjoy a lovely view of Bénodet and the Odet. There is a ferry for people on foot crossing between Ste-Marine and Bénodet.

Go over the Cornouaille Bridge (p 60). Splendid view over Bénodet and the Odet.

★ **Bénodet.** – *P 59.*

The return road is further inland from the left bank of the Odet.

Le Drennec. – Pop 1 529. Standing in front of the chapel beside the road is a charming 16C fountain. A trefoil niche beneath a crocketed gable contains a *Pietà*.

Pass through Moulin-du-Port to return to Quimper by the D 34.

BOAT TRIPS

★★ **Down the Odet.** – The woods and castle parks which lie along the river, form a fine, ⊙ green landscape. The port of **Corniguel**, at the mouth of Kérogan Bay, is modern.

★ **Kérogan Bay.** – The estuary at this point looks like a lake.

★★ **The Vire-Court.** – The Odet here winds between high, wooded cliffs. This wild spot has its legends. Two rocks at the narrowest point of the gorge are called the Virgin's Leap (Saut de la Pucelle). Another rock is called the Bishop's Chair (Chaise de l'Évêque). Angels are said to have made it in the shape of a seat for the use of a saintly prelate of Quimper who liked to meditate in this lonely place. A little farther on the river bends so sharply that a Spanish fleet, coming up to attack Quimper, did not dare to go through. After having taken on water at a fountain now called the Spaniards' Fountain, the ships turned back. On the right bank, before Pérennou, ruins of Roman baths can be seen.

★ **Bénodet.** – *P 59.*

★★ **Up the Odet.** – *Boat trips starting from Beg-Meil or La Forêt-Fouesnant (Port-la-* ⊙ *Forêt).*

Michelin map 58 fold 12 or 230 fold 34

This little town is prettily situated at the junction *(kemper)* of the Ellé and the Isole Rivers, which join to form the Laïta. It consists of an upper town, dominated by the Church of Notre-Dame-de-L'Assomption, and a lower town grouped about the former Abbey of Ste-Croix and the Rue Dom-Morice.

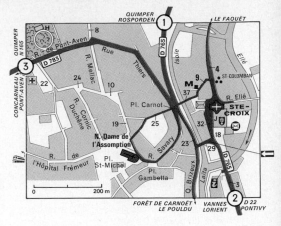

SIGHTS

Start from the Place Charles-de-Gaulle and take the Rue de la Paix.

One skirts the buildings of the former Abbey of Ste-Croix (18C), which houses the police station and the Law Courts. Enter the first door on the right to glance at the main staircase and the cloister with its flowers. This was where Lancelot, one of the "Gentlemen of Port-Royal" and Racine's teacher, died in exile.

★★ **Ste-Croix.** – The church, which is interesting archaeologically, was first built in the 12C, but had to be rebuilt, except for the apse and the crypt, in 1862, when its belfry collapsed. The new belfry (campanile) stands alone.

The plan is copied from that of the Holy Sepulchre at Jerusalem. It includes a rotunda with three small apsidal chapels opening into it and a porch, the whole forming a Greek cross.

The **apse**★★, with its blind arcades, columns, capitals and windows, is the finest specimen of Romanesque art in Brittany. A Renaissance stone **altarpiece**★ stands against the façade.

The **crypt**★★ has remarkable capitals and two 15C tombs. *Enter by the wrought iron grilles under the chancel.*

In the gallery dividing the church and the sacristy, there is a 16C Entombment carved in stone.

On leaving the church, take the Rue Ellé which skirts the north side and affords a good view of the east end and the belfry.

Rue Brémond-d'Ars (4). – There are some half-timbered and old 17C houses at Nos 8, 10, 11 and 12. At No 15 bis note the staircase of the Présidial, a former law court.

Level with the ruins of the Church of St Colomban, at the corner of No 9 turn into the Rue Dom-Morice.

★ **Rue Dom-Morice (9).** – This narrow alley is lined with 16C half-timbered or corbelled houses; No 7, the archers' house (1470) is noteworthy.

⊘ **Museum (M).** – Housed in the Archers' House, the museum traces the history of the house and of the archers who lived there. Two floors are devoted to Quimperlé, its activities, famous men and regional costumes.

Cross the Pont Salé and take the Rue Savary, going up.

This leads to the Church of Our Lady of the Assumption.

⊘ **Notre-Dame-de-l'Assomption** or **St-Michel.** – A 13 and 15C church, surmounted by a large square tower. Pass under the archway built into one of the buttresses to get a glimpse of the fine carved porch (1450). Inside look at the oak panelled vault with a sculptured cornice, magnificent Flamboyant piscinas and, near the north door, a 15C font. Among the more interesting wooden statues, note that of Our Lady of Good Tidings (16C) and a 12C Pietà (first pillar to the left).

Take the Rue de Madame-Moreau, which descends and is interrupted by steps to the Place Carnot. Turn right into the Rue La-Tour-d'Auvergne, and cross the Moulin-de-la-Ville Bridge. Return to the Place Charles-de-Gaulle.

EXCURSIONS

Round tour of 43 km - 27 miles. – *Time: about 2 1/2 hours. Leave Quimperlé by the Quai Brizeux and the D 49, the road to Le Pouldu.*

Carnoët Forest. – The State Forest of Carnoët (750 ha - 1 852 acres) planted with beech and oak and bounded by the Laïta River, offers pretty sites and pleasant walks (lanes reserved for walking and riding). On the edge of the forest at Toulfoën, a *pardon* is held, which is still known as the Bird Festival *(p 226)*.

500 m - 1/3 mile beyond Toulfoën, turn left towards the Rocher Royal.

The road winds through the forest to the banks of the Laïta where can be seen the **Rocher Royal**, a rocky ridge towering above the river, and the ruins of Carnoët Castle. This is the legendary dwelling of the Count of Commore, the Bluebeard of Cornouaille. After hearing a prediction that he would die by the hand of his son, he put his four wives to death as soon as they conceived. The fifth wife, Triphine, before she died, was able to save her son, who became **St Trémeur**. Commore, meeting the Saint, was struck by his resemblance to his mother and immediately had him beheaded. Then, says the legend, Trémeur picked up his own head, walked towards his father's castle and threw a handful of earth against the building, which collapsed burying Commore alive.

Return to the D 49, turn left and at a major junction, left again.

St-Maurice Bridge. – The bridge over the Laïta gives a fine **view**★ of the river and its steep banks.

Turn round and after 700 m - about 1/2 mile, turn right.

St-Maurice. – It stands in a green and pleasant **site**★: the river Laïta is on the right with a pond on the left. Nearby are remains of the chapterhouse of the former Abbey of St-Maurice, founded in 12C.

Make for Le Pouldu.

Le Pouldu. – Facilities. This small port lies at the mouth of the River Laïta.

⊙ The **Notre-Dame-de-la-Paix Chapel** near Grands Sables beach, stands in a grassy close, the entrance of which is flanked by a monument to Gauguin. Transported 26 km - 16 miles and rebuilt here, the chapel was consecrated in 1957. The bays have flame and lily shaped tracery with stained glass by Manessier and Le Moal. Below the timber roof the rood-beam carries a Christ with a red loincloth and a second group depicting a *Pietà*.

Follow the road D 124 along Grands Sables beach then the D 24 and turn left into the D 16 towards Doëlan.

View of Groix Island and Talud Point.

Go round the port of Doëlan to the village.

Doëlan. – A small fishing port commanding the entrance to a deep, sheltered estuary.

Return to Quimperlé by the D 316, Clohars-Carnoët and the D 16.

Round tour of 37 km - 23 miles. – *Time: about 1 1/2 hours. Leave Quimperlé to the southwest by the D 16 and at Gare-de-la-Forêt, bear right into the D 116.*

Moëlan-sur-Mer. – Pop 6 501. In the **church**, note the five 18C confessional boxes in the German style. Pass along the south side of the church and by the chevet, take the lane ⊙ leading to **St-Philibert-St-Roch Chapel** which is picturesquely placed near a 16C Calvary. Alongside is the St-Roch fountain. A *pardon* takes place on the second Sunday following the 15 August.

Proceed to Brigneau. A menhir stands on the left hand side of the road (signposts). There is a fine view over Brigneau Bay.

Brigneau. – A tiny fishing port where pleasure craft also find shelter.

The road follows the coastline. Thatched-roofed houses are dotted along the way.

At Kergroès, bear left into the D 116.

Kerfany-les-Pins. – On the Bélon River, this small seaside resort has a pretty site and a sandy beach. Fine view over Port-Manech and the Aven estuary.

Take the uphill road beyond the beach and at Lanriot, turn left.

Bélon. – This locality, on the south bank of the Bélon, is famous as an oyster-farming centre *(p 20)*. The oyster-beds on the north bank can be seen at low tide.

Return to Quimperlé on the D 116 via Moëlan-sur-Mer.

★ **The Devil's Rocks (Rochers du Diable).** – *12 km - 7 miles NE, plus 1/2 hour on foot Rtn. Leave Quimperlé on the D 790 towards Le Faouët and after 4.5 km - 3 miles turn right and go through Locunolé.*

There is a pretty run as the road descends towards the Ellé. *Cross the bridge and turn left towards Meslan; after 400 m - about 1/4 mile, leave the car in the car park to the left.* Paths lead up to the top of the rocks which drop vertically to the fast-flowing waters of the Ellé.

QUINTIN

Pop 3 223

Michelin map **59** folds 12, 13 or **230** fold 22

In the past, Quentin was well known for its fine linen which was used for head-dresses and collars. In the 17 and 18C the industry expanded to the manufacture of Brittany cloth which was exported to America but decline set in at the Revolution when there were 30 000 weavers in the town.

The old houses of Quintin rise in terraces on a hill at the foot of which the Gouët River forms a fine stretch of water.

Basilica. – The relics of St Thuriau and a piece of the Virgin's girdle, brought from Jerusalem in the 13C by a lord of Quintin, are kept in the basilica. There are also four stoups made of shells from Java and, under the porch, the old crowned statue of Our Lady of Safe Delivery, which is specially venerated by expectant mothers, a 14C font in the north transept and two 14C effigies in the chancel. The *pardon* of Notre-Dame-de-Délivrance takes place on the second Sunday in May.

At the east end of the basilica stands the New Gate (Port Neuve - 15C), all that remains of the ramparts which surrounded the town. In the Rue Notre-Dame beyond the parvis, is the 15C fountain of Notre-Dame-d'Entre-les-Ponts with two former chapter houses with decorated façades opposite at Nos 5 and 7.

Old houses. – There are fine 16-17C corbelled houses lining the picturesque Place 1830, the Rue au Lait (Nos 12, 13) and the Grande Rue (Nos 37 and 43). In Place du Martray, the Hôtel du Martray, the town hall and the house at No 1 date from the 18C.

Castle. – *Access from the Place 1830.*
Only the imposing corner pavilion and the fine terrace overlooking the lake remain of the original 16C building. The main building and the outbuildings lining the gardens are 18C.

Pierre Longue Menhir. – *800 m - 1/2 mile farther on by the road beyond the Calvary which skirts the pool.*
At the top of the hill, a menhir 4.70m - 14ft high stands in a field to the left.

⊙ **Robien Castle.** – *2 km - 1 mile by the road to Corlay.*
The 18C château stands on the site of two others, which were successively destroyed. Of the first, there remain only the ruins of a 14C chapel near the present building. The austerity of the granite façades is relieved by a central rotunda and projecting wings at either end. A pleasant walk may be enjoyed in the park which is planted with different species of trees and through which flows the Gouët.

RANCE Tidal Power Scheme (USINE MARÉMOTRICE DE LA RANCE)

Michelin map **59** fold 6 or **230** fold 11

The use of tidal power is nothing new to the Rance Valley. As early as the 12C, riverside dwellers had thought up the idea of building little reservoirs which, as they emptied with the ebb tide, drove mill wheels. To double the output of a modern industrial plant, it was tempting to try to work out a means of using the flow as well as the ebb tide. The French electricity authority (EDF), therefore, searched for new technical methods of producing electricity and successfully set up, between the headlands of La Briantais and La Brebis, a hydro-electric power scheme operated by both the flow and ebb of the tide.

The Rance estuary is closed by a dam 750 m - 800 yds long, making a reservoir of 22 sq m - 8 sq miles. The D 168 which connects Dinard and St-Malo runs along it. The lock is 65 m - 69 yds long and enables boats to pass through the dam. The road crosses the lock by means of bascule bridges.

⊙ The **power station** is in a huge tunnel nearly 390 m - 400 yds long in the very centre of the dam. Here, each in a reinforced pit, are the 24 AC generators of a combined capacity of 240 000 kW which can produce 550 million kW per year.
Walk along the dam to the platform. From there the **view★** extends over the Rance estuary as far as Dinard and St-Malo. The dam lies between the power station and the right bank with its centre on the small island of Chalibert. There are six sluice-gates at the eastern end which can regulate the emptying and filling of the reservoir thus controlling the water supply to the power station.

Gourmets ...

The region's gastronomic specialities are described on page 41.

Each year the Michelin Red Guide France proposes a revised selection of establishments renowned for their cuisine.

★★ RANCE Valley

Michelin map **59** folds 5, 6, 15, 16 or **230** folds 11, 25

The Rance estuary, lying between St-Malo and Dinard, is among the places most frequented in Brittany. Farther upstream, Dinan is a typical old inland town.
The Rance is a perfect example of a Breton river. It forms a deep gulf between Dinan and the sea, flowing with many branches and inlets over a level plateau. This curious gulf is due to the flooding by the sea of an ordinary but steep sided valley: the stream itself and the bottom of the valley have been "drowned" by a mass of tidal water. All that remains visible of the original valley is its steep sides, sloping into the sea. The Rance proper is a small river without much water, which winds along above Dinan. The exceptional volume of the tides makes it the very place for a tidal power station.

★★ BOAT TRIP

⊙ *5 hours Rtn – not counting the stop and tour of Dinan*

The boat follows the Noires breakwater (Môle des Noires) and crosses the Rance estuary for a brief stop at Dinard. It enters the Rance, leaving the Aleth Corniche on the left (St-Servan), passes in front of Vicomté Point and Bizeux Rock and then enters the lock of the Rance dam. You will go up the river, between its great banks, through a series of narrow channels and wide pools. After the Châtelier Lock the Rance gets narrower and narrower and becomes a mere canal just as you come within sight of Dinan, perched on its ridge.

★★ **Dinan.** – *P 86.* Your boat will stop for a longer or shorter time according to the tide – 8 hours or only 1/4 hour.
The scenes on your way back will be changed by the difference in the direction of the light and its intensity.

★ROUND TOUR STARTING FROM ST-MALO

87 km - 54 miles – allow one day

★★★ **St-Malo.** – *Time: 2 1/2 hours. Description p 193.*

    Leave St-Malo by ③, the N 137. Turn right by the aerodrome into the D 5.

La Passagère. – Fine view over the Rance.

    Make for the Chapel of Le Boscq and St-Jouan. The D 117, on the right, takes you to St-Suliac. On the right notice the Boscher mill, a former tidal mill (p 175). In St-Suliac before the church bear left in the direction of Mount Garrot. 1 km - 1/2 mile farther on leave the car near an old crenellated watchtower. From the foot of the tower there is a wide **panorama★** *of St-Suliac cove, St-Malo, the Dol countryside, the Rance River and St-Jean Bridge.*

Mount Garrot. – *15 min on foot Rtn.* A path to the right leads to the point, passing behind a farm. Notice the views of the Rance Valley on the way.

    From La Ville-ès-Nonais continue onto the St-Jean Bridge.

St-Jean Bridge (Pont St Jean). – From this suspension bridge there is a pleasant view of the Rance, the Port St-Jean slipway and, on the rocky bank opposite, the St-Hubert slipway.

    Return to La Ville-ès-Nonais, bear right. In Pleudihen bear right towards Mordreuc.

Mordreuc Slipway (Cale de Mordreuc). – From this lovely place there are good views of St-Jean Bridge downstream, the deepening valley upstream and just opposite a promontory on which lie the ruins of an old castle.

Lanvallay. – Pop 2 531. A remarkable **view★** of the old town of Dinan, its ramparts and its belfries. Below, flows the Rance spanned by a long viaduct.

★★ **Dinan.** – *P 86.*

    Take the road which passes under the Dinan viaduct and skirts the harbour.

Taden. – Pop 1 718. When you cross the village, on your way to the slipway, glance at the porch and keep which is flanked by a 15C turret. The towpath, which used to link Dinan to the Chatelier Lock, is a favourite spot for fishermen and a pleasant place to stroll.

    Return to the D 12 towards Dinard. As you leave La Hisse turn right before the level crossing.

Chatelier Lock (Écluse du Chatelier). – It regulates the Dinan basin.

Continue onto **Plouër-sur-Rance.** On either side of the porch of the 18C church are carved tombstones.

    After Plouër-sur-Rance and Le Minihic bear right onto the D 114 and then 250 m farther the D 3.

La Landriais. – The port contains naval dockyards. The walk along the Hures Promenade, from the car park and, as it skirts the Rance for 2 km - 1 mile affords fine views.

    On your way back, take the D 114 again after 1 200 m - 3/4 mile then turn right after 1 km - 1/2 mile onto the D 5, a fine coast road.

Jouvente Slipway (Cale de la Jouvente). – Across from la Passagère. There is a nice view of the Rance and Chevret isle.

La Richardais. – Pop 1 381. The church is dominated by its pierced tower and the Calvary surmounting it. On the walls of the nave runs a fresco (1955) depicting the Stations of the Cross by Xavier de Langlais. From the fine wood vaulting resembling the upturned keel of a ship, 4 lamps in the form of wheels hang down. Five stained glass windows are by Max Ingrand.

On leaving La Richardais by the north, you get a viewpoint of the tidal power scheme and the Rance estuary.

    Reach Dinard by the D 114 and ① on the town plan.

★★★ **Dinard.** – *P 81.*

The Rance Tidal Power Scheme (Usine marémotrice de la Rance). – *P 175.*

    Return to St-Malo by the direct route (D168 and N 137).

Michelin map 58 fold 13 or 230 fold 16 – Local map p 81

Raz Point, at the tip of Cornouaille, is in a very attractive setting. Walk round the signal station in front of which stands a statue of Our Lady of the Shipwrecked (Notre-Dame-des-Naufragés) to ⊘ enjoy a wide **panorama**★★ of the horizon: straight ahead is Sein Island and beyond, in clear weather, the Ar Men Lighthouse. Between Sein Island and the mainland is the fearful Raz du Sein or tide race which, so an old saying has it, "no one passes without fear or sorrow"; to the northwest can be seen the Trévennec Lighthouse standing on an islet.

It is well worth walking round the point. The path follows the edge of deep chasms *(safety rope)*, the deepest of which is the Plogoff Inferno (Enfer de Plogoff) with its sheer walls against which the waves crash deafeningly. The long, narrow spur, cut

(A. Gaël)

Raz Point

away by the sea, towers more than 70m - 220ft above the waves. It reaches out into the ocean by a chain of reefs on the very last of which is perched the Vieille Lighthouse. The setting is particularly impressive in stormy weather.

REDON   Pop 10 252

Michelin map 63 fold 5 or 230 folds 38, 39

This river port at the crossing of the Vilaine and the Nantes-Brest canal, has a wet dock which links these two waterways. It is also a local farming centre with its markets on Mondays and fairs. The **Foire Teillouse** *(fourth Saturday in October)* is renowned for its chestnuts. The town's industries include mechanical engineering, plastics, foundries, cold stores and the production of cigarette lighters..

St-Sauveur (Y B). – This former abbey church, founded in 832 AD, was a great pilgrimage centre throughout the Middle Ages and until the 17C. This accounts for the impressive size of the building. In 1622 Richelieu was the commendatory abbot. It was cut off from its 14C Gothic bell tower by a fire in 1780. A remarkable Romanesque sandstone and granite **tower**★ stands at the transept crossing. From the neighbouring **cloister** (17C) occupied by the College of St Saviour, the superimposition of its arcades can be seen. From the esplanade planted with chestnut trees and overlooking the Rue Richelieu, one has a good view of the chevet with its buttresses.

The **interior** reveals a dimly lit low nave (11C) with wood vaulting separated from the side aisles by flat pillars. The 12C vaulting at the transept reveals remains of frescoes; note the carved pillars in the transept crossing. A 17C altarpiece in stone and marble takes the form of the tall, illuminated chancel, which with the ambulatory, is 13C.

The Old Town. – The old town contains elegant 15-18C town houses. Leave from St-Sauveur Church and walk along the Grande Rue, noting Nos 22, 25, 38, 44, 52 and 54; look down Rue d'Enfer and Rue Jeanne-d'Arc. Cross the flower decorated bridge which spans the Nantes-Brest canal. In the Rue du Port across from No 6, Hôtel Camoy, are three corbelled houses. Go into the Rue du Jeu de Paume which has, at No 10, the old customs barracks, a 4 storey building, with a severe façade. Return to Rue du Port where former old salt houses (No 40) can be seen; occupying No 3 Rue du Plessis is the Hôtel Richelieu. The Quai Duguay-Trouin is lined with stately ship-owners homes of which Nos 15, 7, 6 and 5 are worth looking at. By way of the Quai St-Jacques, where ramparts in ruins still stand and the Rue de Richelieu, you return to the church.

EXCURSIONS

Rieux. – Pop 2 263. *7 km - 4 miles S by* ③, *the D 775 towards Vannes, after 4.5 km - 3 miles take the road on the left.* The **church** (1952) has a slim belfry built against the side of the main vessel. The groined brick vaulting springs from roughly hewn capitals supported by short columns. The unfaced stonework of the walls is interrupted only by the vividly coloured **stained glass windows**★ of unevenly cut glass by Job Guével.

On entering the village, in a bend, take the road to the left which takes you to a car park, from where there is a pleasant view of the Vilaine Valley and Redon; occupying the wooded promontory are castle ruins.

REDON

*The main throughroutes
are clearly indicated
on all town plans.*

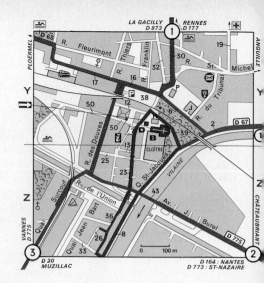

St-Just. – Pop 1 024. *9 km - 5 miles NE. Leave Redon by ① on the town plan, the D 177 to Rennes and at Renac bear left towards St-Just.* This little town lies at the centre of an area rich in megaliths, especially in the Cojoux moor (signposted path).

Pies Island. – *12 km - 7 miles NW. Leave Redon by the D 65 and then the D 764 to Ploërmel* **(Y)**; *at St-Vincent-sur-Oust, turn right.* The road leads to the bank of the Oust, a peaceful river, partly canalized, flowing through verdant countryside. A path to the left gives a view of Pies island.

★★ RENNES   Pop 200 390

Michelin map **59** fold 17 or **230** fold 26

Rennes, the capital of Brittany and once a calm provincial city is now a booming town and its population has increased two fold since World War II. The Classical style which prevails in the town centre, gives the streets, buildings and houses a rather cold dignity. The mediaeval streets spared by the 1720 fire *(p 179)* add character to this quarter with its pretty half-timbered houses. This area (bordered on the south by the Vilaine) is where the people of Rennes congregate.

The new city on the left bank of the Vilaine includes the station, hotels and sports, radio and cultural centres. The new residential suburbs on the outskirts of the city include three industrial zones which have attracted many plants manufacturing cars, railway equipment, the building industry and public works and transportation, etc.

Recently Rennes has become a centre of the electronics and communications industry. Rennes is also a university city: two universities, a medical school and several other specialized schools, with a total student enrolment of 27 000.

HISTORICAL NOTES

Du Guesclin's Beginnings (14C). – Bertrand Du Guesclin was born in the Castle of La Motte-Broons (now disappeared) southwest of Dinan. He was the eldest of ten children, and by no means handsome. On the other hand, he was bursting with energy and good sense. Bertrand spent his childhood among peasant boys whom he taught to fight. In this way he acquired strength, skill and cunning – and rough manners. His family were ashamed of him and kept him out of sight.

In 1337, when Du Guesclin was seventeen, all the local nobles met for a tournament at Rennes. Our hero went to it in peasant's dress, mounted on a draught horse. He was kept out of the lists. His despair at this was such that one of his cousins from Rennes lent him his armour and his charger. Without giving his name, Bertrand unseated several opponents. At last a lance thrust lifted his visor. His father recognized him. Delighted and proud, he exclaimed: "My fine son, I will no longer treat you scurvily!" *Other details pp 24, 52, 86, 104 and 113.*

The Duchess's marriage (1491). – In 1489, when François II died, his heiress, Anne of Brittany, was only twelve, but this did not prevent wooers from coming forward. Her choice fell on Maximilian of Austria, the future Emperor. The religious marriage was performed by proxy in 1490.

Charles VIII, who had an unconsummated marriage with Margaret of Austria, daughter of Maximilian, asked the Duchess's hand for himself; he was refused, but laid siege to Rennes in August 1491. The starving people begged their sovereign to accept the marriage. She agreed and met Charles VIII. Anne was small and thin and slightly lame, but she had gaiety and charm; she knew Latin and Greek and took an interest in art and letters. Charles was short and ill favoured, with large, pale eyes and thick lips, always hanging open; he was slow witted, too, but he loved power and had a taste for pomp. Quite unexpectedly the two young people took a liking to each other, which grew into tender affection. Their engagement was celebrated at Rennes. There remained, however, the problem of freeing the fiancés. The Court of Rome agreed and the wedding took place in the royal Castle of Langeais, in the Loire Valley, on 6 December 1491. The marriage united Brittany to France. *See other details about Anne of Brittany pp 140 and 213.*

The great fire of 1720. – At the beginning of the 18C the town still looked as it did in the Middle Ages, with narrow alleys and lath and plaster houses. There was no way of fighting fire, for there was no running water. In the evening of 22 December 1720, a drunken carpenter set fire to a heap of shavings with his lamp. The house burned like a torch and immediately other houses caught fire.

The ravaged quarters were rebuilt to the plans of Jacques Gabriel, the descendant of a long line of architects and himself the father of the Gabriel who built the Place de la Concorde in Paris. A large part of the town owes its fine rectangular street pattern and the uniform and rather severely distinguished granite houses, to this event. In order that they might be inhabited more quickly, new houses were divided into apartments or flats which were sold separately. This was the beginning of co-ownership.

The La Chalotais affair. – In 1762 the Duke of Aiguillon, Governor of Brittany, clashed with Parliament over the Jesuits. The Jansenist lawyers *(robins)* opposed the Society of Jesus, whose colleges made it very powerful in Brittany – that of Rennes had 2 800 pupils. La Chalotais, the Public Prosecutor, induced Parliament to vote for the dissolution of the Order. His report had a huge success: 12 000 copies were sold in a month. Voltaire wrote to the author: "This is the only work of philosophy that has ever come from the Bar."

Aiguillon, who defended the Jesuits, asked Parliament to reverse its vote. It refused. Louis XV summoned the Councillors to Versailles, scolded them and sent three into exile. On returning to Rennes the Members of Parliament resigned rather than submit. The King had La Chalotais arrested and sent him to Saintes; the other Councillors were scattered over various provinces, but the Paris Parliament took the side of the Rennes Parliament and Louis XV hesitated to go further. Aiguillon, lacking support, retired in 1768. The Assemblies had defeated the royal power. Revolution was on the march.

A great mayor: Leperdit. – In 1793, before going to Nantes, where he became notorious *(p 142),* **Carrier** was appointed to represent the Convention at Rennes. There he found a Mayor named Leperdit, who was a working tailor and a simple fellow but a man of great character and coolness. The Convention man wanted to execute prisoners. Leperdit stood up to him bravely. "No mercy," said Carrier; "those people are outside the law." "Yes," answered the Mayor, "but not outside humanity." Fortunately for Rennes and its Mayor, Carrier did not stay long.

In 1794, when Leperdit was addressing a crowd who were demanding bread, stones were thrown and he was wounded on the forehead. Bleeding but still calm, he said to the ruffians: "I cannot, like Christ, change these stones into bread; as for my blood, I would give the last drop if it would feed you."

★★ LAW COURTS (PALAIS DE JUSTICE) (BY) *time: 1 hour*

⊙ The Law Courts, the former Houses of Parliament of Brittany, stand in the Place du Palais, a square, lined by 17 and 18C houses.

The building with its sweeping, sober lines is worthy of the powerful assembly that had it built between 1618 and 1655 to the plans of Salomon de Brosse, the architect of the Luxembourg Palace in Paris *(see Michelin Green Guide to Paris)*. Funds for the building were found by levying a tax of one *sol* per litre of wine and three *deniers* per litre of cider (a builder's mate then earned seven to twelve *sols* a day).

The Parliament was the supreme court of the 2 300 Breton tribunals. It also played a legislative and political role. Most of the 100 to 120 Councillors and Presidents were drawn from the noble families of the province. A seat could be bought for a small sum. Salaries were low, but the judges received the famous "spices" (consisting originally of sweets and preserves) from their clients.

Members of Parliament were much respected at Rennes; they ruled over thousands of lawyers; by tradition, they had large families: a president to whom his wife presented thirty-two children hardly caused a stir.

Enter the **Hall of the Great Pillars**★ (Salle des Gros Piliers), a large vestibule with columns. It was formerly cluttered with sales-booths which were removed in 1840.

Pass through a series of magnificently decorated rooms, on which 17C painters such as Jouvenet and Coypel worked. The most impressive is the **Grand'Chambre**★★, the former parliamentary debating chamber. It is 20m long, 10m wide and 7m high - 66ft × 33ft × 23ft. The coffered ceiling, paintings and woodwork are amazingly rich. The walls are covered with ten modern tapestries representing scenes from the history of Brittany, which the Gobelins manufactory took 24 years to weave. Charming loggias or boxes, finely decorated, enabled important visitors to follow the debates. Mme de Sévigné came there several times during her visits to Les Rochers *(p 185).*

★ OLD TOWN (VIEUX RENNES) (ABY) *time: 1 hour*

This is the part of the old town which escaped the fire. It contains a maze of 15 and 16C houses with overhanging storeys and lordly mansions with sculptured façades which can be seen as you stroll in the cathedral quarter.

> *Follow the itinerary indicated on the town plan starting from the St-Sauveur Church (p 181).*

At no 6 **Rue St-Sauveur** stands a 16C canon's residence.

At no 3 **Rue St-Guillaume** a beautiful mediaeval house, said to be the **house of Du Guesclin,** contains the restaurant Ti Koz.

The **Rue de la Psalette** which skirts the cathedral is lined with old houses.

No 22 **Rue du Chapitre** is a Renaissance house, no 8 is the Hôtel de Brie (17C) and no 6 the 18C **Hôtel de Blossac** with a fine staircase *(on the left on entering).*

Nos 6 and 8 **Rue St-Yves** are 16C houses.

The restored no 10 **Rue des Dames** is the Hôtel Freslon de la Freslonnière.

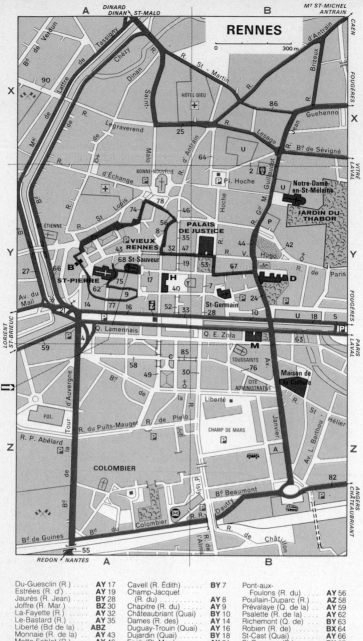

RENNES

0   300 m

The **Mordelaise Gate** (Porte Mordelaise) (**AY B**) is all that remains of the 15C ramparts. Go through the gate to see the outside face. The Dukes of Brittany passed through it on their way to the cathedral for their coronation. In 1598 the silver-gilt keys of the city were presented there to Henri IV. At this kind of ceremony the Béarnais made a statement which always went down well: "These are beautiful keys," he would say, "but I would rather have the keys to the hearts of your citizens."

The **Place des Lices** was where jousts and tournaments were held. Nos 26 and 28 are 17C hotels with large staircases capped with domes.

The **Rue St-Michel** is lined with half-timbered houses.

Looking onto the **Place Ste-Anne** are 16C houses. Leperdit, the mayor, lived at no 19.

The shopping street, **Rue du Pont-aux-Foulons** is lined with half-timbered houses.

The **Rue du Champ-Jacquet** leads to an oddly shaped triangular square, of the same name. The façade of the former Hôtel de Tizy (no 5) gives onto it.

On the **Rue St-Georges** all the houses are old. The half-timbered houses, nos 8, 10 and 12 form an exquisite ensemble of 17C half-timbered houses.

The Hôtel de Moussaye (16C), no 3, has a Renaissance façade with sculpted pilasters.

180

ADDITIONAL SIGHTS

⊙ **Museums (Palais des Musées) (BY M)**. – This former university houses two museums: the Museum of Brittany (Musée de Bretagne) on the ground floor and the Fine Arts Museum (Musée des Beaux-Arts) on the 1st floor.

★★ **Museum of Brittany.** – This museum recalls the history of Brittany. Through the exhibits (objects, models, carved figures) different eras are evoked: geological, prehistoric, Gallo-Roman Armorica, mediaeval Brittany and Brittany of the *ancien régime*.
In the second last gallery, concerned with the period from 1789 to 1914, costumes, everyday objects, tools and furnishings characteristic of Brittany are displayed. An audio-visual programme presenting Brittany of today occurs in the last gallery.

★★ **Museum of Fine Arts.** – The museum contains an important collection of works covering the 14C to the present. Among the early masters are Veronese *(Perseus Rescuing Andromeda)* and Maerten van Heemskerk *(St. Luke Painting the Portrait of the Virgin)*. The 17C is well represented (Rubens, Jordaens, and Champaigne); *The Newborn* by Georges de La Tour is captivating.
The 18C is exemplified by the works of Chardin *(The Basket of Plums; Peaches and Grapes)* and Greuze *(The Portrait of a Young Girl)*.
Among the 19C canvases are Jongkind, Corot, Boudin and Sisley. Works of the members of the Pont-Aven school are also on display: Bernard, Gauguin *(Oranges)* and Sérusier.
The last gallery concerned with the 20C contains works by Laurent, Picasso, Utrillo and Vlaminck.
Old drawings, porcelain (18C Rennes, Le Croisic, Dinan, Quimper) and fine Egyptian, Greek and Etruscan archaeological artefacts complete the museum's exhibits.

⊙ **St Peter's Cathedral (Cathédrale St Pierre) (AY)**. – This, the third cathedral built on this site since the 6C, was finished in 1844 after fifty-seven years' work. The previous building collapsed in 1762 except for the two towers in the Classical style flanking the façade.
The interior is very rich, its stucco facing covered with paintings and gilding. The cathedral contains a masterpiece: the gilded and carved wood **altarpiece**★★ in the chapel before the south transept. Both in size and in execution, this 16C Flemish work is one of the most important of its kind. The scenes represent the life of the Virgin.

The Mordelaise Gate *(p 180)* and quarters of the old town *(p 179)* can be seen near the cathedral.

St-Sauveur (AY). – 17 and 18C. Inside are a fine gilded wooden canopy and an organ loft (17C). To the right is a chapel consecrated to Our Lady of Miracles who saved Rennes from the English during the siege of 1357.

⊙ **Town Hall (Hôtel de Ville) (AY H)**. – The Town Hall was built to the plans of Jacques Gabriel in 1734-43, after the fire of 1720. A central tower, standing back from the façade, carries the great clock – "le gros", as the townspeople call it – and is joined by two curved buildings to two large annexes. Inside are the former chapel and a lovely 17C Brussels tapestry. The right wing contains the Pantheon of Rennes, a hall dedicated to the memory of men who have died for France. Provided no official reception is being held, the public are admitted to the left wing of the building and can see the monumental staircase, the 18C Brussels' tapestries and the hall where the civil ceremony of a wedding is performed.

St-Germain (BY). – This Flamboyant church (15-16C) with its 17C gable (on the south side) retains certain characteristics typical of a Breton cathedral: wood vaulting and its beams with sculpted ends. In the south transept the beautiful 16C **stained glass window** recounts the life of the Virgin and the Passion.

(Christiane Olivier, Nice)

Rennes. – Thabor garden

Palais St-Georges (BY D). – Preceded by a beautiful garden, this former Benedictine abbey (1670) now houses administrative services.

Notre-Dame-en-St-Melaine (BY). – This church was rebuilt in the 14 and 17C. The tower and transept, both of the 11C, are all that remains of the former St-Melaine Abbey's church.
In the south arm of the transept a 15C fresco represents the Baptism of Christ. The decoration inside the church is modern: stained glass windows by Le Moal and a tapestry and a painting (1942) by Mériel-Bussy.

Go round the building, on the left, to see the 17C cloister which has been restored, adjoining the north side of the church, with its gallery decorated with beautiful carvings and a well.

To the left of the square is the former bishop's palace (17-18C).

★ **Thabor Garden** (Jardin du Thabor) (BY). – The former garden of the Benedictine Abbey of St-Melaine formed the nucleus of this park, which now covers nearly 11 ha - 27 acres. It includes a formal French garden, a botanical garden, a landscape garden, a rose garden and animal enclosures.

⊘ **Cultural Centre** (Maison de la Culture) (BZ). – Designed by the architects Carlu (he also designed the Palais de Chaillot in Paris, *see Michelin Green Guide to Paris*) and Joly, it contains various halls: theatre, cinema, conference hall. Also included are an exhibition gallery and a discotheque.

EXCURSIONS

★ **Brittany Car Museum** (Musée Automobile de Bretagne). – *4 km - 2 1/2 miles NW. Leave*
⊘ *Rennes by the Rue J.-Guéhenno* (BX).
Some 70 cars all in perfect condition and in working order are exhibited in this museum. Among the different makes represented are a Hurtu (1898), a Dion-Bouton (1899) – where the steering wheel was in the middle and the passengers sat on either side of the driver – a taxi (1911) requisitioned by the government to transport troops during World War I and a Licorne (1919). Turn of the century fire trucks, as well as cycles, motorcycles and horsedrawn vehicles complete the collection.

Forest of Rennes. – *11 km - 7 miles NE.* In this 3 000 ha - 7 410 acres State Forest, forest roads and a long distance footpath (GR 39) wind through the beautiful oak, beech, pine, birch and chestnut trees.

Vilaine Valley. – *Round tour of 36 km - 23 miles – about 1 hour. Leave Rennes by the Boulevard Georges-Pompidou* (AZ 55).
Cross the river at Pont-Réan in beautiful surroundings. As you leave the town, turn left.

Le Boël. – You can enjoy a pleasant walk by the river which runs between rocky hills in a verdant setting. A small lock and a dam seem to link the right bank to the old mill on the far bank.

Return to Pont-Réan and after crossing the bridge over the Vilaine, turn right.

Bruz. – Pop 8 018. This country town is an example of successful planning in rural surroundings with its tiny square on the north side of the church. The **church**★ (1950), which is built of rose veined schist, is beautiful. A pointed spire rises above the square tower that forms the porch at its base. The interior blends well; daylight enters on all sides through square panes of glass decorated with a picture of three fishes within a circle; in the apse through stained glass windows depicting the Seven Sacraments and in the two arms of the transept through windows, to the south of the Crucifixion and to the north of the Virgin Mary. The organ is flanked on either side by the long, narrow stained glass windows of unequal height that can be seen in the façade.

From Bruz one can reach the old Boël mill (4 km - 2 1/2 miles) by taking the D 77 S and 3 km - 2 miles farther bear right and then turn left before the level crossing.

Return to Rennes by the D 44 to Chartres-de-Bretagne and the N 137.

La ROCHE-BERNARD   Pop 838

Michelin map 🔢 fold 14 or 🔢 fold 52

This little old town, picturesquely sited on the spur of La Garenne, overlooks the Vilaine River. Its naval dockyards were famous in the 17C.
The port stands on a tributary of the river. It was very prosperous in the past due to its trade of wood, wheat, wine, salt and spices. It has now become a pleasure boat harbour.

A real Republican. – The town of La Roche-Bernard welcomed the Revolution and opposed the Chouans. In 1793, 6 000 "Whites" easily defeated the 150 "Blues" who were defending the town. The Mayor, Sauveur, refused to flee. He was ordered to shout, "Long live the King!" and he replied, "Long live the Republic!" He was shot down. The Tree of Liberty was set on fire and the dying man was thrown into the flames. The next day his stoical father wrote to the authorities at Rennes: "My son died at his post; the barbarians could not rise to the level of a true Republican." The town was named La Roche-Sauveur until 1802.

★ **Bridge.** – The suspension bridge, built in 1960, stands more than 50m - 160ft above the river. Stop at either end or on the *corniche* roads upstream to see how it blends with the landscape.

★ **Viewpoint.** – From a bend in the D 774 towards La Baule, a belvedere (23 steps) dominates the Vilaine Valley extending its views, onto the wooded slopes, on the right the suspension bridge and on the left the pleasure boat harbour on the Rhodoir. On a rock a commemorative plaque for the launching of *La Couronne* (1634) has been placed.

Old Quarter. – Across from the viewpoint and on the other side of the D 774 begins the **Promenade du Ruicard,** which overlooks the port. It goes into the Rue du Ruicard and leads through a maze of small streets, some of which are stepped. Houses of the 16 and 17C follow: nos 6 and 8 are well restored, no 11 has an interesting doorway, no 12 has a turret.

The Passage de la Quenelle, with its dormer windows surmounted by sculpted pediments, leads to the **Place Bouffary** where the guillotine stood in 1793. Situated on the square is the town hall, which is also known as the "House of the Cannon" (1599) because of the cannon placed in the corner. On the left opens the Rue de la Saulnerie with a 15C house.

In the Rue Haute-Madame stands the small 11C Chapel of Our Lady, rebuilt in the 16 and 19C. The first church built in the city, it was converted into a Protestant church in 1561, and then during the Terror used to store fodder; it once again became Catholic in 1827.

⏱ **Boat Trip on the Vilaine River.** – Boats go down the Vilaine to the Arzal Dam or up to Redon.

EXCURSIONS

Missillac. – Pop 3 886. *13 km - 8 miles by the N 165 SE and D 2 on the left.*
The 19C church, built in the Gothic style, contains in its north apsidal chapel a graceful 17C wood **altarpiece★** with small twisted columns ornamented with angels and Prophets.
Separated from the town by a small stretch of water beside the wood, the 15C **Bretesche Castle** with its low crenellated ramparts and water filled moat stands in an outstanding **site★**.

Arzal Dam. – *Round tour of 19 km - 12 miles by the N 165 NW and after 2 km - 1 mile the D 148 to the left.*
This dam on the Vilaine forms a freshwater reservoir thus eliminating the effect of the tides and making the trip easier for the coasting vessels that ply upstream to Redon. It is also an attractive stretch for pleasure craft. The D 139 follows the crest of the dam over the river.

Past the dam, turn left onto the D 34 to return to La Roche-Bernard.

Branféré Zoological Park. – *18 km - 11 miles NW. Take the N 165 in the direction of Muzillac, after 5 km - 3 miles turn right: follow the new "Blue Route" signposted and arrowed, for the park and château.*

Le Guerno. – Pop 512. The village, once a popular place of pilgrimage, has a 16C church built where a Templars' Chapel once stood. The church's exterior has on its south side a pulpit, stalls and bench (reserved for the clergy); the altar is backed against the Calvary (on the square). The round tower, on the west side, is capped by an 18C lantern turret.
The inside is decorated by 16C stained glass windows and choir stalls. 22 carved panels ornament the loft. At the transept two cylindrical columns support the vaulting. The trunk of the column on the left is hollow to collect offerings.

Once outside Le Guerno bear right then left onto the avenue which goes to the Branféré Château.

On the way note two lovely 18C fountains dedicated to St Anne and St Mary, respectively.

⏱ **Branféré Zoological Park.** – The château stands in 50 ha - 124 acres of parkland, where over 200 species of exotic animals and countless birds roam amidst the trees and a series of lakes.

Léhélec Château. – *18 km - 11 miles to the north. Return to Péaule, then take the D 20 in the direction of Redon and after 8 km - 5 miles turn right.*

Foleux. – The pleasure boat harbour is located in a lovely site at the confluence of the Vilaine and Trévelo Rivers.

After Foleux skirt the Vilaine – from here there is a good view of the wide valley. Bear right then turn left three times before taking the road which leads to the château.

⏱ **Léhélec Château.** – Surrounded by woodland this manor house built of ferruginous schist offers on its south front an attractive perspective of the three courtyards bordered by the 16 and 18C outbuildings. One of these buildings houses a small rural museum containing regional furniture and everyday objects. Visitors are also admitted to two rooms lit by tall windows – the salon and dining room on the ground floor.

Michelin Guides

The Red Guides (hotels and restaurants)
  Benelux - Deutschland - España Portugal - Main cities EUROPE - France - Great Britain and Ireland - Italia

The Green Guides (beautiful scenery, buildings and scenic routes)
  Austria - Canada - England: the West Country - Germany - Italy - London - New England - New York City - Portugal - Rome - Scotland - Spain - Switzerland and 7 guides on France

Michelin map **63** fold 4 or **230** fold 38

A charming small old town in a picturesque **site**★ on a promontory between deep dells. This landscape of rocks, woods, ravines, orchards and old houses bright with geraniums attracts many painters.

★ **Old houses.** – In the heart of the city stand old 16 and 17C town houses which you can see as you stroll along Rue du Porche, the Place des Halles and Place du Puits. They have elegant flower-decked granite façades and, often, corner turrets. At the Place du Puits note the former law court, the entrance of which is surmounted by a scale.

(J. Labbé/Azimut)
Rochefort-en-Terre. – Old houses

⊙ **Castle.** – The only features that remain of the castle, destroyed in 1793, are the imposing entrance fort, sections of the walls, the bases of the towers, the underground passages and the outbuildings. They were restored at the turn of the century with parts from the former 17C Kéralio Manorhouse near Muzillac.
The tour takes you through the main hall, a salon and two more rooms. They are furnished with 16 and 17C chests, wardrobes and chairs and decorated with 16C Flemish tapestries, modern paintings, and a collection of Quimper porcelain Virgins (13 and 14C).
The hunting pavilion, in the garden with its ivy-decked well, houses a collection of tools and domestic objets which recount the past way of life of the people of the region.
From the terrace, behind the castle there is a fine view of the Gueuzon and the Grées schistous plateau.

Notre-Dame-de-la-Tronchaye. – The 12, 15 and 16C church has a façade embellished with four gables pierced with Flamboyant bays. Inside, the chancel contains 16C stalls and, left of the high altar, a white stone Renaissance altarpiece. In the south arm of the transept, a 17C altarpiece behind a fine 18C wrought-iron grille, bears the venerated statue of Our Lady of La Tronchaye, which was found in the 12C in a hollow tree where it was hidden at the time of the Norman invasions. The statue is the object of a pilgrimage on the Sunday after 14 August. In the north arm of the transept is a wrought iron baptismal font and white stone Renaissance altarpieces; one of the altarpieces is decorated with 3 niches each of which contains a painted wood statue. At the back of the nave the magnificent gallery in finely carved wood comes from the old roodscreen as does the canopy over the high altar.
On the square stands a small 16C Calvary with three tiers of carved figures: the scenes of the Passion, the Crucifixion and the Deposition of the Cross (both at the top) are represented.

★ **ROCHE-JAGU Castle**

Michelin map **59** fold 2 or **230** fold 7

Take a road to the right branching off the D 787 towards Lézardrieux, 5.5 km - 3 1/2 miles from Pontrieux.

⊙ The castle was built in the 15C at the top of the steep wooded slopes which form the left bank of the Trieux River. It was restored in 1968. Together with other fortresses, no longer extant, it commanded the river and thus retains its defensive aspect. On the west façade, note the corbels which supported the former wall-walk and its five doors. The tour includes several rooms with French-style ceilings and large chimneys, the small chapel and its two oratories. There is a magnificent view of the **setting**★ of the Trieux from the terrace in front of the east wall and from the windows facing east and the covered wall walk on the second storey. The river forms a steep sided loop at the foot of the castle which can be reached by a footpath to the right. Notice the ornate chimneys on top of the building.

To choose a hotel, restaurant or camping site
use the annual Michelin Guides

   France and

   Camping Caravaning France

La ROCHE-MAURICE

Michelin map **58** fold 5 or **230** fold 4

The village, situated on a hillside and dominated by the ruins of a castle, has a fine parish close.

★ PARISH CLOSE
time: 1/2 hour

Three crosses featuring Christ and the thieves mark the entrance.

Church. – An elegant, twin-galleried belfry crowns the 16C building. The **south porch★** is delicately carved with bunches of grapes and statuettes of saints.
Inside, note the Renaissance **rood-screen★** decorated on the side facing the nave with twelve statues carved in the round, including nine Apostles and three popes, and on the chancel side with low-reliefs of saints. Behind the high altar, a large **stained glass window★** (1539) illustrates the Passion and the Resurrection of Christ. Also of interest is the pannelled ceiling adorned with angels and coats of arms, carved friezes and beams.

★ **Ossuary.** – It dates from 1640 and is one of the largest in Brittany. Above the outside font, Death (Ankou) is shown armed with an arrow, threatening small figures framed in medallions representing all social classes: a peasant, a woman, a lawyer, a bishop, St Yves, a pauper and a rich man with an inscription « *Je vous tue tous* » (Death comes to all).

(After R. Le Thomas/Azimut photo)
La Roche-Maurice. – Ankou

★ ROCHERS-SÉVIGNÉ Château

Michelin map **63** fold 8 or **230** N of fold 42

The Rochers-Sévigné Château, which was the home of the Marquise de Sévigné, is a place of literary interest. Admirers of the famous *Letters* will enjoy visiting the castle and park.

The Marquise de Sévigné at Les Rochers. – The Marquise used to stay frequently at the château, largely to save money as her husband and her son had spent three-quarters of her fortune, and after 1678 she virtually lived there until she died in 1696 at Grignan in the Drôme.
Her letters give a picture of life as it was led at Les Rochers. Up at eight o'clock, Mass in the chapel at nine, a walk and then lunch. In the afternoon, needlework, another walk, talks and letter writing. Charles, the lady's son, used to read learned books aloud. Sometimes the readings would go on for five hours. The reader's stamina and the audience's staying-power seem worthy of admiration. Supper at 8pm. After dinner Charles would read again, this time from amusing books "to keep himself awake". The circle broke up at 10pm, but Mme de Sévigné went on reading or writing in her room until midnight.
The only variety in this country life was that created by the visits of local ladies and gentlemen or a little trip to Vitré when the legislative bodies of the district met there. The Marquise describes, sometimes with a touch of malice, the provincial nobility, their dress, their airs and graces and their faults. The official banquets, at which 400 bottles of wine were emptied, filled her with astonishment. "As much wine passes through the body of a Breton", she wrote, "as water under the bridges."
The noble lady took an interest in repairs to the building. She felt dizzy when she saw carpenters perched on the roof: "One can only thank God", she wrote, "that some men will do for 12 *sous* what others would not do for 10 000 *écus.*" That did not prevent her from keeping a sharp eye on the accounts and deploring the high cost of living.

Château. – The château was built in the 15C and remodelled in the 17C. It consists of two wings set at right angles. On the left, as you enter, is the chapel (1671), built by the "very good" Abbot of Coulanges, the Marquise's maternal uncle.
The only parts which are open to visitors are the chapel and two rooms in the big north tower: the room on the ground floor was known as the Green Room *(Cabinet Vert).* It contains Mme de Sévigné's furniture, personal possessions, family pictures and her portrait; there is a collection of autographs and documents in a glass case. The 16C chimneypiece is adorned with the Marquise's initials (Marie de Rabutin-Chantal – MRC).

Garden. – In the garden at the end of the main avenue, at the Place Coulanges, is the semicircular wall that Mme de Sévigné called "that little wall that repeats words right into your ear" because of its double echo (stones mark the places where the two conversationalists should stand).

Park. – Beyond the garden lies the large, wooded park, which is crossed by avenues the names of which recall the Marquise and her literary environment: the Mall, the Lone Wolf, Infinity, the Holy Horror, My Mother's Whim, My Daughter's Whim, Royal Avenue.

ROSANBO Château

Michelin map **58** fold 7 or **230** fold 6 – 8 km - 5 miles W of Plouaret

The road to the castle branches off to the right from the D 32, which links Lanvellec to Plufur.

⊘ The château stands on the site of a former fortified castle built on a rock overlooking the Bo – from which the name is derived: *ros* = rock, *an* = on the, Bo = the name of the stream.

As you enter the courtyard you see all the different periods of construction. The oldest part is 14C and consists of the buildings on the right of the courtyard up to the tower; the part opposite is 15C and partly remodelled in 17C and that on the left, 19C.

The ground floor rooms contain fine Renaissance Breton and Florentine furniture, Italian and English silverware and 17C Aubusson and 18C Flemish tapestries. Church and sacristy furnishings have been assembled in a great hall and gallery.

The **library**, which contains over 8 000 volumes including a large collection of 17C books, looks on to a terrace ornamented with a pond. A second terrace, communicating with the first, is decorated with a formal garden of box hedging whose geometrical design was inspired by the work of Le Nôtre. From this terrace there is a sheer drop to the Bo Valley.

On the entrance side and sweeping away into the distance is the French **garden**. It is terraced and consists of lawns. The end of the garden, shaded by trees, is divided into "green apartments"; there is a Salon of the Four-Seasons, each represented by a cherub, the "triangle" with Tuscan vases, a former open-air theatre beneath a fine arch of trees and a lawn known as "the lawn of the lion overcoming the serpent" after the statue by Barye which stands upon it. The whole is divided off from the main garden by two arbours separated by a path.

On the lawn before the 14C façade there is a statue of a wild boar cut in rose granite.

★ ROSCOFF   Pop 3 787

Michelin map **58** fold 6 or **230** fold 5 – Facilities

Roscoff is a much frequented seaside resort and a medical centre using sea water treatment; it is also a fishing port for lobsters and spiny lobster, a pleasure boat harbour and a great vegetable market and distribution centre to England. A pier to the east of Bloscon Point closes off the deep water harbour from which car ferries to and from Plymouth and Cork operate.

The University of Paris owns a laboratory in the town for oceanographic and biological research.

SIGHTS

★ **Notre-Dame-de-Kroaz-Batz**. –
⊘ Built in the 16C, this church has a remarkable Renaissance lantern turret **belfry**★, one of the finest in Finistère. The outside walls and the tower are adorned with sculptured ships and cannon, for Roscoff was a base for privateers as well as a trading port in the 16-17C. Inside note the seven 15C alabasters in the **altarpiece**★ of the altar in the south aisle depicting scenes from the Passion; the church has other altarpieces – particularly interesting is the one (17C) at the high altar adorned with statuettes, angels and medallions.

In the church close are a funerary chapel and an ossuary. The latter is larger and in early 17C style.

★ **Charles Pérez Aquarium** (B). – The
⊘ aquarium has a central pool and several basins in which most of the creatures to be found in the Channel are shown in their natural state. The 1st floor is devoted to the history of the biological centre and oceanographic research.

(Jacques Guillard/Scope)

Roscoff. – Belfry of Notre-Dame-de-Kroaz-Baz

Old houses. – The houses in the Place Lacaze-Duthiers (8) and Rue Amiral-Révellière (13) date from the 16 and 17C. In the latter the so-called House of Marie Stuart (**E**) with its elegant façade adorned with ogee arches, is noteworthy.

Ste-Barbe Chapel. – *Go preferably at high tide. Go round the old fishing port and leave the car in the car park on the left.*
From the chapel *(viewing table)* a fine view extends over the town and port, Batz Island, Primel Point and the deep water harbour. Below the chapel can be seen the fish farm.

⊘ **Fish farm** (Viviers). – There are walkways amidst the pools containing salmon trout, salmon, lobster, spiny lobster and crab.

Go round the bluff on which stands the chapel.

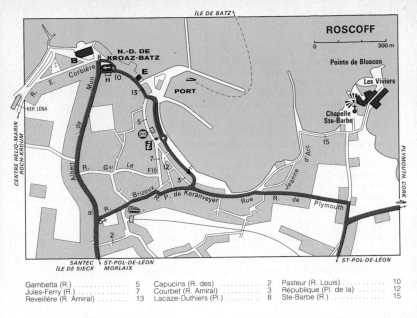

EXCURSIONS

Batz Island. – *Boat trip, crossing: 20 minutes. Description p 53.*

Sieck Island. – *6.5 km - 4 miles W. On leaving Roscoff, take the road on the right to Santec.* It runs along a small bay bounded by Perharidy Point where is the Helio therapy treatment centre, crosses Santec and leads to Dossen through a market-garden area. *At Dossen, turn right, then left to reach the car park.* Sieck Island which can be reached on foot at low tide, has lovely beaches of fine sand and affords views to the east of Batz Island fringed with reefs, to the west over the coast towards Moguériec.

ROSPORDEN   Pop 3 842

Michelin map 𝟻𝟾 fold 16 or 𝟸𝟹𝟶 fold 33

This little town stands by a pool formed by the Aven River, in which the east end of the church is reflected. There are many canning factories in the town which is also famous for its mead (*chouchen* in Breton).

Church. – The 14-15C building, remodelled in the 17C, has a fine square **bell-tower★** with four pinnacles and four windows decorated with tracery framing the octagonal spire. Go through the 14C porch to see inside the gilded 17C high altar above an Entombment, a Virgin and Child (15C) and a Mary Magdalene (16C).

EXCURSION

St-Yvi. – Pop 2 176. *9 km - 5 miles W. Leave Rosporden by the D 765, the Quimper road.* The town has a small parish close with a simple Calvary-cross with a wreathed column and a late 15C ossuary adorned with six trefoil arches. The early 16C **church** has an elegant pierced belfry with two gallerles. Inside, note the 17C retable at the high altar and the altarpiece of the Rosary (18C) to the left of the chancel.

ROSTRENEN   Pop 4 391

Michelin map 𝟻𝟿 fold 11 or 𝟸𝟹𝟶 fold 21

This pretty little town is situated on a hillside.

Notre-Dame-du-Roncier. – The church is the former castle's chapel. Built in 14C and remodelled in 18 and 19C, it has a beautiful Gothic-Renaissance porch. Close by is an interesting 17C sacred fountain. A *pardon* is held on 15 August.

Le Miniou. – Take the D 764 towards Pontivy, then a road to the right and up the hill turn left to reach a weather centre (station climatologique) situated at an altitude of 263m - 928ft. The panorama extends over Rostrenen and the area round Callac to the northwest and Loudéac to the east; from the terrace, there is a view over the Guéméné region to the south and the Noires Mountains to the west.

EXCURSIONS

Round tour of 45 km - 28 miles. – *Time: about 2 1/2 hours. Leave Rostrenen by the D 790, the St-Brieuc road.*

St-Nicolas-du-Pélem. – Pop 2 214. The town includes a 15-16C church with two fine stained glass windows depicting the Passion (1470) at the east end. Go round the north side of the church to see the 17C fountain of St-Nicolas which abuts on to a house.

Proceed to Lanrivain on the D 50 through the smiling Faoudel Valley.

Lanrivain. – *P 127.*

Take the D 87 towards Trémargat and after 1.5 km - 1 mile bear left.

★ **Toul Goulic Gorges.** – *1/4 hour on foot Rtn.* At the far end of the car park overlooking the wooded valley of the Blavet, take the steep path leading downhill through the woods to the cleft in which the Blavet disappears. The river is still full at the beginning of the cleft (north side) but has completely vanished by the time you reach the middle of the cleft and flows, rumbling, beneath a mass of huge rocks.

Turn back and bear left.

Between Trémargat and Kergrist-Moëlou, the landscape is studded with great boulders.

Kergrist-Moëlou. – On the *placître* (church square, *p 37*), shaded by fine old yew trees, stands a Calvary (1578) with some 100 figures in Kersanton granite resting on its octagonal plinth. The figures were damaged during the Revolution and have been replaced haphazardly. The imposing 16C church has a twin transept and in the chancel the stained glass windows are decorated with the coat of arms of the Rostrenen family, the church founders. On the south side is a small ossuary with trefoil arches.

Take the D 31 through St-Lubin to return to Rostrenen.

Nantes-Brest Canal. – *Round tour of 20 km - 12 miles – about 2 1/2 hours.* Leave Rostrenen by the N 164 towards Carhaix-Plouguer and after 3.5 km - 2 miles, turn left into the D 3, the Gourin road. The road reaches the canal, built between 1823 and 1834, at the summit level (alt 184m - 604ft). Walk along the towpath to the right of the bridge, leading to the canal cutting and affording a view of the series of forty-four locks through which boats climb or descend 120m - 384ft in 17 km - 11 miles to Carhaix-Plouguer.

Proceed to Glomel and then turn right into the D 85 towards Paule; after 1.8 km - 1 mile, bear right.

On the canal banks, the former lock keeper's house stands in a pretty **site★**. A pleasant walk along the towpath upstream and downstream from the bridge.

Continue to La Pie and turn right into the N 164 to return to Rostrenen.

RUMENGOL

Michelin map 🔢 fold 5 or 🔢 fold 18 – Local map p 50

The village, situated in the Châteaulin basin, is at its most interesting on *pardon* days *(p 226)*. People come from all over Brittany to attend these festivals dedicated to Our Lady of all Remedies, the most colourful is on Trinity Sunday and another is held on 15 August. Rumengol dates from the time of King Gradlon *(p 25)*, who built a chapel there in the 5C.

Church. – The church is 16C as shown by the south porch and the magnificent west front in Kersanton granite but significant alterations were made in the 17 and 18C. Inside, a 15C statue of Our Lady on the left stands at the entrance to the chancel. The two **altarpieces★** and altars date from 1686.

In the centre of the village, near the chancel apse, is a sacred fountain (1792).

On a grassy area surrounded by fir trees stands an oratory where services are held on the two great *pardon* days. Behind the oratory, note the 15C Calvary in the cemetery.

RUNAN

Michelin map 🔢 fold 2 or 🔢 fold 7 – 5 km - 3 miles W of Pontrieux

Runan, which stands on a plateau in the Tréguier region, has a large church which belonged to the Knights Templar and then to the Hospitallers of St John of Jerusalem.

★ **Church.** – The 14-15C church is richly decorated. The south side has four gables pierced with broad windows and emblazoned façades. The porch gable is adorned with a sculptured lintel depicting the Annunciation and a Descent from the Cross. The superimposed figures of the twelve Apostles join to form the keystone of the vaulting. The ossuary adjoining the church dates from 1552; the outdoor pulpit from the time of St Vincent Ferrier *(p 214)*.

Inside, the building is roofed with panelled vaults resting on decorated friezes: signs of the Zodiac to the left of the nave, animals on the right. The Commandery Chapel (right) contains slim sculptured pillars. The furnishings are remarkable: the great stained glass window depicting the Crucifixion in the east end (1423) is beautifully designed. The old altarpiece of the font chapel of the same period includes exceptionally delicate figures (five scenes from the lives of Christ and the Virgin) made of bluish Tournai stone, Christ and a *Pietà*.

ST-AUBIN-DU-CORMIER   Pop 2 433

Michelin map 🔢 fold 18 or 🔢 fold 27

This city of the Breton marshland witnessed in 1488 the decisive battle *(p 22)* waged by Breton troops under Duke François II of Brittany and the army of the King of France led by the Duke de la Trémoille. François II was defeated and signed the Treaty of Verger renouncing Brittany's sovereign rights.

Castle ruins. – The impressive 13C fortress stands, still an imposing ruin, between the pool and the deep ravine which formed its natural defences.

Bécherel Rocks. – Beyond the ruins, a path on the left of the road winds through a mass of rocks in a wooded setting.

Michelin map 59 fold 3 or 230 folds 8, 9

The town is built 3 km - 2 miles from the sea on a plateau deeply cleft by two watercourses: the Gouëdic and the Gouet. Bold viaducts span their valleys. The Gouet is canalized and leads to the commercial and fishing port of Légué.

St-Brieuc is the administrative, commercial and industrial centre of the department (Côtes-du-Nord). The markets and fairs of the town are much frequented, especially the Fair of St Michael on 29 September and another fair also in early September.

An industrial zone has been established southwest of the town, where there are already many factories and great refrigerated depots intended for the storage of local products. The *pardon* of Notre-Dame-d'Espérance takes place the last Sunday in May.

SIGHTS

★ **St Stephen's Cathedral** (**Cathédrale St-Étienne**) (**AY**). – This great building of the 13 and ⊙ 14C has been reconstructed several times and restored in 19C; its mass bears striking witness to its original role of church fortress. The front is framed by two great towers complete with loopholes and machicolations and supported by stout buttresses. The two arms of the transept jut far out and are protected by towers with pepperpot roofs.

ST-BRIEUC

		Abbé-Garnier (R.)	**AX** 2	Martray (Pl. du)	**AY** 33
		Commune (Bd de la)	**BY** 12	Piélo (Bd de)	**BV** 34
		Corderie (R. de la)	**AX** 13	Quinquaine (R.)	**AY** 38
Chapitre (R. du)	**AZ** 3	Ferry (R. Jules)	**AX** 16	Résistance (Pl. de la)	**AY** 39
Charbonnerie (R.)	**AY** 4	Gambetta (Bd)	**AV** 17	Rohan (R. de)	**AYZ** 40
Glais-Bizoin (R.)	**ABY** 20	Hérault (Bd)	**AV** 23	St-Gouéno (R.)	**AY** 44
Jouallan (R.)	**AY** 26	Le-Gorrec (R. P.)	**AZ** 28	Victor-Hugo (R.)	**BX** 50
St-Gilles (R.)	**AY** 43	Libération (Av. de la)	**BZ** 29	3-Frères-Le-Goff (R.)	**AY** 52
St-Guillaume (R.)	**BZ** 46	Lycéens-Martyrs (R. des)	**AZ** 32	3-Frères-Merlin (R.)	**AY** 53

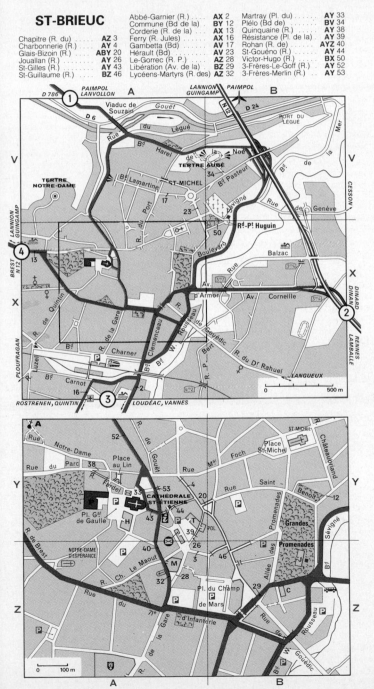

Go into the church through the Gothic porch in the front.

The lofty nave with its seven bays was rebuilt in the 18C. The harmonious three-sided chancel has an elegant triforium with quatrefoil balustrade and trilobed arches above the great arcades.

In the south aisle, note the carved wooden altar by Corlay (*c* 1745) in the Chapel of the Holy Sacrament. The north arm of the transept is lit by fine 15C stained glass windows and in the small chapel stands the tomb of St William (died 1231). The apsidal chapel contains a graceful 15C alabaster Virgin. The 16C organ loft, the 18C pulpit and the Stations of the Cross carved in granite by Saupique (1958) are also noteworthy.

Old houses (AY). – The quarter to the north of the cathedral still retains many 15-16C half-timbered and corbelled houses. Walk through the Place au Lin: the Ribeault mansion; at No 15, the house known as the "mansion of the Dukes of Brittany"; and Nos 17, 19, 27, 29, 31, 32, 34), the Rue Quinquaine (No 9) and the Rue de Gouet (Nos 6, 16, 22).

★ **Aubé Hill (Tertre Aubé) (ABV).** – The hill commands a fine **view★** of the Gouet Valley, crossed by the viaduct which carries the road to Paimpol; also of the partly hidden port of Légué, below, and, to the right, of the Bay of St-Brieuc. On a hill to the right is the ruined tower of Cesson.

Grandes Promenades (BYZ). – These walks encircle the Law Courts. Among the statues are a bust by Elie Le Goff Sr. of the writer Villiers de l'Isle-Adam, who was born at St-Brieuc, *Form arising from matter* by Paul Le Goff and *La Bretonne du Goëlo* by Francis Renaud.

Huguin Roundabout (Rond-point Huguin) (BX). – From the roundabout, on which stands a monument to the folklorist, Anatole Le Braz *(p 29)*, there is a view of the Gouëdic Valley and its two viaducts with the village and tower of Cesson perched high above, St-Brieuc Bay and the coast as far as Cape Fréhel.

St-Brieuc Fountain (AY A). – The fountain, which is sheltered by a 15C porch, stands against the east end of the chapel of Notre-Dame-de-la-Fontaine which was rebuilt in the 19C. The Welsh monk, Brieuc (Brioch), is believed to have lived there when he came to preach in the area in the 5C.

Tour du Saint-Esprit (AY P). – The tower is an interesting Renaissance structure with a pepperpot octagonal corner tower, restored in 1962 and contains the Préfecture.

EXCURSIONS

Round tour of 25 km - 15 miles. – *Time: about 2 hours. Leave St-Brieuc N by the Port du Legué; follow the quay on the left bank.* On the right, the ruined tower of Cesson is outlined amid the greenery; as the road climbs there is a good view over the Guettes Point at the far end of the bay and the coast as far as Erquy Point. *Cross St-Laurent-de-la-Mer and at Ville-Agan, take the Rue du Roselier on the right.*

★ **Le Roselier Point.** – Take a path on the right of the telescope to go round the point. Fine **views★** extend over St-Quay-Portrieux and the coast; the path passes near an old oven used for turning cannon balls red-hot, and skirts a villa. The view takes in Cesson Point, the far end of St-Brieuc Bay and the Guettes Point with its mussel-poles, and the coast towards Le Val-André. Paths cut in the cliff side lead back to the starting point.

Turn back and after 2 km - 1 mile, bear right.

Martin Beach. – This pretty beach lies between Le Roselier Point and the Tablettes Reef (Rocher des Tablettes).

The road then climbs steeply and at Ville-Fontaine, bear right into a pleasant little road descending between wooded embankments.

Les Rosaires Beach. – The beach is framed between wooded cliffs some 100m - 320ft high. The view includes the whole of the Bay of St-Brieuc from St-Quay Point to Cape Erquy.

The D 1^B leads straight back to St-Brieuc.

★★ ST-CAST-LE-GUILDO   Pop 3 246

Michelin map 59 fold 5 or 230 folds 10, 11 – Local map p 96 – Facilities

This seaside resort, which is much frequented, is formed by three settlements: Le Bourg, L'Isle and La Garde. A fine beach is bounded by La Garde and St-Cast Points. The port shelters a small fishing fleet which specializes in scallops and clams.

★★ **St-Cast Point.** – There is a superb **view★★** of the Emerald Coast from the point *(viewing table – table d'orientation – beside the signal station).* At the tip of the point a monument to the Escaped Prisoners of France (Monument aux Évadés) can be reached by a cliff path which follows the shore, passes another monument dedicated to the crew of the frigate *Laplace,* mined in 1950, and rejoins the St-Cast road at La Mare beach.

★★ **La Garde Point.** – At the end of this point there is a very fine **view★★** of the beaches of St-Cast and Pen Guen and the coast as far as La Varde Point; also a statue of Notre-Dame-de-la-Garde by Armel Beaufils. A scenic path goes round the point by way of the Corniche de la Plage near the Hôtel Ar Vro, passes beside the oratory, follows the cliff along the point and, on the south shore, joins the road leading to the slipway near the oratory.

Commemorative column. – From the base of the column there is a nice **view** of the harbour, the beach (Grande Plage) and the coastline towards St-Malo.

The column is surmounted by a greyhound for France, trampling the English leopard. It recalls the failure of a British attack on St-Malo in 1758, during the Seven Years War, when 13 000 British troops returned to embark in warships anchored in the Bay of St-Cast. They were attacked by the Duke of Aiguillon, Governor of Brittany, and lost 2 400 men. The Duke directed the battle from the mill of Anne de la Vieuxville. When La Chalotais *(p 179)* Procurator of the Rennes Parliament, was told that the Duke "covered himself with glory" he commented sardonically: "Yes, and especially with flour". This did not improve relations between the Procurator and the Governor.

Church *(at Le Bourg).* – The modern church contains a 16C stoup and some 17C statues. In the north arm of the transept a modern stained glass window depicts the Battle of St-Cast *(see above).*

Ste-Blanche *(at L'Isle).* – Above the high altar is an old statue of St Blanche (Gwen) – the mother of St Guénolé, St Jacut and St Venec *(p 172)* – which is an object of great veneration. There are also some 17C statues.

★ ST-FIACRE Chapel

Michelin map 🗒 fold 17 or 🗒 fold 20 – 2.5 km - 2 miles S of Le Faouët

The chapel is a fine 15C building. The façade has one of the best gable-belfries in Brittany *(details and illustration p 35).*
Inside, the **rood-screen**★★ of lace-like woodcarving, is a Flamboyant work of 1480 *(photo p 36).* On the nave side scenes of the Temptation of Adam and Eve, the Annunciation and the Calvary are related. The most curious figures are on the chancel side; they picture theft (a man picking fruit from a tree), drunkenness (a man vomiting a fox), lust (a man and a woman) and laziness (a Breton peasant playing bagpipes and a bombard). The decoration of the panels of the gallery and the brackets is very varied. The stone altarpiece against the left pillar shows the martyrdom of St Sebastian. There are old statues and 16C **stained glass windows** in the chancel and transept. These include The Passion (chancel), The Life of St John the Baptist (south transept), The Tree of Jesse and The Life of St Fiacre (north transept). The statues of St Apollinia, St Fiacre (in a painted wooden niche) and a Breton duke in court dress date from the 15 and 16C.

ST-GEORGES-DE-GRÉHAIGNE   Pop 348

Michelin map 🗒 fold 7 or 🗒 fold 13

Before the polders were reclaimed the sea came to within 1 km - 1/2 mile of the village. The Benedictine **church** was built in the 15C on the hilltop on the former site of a chapel that had been dedicated to St George in 1030. The interior, with its oak roof is adorned by several large statues, the oldest being one of St Samson (in the nave across from the entrance). The central aisle paved with tombstones leads to the narrower chancel lit by a 15C window showing the Virgin as a Breton peasant. On looking between the trees behind the church one can distinguish Mont-St-Michel beyond a distant row of poplar trees.

EXCURSION

ⓥ **Miniature Mont-St-Michel (Petit Mont-St-Michel).** – *9 km - 5 1/2 miles NW on the D 797 and then bear left on the road to St-Marcan.*
On the hillside, in an enclosure, monuments of the region are presented at a 1 to 50 scale reduction: the Church of Pontorson, Mont-St-Michel, Fougères, etc. Stroll along the pathways from where the views open onto the bay of Mont-St-Michel. Playground for children.

ST-GILDAS-DE-RHUYS   Pop 1 064

Michelin map 🗒 fold 12 or 🗒 fold 50 – Local map p 138

This village owes its origin to a monastery founded by St Gildas in the 6C. The most famous of the abbots who governed it was Abélard in the 12C.

Abélard. – It was after the adventures with Héloïse, that the learned philosopher tried to find peace in this Breton solitude. His disillusion was quick and cruel: "I live", he wrote to Héloïse, "in a wild country whose language I find strange and horrible; I see only savages; I take my walks on the inaccessible shores of a rough sea; my monks have only one rule, which is to have none at all. I should like you to see my house; you would never take it for an abbey; the only decorations on the doors are the footmarks of various animals – hinds, wolves, bears, wild boars – or the hideous remains of owls. Every day brings new dangers; I always seem to see a sword hanging over my head." However, the monks used poison, not a sword, to get rid of their Abbot. It was a wonder he survived and managed to escape through a secret passage in 1132.

★ **Church.** – *Time: 1/2 hour.* This is the former abbey church built at the end of the 11C and largely rebuilt in the 16 and 17C. The Romanesque chevet has pure, harmonious lines; it is ornamented with brackets; note a small carving depicting a tournament. Inside, the Romanesque **chancel**★ is remarkable. Behind the Baroque high altar is the tomb of St Gildas (11C). Other tombs in the north transept and the ambulatory are lit by modern stained glass windows. There are also the gravestones of St Goustan (11C) and the children of Brittany (13C). At the end of the nave is a stoup made up from two ⓥ carved capitals. Another capital is found in the south aisle. The **treasury**★ contains valuable and well displayed old objects: shrines, reliquaries (15C) containing the arms and legs of St Gildas, and his embroidered mitre, a 17C silver-gilt cross bejewelled with emeralds, etc.

ST-GONÉRY

Michelin map 🗏 fold 2 or 🗏 fold 7 – Local map p 209

This little town in the Trégorrois region has a fine 15C chapel.

★ **St-Gonéry Chapel.** – The chapel has a curiously leaning lead steeple (1612) on a 10C
🕓 tower.

Inside the painted wood vaulting depicts scenes from the Old and New Testament;
these **paintings** which date from the late 15C, were restored in the 18 and 19C.

In the chapel on the right of the chancel, there is a 16C **Reliquary cupboard★**, a finely carved
canopied type of chest. The left chapel contains the 16C **mausoleum★** of a bishop of
Tréguier; the recumbent figure rests on a great marble slab decorated with mouldings
and supported on four lions. A 15C Virgin in alabaster stands in the nave.

Under the belfry porch are the sarcophagus and tomb (1614) of St Gonery, a hermit
who preached in the region in the 6C. An opening in the tomb's arches enabled sailors
and soldiers leaving for a long journey to remove a handful of earth which they
promised to restore on their return.

A small Calvary and an octagonal 16C pulpit stand in the cemetery.

★ **ST-JEAN-DU-DOIGT**   Pop 656

Michelin map 🗏 fold 6 or 🗏 folds 5, 6

This picturesque village owes its name to the relic kept in its church since the 15C. It
celebrates its *pardon,* which is attended particularly by people suffering from
ophthalmia, the last Sunday in June.

Parish Close. – *Time: 3/4 hour.* It has a 16C triumphal gateway and, on the left, a pretty
Renaissance **fountain★** dominated by God the Father blessing the baptism of His Son
performed by St John the Baptist. To the right of the church porch is a small chapel
(1577) adorned inside with a frieze and sculpted beams.

★ **Church.** – St John's finger, which was brought to the Chapel of St Meriadoc *c* 1420,
worked miracles. A great church was started in 1440, but the building went slowly and
was finished only thanks to the generosity of Anne of Brittany in 1513.

The church, built in the Flamboyant style, has a flat east end. The belfry which has lost
its spire, abuts on to the first bay in the nave which includes eight bays in all. The rich
furnishings were completely destroyed by a fire in 1955 and the whole building was
badly damaged but it has now been restored.

At the base of the tower, abutting on to the buttresses, are two small ossuaries; one,
on the right is Gothic, the other, Renaissance in style.

★★ **Treasury.** – The treasury contains several reliquaries, one of which holds the first joint
🕓 of the index finger of St John the Baptist. There is also a **processional cross★**. The finest
piece is a silver-gilt Renaissance **chalice★★**.

★★ **ST-LUNAIRE**   Pop 2 020

Michelin map 🗏 fold 5 or 🗏 fold 11 – Local map p 97

This smart resort has two beaches: to the east that of St-Lunaire, which is the more
frequented facing St-Malo, and to the west that of Longchamp, which is the larger
opposite Cape Fréhel.

SIGHTS

★★ **Décollé Point.** – The point is joined to the mainland by a natural bridge crossing a
deep fissure and known as the Cat's Leap (Saut du Chat); the Décollé Promenades are
laid out beyond the bridge.

> *To the left of the entrance to the Décollé Pavilion, take the road leading to the point,
> on which stands a granite cross.* From here the vantage point affords a very fine
> **view★★** of the Emerald Coast, from Cape Fréhel to the Varde Point.

★ **The Sirens' Cave** (Grotte des Sirènes). – From the bridge crossing the cleft through which
it opens to the sea, you can see the bottom of the grotto. The wash of the sea at high
tide is spectacular.

🕓 **Old Church.** – The church stands among the trees in a former cemetery. The nave
is 11C; the side aisles and canted chancel were rebuilt in the 17C. In the middle of the
nave lies the tomb of St Lunaire with the recumbent figure of the saint (14C) resting
on a Gallo-Roman sarcophagus. The transept contains seven tombs; in the Pontbriand
Chapel in the north arm, note the tombs of a squire and a lady (15C), in the Pontual
Chapel in the south arm, the tomb of a lady of the Pontual family (13-14C), richly carved
in high relief.

The Michelin Guide France

revises annually its selection of establishments offering

- *a good but moderately priced meal*
- *prices with service included or net prices*
- *a plain menu for a modest price*
- *free overnight parking*

Michelin map **59** fold 6 or **230** fold 11 – Local maps pp 97 and 176

St-Malo, St-Servan, Paramé and Rothéneuf (facilities) have joined together to form a single administrative district which is known as the commune de St-Malo. The **site★★★** of St-Malo is unique in France and makes it one of the great tourist centres of Brittany.

The Port. – The port has four wet docks (Vauban, Duguay-Trouin, Bouvet and Jacques Cartier) and an outer harbour.

Imports of coal, fertilizers, granite, wood and pulp for paper, wine, foodstuffs for cattle, hydrocarbons and phosphates keep it busy. Its main export is wheat from the hinterland.

It is the only Breton port to still have a cod fishing fleet *(details p 20)* and is the port from which passengers cross from France to the Channel Islands.

Pleasure boat harbours have been made in the Vauban dock and in the Sablons Bay and attract many sailing enthusiasts.

HISTORICAL NOTES

Origin. – St Malo, returning from Wales in the 6C, converted the Gallo-Roman settlement Aleth (St Servan) to Christianity and became its bishop. The neighbouring island on which the town of St-Malo is built today was then uninhabited. Later, people settled there because it was easy to defend from Norman attacks, and it became important enough for the Bishopric of Aleth to be transferred to it in 1144. It took the name of St Malo while Aleth put itself under the protection of another local saint – St Servan.

The town belonged to its bishops, who built ramparts round it. It took no part in provincial rivalries. At the time of the League, St-Malo declared itself a republic and was able to keep its independence for four years. This principle was reflected in the device: "Ni Français, ni Breton, Malouin suis" (I am neither a Frenchman nor a Breton but a man of St-Malo).

Famous men of St-Malo. – Few towns have had as many famous sons as St-Malo over the centuries.

Jacques Cartier left in 1534 to look for gold in Newfoundland and Labrador: instead he discovered the mouth of the St Lawrence River, which he took to be the estuary of a great Asian river. As the word *Canada,* which means "village" in the Huron language, was often used by the Red Indians he encountered, he used the word to name the country.

Cartier took possession of the land in the name of the King of France in 1534, but it was only under Champlain that the colonization of Canada began and that Quebec was founded (1608).

Porcon de la Bardinais, who had been charged in 1665 by the St-Malo shipowners to defend their ships against the Barbary pirates, was captured and taken before the Dey of Algiers. The Dey sent him to Louis XIV with peace proposals on condition that if these were not accepted he would return to Algeria. The Dey's proposals were refused, so Porcon went to St-Malo to put his affairs in order, said farewell to his family and returned to Africa, where he was executed.

Duguay-Trouin (1673-1736) and **Surcouf** (1773-1827) are the most famous of the St-Malo privateers. These bold seamen received "letters of marque" from the king which permitted them to attack warships or merchantmen without being treated as pirates, that is, hanged from the main yard. In the 17 and 18C the privateers inflicted heavy losses on the English, the Dutch and the Spanish.

Duguay was the son of a rich shipowner and had been destined for the priesthood; but by the time he was 16 the only way to put an end to his wild living was to send him to sea. His gifts were such that at 24 he entered the so-called Great Corps of the French Navy as a commander and at 36 he was given a peerage. When he died he was a Lieutenant General in the seagoing forces and a Commander of the Order of St Louis.

Surcouf's history is completely different, but quite as outstanding. He answered the call of the sea when very young and soon began a prodigious career of fabulous exploits. First as slaver then as privateer he amassed an enormous fortune. At 36 he retired! He continued, however, to make money by fitting out privateers and merchantmen.

Chateaubriand and Lamennais brought the flavour of the Romantic Movement to their native St-Malo.

François-René de Chateaubriand (1768-1848) was the tenth and last child of a very noble Breton family who had fallen on evil times. His father went to America in search of fortune and was able, on his return, to set up as a shipowner at St-Malo. In a room on the 2nd floor of a modest townhouse (maison natale de Chateaubriand – it gives onto the courtyard of the Hôtel France et Chateaubriand and is near the Quic-en-Groigne tower) René was born. From its window he could look out to sea beyond the ramparts and dream...

The future poet spent his early years in roaming about the port, then went in succession through schools at Dinan, Dol, Rennes and Brest, dreaming sometimes of the priesthood, sometimes of the sea.

He spent two years in exile at Combourg *(details p 77)* with his father, his mother and his sister Lucile. It was through the profession of arms that he began, in 1786, the adventurous career which ended in 1848 in the solitary grandeur of Grand Bé *(p 196)*.

Lamennais (1782-1854), another St-Malo shipowner's son, also had a place in the Romantic Movement. He became an orphan early and was brought up by an uncle at the Castle of Chesnaye, near Dinan. At 22 he taught mathematics in the College of St-Malo before entering the seminary of that town.

He was ordained a priest in 1816 and had a great influence on Lacordaire and Montalembert. His writings and violent quarrels got him into trouble with Rome which led him to renounce the Church.

He retired to Chesnaye and published, in 1834, the famous *Paroles d'un Croyant* (Words of a Believer). Owing to his advanced political ideas he was sentenced to a year's imprisonment in 1840 but won a seat in the National Assembly in 1848.

To the famous men of St-Malo already mentioned should be added **Mahé de la Bourdonnais** (1699-1753), a great colonist and the rival of Dupleix in the Indies; **Broussais** (1772-1838), who transformed the medical science of his time; **Gournay** (1712-59), the economist to whom the formula "laissez faire, laissez passer" (let it be, let it go) is attributed; and finally that saintly figure of **André Desilles.** In 1790 the garrison of Nancy, to which this 23 year old Lieutenant belonged, revolted against the National Assembly. Troops were sent to subdue it. To prevent the fraticidal struggle, Desllles threw himself in front of the guns and fell, mortally wounded.

As Chateaubriand commented of his home town: "It's not a bad record for an area smaller than the Tuileries Gardens."

Destruction and Renaissance of St-Malo. – St-Malo and the area around was turned into an entrenched camp by the Germans and became the prize for which a merciless battle raged from 1 to 14 August 1944. The town was left in ruins. With a great sense of history, its restorers were determined to bring the old city back to life. They have been completely successful.

★★★ THE RAMPARTS (REMPARTS) *time: 1 hour*

Leave your car on the St-Vincent Esplanade (DZ).

The statue near the esplanade, at the entrance to the Casino garden, is of Chateaubriand by Armel-Beaufils. It was erected up in 1948 on the centenary of his death. Pass under the St Vincent Gate (Porte St-Vincent) which consists of twin gates; then take the staircase to the right leading to the ramparts.

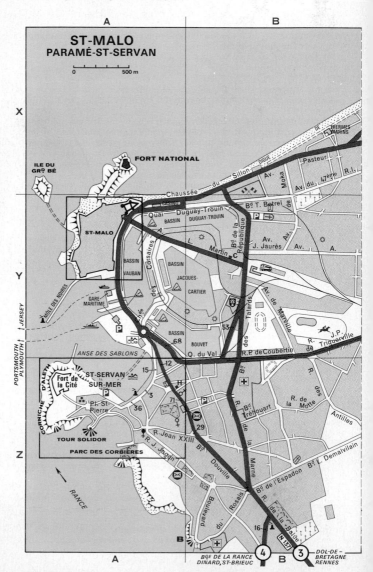

The ramparts, started in the 12C, were enlarged and altered up to the 18C and survived the wartime destruction. The rampart walk commands magnificent views especially at high tide of the coast and islands.

From the St-Vincent Gate to the St-Louis Bastion. – Directly after the Grande Gate (Grande Porte), which is crowned with machicolations, the view opens out over the narrow isthmus which joins the old town to its suburbs, the harbour basins and, in the distance, St-Servan.

From the St-Louis Bastion to the St-Philippe Bastion. – The rampart skirts the houses where lived the rich shipowners of St-Malo; two, near the St-Louis Bastion, are still intact but the following walls and façades are reconstructions of buildings carefully dismantled.

This fine group of houses including the high roofs, surmounted by monumental chimneys, standing up from the ramparts, once more gives this part of the town its old look.

The view extends over the outer harbour; to the Aleth Rock, crowned by the Cité Fort, and the mouth of the Rance estuary; to Dinard, with the Prieuré beach and the Vicomté Point.

From the St-Philippe Bastion to the Bidouane Tower. – A very fine view of the Emerald Coast west of Dinard, and of the islands off St-Malo. To the right of the Moulinet Point you can see part of the great beach at Dinard, the Étêtés Point separating Dinard from St-Lunaire, the Décollé Point, the Hébihens Archipelago, the St-Cast Point and Cape Fréhel; nearer, on the right, are Harbour Isle and, farther to the right, the Grand Bé *(p 196)* and Petit Bé Islands; then, in the background, Cézembre Island and Conchée Fort.

From the Bidouane Tower to the St-Vincent Gate. – From this point you can see the National Fort *(p 196)* and the great curve which joins St-Malo to the Varde Point, passing through the beaches of Paramé, Rochebonne and Le Minihic.

At the end of the ramparts take the stairway going down near the St-Thomas Gate (Porte St-Thomas) – this gate opens on the main beach which joins the immense Paramé beach.

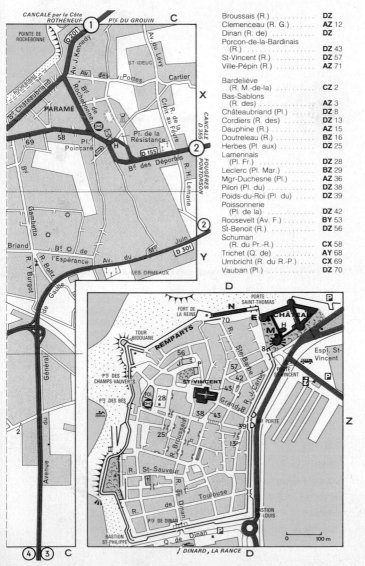

ST-MALO★★★

★★ CASTLE (CHÂTEAU) (DZ) *time: 1 1/2 hours*

> *You can enter the courtyard and see the façades of the former 17-18C barracks (now the town hall), the well, the keep and the gatehouse.*

The little keep was built as part of the ramparts in 1395. The great keep (1424) dominates the castle; and corner towers were constructed in the 15 and 16C. The chapel and the Galley date from the 17C.

★ **St-Malo Museum (M)**. – The museum, which is installed in the great keep and gate-
⊙ houses records the development of the city of St-Malo and its celebrities (Jacques Cartier, Duguay-Trouin, La Bourdonnais, Surcouf, Chateaubriand, Lamennais and the mathematician Maupertuis). Documents, ship models, paintings and arms trace St-Malo's sea-faring tradition. To end the visit climb up to the watch towers of the keep, from which you will see an impressive **panorama★★** of the town, the harbour, the coast and the sea.

★ **Quic-en-Groigne (E)**. – This tower (68 steps) which is located in the left wing of the
⊙ castle, bears the name Quic-en-Groigne from an Inscription Queen Anne had carved on it in defiance of the bishops of St-Malo: "Qui-qu'en-groigne, ainsi sera, car tel est mon bon plaisir." (Thus it shall be, whoever may complain, for that is my wish.) It contains a **waxworks museum** with reconstructions of historic scenes and the celebrities of St-Malo.

ADDITIONAL SIGHTS

St-Vincent Cathedral (DZ). – The building was started in the 11C and completed in the 18C. The nave is roofed with quadripartite vaulting typical of the Angevin style; dark and massive it contrasts with the slenderly built 13C chancel. Lit by magnificent **stained glass windows★** by Jean Le Moal, the chancel becomes a kaleidoscope of colours. In the transept restored in the 17C style the stained glass windows are muted in colour while in the side aisles the windows by Max Ingrand are brighter. The north side aisle has preserved its original vaulting.
The Chapel of the Sacred Heart (south side) is a very successful piece of reconstruction with its wooden vault and granite altar. A 16C Virgin, Notre-Dame-de-la-Croix-du-Fief, which comes from a mediaeval house, is kept in the second chapel north of the ambulatory together with the remains of Duguay-Trouin. The neighbouring chapel houses the tomb of Jacques Cartier.

⊙ **Aquarium (DZ N)**. – A gallery 120m - 394ft long with some 100 aquariums, built into the walls of the ramparts in the Place Vauban near the St Thomas Gate, contains a collection of salt and freshwater specimens, particularly fish and fauna native to the St-Malo Bay, North Sea, Mediterranean coasts and coral reefs. Note a blue lobster, a couple of king crabs, seahorses and a collection of anemones. In the exotarium varans, crocodiles, snakes and batrachians can be seen.

★ **National Fort (Fort national) (AX** – *town plan p 195)*. – *Access by the Plage de l'Éventail*
⊙ *at low tide, 15 min on foot Rtn.*
Built by Vauban in 1689, the Royal Fort became the National Fort after the Revolution (1789) and then private property. Built on the rock, this stronghold assured the protection of the city. The **view★★** of the ramparts is remarkable. The fort commands extensive views of the coast and the islands: St-Malo, St-Servan, the Rance estuary, Dinard, the Grand and Petit Bé Islands, Harbour Island, the Grand Jardin Lighthouse, the Conchée Fort and in the distance the Chausey Islands. The visit to the dungeon is worthwhile. The fort played an important part in 1692 against the English and Dutch fleet.

Grand Bé Island (AX – *town plan p 195)*. – *3/4 hour on foot Rtn. Only at low tide. Leave St-Malo by the Champs-Vauverts Gate and cross the beach diagonally to the causeway. Follow the road that skirts the right side of the island.*
Chateaubriand's tomb is on the seaward side; it is a plain, unnamed flagstone surmounted by a heavy granite cross. Edouard Herriot based an interesting character sketch of Chateaubriand on the loneliness of this place. "He was a giant of letters, living in splendid isolation. And though it may surprise us at first, we can understand why he wished to be buried on his lonely rock, with nothing around him but the sea that inspired his first dreams. At the meeting-point of two centuries he stands like an island, destined to know the convulsions of war even after his death, rugged by nature, remote from ordinary men, preferring to their society, which he scorned, the lofty pleasures of communion with his friend the Ocean."
From the highest point on the island there is a beautiful **panorama★★** of the entire Emerald Coast.

> *Cross the open space, go down a few steps and turn left along a road leading back to the causeway by which you came.*

BOAT TRIPS

★★★ **Dinard.** – *P 89.*

★★★ **Cruise to Cape Fréhel.** – *P 102.*

★★ **The Rance Valley.** – *P 176.*

Cézembre Island. – *P 90.*

★ **Chausey Islands.** – *The sights are described in the Green Guide to Normandy.*

Jersey. – *The sights, hotels and restaurants are listed in the Michelin Red Guide Great Britain and Ireland.*

★ST-SERVAN-SUR-MER

The resort of St-Servan-sur-Mer is gay with many gardens, in striking contrast to the walled town of St-Malo. Its main beach is formed by the Sablons Bay, although there are also smaller beaches along the Rance. The town has three ports: the Bouvet dock, a trading and a fishing port, linked with that of St-Malo, the Solidor, a former naval base, and the Saint-Père.

Jeanne Jugan, humble servant of the poor (1792-1879). – The name of Jeanne Jugan recalls a humble, devoted life, a faith to move mountains and an admirable work of charity. Jeanne was the daughter of a Cancale fisherman who lost his life at sea, leaving a widow and seven children. Jeanne found a place as a domestic servant with an old spinster at St-Servan-sur-Mer, and while taking care of her for eighteen years she helped the poor and lonely old people of the neighbourhood. In 1835 her mistress died, leaving her 400 francs. The great hearted serving woman bought a hovel in which she sheltered old people with the help of three friends who were also domestics or working women. In 1840 these holy women formed a sort of religious society of which the Vicar of St-Servan-sur-Mer, the Abbé Le Pailleur, became chaplain. The society, in due course, became the Congregation of the Little Sisters of the Poor.

To feed her people Jeanne went out begging every day, in all weathers, with her basket on her arm, well received by some, rebuffed by others. One day an angry boor struck her. "The blow is for me, my good man," she said with a smile, "now give me something for my paupers." By the rules of the Congregation, this daily quest was, until the last World War, its only means of subsistence. Jeanne Jugan died at the age of 87. Today the 6 500 Sisters are scattered all over the world, in more than 300 establishments.

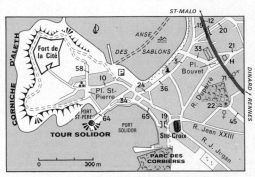

★★ **Aleth Corniche** (AY). – This walk offers magnificent **views★★**. Leave your car in the Place St-Pierre, where in a garden stand the ruins of the former cathedral of Aleth.

Take the Rue St-Pierre at the east end of the church and follow on the left the corniche pathway.

First comes a remarkable view of St-Malo. Farther to the left can be distinguished the Petit Bé, the Grand Bé and Cézembre Islands. Bear left and skirt the seashore. Go round the fort *(below)*. The whole harbour is now visible: to the right of Cézembre Island, in the distance, is the fortified Island of Grande Conchée; on the left, the Grand Jardin Lighthouse, Harbour Island and its fort and, in the distance, Cape Fréhel and the Décollé Point, followed by a maze of reefs. Finally take a steep downhill path to the right to enjoy a very fine view of the Rance estuary, barred by the Bizeux rock, on which stands a statue of the Virgin, and beyond, of the tidal power scheme *(p 175)*.

★ **Solidor Tower.** – This tower, which commands the Rance estuary, was built in 1382 and restored in the 17C. It consists of three contiguous towers and its three storeys were long used as a prison. It now houses the International Museum of Cape Horn Vessels.

★ **International Museum of Cape Horn Vessels** (Musée International du Long Cours Cap Hornier).
⊙ – The life of the great navigators (16-20C) who sailed to Cape Horn is recounted in the museum. Throughout the galleries the history, techniques, traditions and life on board are evoked. Note the model of *Victoria*, the first ship which sailed round the world in 1 084 days from 1519 to 1522. A succession of exhibits at different levels leads to the wall walk (104 steps) which commands a **view★** of the estuary, St-Servan-sur-Mer, St-Malo, Dinard and the Rance.

Corbières Park (Parc des Corbières). – It is a wooded park left in its natural state with trees of different species. Bear right, follow the cliff path which goes round Corbières Point, affording fine **glimpses★** of the Rance estuary and the tidal power scheme.

City Fort (Fort de la Cité). – The City Fort was built in 1759 on the orders of the Duke of Aiguillon. It was modernized and used by the Germans in the last war. Around the inner courtyard is a chain of blockhouses joined by over a mile of underground passages, which also serve the barracks, the hospital and all the offices of this little town, built on several storeys.

⊙ **Ste-Croix.** – The church is in the Greco-Roman style. The interior is decorated with frescoes (1854) and stained glass windows (1962).

★ **Rosais Belvedere** (BZ B – *town plan p 194*). – The belvedere is near the little marine cemetery on the side of a cliff overlooking the Rance and which contains the tomb of Count and Countess of Chateaubriand, the writer's parents. **View★** of the Rance dam, the Bizeux rock with a statue of the Virgin atop it, Vicomté Point and Dinard.

ST-MALO★★★

★★ PARAMÉ

Paramé, a much frequented seaside resort, possesses a salt-water thermal establishment. It has two magnificent beaches extending for 2 km - 1 1/2 miles: the Casino Beach, which continues that of St-Malo and the Rochebonne Beach. The splendid seafront promenade, 3 km - 2 miles long, is the chief attraction for the passing tourist.

ROTHÉNEUF by ① of the town plan

This seaside resort has two beaches which widely differ. That of the Val is wide open to the sea. That of Rothéneuf Cove lies on an almost landlocked bay like a large lake surrounded with dunes, cliffs and pines.
Near Rothéneuf is **Le Minihic,** with its own beach and villas.

★ **Jacques Cartier's Manorhouse.** – *Place du Canada.* After his expeditions to Canada, ⊘the explorer, Jacques Cartier, bought a farm which he extended and called *"Limoëlou"* (bald hillock). This 16C house and its 19C extension have been restored and furnished in contemporary style. The tour includes an audio-visual presentation on the explorer's expeditions and of the colony of "Nouvelle France" also known as Canada.

⊘**Sculptured Rocks (Rochers sculptés).** – From 1870 onwards, some rocks along the coast have been sculptured with patience by a priest, the Abbé Fouré, who spent twenty-five years of his life on the task. There are some 300 small carvings.

⊘**Sea-water Aquarium.** – This has interesting specimens of live salt-water creatures and a big collection of shells.

★★ ST-MATHIEU Point

Michelin map 🗺 fold 3 or 🗺 fold 16 – Local map p 44

St-Mathieu, which was an important town in the 14C, is now only a village known for the ruins of its abbey church, its site and its lighthouse.

⊘**The Lighthouse.** – The lighthouse has a considerable system of lights; two auxiliary lights are reserved for air navigation. There is also a radio beam. The main light is served by a 1 500 watt lamp, giving it an intensity of about 5 000 000 candlepower, with a range of 55 to 60 km - 34 to 37 1/2 miles.
From the top (167 steps) there is a superb **panorama★★**; from left to right – the mouth of the Brest Sound; the Crozon Peninsula; Raz Point; Sein Island (in clear weather); the Pierres Noires reef; and the Islands of Béniguet, Molène and Ushant. Beyond Béniguet, 30 km - 18 1/2 miles away, you can sometimes distinguish the Jument lighthouse.

★ **Abbey Church.** – The ruins are the remains of a monastery (6C) which, according to legend, had as a relic the head of St Matthew, brought from Africa by seamen.

Go inside the lighthouse enclosure. An opening in the flat chevet gives access to the ruins.

The 13C chancel, which has ogive vaulting, is flanked by a square keep. The nave with rounded or octagonal pillars, has a single aisle on the north side and two 16C aisles on the south side. The church has a 12C façade pierced by a round arched doorway and three narrow windows.
In front of the restored Notre-Dame-des-Grâces Chapel, note the 14C porch, a relic of the former parish church.

Go round the lighthouse enclosure to reach the tip of the point.

At the tip of the point, a column, erected to the memory of the French sailors who died in the First World War, is the work of the sculptor Quillivic. There is a magnificent **view** from the edge of the cliff.
At a point 300m - about 1/4 mile from St-Mathieu going towards Plougonvelin are two Gallic **steles** (on the left near a house) surmounted by a cross and known as the Monks' Gibbet (Gibet des Moines).

ST-MÉEN-LE-GRAND   Pop 3 945

Michelin map 🗺 fold 15 or 🗺 fold 24

In the 6C, St Méen (Mewan), a monk from Great-Britain, founded an abbey on this site, which was several times reconstructed from the 11 to the 18C. A seminary is now housed in the abbey buildings. The church retains a fine 16C square tower and a Gothic chancel with a flat chevet. Inside, note in the south aisle, the tombstone, and in the south transept, the statue and funerary monument of St Méen, all from the 15C.
In the cemetery, beside the church, are the saint's tomb, a basin, recumbent figures and tombstones. There is a large brick factory in the town.

EXCURSION

⊘**Montauban Castle.** – *12 km - 7 miles NE. Take the N 164, then the N 12 in the direction of Rennes. At Montauban bear left into the D 61 towards Médréac.* The castle stands near a pool to the left of the road. The domain of the lords of Montauban included nine parishes in the 12C. Philippe de Montauban was the Duchess Anne's chancellor in the late 15C. All that remains of the imposing 15C mansion are the tall guard towers with pepperpot roofs, a corner tower, and some buildings. The guard room, saloon and two bedrooms contain furniture, archives and mementoes of the castle's past history.

Michelin map 📖 fold 15 or 📖 fold 52

A visit to St-Nazaire, which is above all a great shipbuilding centre, is particularly interesting. Originally a small fishing port in the 15C, the town developed rapidly, in 1856, when large ships, finding it difficult to get up to Nantes, stopped at its deep water port.

St-Nazaire during the War. – The Allied forces landed here during World War I, during World War II it became a German submarine base. On 27 March 1942 a Canadian-British commando caught the enemy by surprise, while the destroyer *Campbeltown* knocked down the entrance lock Louis-Joubert and the following day neutralised the lock by blowing itself up. A stele, reminding us of this heroic act, faces the sea on Boulevard de Verdun.

The obvious target for aerial bombardment between 1940 and 1945, the town got caught up in the fighting for the St-Nazaire Pocket and consequently was desolate when finally liberated.

A monument to commemorate the Surrender of the St-Nazaire Pocket (May 1945) stands west of Bouvron, a place on the N 771 between Savenay and Blain, 36 km - 22 miles from St-Nazaire.

St-Nazaire today. – Rebuilt after the war, the town is now divided into two distinct quarters: to the east is the **harbour and industrial zone** and to the west the **residential quarter** opened with wide avenues following the plans of the architect, Lemaresquier. In the town centre, the town hall (1969) stands amidst a fine square decorated with fountains; the rectangular basin faces the Avenue de la République.

Farther west the Avenue Léo-Lagrange separates the **park**, with its pond, from the **sports ground.** Beyond are the hospital centre and schools. Near the coast, modern buildings have been built in the Kerledé quarter.

To the east of St-Nazaire, near the mouth of the Brivet the **St-Nazaire-St-Brévin Bridge★** *(toll)* spans the Loire, a distance of more than 2.5 km - 1 1/2 miles, and it stands 61m - 200ft above mean high water at midpoint. It provides a link between the town of St-Nazaire and the Retz country, the Vendée and the Charentes and promotes industrial development on both banks of the Loire.

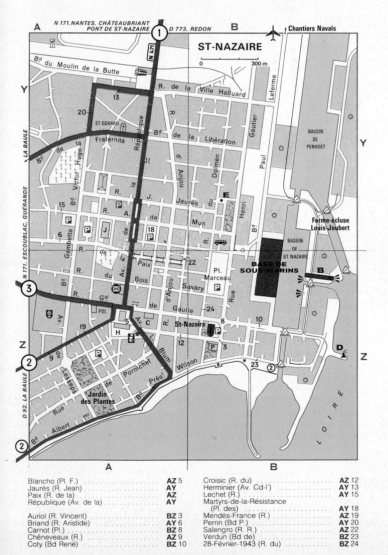

THE PORT *time: 1 1/2 hours*

Tourists may walk along the harbour roadways but it is particularly difficult to do so when the men of the naval yards are coming in to work or leaving. The roadways offer views of the undermentioned works.

★ **Panorama** (BZ B). – On the submarine exit *(see below)*. This terrace offers a remarkable ⊙ overall view of the harbour, the Loire Estuary, and the St-Brévin-les-Pins Suspension Bridge on the other side of the river.

Harbour Installations (BYZ). – The **St-Nazaire Basin** (9 ha - 22 acres) was established in 1856, when St-Nazaire was only an annexe of Nantes. The port became autonomous in 1879. Two years later the magnificent **Penhoët Basin** (22 ha - 54 acres), one of the largest in Europe with three types of dry dock, was opened. The port is governed jointly wIth that of Nantes by the Autonomous Port Authority of Nantes-St-Nazaire. Three works deserve attention: the entrance lock, the submarine base and the exit for submarines. The **entrance lock, Louis-Joubert** (Forme-écluse Louis Joubert), was built between 1929 and 1932, to allow for the increase in tonnage of great Atlantic liners such as the *Normandie*. The lock is 350 by 50m and 15m deep (1 148 × 164ft and 49ft deep). It has three functions: first as a dry dock for the repair and careenage of very large ships; second as a lock allowing ships drawing not more than 12.50m - 40ft to pass from the Penhoët dock directly to the Loire estuary at high tide; finally the lock can also serve as a loading and unloading berth. This lock supplements, for the larger ships, the lock at the southern entrance to the port. This measures 211 × 30m - 692 × 96ft.
The **submarine base★** (Base de sous-marins), which was built, during the occupation, is a very large reinforced concrete structure covering an area of 37 500 sq m - 44 830 sq yds and measuring 300 × 125m - 960 × 400ft. It had fourteen bays, which together could take some twenty submarines. Machine shops were installed at the back of the bays. In spite of much bombing the base came through the war undamaged and is now the site of various industries.
The **submarine exit★** (BZ B), opposite the base, is a covered lock. This was to provide shelter from air attack and to allow the German submarines to enter and leave the base in secret (it is no longer used). It adjoins the port's former entrance (53m long by 13m wide - 170 × 42ft), now used for the Loire river traffic and for fishing craft.

The shipyards. – Between the Penhoët Basin (BY) and the Loire lies the Atlantic Dockyard (Chantiers de l'Atlantique), made up of the former Loire workshops and the Penhoët dockyard which had been linked together in 1956 and which since 1976 have been incorported with Alsthom. Among the ships which have come from the Atlantic Dockyard are the battleship *Jean Bart,* the oceanliners *Normandie* and the *France*. Cargo boats, container ships, ore carrying ships and tankers (550 000 tons capacity) for French and foreign use are also built in the yards.
The Atlantic Shipyards are equipped to build several ships simultaneously. This method substitutes for the conventional slipway, a huge dry dock divided into sections in which stand the ships under construction. Launching the completed ship is achieved by filling the section with water and floating her out. A new dock enables ships of 500 000 tons to be built. Near the naval repair dock is a 450 × 95m - 1 476 × 312ft dock for battleships.

ADDITIONAL SIGHTS

Lighthouse (BZ D). – Standing on the old pier, the lighthouse commands a view of the shipyards and the Loire estuary.

Dolmen (BY E). – In a little shaded square two high stones support a granite table. Alongside is a menhir which was moved here from elsewhere.

⊙ **Ste-Anne.** – The church (1957) stands between the Rue du Soleil-Levant and the Boulevard Jean-Mermoz, which you reach by ③ on the town plan. The belfry stands separately to the left of the façade. The entrance is surrounded by great mosaics by Paul Colin depicting work in the St-Nazaire naval dockyard. Inside the stained glass windows contrast vividly with the bare concrete walls; to the left, the chapel with blue stained glass windows, contains a statue of St Anne.

St-Nazaire (BZ). – This vast 19C Gothic style church with its slate topped belfry, was restored in 1945. Sculpted round the side aisles is a Stations of the Cross with a series of expressive figures. The transept is lit by fine rose windows with modern stained glass. In the chancel is an elegant 18C gilt wooden altarpiece adorned with scenes of the Gospel and statues of the Prophets.

Beaches. – The Grand and Petit Traict sand beaches extend for over 2 km - 1 mile between the outer harbour *(avant-port)* jetty and the Ville-ès-Martin Point. They are skirted by the Président-Wilson and Albert I Boulevards and separated by a rock. The view from the beach extends over the Loire Estuary to the south as far as St-Gildas Point.

Botanical Gardens (Jardin des Plantes) (AZ). – Across from the Loire Estuary the gardens with their shaded alleys and colourful flower beds offer a pleasant resting spot near the Grand Traict beach.

⊙ **Notre-Dame-d'Espérance.** – Standing to the south of Place Pierre-Bourdan, near the Rue de Pornichet (by ② on the town plan) this 1965 church has a white façade with oblique buttresses and a bare interior showing uncovered stonework.

EXCURSION

★ **From St-Nazaire to La Baule by the coast.** – *Round tour of 38 km - 24 miles – about 2 hours. Leave St-Nazaire by ②, D 92. Turn left onto the D 292. The road in the opposite direction is described on p 55.*

Michelin map 58 fold 6 or 230 fold 5

This little town, which St Paul, known as the Aurelian, made the first bishopric in Lower Brittany, offers the tourist two of the finest buildings in Brittany: the former Cathedral (the bishopric did not survive the Concordat) and the Kreisker Belfry.
From January to September, during the season for cauliflowers, artichokes, onions and potatoes, St-Pol is extremely busy. Numerous lorries, vans and tractors with trailers arrive, bringing these famous Breton products to the market for many transporters and agricultural cooperatives.

★★FORMER CATHEDRAL (ANCIENNE CATHÉDRALE)
time: 1 hour

Built on 12C foundations the cathedral was erected in the 13 and 14C (nave, aisles, façade and towers) and in the 15 and 16C (side chapels, chancel, apse and remodelling of the transept). The building is neither very large nor very tall (80m - 256ft long and 16m - 51ft high) but it is beautifully proportioned and plainly elegant. The architects were inspired by the cathedral at Coutances and used Norman limestone to build the nave; the traditional granite was used for the façade, the transept and the chancel. The Breton influence can be found in the bell turrets on the transept crossing and also in the porches (p 35).

Exterior. – From a small public garden, on the north side between the church and the former bishop's palace (now the town hall), is a view of the north transept wall with Romanesque characteristics. The south side which faces the main square has a fine porch. The transept contains a remarkable rose window with above it a sort of pulpit from which sentences of excommunication used to be read.
The façade is dominated by two towers each 50m - 160ft high. The spires differ slightly, the general outline of the left tower is slenderer. The terrace which surmounts the porch was used by the bishop to bless the people; the small door under the right tower was reserved for lepers.

Interior. – *Enter the church through the south porch.* To the left is a Roman sarcophagus which serves as a stoup. Starting the tour from the right, note a Renaissance stained glass window (1560) and in the transept the 15C rose window. Around the chancel there are tombs of local bishops and two 17C altarpieces. The carved **stalls★** of the chancel date from the 16C. Over the high altar, a palm tree in carved wood bent in the shape of a crozier, contains a ciborium for the Host.
In wall niches against the chancel to the left, 34 wooden reliquaries contain skulls. Opposite, kept in a gilded bronze shrine are relics of St Paul the Aurelian.

ST-POL-DE-LÉON

Leclerc (R. Gén.)	6	Croix-au-Lin (R.)	4
Parvis (Pl. du)	8	Kreisker (Pl. du)	5
		Minimes (R. des)	7
		Psalette (R. de la)	10

ADDITIONAL SIGHTS

★ **Kreisker Chapel (Chapelle du Kreisker).** – It was, at one time, in this 14-15C chapel that the town council used to meet; today it is the college chapel. What makes it famous is its magnificent **belfry★★** *(illustration p 35)*, 77m - 246ft high. This was inspired by the spire of St Peter's at Caen (destroyed during the war – *see Michelin Green Guide to Normandy*), but the Breton building in granite surpasses the original. The Kreisker belfry has served as a model for many Breton towers.
The chapel aisles are formed of a series of gables over fine, tall windows. The west front and the flat east end are pierced with very large bays.

Enter through the north porch.

The 15C gable is surmounted by a statue of Notre-Dame-de-Kreisker (11C). The church is roofed with wooden cradles. The only stone vault joins the four huge uprights which support the belfry at the transept crossing. In the south aisle is a vast 17C carved wood altarpiece depicting the Visitation.
You may climb the tower (169 steps). From the platform you will get a circular **view★★** of the town, Batz Island, the coast as far as the Bretonne Corniche and the Arrée Mountains inland.

Rue Général-Leclerc (6). – There are interesting old houses in this street: note the slate-faced wooden façade at No 9; a Renaissance house with a corbelled turret at No 12; a mansion with a fine porch and ornate dormer windows (1680) at No 30.

Cemetery. – Small arched ossuaries are built into the walls. In one corner is the Chapel of St Peter (**E**) in the Flamboyant style lit by modern stained glass windows. Opposite the porch, at the end of an alleyway, is a war memorial by the sculptor Quillivic, backed by a semicircular wall adorned with low reliefs.

Prébendal House (D). – This was the 16C residence of the canons of Léon. The façade is emblazoned.

Champ de la Rive. – *Access by the Rue de la Rive.* A pleasant shaded walk. Take the metalled path on the right to reach the top of a hillock crowned by a modern Calvary. From the viewing-table there is a fine view of Morlaix Bay.

St Anne's Rock (Rocher Ste-Anne). – *Access by the Rue de la Rive and Rue de l'Abbé Tanguy.* As the road descends, there is a **view★** over Morlaix Bay and its islands. A dyke leads to St Anne's Rock and the Groux harbour. From the rock which forms a remarkable viewpoint (seats), the **view** extends from Roscoff as far as Primel Point.

EXCURSION

★ **Kérouzéré Castle.** – *8 km - 5 miles to the west by ③ on the town plan, the D 788* ⊙ *towards Lesneven, then the D 10 to the right to Plouescat. At Sibiril, turn right towards Moguériec and after 500m - 1/3 mile left towards the castle.*
This granite feudal castle is an interesting specimen of 15C military architecture. Three of the massive machicolated corner towers remain standing, the fourth was demolished in 1590 after a siege. A central stone staircase gives access to the three floors which were used by soldiers and included large bare rooms with deep window recesses and stone seats, a wall walk and a guard tower. The castle also retains pepperpot roofs, the oratory frescoes, some tapestries and fine Breton furniture, all dating from the 17C.

★ ST-QUAY-PORTRIEUX   Pop 3 399

Michelin map 𝟻𝟿 fold 3 or 𝟸𝟹𝟶 folds 8, 9 – Facilities

St-Quay-Portrieux, a popular resort, is named after the Welsh hermit, St Quay, who landed on this coast about 472 AD. Its fine beaches are fringed by the St-Quay rocks.

Port. – The little port of Portrieux used to be a deep sea fishing base. Nowadays, the fishing fleet sails in St-Brieuc Bay and catches mackerel, plaice, bass, concentrating on scallops and crustaceans from November to April. A large deep sea harbour is being built in front of the jetty on which stands the lighthouse.

Coast road (Chemin de ronde). – *1 1/2 hours on foot Rtn, preferably at high tide.*
This former customs officers' path starts from the Portrieux port, beyond the town hall, skirts the Comtesse beach, passes in front of the Viking monument and goes round the signal station, affording a fine **view★** of St-Brieuc Bay, from Bréhat to Cape Fréhel. The road then continues along the terrace overlooking the Châtelet Beach, round the sea water pool and reaches the Casino. The walk may be extended as far as St-Marc beach *(plus about 2 hours on foot Rtn).*

EXCURSIONS

From St-Quay-Portrieux to Paimpol by the coast road. – *66 km - 41 miles – about 3 1/2 hours. Leave St-Quay-Portrieux NW by the D 786, the Paimpol road. At the entrance to Plouha, turn right into the D 32 which follows the Corzic.*
La Palus-Plage. – A lovely cove. To the left of the beach, a stairway cut in the rock leads to an upper path from which there are good views of St-Brieuc Bay.
Return to Plouha.
Plouha. – Pop 4 263. This little town has many villas which belong to Navy pensioners.
★ **Kermaria** and **Lanleff.** – *10 km - 6 miles from Plouha. Descriptions p 121.*
At Plouha, take the road to Port-Moguer.
Port-Moguer. – A large rocky creek in a pretty setting. Follow the dyke, paved in pink granite, to the rocky islet to enjoy a view of the coast with cliffs up to 100m -320ft high.
Return to Plouha and bear right towards Paimpol; at a place called "le dernier sou", bear right.
Plage Bonaparte. – From this beach at the bottom of Cohat Bay, reached by a tunnel cut through the cliff, allied pilots, brought down on French soil, were taken back to Great Britain. To reach the monument commemorating this event, take the stairway to the right of the beach car park, then the path up to the top of the cliff or if you go by car, drive along the road leading off to the right before the beach. From the platform, there is a good **view** over St-Brieuc Bay and Cape Fréhel, Port-Moguer cove to the right and Minard Point to the left.
Turn back and bear right towards Lanloup. The rest of the excursion along the Goëlo coast is described in the opposite direction on p 151.
Étables-sur-Mer. – *5 km - 3 miles S – about 3/4 hour. Take the D 786 in the direction of St-Brieuc.*
The road goes towards the coast which it finally overlooks and follows closely.
⊙ **Notre-Dame-de-L'Espérance.** – Built after the cholera epidemic of 1850, the restored Chapel of Our Lady of Hope, decorated with stained glass windows in blue tones and two paintings by Jean Michau and a tapestry depicting the Virgin and Child by Toffoli, stands on the Étables cliff, overseeing St-Brieuc Bay.
Étables-sur-Mer. – Pop 2 039. The town, built on a plateau and possessing a fine public park, overlooks the quiet, family resort on the coast. The two parts of the town are linked by an avenue lined with villas. There are two sheltered, sandy beaches.

After the road has left the shore, you get a good view of Binic *(p 61)* beyond Etables.

⊙ BOAT TRIPS

★★ **Bréhat Island.** – *Boat services operate in summer.*

Michelin map **58** fold 6 or **230** fold 5 – Local map p 153

This village has a magnificent parish close *(details on parish closes and illustration p 37)*, the ossuary and the church being the key features of this rich 16-17C Renaissance group.

(After Christiane Olivier, Nice, photo)

St-Thégonnec. – Parish close

★★ PARISH CLOSE *time: 3/4 hour*

★ **Triumphal Arch.** – A rounded arch surmounted by small lantern turrets (1587).

★ **Funerary Chapel.** – The chapel was built from 1676 to 1682. Inside is a 17C altarpiece (restored) with spiral columns. In the crypt, under the altar, is a **Holy Sepulchre★** with figures carved in oak and painted (1699-1702), the work of a Breton sculptor, Jacques Lespaignol.
The treasury which contains gold and silver plate is situated at the far end of the ossuary.

★★ **Calvary.** – The Calvary was erected in 1610. On the base are groups of figures depicting the Passion. Below, a small niche shelters St Thégonnec with the wolf he harnessed to his cart after his donkey had been devoured by wolves.
The platform is surmounted by a double armed cross bearing figures and two simple crosses for the thieves. Notice the angels collecting blood running from Christ's wounds.

★ **Church.** – The church has been remodelled several times. The only trace of the old building is the gable belfry (1563) on the left of the tower. The Renaissance tower is crowned with a dome with lantern and corner turrets.
Over the porch is a statue of St Thégonnec; in niches in the corner buttresses there are statues of the Annunciation, St John and St Nicholas; inside the porch, four statues of Apostles.
Inside, the **pulpit★★** is one of the masterpieces (1683) of Breton sculpture. The corners are adorned with the four Cardinal Virtues, while the Evangelists are depicted on the four panels. On the medallion at the back, God is giving the Tables of the Law to Moses. The sounding board (1732) decorated with angels and roses, is surmounted by The Angel of Judgment blowing a trumpet.
In the north aisle, against a pillar of the transept stands a statue of St Thégonnec; the folding panels relate the saint's life.
In the entrance of the Apostles' porch is a statue of the Virgin carrying the Child Jesus, framed in a Tree of Jesse.
The apse and both arms of the transept are covered with **woodwork★** dating from the 17 and 18C which have been restored. The panels of **Rosary altarpiece★**, on the left, represent below and in the centre, the Virgin and the Child, Jesus giving a rosary to St Dominic and St Catherine; above, the Virgin and St Lawrence give Christ a soul saved from the flames of Purgatory.
The organ (1670-1676) was restored in 19C.

Times and charges for admission to sights described in the guide are listed at the end of the guide.

The sights are listed alphabetically in this section either under the place – town, village or area – in which they are situated or under their proper name.

Every sight for which there are times and charges is indicated by the symbol⊘ in the margin in the main part of the guide.

★ STE-ANNE-D'AURAY

Michelin map **63** fold 2 or **230** fold 36

Ste-Anne is the outstanding Breton place of pilgrimage. The first *pardon* takes place on 7 March; then, from Easter until Rosary *(the first Sunday in October),* there are parish pilgrimages *(especially Wednesdays and Sundays from 14 July to end of August).* The *pardon* of St Anne on 26 July *(p 226)* and on 15 August is the most frequented, together with the Rosary *(details on pardons p 27).*

In 1623 St Anne appeared to a ploughman, Yves Nicolazic, and asked him to rebuild a chapel which had previously been dedicated to her in one of his fields. On 7 March 1625, Yves unearthed, at the spot she had indicated, an old statue of St Anne. A church was built there the same year. The present basilica, in the Renaissance style, took its place in the 19C.

PILGRIMAGE CLOSE *Correct dress required*

Basilica. – Built from 1866 to 1872, it took the place of the 17C chapel. At the south transept is a modern statue of St Anne; part of the face of the original statue, which was burnt in 1796 is set in the base.

★ **Treasury.** – It contains a relic of St Anne presented by Anne of Austria in thanks for the birth of Louis XIV. There are also gold and silver plate and the cloak of the old statue, and, in a glass case in the centre, ornaments given by Anne of Austria, surrounded by numerous votive offerings.

A Breton art gallery contains old statues (15-19C), small faïence statues of Quimper, Gien, Nevers, and votive offerings.

Scala Sancta. – Old doorway from the square with a double staircase which pilgrims climb up on their knees.

War Memorial (Monument aux morts). – The memorial was raised by public subscription all over Brittany to the 250 000 Breton soldiers and sailors who died in the First World War. It has become the memorial to all dead during the wars which have occurred in the 20C.

Not far away, on the other side of the D 102, a national cemetery contains the graves of 1 338 soldiers of whom 370 were Mohammedans.

Miraculous Fountain. – The fountain consists of a basin and a column adorned with smaller basins and surmounted by a statue of St Anne.

SIGHTS

St Anne Diorama (Historial de Sainte Anne). – This retrospective exhibit, which includes wax figures in period costume, brings the visitor into the atmosphere of old Brittany and shows the origins of the annual pilgrimage.

Nicolazic Museum. – *To the right of the war memorial.*
Old statues and dolls in Breton costumes, furniture and Breton dress.

House of Nicolazic. – It was in this house that St Anne appeared to the pious peasant. Inside are a chapel and some old furniture.

STE-BARBE Chapel

Michelin map **58** fold 17 or **230** fold 20 – 3 km - 2 miles NE of Le Faouët

This Flamboyant-style chapel is built in a rocky cleft on the side of a hill. The **site★** is very pretty; from a height of some 100m - 300ft, it overlooks the little Ellé Valley. The great stairway (78 steps), built in 1700, leading up to the chapel, is linked by an arch to the St Michael Oratory crowning a rock spur. Nearby, in a little building, is the bell tolled by pilgrims to call down blessing from heaven.

Owing to its position and orientation, the chapel has only a single aisle and a small apse. Inside are Renaissance stained glass windows and a gallery with finely carved panels. Two *pardons* are held every year.

Paths lead down to the sacred fountain, below the chapel.

From a rocky platform reached by a path starting on the right half-way along the car park, there is a good view of the sunken, wooded Ellé Valley.

STE-MARIE-DU-MÉNEZ-HOM Chapel

Michelin map **58** fold 15 or **230** fold 18 – 3.5 km - 2 miles N of Plomodiern

The chapel stands in a small parish close at the entrance to the Crozon Peninsula. The close has a very plain rounded doorway dated 1739 and a Calvary with three crosses rising from separate bases. The chapel, which has a twin-gabled façade, is entered by a doorway beneath the elegant galleried belfry, topped by a cupola which gives an upward sweep to the massive building.

Inside, the ornate **altarpieces★** take up the whole of the east wall but not covering over the window apertures. While both the central altarpiece, with the family and life of the Virgin as its theme, and the north altarpiece depicting the saints, have figures which are rather heavy and expressionless, the figures of the Apostles on the south altarpiece show life and elegance. The skill with which they were carved, marks a step forward in Breton sculpture. The lovely friezes in the north transept, adorned with animals and various scenes, a remarkable St Lawrence, a graceful St Barbara in wood are also noteworthy.

★ SEIN Island   Pop 504

Michelin map 58 fold 12 or 230 folds 15, 16

Sein Island makes a picturesque excursion. It is less than 1 km² - 1/2 sq mile in area and lies very low; the sea sometimes covers it as it did in 1868 and 1896. The island is bare: there are no trees or even bushes; old fields are enclosed by low, drystone walls.

Men and their work. – For centuries the island was an object of superstitious dread. In the 18C its few inhabitants lived in almost total isolation. The islanders were great wreck looters. Today they are among the most active lifesavers. The women do all the manual labour, the men are sailors or fishermen. Fishing is the island's only means of livelihood.

A fine page of history (1940-44). – Directly after General de Gaulle's appeal of 18 June 1940, the men of Sein Island (altogether 130 sailors and fishermen), put to sea and joined the troops of Fighting France in England. Moreover, nearly 3 000 French soldiers and sailors also reached the island and embarked for England. When the Germans arrived on Sein they found only women, children, old men, the Mayor and the priest. For several months fishing boats brought or embarked Allied officers. Of the sailors from the island who went to England twenty-nine were killed on the battlefields. A commemorative monument stands to the right of the road to the lighthouse. General de Gaulle came in person in 1946 to award the Liberation Cross to the Island.

TOUR

The village. – Its small white houses with brightly painted shutters stand along alleys barely a yard wide for protection from the wind. On a hillock near the church, two menhirs rise side by side, hence known as "The Talkers". Beyond the church, the Nifran Calvary is a simple granite coss resting on a tiered plinth. Behind it is the only dolmen on the island.

⊙ **Lighthouse (Phare).** – 249 steps. The lighthouse, on the island's western tip, is equipped with a light 6 kW which has an average range of 50 km - 31 miles. From the platform is a vast **panorama**★★ of the island, the coast and the Sein reef. This reef submerged or visible, prolongs the island some 20 km - 12 miles towards the open sea.
On one of these rocks, which is constantly pounded by the sea, the **Ar Men lighthouse**, which took 14 years of super human effort to build, was erected in 1881. Its light has a range of 55 km - 34 miles to warn seamen off the rocks.

Lobster farm. – Left of the lighthouse. This farm has been set up with the aim of replenishing stocks around the island.

Port. – The port provides a good shelter for pleasure craft.

★ TONQUÉDEC Castle

Michelin map 59 fold 1 or 230 fold 7 – 7.5 km - 5 miles SE of Lannion

⊙ The ruins of Tonquédec Castle stand in very fine surroundings on a height overlooking the Léguer Valley. The castle, which was built in the early 13C, was dismantled by order of Jean IV in 1395; rebuilt at the beginning of the 15C, it was again razed by order of Richelieu in 1622.
The entrance gate is opposite a pool now run dry. Enter an outer fortified courtyard. On the right, two towers connected by a curtain wall frame the main entrance to the second enclosure. Pass through a postern into the second courtyard. Opposite, standing alone, is the keep with walls over 4m - 13ft thick. Go up a stairway (70 steps) to a platform to admire the plan of the castle and the local countryside: a wide, fertile and populous plateau intersected by deep, wooded valleys running north and south. These are now almost uninhabited; the old mills that gave them some life are nearly all abandoned.

★ TRÉBEURDEN   Pop 3 228

Michelin map 59 fold 1 or 230 fold 6 – Local map p 67 – Facilities

This seaside resort has several beaches, the two main ones are well situated and separated by the rocky peninsula of Le Castel: the Pors-Termen beach which is a continuation of the Trozoul, which faces the harbour and the Tresmeur which is much larger and more frequented.

★ **The Castel.** – *1/2 hour on foot Rtn. Follow a path along the isthmus (car park) between the two beaches of Trozoul and Tresmeur.*
Le Castel commands an extensive **view**★ of the coast and the Milliau, Molène, Grande and Losquet Islands and in clear weather, the coast of Finistère as far as St-Pol-de-Léon.

★ **Bihit Point.** – *Round tour of 4 km - 2 1/2 miles. The Porz-Mabo road overlooks the Tresmeur beach and offers views of the Grande, Molène and Milliaud Islands. Take the road to the right.*
From the viewing-table there is a fine **view**★ of the coast from Batz Island and Roscoff right over to Grande Island and the Triagoz lighthouse out to sea with Trébeurden and its beaches down below.
The road, which has already covered a quarter circle, goes on to Porz-Mabo.
You can see Locquémeau and Séhar Point in the distance.

Porz-Mabo. – A fine sandy beach.
A road goes from the beach to Trébeurden.

Michelin map **59** fold 1 or **230** fold 6 – Local map p 67 – Facilities

The resort of Trégastel rivals the neighbouring locality of Ploumanach for the beauty and strangeness of its **rocks★★**, which are characteristic of the Bretonne Corniche (p 67).

SIGHTS

◷ **Sea-water Aquarium.**
– It is located in caves, which housed a church in the 19C (Coz Ilis = the old church) under a mass of enormous rocks known as the Turtles. In three rooms are exhibited varieties of fish from Breton waters and tropical seas, stuffed birds including puffins, herring gulls, guillemots, penguins and gannets, all from the Seven Islands (p 156).

At the exit, a stairway (28 steps) leads up to a **statue of the Eternal Father** (Père Éternel). From the belvedere, there is a good **view** of the mass of rocks and the Côte de Granit Rose coastline.

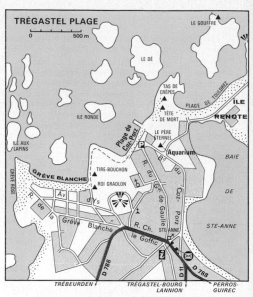

Coz-Porz Beach. – A sandy beach lined with rocks bearing descriptive names: the Turtles, the Witch. At the north end of the beach, beyond the jetty, make for a small beach near two rocks, the Death's Head (Tête de Mort) and the Pile of Pancakes (Tas de Crêpes), both on the right. This last rock, which appears to lie in folds, is a good example of wind erosion. Beyond a sandbank there is a mass of rocks, among which is the Thimble.

★ **The White Shore** (Grève Blanche). – 1 hour on foot Rtn.
Rock enthusiasts will go there from Coz-Porz. The path, which starts from the left end of the latter beach, follows the cliff edge around a promontory from the end of which can be seen the White Shore, Rabbits' Island (Ile aux Lapins) and, out at sea, the Triagoz Islands.

The path continues near the foot of a rock called the Corkscrew (Tire-Bouchon) and reaches the end of the White Shore, dominated by a great rock which is known as King Gradlon (Roi Gradlon) among local people on account of its resemblance to a crowned head.

Viewing table. – Telescope. This permits a circular **view★** of the coast: the White Shore, Grande Island, the Triagoz lighthouse, the Seven Islands; and the hinterland (when weather permits): the Clarté, Pleumeur-Bodou (with its distinctive radar dome) and Trébeurden villages.

★★ **Renote Island.** – Northeast. Leaving the sand bar you will find opposite you Renote Island, formed of huge blocks of granite and now connected with the mainland. Follow the road that crosses the island.
You pass Touldrez beach on your left and approach the Chasm (Le Gouffre) a cavity in the middle of a mass of rocks which can be reached at low tide. As you walk amidst the rocks to the very tip of the peninsula, you get good views of the horizon out to sea and of the Seven Islands looking north; of the Ploumanach coast to the east and the Bay of St Anne to the south.

Trégastel-Bourg. – 3 km - 2 miles S towards Lannion.
The 13C church was remodelled in the 14 and 18C. To the right of the south porch, stands a semicircular 17C ossuary, adorned with balusters and crowned with a domed turret. At the end of the nave is an unusual 14C stoup, a former grain measure. In the cemetery are a small Calvary, an altar for offerings and the tomb of the Breton author, Charles le Goffic (p 29).
Situated 500 m - 1/3 mile beyond the village to the south, a modern Calvary rises on a knoll. Steps lead to the top from which there is a fine **view** of the Côte de Granit Rose.

The Michelin Guide France
revises annually its 500 town plans showing:

– throughroutes and by-passes, traffic junctions and roundabouts,
new roads, car parks and one-way systems

– the exact location of hotels, restaurants and public buildings.

With the help of all this updated information take the harassment out of town driving

Michelin map **59** fold 2 or **230** fold 7 – Local map p 209

The town (evangelized in the 6C by St Tugdual), a former episcopal city, was built in terraces on the side of a hill overlooking the wide estuary of the Jaudy and Guindy Rivers. The port, which provides a magnificent anchorage for yachts, can receive big ships.

One of the great Breton *pardons* takes place in the town of St Yves on 19 May *(p 25)*. This is the "*pardon* of the poor", as well as that of advocates and lawyers. The procession goes from the cathedral to Minihy-Tréguier *(p 208)*.

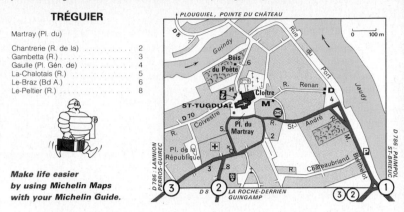

TRÉGUIER

Martray (Pl. du)

Chantrerie (R. de la)	2
Gambetta (R.)	3
Gaulle (Pl. Gén. de)	4
La-Chalotais (R.)	5
Le-Braz (Bd A.)	6
Le-Peltier (R.)	8

Make life easier by using Michelin Maps with your Michelin Guide.

Place du Martray. – The square is the heart of the town. It has kept picturesque old houses. A statue of Ernest Renan (1823-92) stands in the square to commemorate the writer's birth in Tréguier and his attendance at the local college *(p 29)*.

★★St-Tugdual Cathedral. – The cathedral, which dates from the 13 to the 15C, is one of the finest in Brittany. The transept is surmounted by three towers; the tower of the south arm roofed by an 18C pierced spire rises 63m - 202ft. At its base under a fine Flamboyant **window★** is a porch (1438). Every fifteen minutes five bells peal St Yves' canticle. The Gothic tower of the sanctuary, uncompleted, rises above the crossing. The Romanesque Hastings Tower is all that is left of the 12C church.

Enter by the main porch.

Steps lead down towards the luminous nave with its Gothic arches worked delicately in the granite. A sculpted frieze runs under the triforium. The ribbed vaulting in the Tudor style is lit by the clerestory windows. The magnificent 15C windows made from the Tréguier workshops were broken in 1793. They were replaced for the most part in 1971 by modern stained glass, the work of the master glazier Hubert de Sainte-Marie, portraying Biblical themes (to the left scenes from the Old Testament, to the right scenes from the Gospel).

Start from the north aisle.

The tomb of St Yves is an 1890 copy of the monument built by Jean V, Duke of Brittany, in the 15C. The recumbent figure of Jean V sculpted in 1945 is located in the Duke's Chapel, lit by stained glass donated in 1937 by American, Belgian and French lawyers. The north arm of the transept is cut off by the Hastings Tower in Norman limestone. The doors of the sacristy and cloister open under handsome Romanesque arches which rise above a heavy pillar, coupled by columns with sculpted capitals and surmounted by an arcature with pilaster strips.

In the ambulatory, the third chapel houses a 13C Christ carved in wood. The chancel with slender columns has 18C painted vaulting. It holds 46 Renaissance **stalls★**.

The **stained glass window★** brightens the south transept. It recounts the story of the Vine (symbol of the Church) which winds round the founders of the seven Breton bishoprics among them St Tugdual, around the saints of the land and around the Breton trades. Near the south doorway an interesting 15C group carved in wood represents St Yves between the Rich and the Poor.

⊘ **Treasure.** – The sacristy contains the treasure, which includes the head reliquary (19C) of St Yves in gilded bronze placed against the foundation wall of the Hastings Tower, which is thought to date from the 11C. Also of interest are a cupboard reliquary, a vestiary with revolving drawers (1650), old statues and a 15C manuscript.

⊘ **Cloister** (Cloître). – The 15C cloister abuts the former bishop's palace and the cathedral chevet cuts across the north gallery. The Flamboyant arches in Breton granite, roofed with slate, frame a cross rising on a lawn. Under the wooden vaulting with its sculptured frieze, there are 15 to 17C recumbent figures in the ambulatory.

⊘ **Renan's House** (M). – The 16C half-timbered house has been turned into a museum, and there you may see the room where Renan was born, his room as a schoolboy (fine view over the town), a reproduction of his study at the Collège de France and his library. A gallery has been arranged in honour of Renan's *Prayer on the Acropolis* following a visit by the philosopher to Greece. Also displayed are manuscripts and portraits.

War memorial. – *N of the cathedral.* A sober and moving work by F. Renaud.

Old town gates (D). – The gates lined with tall half-timbered houses are at the corner of the Rue du Port and Rue Renan.

Bois du Poète. – The wood overlooks the Guindy River and contains a monument to the writer Anatole Le Braz *(p 29)*. Pleasant walk.

EXCURSIONS *local map p 209*

Minihy-Tréguier. – Pop 790. *1 km - 1/2 mile S. Leave Tréguier by ② on the town plan, the D 8. Shortly after coming out of the town, turn left.*

The birthplace of St Yves, is the scene of a *pardon* on 19 May. This is called locally "going to St-Yves"; the local priest is even known as the "Rector of St-Yves". The 15C church is built on the site of the former chapel of the manor of Kermartin, where Yves Hélori was born and died (1253-1303 – *p 25*). His will is written in Latin on a painted canvas kept in the chapel. A 13C manuscript kept in the presbytery is called the *Breviary of St Yves.* In the cemetery is a 13C monument pierced in the middle by a very low archway, under which the pilgrims pass on their knees. This is called the "tomb of St Yves", but is probably an altar belonging to the original chapel.

① **Round tour of 37 km - 23 miles.** – *Time: about 2 hours.*

Leave Tréguier by the D 8 to the north and at Plouguiel, bear right.

La Roche-Jaune. – A small port on the Jaudy estuary. Oyster farms.

On leaving La Roche-Jaune in the direction of St-Gonéry, you will enjoy a good view of the Jaudy estuary, the oyster-beds and the islands.

St-Gonéry. – *P 192.*

At St-Gonéry, take the road to Pors-Hir.

Pors-Hir. – A small harbour built between great rocks near a little cove.

The road follows the coastline in a beautiful setting; houses built against huge rocks or nestling between tall boulders add a fairy-like touch.

Château Point. – From the tip of the headland, there are beautiful views over Er Islands, the Heaux Lighthouse and the Seven Islands.

★ **Le Gouffre.** – *1/4 hour on foot Rtn.* A deep cleft in a mass of rocks into which the sea roars furiously.

Turn back and follow the road along the bays, then bear right three times.

From Le Roudour, you can make for **Pors Scaff Bay** bristling with islands.

Beyond Le Roudour, take a coast road in the direction of Gouermel affording fine views.

Buguélès. – A small resort fringed by islands, all inhabited. From the harbour there is a good view of Château Point; inland the Plougrescant belfry stands out on the horizon.

Make for Penvénan and turn right into the D 74 towards Port-Blanc.

★ **Port-Blanc.** – A small fishing port and seaside resort. Under the dunes of the main beach are traces of memorial stones (now covered) which suggest the existence, at one time, of a necropolis.

ⓥ To reach the **Chapel of Notre-Dame-de-Port-Blanc,** go to the great esplanade by the sea, turn left before a group of houses built on the rocks *(car park)*. At the left corner, take an uphill path and a stairway (35 steps). The 16C chapel has a roof that comes down to the ground. Inside, to the right of the chancel, note a group showing St Yves between a rich man and a pauper. There is a Calvary in the close. A *pardon* is held on 8 September.

Return to Tréguier by the D 74 through Penvénan and the D 70.

② **The Wild Peninsula** (Presqu'île Sauvage). – *Round tour of 49 km - 30 miles - about 3 hours.*

Leave Tréguier by ① on the town plan, the D 786 towards Paimpol.

After crossing the bridge over the Jaudy, you will see a glass-blower's workshop on the left.

Lézardrieux. – Pop 1 859. The town is built on the left bank of the Trieux which is spanned by a suspension bridge. The 18C church has an elegant gabled belfry flanked by two turrets and topped by a pinnacle pierced with arcades containing the bells. This particular type of belfry is to be found throughout the peninsula.

Make for the Talbert Spit, skirting the large marina on the Trieux. After 3 km - 2 miles bear right into a downhill road.

Old tidal mill (Ancien moulin de marée). – A ruined mill which was driven by water from a small reservoir upstream. From the dyke, there is a good view over the mouth of the Trieux.

Return to the D 20 towards Talbert Spit and turn right.

Bodic Lighthouse (Le Bodic). – A small lighthouse commanding the mouth of the Trieux. A path on the left leads through fields to a belvedere from which the **view★** extends over the Trieux estuary and Bois Island in the foreground and Bréhat Islands in the distance.

The road then passes near the Pommelin Bay, crosses Lanmodez and Larmor-Pleubian.

Talbert Spit (Sillon de Talbert). – This long, narrow tongue of land, surrounded by reefs, consists of sand and shingle washed by the currents of the Trieux and the Jaudy; it is possible to go round on foot. Seaweed is collected and dried on the spot and then sent to a factory nearby for processing.

Return to Larmor-Pleubian and bear right towards Pors-Rand beach.

Creac'h Maout viewing table. – From the viewing table in front of the war memorial and the signal station there is a wide **panorama★** over Arcouest Point, Bréhat, Talbert Spit, Heaux Lighthouse (built 1836-1839, 56m - 184ft high, average range 35 km - 22 miles), Château Point and the Jaudy estuary.

Go through St-Antoine to the entrance of Pleubian and bear right.

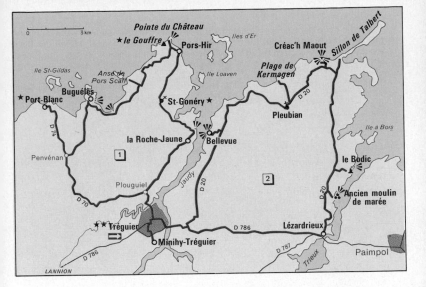

Kermagen Beach (Plage de Kermagen). – It faces Château Point and Er Islands.

Pleubian. – Pop 3 293. On the north side of the church with its characteristic belfry, is a fine 16C round **pulpit★** surmounted by a cross and decorated with a frieze depicting the Last Supper and scenes from the Passion: Judas's Kiss, the Flagellation, Christ bearing the Cross.

At Pleubian, take the direction of Kerbors by the coast road.

The road passes near the covered alleyway at Men-ar-Rompet, partly hidden in the greenery, and by Poule Island.

At Kerbors, turn left before the church.

Bellevue. – It is located on the bank of the Jaudy. On the right the view extends over the Jaudy estuary, on the left over the valley and site of Tréguier dominated by the cathedral towers; opposite La Roche-Jaune rises in terraces. There are trout and salmon farms along the Jaudy, which is tidal, as fish farming develops in the region.

The road winds through fields growing early vegetables and descends towards the Jaudy Valley and Tréguier.

La TRINITÉ-LANGONNET

Michelin map **58** fold 17 or **230** fold 20 – 13 km - 8 miles E of Gourin

This village in the Noires Mountains possesses a fine Flamboyant-style **church** with a three-sided chevet. The west gabled doorway has twin doors; the south porch added in 18C is also of interest. Inside, the **timbering★** dated 1568 and decorated with Renaissance designs shows great craftsmanship and enhances the lofty, well-lit nave. In the richly ornamented chancel, note the carved recesses, brackets and friezes; and on the left of the chancel, a sacrarium, a fine stone cupboard, placed under a Trinity.

La TRINITÉ-SUR-MER   Pop 1478

Michelin map **63** fold 12 or **230** folds 35, 49 – Facilities

The village, built on a height, now extends some 800 m - 1/2 mile down the slope to the harbour and beaches on the Crach River estuary which is lined with oyster-beds *(p 18)*. A small fishing port, a busy pleasure harbour and naval yards add to the activity of this resort which has fine beaches along the Kerbihan Peninsula.

Kerisper Bridge. – From this great bridge over the Crach River there is a good **view★** of the estuary, the town and the port installations.

Join us in our never ending task
of keeping up to date.

Send us your comments
and suggestions, please.

Michelin Tyre Public Limited Company
Tourism Department
Lyon Road – HARROW – Middlesex HA1 2DQ

An excursion to the island of Ushant by sea is of the greatest interest, since it enables you to see the Brest Channel, the St-Mathieu Point, the Four Channel, the famous Black Stones (Pierres Noires) reef and that of the Green Stones (Pierres Vertes), the Islands of Béniguet and Molène, and the Fromveur Channel. The island itself is extremely curious.

On the way to Ushant the boat usually anchors off and sometimes calls at **Molène.** There the pastures on the rare patches of earth in this archipelago are so small that, according to a local jest, a Molène cow which has her four feet in one field, grazes from another and manures a third.

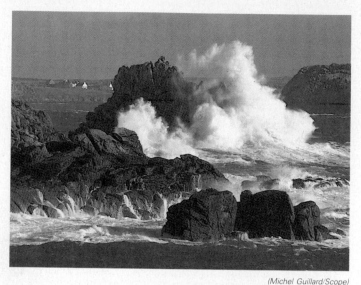

(Michel Guillard/Scope)

Ushant. – Rocks

Nature. – Ushant is 7 km - 4 miles long and 4 km - 2 1/2 miles wide and its highest point is 60m - 197ft above sea level. It is famous in marine history for the danger of its waters due to frequent fog, strong currents (the Fromrust to the northwest and the Fromveur to the southeast) and countless reefs.

In winter the wind is master and hurls the waves against the broken and rocky shores with the utmost fury for as much as ten days on end. The scene is often sinister when the fog comes down and the mournful howl of the foghorns mingles with the roar of the storm.

Few tourists know the island in this inhospitable guise, for the summer season brings calm and a quieter atmosphere, similar to that of the coasts of Brittany. The climate is mild. In January and February, Ushant has the highest mean temperature in France.

The colonies of sea birds that nest on the island's cliff and on the neighbouring islets are particularly numerous in the autumn when the migrants from northern Europe fly in.

The **Armorique Regional Nature Park** *(p 49)* to which Ushant has been attached since 1969, helps maintain its traditional character.

The men and their work. – The men either work the land (as do the women), fish, or work for the Navy or Merchant Marine. Only one-tenth of the island can be cultivated; there are a few fields of potatoes and a little wheat. However, in recent years, with the aid of a branch of the Armorique Regional Nature Park about 100 ha - 247 acres are being recultivated (wheat, potatoes and fodder crops).

Small sheep, some with brown wool, crop meagre salt pastures; their meat is good. They live in the open and take shelter from northwesterly or southwesterly gales behind low dry-stone walls built in a star formation or wood shelters. Though from early February for lambing to late September they are tethered in twos to a stake they wander freely the rest of the year, their owner's mark being nicked on their ears. Dairy cattle have been reintroduced to the island with the aim of achieving self-sufficiency.

Tradition. – The important part played by the women of Ushant in family life was recognized by an old custom by which it was the girls who proposed marriage. Women's dress is severe and not often worn, it is made of black cloth and consists of a short skirt and a small *coiffe;* the hair is combed back and falls on the shoulders. The character of the people is reflected in the customs which were observed until 1962 when a member of a family was lost at sea. The friends and relatives met at the man's home to pray and watched over a little wax cross that stood for him; the sad vigil lasted all night. The next day, at the funeral service, the cross was deposited in a reliquary in the church. Later, at some major ceremony, it would be put in a mausoleum in the cemetery where the crosses of all the missing are assembled. These little wax crosses are called *Proëlla* crosses. The word means "the homecoming of souls".

⊘ TOUR

Roads from Lampaul lead to the best sites but many paths and tracks enable the visitor to criss-cross the island, to reach the fine cliffs, the pretty little creeks, to discover the flora as well as the marine fauna: herring gulls, crested cormorants, oyster catchers, puffins, terns, etc.

Lampaul. – This is the island's capital. Note the old houses kept in excellent repair; the shutters are painted in green or blue, the island's traditional colours. A small monument containing the *Proëlla* crosses *(p 210)* stands in the cemetery next to the church.

The tiny port, west facing, is picturesque, while the sandy beach of Le Corce nearby extends to the south.

★★★ **The North-West Coast.** – *Leave Lampaul W by an uphill road; after 500 m - 1/3 mile, bear right.*

⊘ **Ushant Folk Centre** (Maison Ouessantine). – At the hamlet of **Niou-Uhella,** two traditional houses have been restored and rearranged by the Armorique Regional Nature Park. Visitors will see in one of them furniture typical of the island built of wood from wrecked vessels and in the second a display of farm and domestic implements and costumes, etc which depicts aspects of life on Ushant.

Proceed towards the coast.

Karaes Mill (Moulin de Karaes). – This is the island's last mill (restored) with its round stone base. It was used to mill barley from which bread was still made at the beginning of the 20C.

Creac'h Lighthouse (Phare de Creac'h). – This lighthouse, with that at Land's End, marks the entrance to the English Channel; it has two tiers of revolving beams. The light is cast by four lamps giving a total of 16 million candlepower and an average range of more than 60 km - 37 miles.

Go round the lighthouse to the right to view the coast.

Its extraordinarily jagged **rocks**★★★ *(rochers – illustration p 210)* pounded by the sea are very impressive. A gangway in front of the lighthouse gives access to Creac'h Beach where stands the fog-horn. Cargo boats and oil tankers can be seen on the horizon; some 300 ships pass in the area which is patrolled day and night by the French Navy.

Turn back and bear right towards Pern Point.

Notre-Dame-de-Bon-Voyage. – Also known as the Chapel of St-Gildas after the English saint who came here in the 5C, it was built at the end of the 19C. The people of Ushant come to the chapel every year for the island's *pardon* on the first or second Sunday in September.

★ **Pern Point.** – This, the western-most point of the island extends into the sea in a series of rocks and reefs lashed by the rollers. In the distance is the unmanned Nividic Lighthouse (Phare de Nividic).

Feunteun Velen Peninsula. – *At Lampaul, take the road skirting the cemetery.* Pass near the small port of Lampaul where the boat from Brest sometimes drops anchor. The jetty gives shelter to the fishing boats.

The road goes round the deep Lampaul Bay bounded by the Le Corce and Le Prat beaches and with the Le Grand Truk and Youc'h Corz bristling in the centre, then descends gently towards Porz Doun Point. Note on the left the white pyramid of Le Runiou (Pyramide du Runiou), a landmark for shipping; on the right is the great cove of Porz Coret.

Porz Doun Point. – The cliff-lined point at the southern tip of the island affords a fine **view** over Lampaul, the Pern Point and the Jument lighthouse (built from 1904 to 1912) which reaches a height of 42m - 138ft and houses a fog-horn.

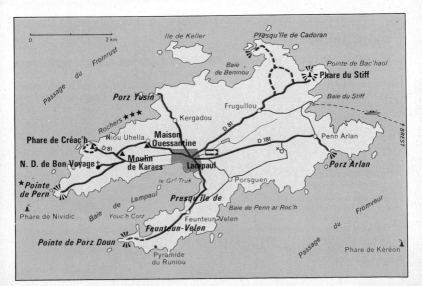

ⓥ **Stiff Lighthouse (Phare du Stiff).** – *Leave Lampaul by the road running along the south side of the church.*

The road rises gently to the island's highest point at an altitude of 60m - 197ft, the Bac'haol Point.

The lighthouse built by the military architect Vauban in 1695, comprises two adjoining towers, one containing a spiral staircase (126 steps) and the other three small superposed rooms. The light has a range of 50 km - 31 miles thanks to a lamp of 6 000 W giving a total of 1.2 million candlepower. From the top a vast **panorama★★** unfolds over the islands, the mainland from the Vierge lighthouse to Raz Point.

Nearby stands the new radar-tower (height 140m - 459ft) which controls the sea lane off the island.

Paths lead to the tip of the **Cadoran Peninsula** (Presqu'île de Cadoran) from which may be enjoyed a pretty view of Beninou Bay sometimes frequented by a seal colony, and Keller Island favoured by nesting birds.

Porz Yusin. – *Leave Lampaul N by a road running past the island's electricity generating plant.*

The road passes several hamlets with white houses adorned with brightly coloured shutters and surrounded by small gardens, on the way to Porz Yusin, one of the few sheltered spots on the north coast.

This pretty rocky setting is ideal for birdwatching. There are also very fine varieties of algae.

Porz Arlan. – *Leave Lampaul by the road skirting the cemetery, then turn left.*

The road runs across the plateau, leaving on the right the Chapel of Our Lady of Hope (dating from 1863) and on the left the airfield before bearing right towards picturesque Porz Arlan.

In this creek nestle a tiny sandy beach and a small port sheltered by a jetty. From this charming site the beautiful **view** extends over the rocky coastline, Fromveur and Kéréon lighthouse, and Bannec Island.

The Maps, Red Guides and Green Guides are complementary publications. Use them together.

★★ **Le VAL-ANDRÉ**

Michelin map 🟦59 fold 4 or 🟦230 fold 9 – Local map p 96 – Facilities

The resort has one of the finest sand beaches on the north coast of Brittany.

★ **Pléneuf Point.** – *15 min on foot Rtn. From the car park at the port of Piégu starts this walk at the foot of the cliff.* It leads to a small belvedere (bench) facing Verdelet Island, a bird sanctuary.

By skirting the Pléneuf Point it is possible to reach the Vallées Beach (allow 1/2 hour on foot). Leave from the port of Piégu and go up the steps which end in the Rue de la Corniche.

This very pretty walk, on a cliff path overlooking the sea, affords superb **views★★** of St-Brieuc Bay and the beach and resort of Le Val André.

★ **The Watch-path Walk (Promenade de la Guette).** – *1 hour on foot Rtn.* At the southwest end of the quay at the juncture with the Rue des Sablons, two arrows point the way to the Guette pathway, the Corps de Garde and the Batterie.

Go round the Anse du Pissot, down the stairs to the beach and along the Corps de Garde which is now in ruins. Soon after there is an extensive **view★** of St-Brieuc Bay. From the statue of Our Lady of the Watch go down to **Dahouët**, a fishing port and pleasure boat harbour.

Follow the Quai des Terre-Neuvas and take, across from the pool, after the bridge, the Mocquelet Path to the Val-André quay.

EXCURSION

Round tour of 19 km - 12 miles. – *Time: about 1 1/2 hours. Leave Le Val-André by the D 786 towards Erquy. After 5 km - 3 miles, turn right.*

ⓥ **Bienassis Château.** – At the park entrance take the main tree-lined avenue which affords good views of the building, as it leads up to the château. Go through an opening in the crenellated wall, all that remains of the 15C enclosure; its corner towers and turrets were added in the 17C when the château was rebuilt.

The ground floor includes a great saloon, the former guardroom and the dining room adorned with porcelain from China, Japan and Bayeux, and furniture in the Louis XIV and Breton Renaissance styles. The north façade overlooking the garden retains two 15C towers.

On leaving the park, bear left in the direction of St-Brieuc and after 3 km - 2 miles, turn left towards St-Jacques-le-Majeur.

ⓥ **St-Jacques-le-Majeur.** – The 13C Chapel of St James the Major, restored in 16C, stands at the crossroads. Its elegant doorway is adorned with clustered columns crowned with carved capitals.

The bare interior lit by modern stained glass windows, contains a charming statue of a Virgin and Child (14C) known locally as Our Lady of Safe Return (Notre-Dame-du-Bon-Voyage), a Stations of the Cross carved in granite by Saupique, a contemporary sculptor from Rennes.

Take the direct road back to Le Val-André.

Michelin map **63** fold 3 or **230** folds 36, 37 – Local map p 138

Vannes is built in the shape of an amphitheatre at the head of the Morbihan Gulf. The town, an important agricultural centre, is also developing industrially. There is a Michelin tyre factory to the east of the town.

The old quarter, enclosed in its ramparts and grouped around the cathedral, is picturesque. It is a pedestrian zone where elegant shops have established themselves in old town houses.

HISTORICAL NOTES

Nominoé, founder of Breton unity (9C). – Nominoé, a Breton of modest origin, was discovered by Charlemagne, who made him Count of Vannes. Becoming Duke of Brittany (826) under Louis the Pious, he had decided to unite all the Bretons in an independent kingdom *(p 22)*. When Louis died, he went into action. In ten years unity was achieved: the Duchy reached the boundaries which were to be those of the Province until 1789. From the first Vannes was the capital of the new Breton kingdom, which reverted later to the status of a Duchy.

The union with France (16C). – Anne of Brittany, who married successively Charles VIII *(details p 178)* and Louis XII, remained the sovereign of her duchy.

When she died in 1514 at the age of 37 without leaving a male heir, Claude of France, one of her daughters, inherited Brittany. A few months later Claude married the heir to the throne of France, François of Angoulême, and after a few months, on 1 January 1515, became Queen of France. The King easily persuaded her to yield her duchy to their son, the Dauphin. Thus Brittany and France would be reunited in the person of the future king.

The last step was taken in August 1532. The States (councils), meeting at Vannes, proclaimed "the perpetual union of the Country and Duchy of Brittany with the Kingdom and Crown of France". The rights and privileges of the duchy were maintained: taxes had to be approved by the States; the Breton Parliament kept its judicial sovereignty and the province could maintain an army.

★ THE OLD TOWN time: 2 1/2 hours

Start from the Rue A.-Le-Pontois.

From here there is a very pleasant view of the old Hermine Ducal Castle (rebuilt around 1800) with a pretty flower garden in front of it. The castle houses the Law School.

★ **Ramparts (Remparts).** – After crossing a small bridge, go to the left-hand parapet, from where you can look down on some old **wash houses** with very curious roofing.

From the Frères Jolivet alley in the Promenade de la Garenne *(p 215)* you will get a view★★ of the most picturesque corner of Vannes, with the stream that flows at the foot of the ramparts (built in the 13C and remodelled repeatedly until the 17C), the formal gardens and the old houses with the cathedral in the background.

When you reach the end of the promenade, follow the Rue F.-Decker, bordered by the Préfecture's gardens (Jardin de la Préfecture) which leads to the 15C **Prison Gate,** flanked by a machicolated tower.

Pass through the gate.

The cathedral chevet now comes into full view. Follow the Rue St-Guenhaël, with its old houses, and then turn right into the Place St-Pierre.

To the left of this square, is **La Cohue (B),** a marketplace from the 12 and 14C and where until 1840 fairs were held. On the first floor, the courtroom (restored) dating from 1550, was the seat of the Presidial court of justice.

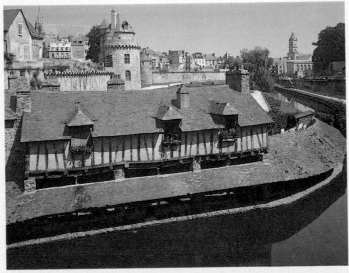

(Christiane Olivier, Nice)

Vannes. – Ramparts and wash-houses

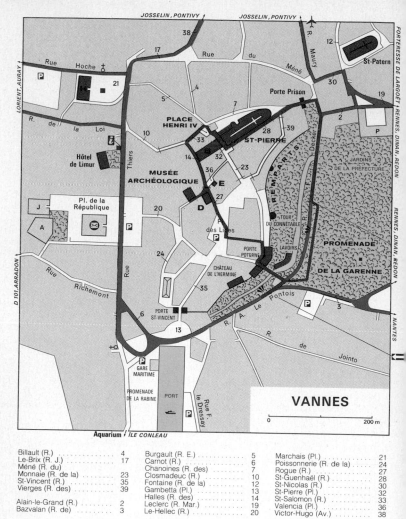

★ **St Peter's Cathedral** (Cathédrale St-Pierre). – Men worked on this building from the 13 to the 19C. The only trace of the 13C construction is the north tower of the façade, which is surmounted by a modern steeple. Cross the cloister's (16C ruins) garden which borders the north side of the cathedral. The rotunda chapel, which juts out, was built in 1537 in the Italian Renaissance style, which is rare in Brittany.

Enter the church by the fine transept door (Flamboyant Gothic, with Renaissance niches). In the entrance, on the left, a painting describes the death of **St Vincent Ferrier**, the Duchess of Brittany is present. This Spanish monk, who was a great preacher, died at Vannes in 1419 and was canonized in 1455. On the right is St Vincent preaching at Granada. In the 2nd chapel of the north aisle, a rotunda chapel, is the tomb of the Saint. On the walls a fine tapestry (1615) depicts the miraculous cures made by Vincent and his canonization.

In the apsidal chapel or Chapel of the Holy Sacrament and nave chapels you will see altars, altarpieces, tombs and statues of the 17 and 18C. In the Baptismal Chapel there is an altar frontal (16C) in stone depicting the Last Supper. The 15C nave has lost some of its original character as the heavy 18C vaulting has reduced its height and masked the panelled woodwork.

The cathedral **treasure** is exhibited in the old chapterhouse which is ornamented with 18C woodwork. It includes a remarkable painted 12-13C chest, a 12C reliquary cross, an ivory cross and pyx, chalices and other vessels.

★ **Place Henri-IV.** – The picturesque square is lined with 16C gabled houses. Glimpse down the Rue des Chanoines.

Walk along the Rue St-Salomon with its old town houses, turn into the Rue des Halles, where the La Cohue's other entrance is situated.

House of St Vincent Ferrier (E). – *No 17 Place Valencia.* In this house, remodelled in the 16C, Vincent Ferrier died in 1419.

House of Vannes (D). – An old dwelling adorned with two carved wood busts of jovial peasants known as "Vannes and his wife" (*see Questembert p 166*).

To return to the car go down Rue Rogue, cross Place des Lices and skirt the ramparts. Pass by the Constable's Tower (Tour du Connétable) to the Postern Gate (Porte Poterne) and the small bridge spanning the Rohan.

ADDITIONAL SIGHTS

★ **Archaeological Museum.** – This museum occupies 3 galleries on the 1st floor of the
⊙ Gaillard Château (15C). It formerly contained the House of Parliament.
The museum is rich in prehistoric specimens, most of which come from the first
megalithic excavations made in the Morbihan region: Carnac, Locmariaquer, and
Rhuys Peninsula. Exhibited are a remarkable collection of necklaces, bracelets, polished
axes, swords etc.; another gallery contains a variety of *objets d'art* (13-18C).

Limur Mansion (Hôtel de Limur). – A late 17C town house with a fine stone staircase.

Town Hall (H). – This building in the Renaissance style, erected at the end of the 19C,
stands in the Place Maurice-Marchais, which is adorned with the equestrian statue of
Constable de Richemont, one of the great figures of the 15C, for it was he who created
and commanded the French army which defeated the English at the end of the Hundred
Years War. He became Duke of Brittany, succeeding his brother in 1457, but died the
following year.

St-Patern. – This church was rebuilt in the 18C; it is topped by an imposing square
tower, completed in 1826.

Promenade de la Garenne. – The park of the former ducal castle of Vannes was
arranged as a public promenade in the 17C. The view of the ramparts (p 213), especially
the Constable's Tower, is attractive. In the upper part of the garden, on a wall, to the
left of the War Memorial, a marble tablet recalls the shooting of the Royalists (details
p 166).

⊙ **Oceanographic and Tropical Aquarium.** – Situated near the pleasure boat harbour,
this vast three-storeyed building is devoted to the link between man and the sea. In
over 50 pools complete with waterfalls live some thousand fishes from the world's seas.
The exhibition also includes the scientific and technical aspects, a laboratory, a
shopping area, etc.

EXCURSIONS

★ **Conleau Island.** – *5 km - 3 miles – plus 1/2 hour on foot Rtn. Leave Vannes by the
Promenade de la Rabine*. After 2 km - 1 mile a good view of the Morbihan Gulf unfolds
before you.

*Cross the estuary of the Vincin on a causeway to reach Conleau Island. Leave your
car (car park). Turn right in the woods on to the path skirting the Vincin.*

Conleau. – A small port well placed at the mouth of the Vincin. From the beach there
is a good view over Boëdic Island between Langle Point, on the left, and Kerguen Point
on the right.

Séné Peninsula. – *10 km - 6 miles S - about 3/4 hour. Leave Vannes by the Rue
Ferdinand-le-Dressay which skirts the harbour's left shore, then bear left towards Séné.*

Séné. – Formerly known for its typical fishing-boats, the *"sinagots"*, the village maintains
its maritime tradition.

On leaving Séné, bear right towards Bellevue and Port-Anna.

Former salt marshes and market gardens may be seen along the road.

Port-Anna. – This little port, frequented by fishing boats and pleasure craft, commands
the narrow channel through which sail boats heading for Vannes.

Return to Bellevue and bear right towards the wharf.

Wharf (Embarcadère). – It is used for goods despatched to Arz Island. From the car park,
the **view★** extends over the Vannes river with Conleau Island to the left and Séné, at
the end of a creek to the right.

Round tour of 55 km - 34 miles. – *Time: about 3 hours. Leave Vannes by the Rue
du Maréchal-Leclerc. After 14 km - 9 miles turn left to the castle.*

★ **Largoët Castle** (Forteresse de Largoët). – *P 128.*

After Elven turn left into the D 1.

The road crosses the Lanvaux moors.

Lanvaux Moors (Landes de Lanvaux). – Contrary to what the name *landes* – moors –
implies, this long crest of flaking rock-land, which was not even cultivated last century,
is now a fertile region. There remain, however, many megalithic monuments which
are worth seeking on foot, particularly around St-Germain, to the left of the road.

On entering **Trédion** turning left you go along the banks of a pool which surrounds a
most attractive Breton manor house.

*Across from it turn right and cross the built up area, then left into the D 133, above
the square.*

The road drops into the rural Valley of the Claie and its tributary the Callac stream.

Callac. – *Turn left.* On the left of the road before a crossroads is a man-made grotto,
a copy of the one at Lourdes. To the left of the grotto a path climbs steeply; on either
side are Stations of the Cross consisting of groups of figures carved in granite. The
path leads to a Calvary from where there is a view on the Lanvaux moors. The descent
is by another path which passes near the chapel. On the other side of the road a stream
flows swiftly at the foot of a hillock at the top of which stands a cross. It is a pleasant
spot.

*Take the left-hand road. When it reaches the D 1, turn left, and 600 m – about 1/3 mile
later bear right. After 2 km - 1 mile take the D 126 on the left, which will bring you
back to Vannes.*

⊙ **St-Avé.** – The **Chapel of Our Lady of Le Loc** (Notre-Dame-du-Loc) rises by the old lie of the D 126. A Calvary and a fountain stand before the 15C building. Inside, note the carving on the frieze which runs along the roof line and the frieze along the nave, which depicts angels, grotesques, and animals; in the centre of the nave stands a Calvary with figures, surmounted by a wooden canopy. There are alabaster panels on the high altar and 15C granite altarpieces at the right and left hand altars. The statues, which date from the 15, 16 and 18C, include a 15C Virgin in white stone.

Go through St-Avé to return to Vannes by the D 126.

Grand-Champ. – *19 km - 12 miles NE. Leave Vannes by the Rue Hoche.* In the doorway stands a display case in which are exhibited 17-19 liturgical objects. In the nave there are two carved wooden panels from Our Lady of Burgo (Notre-Dame-de-Burgo), a ruined chapel in a pretty wooded setting 2 km - 1 mile east of the town.

★★ **The Morbihan Gulf by boat.** – *P 138.*

★★ VITRÉ

Pop 13 491

Michelin map 59 fold 18 or 230 fold 28

This is the best preserved "old world" town in Brittany: its fortified castle *(illustration p 40),* its ramparts and its little streets have remained just as they were 400 or 500 years ago and make a picturesque and evocative picture which is long remembered.

The old town is built on a spur commanding the deep Valley of the Vilaine on one side and a railway cutting on the other. The castle stands proudly on the extreme point. From the 16 to the 18C, Vitré was one of the most prosperous of Breton cities; it made hemp and woollen cloth and cotton stockings which were sold not only in France but in England, Germany, Spain and even America and the Indies.

This prosperity dwindled rapidly in the 19C, but is now reviving with the establishment of knitting mills, tanneries, boot and shoe and agricultural machinery factories, a factory making beds and metal furniture and food processing industries.

The career of Pierre Landais (15C). – About the middle of the 15C, Pierre Landais, a tailor was noticed by Duke François II, who made him his wardrobe master. Being clever and enterprising, he worked his way up and became Grand Treasurer and Counsellor to the sovereign. But the nobles and the clergy hated this conceited upstart who encouraged bourgeois representation in the councils and had feudal rights abolished. With the support of the King of France, a plot was hatched which compelled the Duke to sacrifice his Counsellor: Landais was seized in the castle at Nantes. Under torture he admitted all the charges against him, and died by hanging in 1485.

★★ **Arrival at Vitré.** – Vitré Castle and the houses at its foot are a fine sight. Motorists should pause before going into the town.

Coming from Fougères: Magnificent view of the town coming down the hill on the D 178.

Coming from Rennes: View of the castle from the bend in the road from Brest, N 157.

★★ THE CASTLE (CHÂTEAU) *time 3/4 hour*

⊙ The castle was rebuilt in the 13, 14 and 15C and is an impressive building. The town bought it in 1820 from the La Trémoille family.

The present square used to be the castle forecourt where the stables and outbuildings were. The fortress is tri-angular in plan. The entrance is guarded by a drawbridge and entrance fort flanked by two big machicolated towers. At the south corner stands the main keep or St Lawrence Tower; at the northeast corner stands the Madeleine Tower, and at the northwest corner, the Montafilant Tower. These various works are linked by a wall, reinforced by other towers.

As you enter the courtyard you will see, on the right, a Romanesque porch (1) with archstones, alternating in colour, the town hall (1913) abutting on the

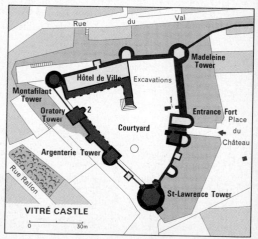

VITRÉ CASTLE

north front, and before you, the Oratory Tower with an elegant Renaissance loggia (2). From the platform of the Montafilant Tower (82 steps) there is a fine view★ of the town, the Tertres Noires and Moines Quarters, the Vilaine River and the old tannery.

Via the curtain wall you arrive at the Oratory Tower which contains a chapel. In this chapel is a beautiful 16C **triptych★** decorated with 32 Limoges enamels.

The Argenterie Tower presents exhibits of the region's natural history. The St Lawrence Tower houses a **museum** containing 15 and 16C sculpture, which comes from the houses of Vitré (a beautiful chimney has been remounted), the 15C tomb of Gui X (a local lord), a 17C chest, 16C Flemish and 17C Aubusson tapestries and engravings of old Vitré.

★ THE TOWN (AB)
time: 1 1/4 hours

> *Starting from the Place du Château, take the Rue Notre-Dame and turn to the right.*

★★ Rue Beaudrairie (A 5). – This, the most curious street in Vitré, gets its name from *baudroyeurs* meaning leather craftsmen. Each house is worth looking at.

Rue d'Embas (A 8). – This street used to lead to the gate (partly destroyed in 1846) of the same name. It is lined with half-timbered houses; note no 10, Hôtel de la Botte d'Argent (1513).

> *Return to the Place de la Liberté by the St-Yves Promenade from where one can see ruins of the ramparts.*
>
> *At Place du Géneral-de-Gaulle (B 13) take the Rue Garangeot.*

Cross the Rue Sevigné: note No 9, a 17C mansion known as "Tour de Sevigné" where the famous writer *(p 185)* lived.

> *Turn right into the Rue Poterie.*

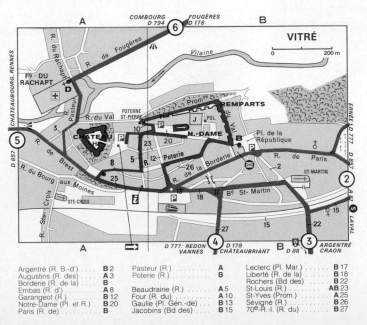

(S. Chirol)

Vitré. – Rue Beaudrairie

Rue Poterie (B). – Picturesque houses: half-timbered or with porches stand on this street.

> *Turn right into the Rue Notre-Dame.*

★ Ramparts (Remparts) (B). – From the Place de la République you will see one of the old rampart towers, the 15C Bridolle Tower (machicolations) (B B).
On the south side of the town the walls follow the line, at a little distance, of the present Rue de la Borderie and the Promenade St-Yves and then join the castle. Only fragments remain, built into private properties. On the north and east sides the ramparts are still intact.
The Rue de Paris, which gives on to the Place de la République, is lined with several old houses.

> *Go through the gate in the Val Promenade to circle the ramparts. At the end of the alley, after passing a gate, take the ramp to the left which passes under the St-Pierre postern; follow the Rue du Four uphill and turn right in the square, then left into the Rue Notre-Dame.*

★ **Notre-Dame.** – The church is 15-16C. Outside, the most curious part is the south side, with its seven gables decorated with pinnacles and its pulpit from which preachers addressed the congregation assembled on the small square and its two finely carved doors.

Inside, you will see many altarpieces and a fine Renaissance stained glass window in the south aisle (third bay) depicting Christ's Entry into Jerusalem.

In the Rue Notre-Dame at no 27 is the former Hôtel Hardy or de la Troussanais (16C) with its finely carved porches and dormer windows.

Turn round and go to the Place du Château.

ADDITIONAL SIGHTS

★★ **Tertres Noirs.** – *Access by the Rue de Brest and the Chemin des Tertres Noirs, to the right after the bridge over the Vilaine.* There is a fine **view**★★ of Vitré, its site and its castle from this shaded terrace.

★ **Public garden.** – *By ④ of the town plan.* A pleasant well kept garden.

Faubourg du Rachapt (A). – During the Hundred Years War this suburb was occupied for several years by the English, while the town and the castle resisted all their attacks. The people of Vitré paid the invaders to go away: hence the name of the suburb *(Rachapt = rachat = repurchase).*

This suburb, lying at the foot of the castle, crosses the Vilaine Valley and rises on the north hill slope. The Rue Pasteur, which affords picturesque views of the town and river, ⊙ leads to the hospital and the 15C **chapel of St-Nicolas** (D).

Enter by the little door on the left and skirt the chapel.

At the end, on the right, go through a pretty door beneath a basket handle arch into the chapel where there is an 18C wooden high altar in gilt. On the right is St Augustine, on the left St Nicholas and 3 children (18C); 16C frescoes have been discovered. The Rue du Rachapt is lined with old houses. Lovely view of the castle.

EXCURSIONS

★ **Rochers-Sévigné Château.** – *6.5 km - 4 miles SE. Leave Vitré by ③, D 88. 6 km - 4 miles from the town, on coming out of a wood, take the château drive on the left. Description p 185.*

★ **Champeaux.** – *9 km - 5 1/2 miles W. Leave Vitré by ⑤, N 157. 2 km - 1 mile from the town turn right onto the D 29. Description p 74.*

Index

Nizon . . . . Towns, sights and tourist regions. Isolated sights (dams, castles, dolmens, points...) are listed under their proper name.

Du Guesclin . . . . People, historical events and subjects.

The Department is given in brackets after the town, see abbreviations below:

C.-du-N. : Côtes-du-Nord
I.-et-V. : Ille-et-Vilaine
L.-Atl. : Loire-Atlantique

N Finistère : Nord Finistère
S Finistère : Sud Finistère

Practical Information

The French Government Tourist Office at 178 Piccadilly, London W1V 0AL, ☎ (01) 491 76 22 and 610 Fifth Avenue, New York, ☎ (212) 757 - 1125 will provide information.

How to get there. – You can go directly by scheduled national airlines, by commercial and package tour flights, possibly with a rail or coach link-up or you can go by cross-Channel ferry or hovercraft and on by car or train. Brittany ferries run daily services from Portsmouth to St-Malo and from Plymouth to Roscoff, and in summer only from Cork to Roscoff.

Enquire at any good travel agent and remember if you are going in the holiday season or at Christmas, Easter or Whitsun, to book well in advance.

Customs and other formalities

Papers and other documents. – A valid national **passport** (or in the case of the British a Visitor's Passport) is all that is required.

For the car you need a valid **driving licence, international driving permit, car registration papers** (log-book) and a **nationality plate** of the approved size. Insurance cover is compulsory and although the Green Card is no longer a legal requirement for France, it is the most effective proof of insurance cover and is internationally recognized by the police and other authorities.

There are no customs formalities for holidaymakers importing their caravans into France for a stay of less than 6 months. No customs document is necessary for pleasure boats or outboard motors for a stay of less than 6 months but you should have the registration certificate on board.

Motoring regulations. – Certain motoring organizations run accident insurance and breakdown service schemes for their members. Enquire before leaving. A **red warning triangle** or hazard warning lights are obligatory in case of a breakdown.

In France it is compulsory for the front passengers to wear **seat belts** if the car is equipped with them. Children under ten should be on the back seat.

The **speed limits,** although liable to modification, are: motorways 130 kph - 80 mph (110 kph when raining); national trunk roads 110 kph - 68 mph; other roads 90 kph - 56 mph (80 kph - 50 mph when raining) and in towns 60 kph - 37 mph. The regulation on speeding and drinking and driving are strictly interpreted – usually by an on the spot fine and/or confiscation of the vehicle. There are tolls on the motorways.

Medical treatment. – For EEC countries it is necessary to have Form E 111 which testifies to your entitlement to medical benefits from the Department of Health and Social Security. With this you can obtain medical treatment in an emergency and after the necessary steps, a refund of part of the costs of treatment from the local Social Security offices (Caisse Primaire de Sécurité Sociale). It is, however, still advisable to take out comprehensive insurance cover.

Nationals of non EEC countries should make inquiries before leaving.

Currency. – There are no currency restrictions on what you can take into France in the way of currency. To facilitate export of currency in foreign bank notes in excess of the given allocation, visitors are advised to complete a currency declaration form on arrival.

Your passport is necessary as identification when cashing cheques in banks. Commission charges vary with hotels charging more highly than banks when "obliging" non-residents on holidays or at weekends.

Duly Arrived

Consulate: British – 6 Rue Lafayette, 44009 Nantes. ☎ 40 48 57 47.
American – direct inquiries to the American Embassy, 2 avenue Gabriel, 75008 Paris. ☎ 42 96 12 02.

Tourist Information Centres or Syndicats d'Initiative 🚹 are to be found in most large towns and many tourist resorts. They can supply large scale town plans, timetables and information on local entertainment facilities, sports and sightseeing.

Poste Restante. – Name, Poste Restante, Poste Centrale, Department's postal number followed by the town's name, France. The Michelin Guide France gives local postal code numbers.

Postage via air mail to: UK letter 2.50F postcard 1.80F
US aerogramme 3.70F postcard 3.15F

Where to stay: In the Michelin Red Guide France you will find a selection of hotels at various prices in all areas. It also lists local restaurants again with prices. If camping or caravaning consult the Michelin Guide Camping Caravaning France. During holidays book well in advance.

Electric Current: Mostly 220-230 volts, in some places, however, it is still 110 volts. European circular two pin plugs are the rule – remember to take an adaptor.

Public holidays in France. – National museums and art galleries are closed on Tuesdays. The following are days when museums and other monuments may be closed or may vary their hours of admission:

New Year's Day

Easter Sunday and Monday

May Day **(1 May)**

Fête de la Libération **(8 May)**

Ascension Day

Whit Sunday and Monday

France's National Day **(14 July)**

Assumption **(15 August)**

All Saints' Day **(1 November)**

Armistice Day **(11 November)**

Christmas Day

In addition to the usual school holidays at Christmas, Easter and in the summer, there are week long breaks in February and early November.

Leisure activities

Seaside cures. – Salt water and sea air cure centres (centres de thalassothérapie) are found on the Channel coast at Paramé and Roscoff and on the Atlantic at Douarnenez.

Sailing and yachting

Yachting and windsurfing. – Perros-Guirec is a stop-over for both yachtsmen and windsurfers (board sailers) on the Round France Races (both in July) and the start of the Figaro's Single-handed Race (July). Brest is the venue for the 24-hour Windsurfing Race (mid-March). The Rum Route Race (autumn) starts from St-Malo while the 1987 Point/Europe I double-handed transatlantic race will leave from Lorient.

Canal boating. – For information consult the Guide des Canaux Bretons, Editions du Plaisancier, available from most sailing specialists or chandlers with a book section.

Rambling. – Topo guides, giving detailed itineraries and useful advice to ramblers, are published by the Fédération Française de la Randonnée Pédestre, Comité national des Sentiers de Grande Randonnée, 8 avenue Marceau, 75008 Paris. ☎ 47 23 62 32.

BOOKS TO READ

In English

BRITTANY Blue Guide – *1978*

THE TASTES OF TRAVEL: NORMANDY AND BRITTANY **Elisabeth de Stroumillo** *Collins – 1979*

PORTRAIT OF BRITTANY **Marion Deschamps** *Robert Hale – 1980*

THE CELTS **T.D.E. Powell** Ancient Peoples and Places Series *Thames & Hudson – 1980*

THE CELTS **Hern Gehard** *Weidenfeld & Nicolson – 1976*

ACCESS IN BRITTANY (Holiday guide for the disabled) *Obtainable from Pauline Hephaistos Survey Projects, 39 Bradley Gardens, West Ealing, London W13*

BRITTANY AND THE BRETONS **Keith Spence** *Gollancz – 1978*

MEGALITHIC BRITTANY: A Guide, **Burl** *Thames & Hudson*

In French

PÊCHEUR D'ISLANDE **Pierre Loti** *Calman-Lévy, Paris*

GUIDE DE BRETAGNE MYSTÉRIEUSE **Le Scouëzec** *Tchou – 1980*

PRINCIPAL FESTIVALS

DATE, PLACE AND NATURE OF FESTIVAL

(no of Michelin map and no of fold given for places not described)

Fourth Thursday and third Sunday before Easter
Nantes .... Carnival

Ascension Day
St-Herbot .... Pardon

Second Sunday in May
Quintin .... Pardon
of N.-D.-de-Délivrance

Third Sunday in May
Tréguier .... Pardon of St-Yves

Whit Saturday and Sunday
Moncontour .... Pardon of St-Mathurin

Whit Sunday and Monday
Quimperlé .... Pardon of Toulfoën
or Bird Festival

Whit Monday
Carantec .... Pardon of N.-D.-de-Callot

Trinity Sunday and eve
N.-D.-du-Crann Chapel .... Pardon
Rumengol .... Pardon

Saturday night and Sunday before midsummer's day
St-Tugen .... Pardon

Last Sunday in June
St-Jean-du-Doigt .... Pardon of the Fire
Plouguerneau .... Pardon
of St Peter and St Paul
Le Faouët .... Pardon of St Barbara

First Sunday in July and preceding Friday and Saturday
Guingamp .... Pardon
of N.-D.-de-Bon-Secours

Second Sunday in July
Locronan .... Petite Troménie
Pont-L'abbé .... Embroidery Festival

Saturday after 14 July
Belle-Isle-en-Terre .... Breton wrestling
match and games

Third Sunday in July
Carantec .... Pardon
of St-Carantec (10am)

26 July
Ste-Anne-d'Auray .... Great Pardon

26 July or following Sunday
Fouesnant .... Pardon of St Anne

Fourth Saturday and Sunday in July
Le Vieux Marché 230 fold 6 ...... Islamic-Christian pilgrimage to the Chapel
of the Seven Saints

Fourth Sunday in July (and preceding days)
Quimper .... ★Cornouaille Festival

Fourth Sunday in July
Bubry 230 fold 35 ... Pardon of St Helen
Paimpol .... Newfoundland
and Iceland Festival

First Sunday in August
Persquen 230 fold 21 .... Pardon
of N.-D.-de-Pénéty
Pont-Aven .... Festival
of the Golden Gorse
Erquy .... Festival of the Sea

First fortnight in August
Lorient .... Interceltic Festival

15 August (and eve)
Perros-Guirec .... Pardon
of N.-D.-de-la-Clarté
Quelven .... Pardon of Notre-Dame

15 August
Plomodiern 230 fold 18 ..... Folk Festival
at Ménez-Hom
Fédrun Islet .... Festival
of the Brière – Barge race

15 August – evening
Pont-Croix .... Pardon
of N.-D.-de-Roscudon
Vannes .... Festival of Arvor
(in front of the ramparts)

Week of 15 August
Guingamp .... Festival of Breton dance
and of St-Loup – National Championship
on last Sunday

Sunday after 15 August
Carantec .... Pardon
of N.-D.-de-Callot
Ploërdut .... Pardon
of N.-D.-de-Crénénan

Penultimate Sunday in August (and evenings of preceding week)
Concarneau .... ★Festival of the Blue Nets

Third Sunday in August
Carnac .... Festival of the Menhirs

Last Sunday in August (eve and following Tuesday)
Ste-Anne-la-Palud .... Great Pardon

First Sunday in September
Camaret .... Pardon of N.-D.-de-Rocamadour – Blessing of the Sea
Penhors .... Pardon
of N.-D.-de-Penhors

First Sunday in September (or second Sunday when the 8th falls on a Sunday)
Le Folgoët .... Great Pardon

8 September
Josselin .... Pardon
of N.-D.-du-Roncier

Second Sunday in September
Carnac .... Pardon of St-Cornély

Third Sunday in September
Notre-Dame-de-Tronoën .... Pardon

Last Sunday in September
Hennebont .... Pardon
of N.-D.-du-Vœu
Plouguerneau .... Pardon of St Michael

Nearest Sunday to 29 September
Mont-St-Michel .... Festival
of the Archangel St Michael

4 December
Le Faouët .... Pardon of St Barbara

First Sunday in December
Paimpol .... Pardon
of N.-D.-de-Bonne-Nouvelle

31 December or 1 or 2 January
Carantec .... Pardon of N.-D.-de-Callot

Times and charges
for admission

As times and charges for admission are liable to alteration, the information below is given for guidance only.

The information applies to individual adults. However, special conditions regarding times and charges for parties are common and arrangements should be made in advance.

Churches do not admit visitors during services and are usually closed from noon to 2pm. Admission times are indicated if the interior is of special interest. Visitors to chapels are accompanied by the person who keeps the keys. A donation is welcome.

When guided tours are indicated the departure time of the last tour of the morning or afternoon will be up to an hour before the actual closing time. Most tours are conducted by French speaking guides but in some cases the term guided tour may cover group visiting with recorded commentaries. Some of the larger and more frequented sights may offer guided tours in other languages. Enquire at the ticket office or book stall. Other aids for the foreign tourist are notes, pamphlets or audio guides.

Every sight for which there are times and charges is indicated by the symbol ⊙ in the margin in the main part of the guide.

a

ARMORIQUE Regional Nature Park
Craft Centre. – Mornings and afternoons. Closed Tuesdays except in July and August and 1 May.

AUDIERNE
Fish farm. – Mornings and afternoons; closed Saturday afternoons, Sundays and holidays (except in July and August). 5F.
Thatched Cottage. – Guided tours (time: 1/2 hour) early April to early October. 15F.

AURAY
Carthusian Monastery. – Guided tours (time: 20 mins) mornings and afternoons; closed 10 days in September and 10 days in October.
Boat trip on the Auray River. – June to mid-September. Apply to Vedettes Vertes, ☎ 97 63 79 99 at Vannes, Place E.-Frick at Locmariaquer, Quai St-Goustan at Auray or at the Tourist Information Centre of Auray, ☎ 97 24 09 75.

AVAUGOUR
Chapel. – Apply to M. Simon (house 100 m from the chapel).

b

BARNENEZ
Tumulus. – Guided tours (time: 20 mins) mornings and afternoons; closed Tuesdays, Wednesdays, 1 January, 1 May, 1 and 11 November and 25 December. 11F.

BATZ Island
Bicycles for hire in July and August.
Church. – Closed Sunday afternoons and frequently during the week.
Lighthouse. – Open to visitors at the keeper's discretion.

BATZ-SUR-MER
St-Guénolé. – Ascent to the tower, mid-May to mid-September, mornings and afternoons. The rest of the year apply at 22 Grande-Rue. 4F.
Salt marsh Museum. – June to September and school holidays, mornings and afternoons; October to March afternoons at weekends only. 8.50F.

BAUD
The Venus of Quinipily. – Mornings and afternoons. 3F.

Times and charges

BEAUPORT

Abbey. – Guided tours (time: 1/2 hour) mornings and afternoons. 11F.

BEG-MEIL

Boat trips. – Apply to M. R. Guillou, ☎ 98 94 97 94. Information from the Tourist Information Centres at Beg-Meil (☎ 98 94 97 47) and at Fouesnant (☎ 98 56 00 93).

BEG-ROHU

National Sailing School. – Apply to the Director for authorisation to visit, ☎ 97 50 27 02, mid-February to late November, mornings and afternoons.

BELLE-ILE

At Le Palais, self-drive cars and bicycles for hire.

Vauban Citadel. – Open all day early June to late September. The rest of the year, opening times are in line with boat timetables. 14 and 20F.

The Great Lighthouse. – Open to visitors at the keeper's discretion.

BÉNODET

Pyramid Lighthouse. – Apply to the keeper at 2 Rue du Phare, for guided tours mornings and afternoons; closed Mondays.

Cornouaille Bridge. – Toll: for rates see the current Michelin Guide France.

Boat trip up and down the Odet River. – 6 departures daily in summer. Apply to Vedettes de L'Odet, ☎ 98 57 00 58.

BERVEN

Church. – Apply to the person whose name is given on the door.

BIENASSIS

Château. – Guided tours (time: 3/4 hour) early June to mid-September, mornings and afternoons. Closed Sundays and mornings from 14 July to 15 August. 10F.

BIEUZY

Church. – Apply at the address given at the church.

BINIC

Museum. – Mid-June to mid-September, mornings, afternoons and evenings. 8F.

BLAIN

La Groulaie Castle. – Only the outside can be seen.

BONNE-FONTAINE

Castle. – Leave the car at the gate. The park only is open, early April to early November, mornings and afternoons; closed Sundays.

BONO

Church. – Apply at the presbytery.

BOQUEN

Abbey. – Daily (not during services) from 11am. Closed Mondays. Visitors are requested to observe silence.

BOTHOA

Mill. – Mornings (except Sundays and holidays) and afternoons. 4F.

BOURBANSAIS

Zoo and Gardens. – Mornings and afternoons. 29F.

Château. – Guided tours (time: 3/4 hour) afternoons; closed early December to end of February. 29F. For information: ☎ 99 45 20 42.

BOURBRIAC

Church. – Apply to Mme Mazevet, 21 Rue Guraz ar Mogn.

BRANFÉRÉ

Zoological Park. – Easter holidays to mid-November, mornings and afternoons. 30F including audio-visual presentation.

BRÉHAT Island

Bicycles for hire at Port-Clos.

Boat trips. – Departures from St-Quay-Portrieux. In July and August, 2 to 3 Rtn trips weekly. For information apply to the agencies running the Bréhat boat services: ☎ 96 20 00 06 Bréhat; ☎ 96 20 82 30 Paimpol.

The Trieux Estuary. – Departures from Arcouest Point, stop-over at Bréhat; depending on the tide. Time: 4 hours.

BRENNILIS

Church. – Open only for services.

BREST

Arsenal and Naval Base. – French nationals only.

Maritime Museum. – Mornings and afternoons; closed Tuesdays and holidays; 12F.

Tanguy Tower. – Early June to late September, afternoons – mornings also in July and August; early January to end of May, Thursday, Saturday and Sunday afternoons.

Museum. – Mornings (except Sundays) and afternoons; closed Tuesdays and holidays.

Boat trips. – Tour of the naval port and of the roadstead (time: 1 1/2 hours); guided tours, April to late September, 3 departures daily.

For the Crozon Peninsula (time: 40 mins), 3 Rtn trips daily mid-March-October; the rest of the year 3 Rtn trips daily on Fridays and Saturdays and 2 Rtn trips on Sundays. Apply to the Compagnie des Vedettes Armoricaines, No 1 Dock, Commercial Port, ☎ 98 44 44 04.

BRIÈRE Regional Nature Park

Lock-Keeper's House. – Early June to late September, mornings and afternoons, 6F.

Nature Reserve. – Early May to late October. 6F.

C

CAMARET-SUR-MER

Notre-Dame-de-Rocamadour. – 1 November to Easter, Sundays only.

Vauban Castle. – Early June to late September, mornings and afternoons. The rest of the year, open afternoons only (except at Easter, Whitsun and on some weekends). For information apply to the town hall. Closed mid-November to mid-December and mid-January to mid-February. 10F.

Boat trips to Les Tas de Pois. – Departure from Quai Téphany (near the fish tanks) early May to mid-September. For information and reservations apply at the harbour office of the Vedettes Sirènes, ☎ 98 26 12 00.

CANCALE

St-Méen Church. – Stairway to the tower's upper platform closed at lunch time (except in July and August), Sunday afternoons and holidays. Tickets available at the Tourist Information Centre.

Museum (Former St-Méen Church). – Early July to late August, mornings (except Mondays) and afternoons; September, Saturdays and Mondays only, afternoons. 6F.

CAOUËNNEC

Church. – Apply to the sacristan, Route de Lanvézéac.

CARADEUC

Park of château. – Mornings and afternoons late March to late October, afternoons only the rest of the year. 7F.

CARANTEC

Church. – Closed Sunday afternoons.

Chapel of Our Lady (Callot Island). – When closed, apply to Mme E. L'Hour (next door).

CAREIL

Château. – Guided tours (time: 1/2 hour), afternoons, early April to late September; late May to mid-September, also mornings. 8F.

CARNAC

Miln-Le Rouzic Museum of Prehistory. – Mornings and afternoons. Closed Tuesdays (except July and August), 1 January, 1 May and 25 December. 12F.

St-Michel Tumulus. – Guided tours (time: 1/4 hour) Easter to late September, mornings and afternoons (no mid-day closing mid-June to mid-September). 3.20F.

Kercado Tumulus. – Early June to early October, mornings and afternoons.

CHAMP DES MARTYRS

July and August. The rest of the year, apply for a guide at the Café de Toul Bahadeu.

La CHAPELLE-DES-MARAIS

Clogmaker's House. – Mid-June to mid-September, mornings and afternoons; the rest of the year, Wednesday afternoons only.

Town Hall. – Closed Thursday and Friday afternoons.

CHÂTEAUBRIANT

Castle. – Guided tours (time: 1/2 hour) mid-June to mid-September, mornings and afternoons. Closed Sunday mornings and Tuesdays. Gardens open all year round.

CHÂTEAULIN

Notre-Dame. – Closed for restoration work; reopening in September 1987.

CLÉDEN-POHER

Church. – When closed apply to Mme Peron in the village.

COËTQUIDAN-ST-CYR

Academy Museum. – Mornings and afternoons. 10F.

COMBOURG

Castle. – Guided tours (time: 3/4 hour) early March to late November, afternoons. Closed Tuesdays and 1 November, 16F; park only (also mornings): 8F.

COMPER

Castle. – Not open. Access to park only: 4F. Closed Wednesdays and Thursdays, Easter to late August, Saturdays and Sundays in winter. Closed also in September, 25 December and 1 January.

CONCARNEAU

Fish Auction Market. – 7 to 10am Mondays to Thursdays.

Ramparts. – Easter to late September. 2.80F.

Shellwork Display Centre. – Early June to late September, mornings and afternoons. 8F.

Fishing Museum. – Mornings and afternoons (all day July and August). 20F.

Marinarium. – Mid-June to mid-September, mornings and afternoons; and during Easter school holidays, afternoons only. 8F.

CORSEUL

Museum. – July and August, mornings and afternoons (except Sundays and holidays). The rest of the year closed Wednesday, Thursday and Saturday afternoons, and Sundays.

Le CROISIC

Fish Market. – In summer, Mondays to Thursdays, sale at 6.30am (fish) and 5am (Norway lobsters); Fridays, 6am (fish) and 4.30am (Norway lobsters).

Côte d'Amour Aquarium. – Mornings and afternoons (all day in July and August). Closed 1 to 15 October and Mondays in winter. 16F.

Naval Museum. – Early May to mid-October, mornings and afternoons, also during school holidays. Closed Tuesdays. 7.30F.

d

DAOULAS

Abbey cloister. – Mornings and afternoons; 5F.

DINAN

Clock Tower. – July and August, mornings and afternoons. Closed Sundays and holidays. 2.50F. The rest of the year, by appointment, 10F. ☎ 96 39 75 40.

Castle. – Early March to late October, mornings and afternoons. The rest of the year, afternoons only. Closed Tuesdays, 25 December and 1 January. 5.50F.

Former Franciscan Monastery. – Open during school holidays, mornings and afternoons.

DINARD

Clair de Lune Promenade and Prieuré Beach. – « Son et Lumière » performance at 10pm, mid-June to late September, Tuesdays, Thursdays, Fridays, Saturdays and Sundays.

Aquarium and Marine Museum. – Whitsun to mid-September, mornings and afternoons. 8F.

Boat trips. – For information, apply at the landing stage or at the Tourist Information Centre, ☎ 99 46 94 12.

Cruise to Cape Fréhel. – In season. Time: 2 1/2 hours.

Cézembre Island. – Crossing: 40 mins Rtn, plus 2 1/2 hours on the island.

Air trips. – Departures several times daily in summer. For information: ☎ 99 81 67 76.

DOL-DE-BRETAGNE

Treasury Museum. – Guided tours (time: 1/2 hour) Easter to late September. Closed Tuesdays (except July and August). 10F.

DOL Mound

Notre-Dame-de-l'Espérance. – Easter to 1 November.

DONGES

Church. – Apply at the presbytery.

DOUARNENEZ

St-Michel. – Apply to Mme Guilloux, 28 Rue Port-Rhu.

Boat trips. – Landing stage at Rosmeur harbour near the fish auction market. Boat trips in the afternoon June to early September; fishing parties mornings July and August. Apply at the Tourist Information Centre, ☎ 98 92 13 35 and 98 92 10 38.

e - f

ECKMÜHL
Lighthouse. – Guided tours (time: 3/4 hour).

ERDRE Valley
Boat trip. – Landing stage: 24 Quai de Versailles at Nantes. Enquiries to the Lebert-Buisson Shipping Company, ☎ 40 20 24 50. Time: 3 hours (or longer with stop-over at Sucé). Boat trip with lunch/dinner on board. Variable departure times and days depending on the season. Apply on the spot for information and bookings.

ÉTABLES-SUR-MER
Notre-Dame-de-l'Espérance. – Afternoons, July and August.

FÉDRUN Islet
Bride's House. – In summer.
Briéron Thatched Cottage. – Early June to late September and Easter holidays, mornings and afternoons. 5F.

Le FOLGOËT
Museum. – Early July to mid-September, all day; Sundays, afternoons only. 5F.

FOUGÈRES
Castle. – Guided tours (time: 3/4 hour or 1 1/2 hours) early March to late October, daily, mornings and afternoons (all day early June to late September). 8F or 13F.
La Villéon Museum. – Easter to late September, Saturday, Sunday and holiday afternoons; early July to mid-September, daily. 5F.

g

GAVRINIS Tumulus
Crossing and tour. – Departure from Larmor-Baden. Daily mid-May to mid-September. The rest of the year on request. ☎ 97 57 03 89. Leave your car at the port opposite the embarkation point. Crossing: 1/4 hour. 13.80F.

GLÉNAN Islands
Boat services. – Leaving from Quimper, Bénodet or Loctudy, apply to Vedettes de l'Odet, ☎ 98 57 00 58 at Bénodet.
Leaving from Beg-Meil or Port-la-Forêt, apply to M. R. Guillou, ☎ 98 94 97 94 at Beg-Meil.
Leaving from Concarneau, apply at the Tourist Information Centre, ☎ 98 97 01 44.

GOUESNOU
Church. – Apply at the presbytery, 1.30 to 2.30pm Saturdays.

GRÂCES
Church of Our Lady. – When closed, apply at the presbytery.

GROIX Island
Bicycles and cars for hire at Port-Tudy.

Le GROUANEC
Church. – Apply at the presbytery or at the catholic school.

GUENGAT
Church. – Closed Sunday afternoons. July and August, guided tour Tuesday afternoons.

GUÉRANDE
St-Michel or Castle Gate. – Easter to late September, mornings and afternoons. 6F.
St-Aubin Collegiate Church. – Guided tours July and August. For information: ☎ 40 24 90 68. Organ concerts at 9.30pm Fridays in season. 35F.

GUERLÉDAN Lake
Boat trips. – Mid-June to mid-October, 8 to 10 departures daily. Time: 1 hour. For information: ☎ 96 28 52 64.

GUINGAMP
Town hall. – The great staircase may be seen during office hours mornings and afternoons. Closed Saturdays, Sundays and holidays.

h

HÉDÉ
Church. – Apply at the presbytery (near the west porch).

HENNEBONT
Notre-Dame-du-Paradis. – Closed Sunday afternoons.
Broërec Gatehouse. – Exhibitions July and August, mornings and afternoons. 7F.
Stud. – Guided tours (time: 3/4 hour). July to mid-September mornings and afternoons at set times. Mid-September to late February afternoons only. Closed Sundays and holidays. 10F. For information: ☎ 97 36 20 27.

HOËDIC Island

Access. – From Quiberon daily services early July to mid-September; the rest of the year daily except Thursdays. For information apply to the Compagnie Morbihannaise de Navigation, ☏ 97 50 06 90.
From Vannes, 2 services per week, Tuesdays and Thursdays, July and August only. Apply to Vedettes Vertes, ☏ 97 63 79 99.

HOUAT Island

Lobster Farm. – Display room planned.

HUNAUDAIE

Castle. – July and August, daily, mornings and afternoons. April, May, June and September, Sundays and holidays only, afternoons. 8F.

j - k

JOSSELIN

Castle. – Guided tours (time: 3/4 hour) late March to mid-September, afternoons; July and August, also mornings. Closed 8 September. 14F.

Dolls Museum. – Early May to late September, mornings and afternoons. Closed Mondays. The rest of the year, Wednesday, Saturday, Sunday and holiday afternoons. 16F.

Ascent of Notre-Dame-du-Roncier bell-tower. – Access by the Place A.-de-Rohan, mid-June to mid-September, mornings and afternoons.

KÉRAZAN-EN-LOCTUDY

Manor. – Early June to mid-September, mornings and afternoons. Closed Tuesdays. 10F.

KERFONS

Chapel. – July and August, mornings and afternoons. The rest of the year, apply at the town hall, ☏ 96 37 05 51.

KERGRIST

Château. – Guided tours (time: 1/2 hour) early July to mid-September, afternoons. Also Saturdays and Sundays from mid-May. Closed Tuesdays. 15F, gardens only 10F.

KERGROADÈS

Château. – Only the outside can be seen.

KERHINET

Briéron Cottage. – Early June to late September, mornings and afternoons. 2F.

KERJEAN

Castle. – Guided tours (time: 3/4 hour) mornings and afternoons. Closed Tuesdays, 1 January, 1 May, 1 and 11 November and 25 December. 16F.

KERMARIA

Chapel of Kermaria-an-Iskuit. – Early May to late September, mornings and afternoons.

KEROUAT

Mill. – Guided tours (time: 1 hour) daily July and August; early April to late November, afternoons only. 13F.

KÉROUZÉRÉ

Castle. – Visit after application in writing or ☏ 98 29 96 05. Closed Sundays. Go along the castle avenue and ring the bell at the main gate.

l

LAMBALLE

Stud. – Guided tours (time: 1 hour) mid-July to early March, afternoons.

Collegiate Church of Notre-Dame. – July and August only.

Local Museum. – Early June to mid-September, mornings and afternoons. Closed Sunday and holiday afternoons. 6F (admittance also to Mathurin-Meheut Museum).

Mathurin-Meheut-Museum. – Early June to mid-September, mornings and afternoons. Closed Sundays and holidays. 3F.

LAMPAUL-GUIMILIAU

Church. – If closed, apply at the Tourist Information Centre at the town hall in Landivisiau.

LANDAL

Castle. – Only the outside and the main courtyard can be seen.

LANDERNEAU

Church of St Thomas of Canterbury. – During school holidays.

LANDÉVENNEC

Ruins of the former abbey. – Afternoons.

Exhibition Room. – Afternoons July and August.

LANGUIVOA

Chapel. – July and August, Easter, Ascension Day and Whitsun.

LANGONNET Abbey

Museum. – Guided tours (time: 3/4 hour) early April to late October, mornings and afternoons. Closed on religious holidays.

LANMEUR

Church. – Not open. Archaeological digs in progress.

LANNÉDERN

Church. – For guided tours, July to mid-September, apply at the Tourist Information Centre in Pleyben.

LANNION

St-Jean-du-Baly. – Closed Sunday afternoons.

LANRIGAN

Château. – Exterior only early June to late August, mornings and afternoons, Wednesdays, Thursdays and Fridays. No cars allowed.

LANRIVAIN

Chapel of Notre-Dame-du-Guiaudet. – Out of season, apply to M. Chenu. Automatic peel of sixteen bells early May to late September.

LARGOËT

Castle. – Closed mid-November to mid-January. 5F. « Son et Lumière » performance: Launcelot of the Lake (Lancelot du Lac) July and August, Fridays and Saturdays, 10.30pm. 45F.

La LATTE Fort

Castle. – Guided tours (time: 1/2 hour) early May to late September and school holidays. The rest of the year, Sunday afternoons. 10F.

LÉHÉLEC

Château. – Early July to late August, afternoons (except Tuesdays). 13F.

LOCARN

Church. – Apply at the town hall (Monday to Friday afternoons only).

Treasury (in the presbytery). – Closed temporarily.

LOCMÉLAR

Church. – Apply at the presbytery in the square.

LOCQUÉMEAU

Church. – Guided tours July and August, afternoons (except Sundays).

LOCRONAN

St-Ronan Church and Chapel of Le Pénity. – Guided tours, mornings and afternoons. 5F. July and August at 9pm with illumination of interior.

Notre-Dame-de-Bonne-Nouvelle. – Guided tours mornings and afternoons.

Craftshop. – Mornings and afternoons.

Museum. – Mid-June to late September, mornings and afternoons. 3.25F.

Glass works. – Workshops open mornings and afternoons. Closed Sundays and holidays and early January to mid-February.

Chapel on Locronan Mountain. – Guided tours mornings and afternoons.

LOCTUDY

Boat trips up the Odet to Quimper. – Apply at the harbour office of Vedettes de l'Odet.

Boat trips to Ile Tudy. – Several trips daily; excluding Sundays mid-September to mid-June. 9F Rtn.

LOQUEFFRET

Church. – Apply at the town hall.

LORIENT

Ingénieur-Général-Stosskopf Submarine Base. – French nationals only.
Dockyard. – French nationals only.
Boat trips. – For information (Mondays to Saturdays) apply at Locmiquélic (☎ 97 33 40 55).

LOUANNEC

Church. – Saturday evenings in summer and Sunday mornings.

LOUDÉAC

Horse Races. – The Sunday two weeks before Easter Sunday, Easter Sunday and Monday and the Sunday after Easter.

m

MAILLÉ

Château. – Exterior daily mid-June to late September. Interior Tuesdays, Wednesdays and Thursdays by prior appointment giving the owner a few days advance notice, ☎ 98 61 44 68. Closed 14 July and 15 August.

La MEILLERAYE-DE-BRETAGNE

Abbey. – Church open for services only. For information, ☎ 40 55 20 01.

MÉNEZ-MEUR

Estate. – Early June to late September, mornings and afternoons; October to May, mornings and afternoons on Wednesdays and Sundays only and local school holidays. 5F.

MOËLAN-SUR-MER

St-Philibert-St-Roch Chapel. – Apply at the presbytery.

MOINES Island (Morbihan)

Access leaving from Port-Blanc. – Service: every 30 mins. Crossing: 5 mins. 6.40F.

MONBOUAN

Château. – Guided tours (time: 1/4 hour) mid-July to late August, mornings and afternoons. 10F.

MONKS' Island (C.-du-Nord)

Lighthouse. – Mid-June to mid-September.

MONTAUBAN

Castle. – Mid-July to mid-September and Easter holidays. 15F.

MONTMURAN

Castle. – Guided tours (time: 3/4 hour) afternoons, daily Easter to 1 November, Saturdays, Sundays and holidays the rest of the year. 12F.

MONT-ST-MICHEL

Ascent to the Abbey. – Leave the car in one of the official car parks: 7F.
Abbey. – Guided tours (time: 1 hour) mornings and afternoons. Closed 1 January, 1 May, 1 and 11 November and 25 December. 22F.
Church. – The Lacework Staircase can be seen only during guided lecture tours (available in English).
Abbey Gardens. – The gate is on the left going down the Grand Degré. 3F.
Historical Museum. – Early February to mid-November, all day. 30F (combined ticket with Mont-St-Michel Historical Museum).
Mont-St-Michel Historical Museum. – Early February to mid-November, all day. 30F (combined ticket with the Historical Museum).
Tiphaine's House. – Early April to mid-November. 7F.

MONT-ST-MICHEL, Miniature

See under St-Georges-de-Gréhaigne.

MORBIHAN Gulf

The Gulf by boat. – For all information, ask at the Gare Maritime des Vedettes Vertes, ☎ 97 63 79 99 at Vannes, at the port at Auray, at the port at Port-Navalo or at the Vedettes Vertes Offices, Place E.-Frick at Locmariaquer.

MORGAT

Big caves. – Boat trip (time: 3/4 hour). Go preferably in clear weather. Departures all day depending on the tide. You will find motor boats in the port. ☎ 98 27 09 54 and 98 27 22 50.

MORLAIX

Museum. – Mornings and afternoons. Closed Tuesdays and most holidays. For information: ☎ 98 88 68 88. 8F.
St-Mathieu. – Closed Sunday afternoons.
St-Mélaine. – Closed Sunday afternoons.

Les MOTTES Lake

Fishing permitted: Thursdays, Sundays and holidays.

NANTES

Ducal Castle. – Mornings and afternoons. Closed Tuesdays (except July and August) and holidays. 5F (free Saturdays and Sundays).

Fine Arts Museum. – Mornings and afternoons. Closed Tuesdays and holidays. 5F (free Saturdays and Sundays).

Natural History Museum. – Mornings and afternoons. Closed Sunday mornings, Mondays and holidays. 5F (free Saturdays and Sundays).

Palais Dobrée. – Mornings and afternoons. Closed Tuesdays and holidays. 5F.

Manoir de la Touche. – Same opening times and admission as the Palais Dobrée.

Regional Archaeological Museum. – Same opening times and admission as the Palais Dobrée.

Notre-Dame-du-Bon-Port. – Closed Sunday afternoons and also Mondays in summer.

Jules Verne Museum. – Mornings and afternoons. Closed Tuesdays and holidays. 5F (free Saturdays and Sundays).

NÉVEZ

Ste-Barbe Chapel. – When closed apply to Mme Glas at a house near the chapel, except Sundays.

NOTRE-DAME-DE-CONFORT

Church. – In season. When closed, apply at the presbytery, 100 m farther on.

NOTRE-DAME-DE-CRÉNENAN

Chapel. – Apply to Mme Le Gouic, in the village.

NOTRE-DAME-DE-LA-COUR

Chapel. – Weekdays only, July and August.

NOTRE-DAME-DE-KÉRINEC

Chapel. – Apply to M. J. Larour, at the farm near the chapel.

NOTRE-DAME-DE-RESTUDO

Chapel. – Apply to M. Mélou, at the house near the chapel.

NOTRE-DAME-DE-TIMADEUC

Abbey. – No visits to the monastic buildings but the public can attend services.

NOTRE-DAME-DE-TRONOËN

Chapel. – June to September, afternoons, also mornings July and August.

NOTRE-DAME-DU-CRANN

Chapel. – July and August, mornings and afternoons, closed Sundays. At other times apply at the town hall.

NOUVOITOU

Church. – Apply at the presbytery.

NOYAL-PONTIVY

Church. – Closed Sunday afternoons.

PAIMPOL

Maritime Museum. – Mid-June to mid-September, mornings and afternoons. 8.75F.

PAIMPONT

Church. – Mornings (except Sundays and holidays) and afternoons.

PENMARCH

St-Nonna Church. – Weekdays early June to late September.

PERROS-GUIREC

Church. – Closed Sunday afternoons.

PETIT MINOU Point

Lighthouse. – Closed temporarily.

PLESTIN-LES-GRÈVES

Church. – Closed Sundays and during services.

PLEUMEUR-BODOU

Space Telecommunications Station. – Guided tours (time: 1 hour) of the installations Easter holidays to mid-October, mornings and afternoons. Closed Saturdays except in June, July and August. For information: ☎ 96 48 41 49. 9F.

PLEYBEN

Funerary Chapel. – Exhibitions mid-June to mid-September, mornings (except Sundays) and holidays.

PLEYBER-CHRIST

Church. – Apply at the presbytery.

PLOARÉ

Church. – Apply to the Rector, 2 Place Paul-Stéphan, at Douarnenez.

PLOËRDUT

Church. – Apply at the presbytery.

PLOËRMEL

La Mennais Museum. – Early April to mid-September, mornings and afternoons.

PLOGONNEC

Church. – Enter by the southeast door.

PLOUBALAY

Water Tower. – Easter to mid-September, daily; early March to Easter and mid-September to mid-November, Sundays and holidays, all day, Saturdays afternoons only. 2.50F.

PLOUGASTEL-DAOULAS

Church. – Closed afternoons.

PLOUHARNEL

Galleon. – Early April to late September, mornings and afternoons (all day July and August). 9F.

PLOUMANACH

Lighthouse. – Guided tours (time: 1/4 hour) early July to late August, afternoons.

PLOUVIEN

Church. – Closed Sunday afternoons.

PLOZÉVET

Chapel of the Holy Trinity. – Apply to M. Bouizec, at the house near the chapel.

PONT-AVEN

Museum. – Early April to late September, mornings and afternoons. 10F.

PONT-CALLECK

Castle. – The park is open to the public. The chapel may be visited when services are not being held (visitors should dress appropriately).

PONTIVY

Castle. – Mornings and afternoons. Closed Mondays and Tuesdays except from mid-June to late September when exhibitions are held. 12.50F in summer, 2.20F in winter.
Notre-Dame-de-la-Joie. – Closed Sunday afternoons.

PONT-L'ABBÉ

Bigouden Museum. – Early June to late September, mornings and afternoons. Closed Sundays. 4F.
Bigouden House. – Early June to late September, mornings and afternoons. Closed Sundays and holidays.
Notre-Dame-de-Tréminou. – July and August, Tuesday and Sunday afternoons.

PONT-SCORFF

Zoo. – Early March to late September, daily; early October to late February, afternoons only Saturdays, Sundays, Mondays and Wednesdays. 20F, children 10F.

PORT-BLANC

Chapel. – July and August, guided tours Mondays and Thursdays at 4pm. When closed apply at the presbytery (first house with brown shutters when coming from Penvénan).

PORT-LOUIS

Citadel. – Mid-December to late October, mornings and afternoons (all day early June to late September). Closed Tuesdays and 1 May. 13F.

PORTZIC

Lighthouse. – Afternoons.

POULDAVID

Church. – Open for services only.

Le POULDU

Notre-Dame-de-la-Paix Chapel. – A keeper accompanies visitors. Apply at the presbytery: ☎ 98 71 56 76.

Le POULIGUEN

Ste-Anne-St-Julien. – Easter to mid-October; out of season apply to the parish priest.

PRIMEL

Fish farm. – Weekdays, late afternoon.

QUELVEN

Chapel. – Apply to Mme Duclos at the nearest café. The opening statue can only be seen by appointment with the Rector: ☎ 97 27 73 64.

QUIMPER

Cathedral. – Visitors not admitted on Sunday mornings and during services.

Quimper workshops. – Guided tours (time: 3/4 hour) mornings and afternoons. Closed Saturdays, Sundays and holidays. 10F.

Keraluc workshops. – Rue de la Troménie. Mornings and afternoons. Closed Saturdays, Sundays (except in June, July, August) and holidays.

Fine Arts Museum. – Mornings and afternoons. Closed Tuesdays and holidays. 4F.

Local Museum. – Closed for reorganisation. Opening in July 1986.

Boat trip down the Odet. – Time: 1 1/2 hours to Bénodet. Departure times vary with the tides. Information about continuing the excursion to Loctudy or the Glénan Islands may be obtained from the Tourist Information Centre at Quimper, 3 Rue du Roi-Gradlon, ☎ 98 95 04 69 or from the Vedettes de l'Odet, ☎ 98 57 00 58 at Bénodet.

Boat trip up the Odet. – Apply to M. R. Guillou at Beg-Meil, ☎ 98 94 97 94.

QUIMPERLÉ

Museum. – Guided tours early July to mid-September, mornings and afternoons. Closed Sundays and holidays. 10F.

Notre-Dame-de-l'Assomption. – Apply at the presbytery.

QUINTIN

Robien Château. – Park only open to visitors, early March to late August.

RANCE Valley

Rance Tidal Power Scheme. – Daily; time: 1/2 hour. Entrance near the lock (downstream side). The scheme is explained by a series of luminous panels and dioramas. From a balcony there is a general view of the generating room.

Boat trip. – For information apply to the Vedettes Offices: at St-Malo ☎ 99 56 63 21, at Dinard ☎ 99 46 10 45, at Dinan ☎ 96 39 18 04 or to the Tourist Information Centres: at St-Malo ☎ 99 56 64 48, at Dinard ☎ 99 46 94 12, at Dinan ☎ 96 39 74 40.

RAZ Point

Car park with attendant: 5F. To tour the point (1 1/2 hours Rtn) ask for the guides at the entrance to the small shopping centre. Wear shoes with non-slip soles.

Le RELECQ

Pardon of Ste-Anne. – Third Sunday in July. Mass in Breton at 11am. Celtic music concert 2.30pm.

RENNES

Law Courts. – Apply to the caretaker at the end of the right corridor.

Museums: Museum of Brittany and Museum of Fine Arts. – Mornings and afternoons. Closed Tuesdays and holidays. 4.20F for one museum, 7F for both (Sundays half price). Every month an explanatory brochure is published on a particular painting.

St Peter's Cathedral. – Closed Sunday afternoons July and August.

Town Hall. – Mornings and afternoons. Closed Saturdays, Sundays and holidays.

St-Germain. – Closed Sunday afternoons.

Cultural Centre. – Afternoons. Closed Mondays all year and also Sundays May to October. Closed also mid-July to late September, 1 January and 1 May.

Brittany Car Museum. – Mornings and afternoons. 15F.

RETIERS

Church. – Closed Sunday afternoons.

La ROCHE-AUX-FÉES

« Son et Lumière » performance: apply at the town hall for information, ☎ 99 47 74 07.

La ROCHE-BERNARD

Boat trip on the Vilaine River. – Boat services July and August. Departures every hour 2 to 5pm. Time: 1 1/2 hours stop at the dam included. 25.30F. The excursion can also start from the dam. Trips with meals on board. Information: ☎ 97 45 02 81. For excursion to Redon, allow one day. Information from Tourist Information Centre: ☎ 99 71 06 04.

ROCHEFORT-EN-TERRE

Castle. – Guided tours (time: 1/2 hour) early June to late September daily, mornings and afternoons; April and May, weekends only. 6F.

La ROCHE-JAGU

Castle. – Mornings and afternoons, Easter to late September; Sundays and holidays only the rest of the year. 15F.

Le ROCHER-PORTAIL

Castle. – Closed to the public.

Les ROCHERS-SEVIGNÉ

Château. – Guided tours (time: 3/4 hour) mornings (except Saturdays and Sundays) and afternoons, mid-February to mid-November. Closed 1 January, Easter Sunday, 1 November and 25 December. 10F.

ROSANBO

Château. – Guided tours (time: 1/2 hour) July and August mornings and afternoons; Easter to late June and September weekends and holidays afternoons only.

ROSCOFF

Notre-Dame-de-Kroaz-Batz. – Guided tours Thursdays in season. Apply at the presbytery. No access to the belfry.

Charles-Pérez Aquarium. – Late March to mid-October, afternoons, and also mornings early June to mid-September. 15F.

Fish farm. – Mondays to Fridays, mornings and afternoons.

ROSTRENEN

Notre-Dame-du-Roncier. – Closed Wednesday afternoons during the school term.

ROTHÉNEUF

Jacques Cartier's Manorhouse. – Guided tours (time: 3/4 hour) mornings and afternoons Wednesdays to Sundays, early June to late September. 8F. ☎ 99 40 97 73.

Sculptured Rocks. – 6F.

Sea Water Aquarium. – 6F.

S

SAILLÉ

Salt-marsh Workers' House. – Early May to late September. 7F. Slide show. Visit to a salt pan Mondays, Wednesdays and Fridays, 5pm (except on rainy afternoons).

ST-ADRIEN

Chapel. – Apply to M. Maho, at a house nearby.

ST-AIGNAN

Church. – Closed July and August.

ST-AVÉ

Notre-Dame-du-Loc. – Apply at the presbytery.

ST-BRIEUC

St-Stephen's Cathedral. – Closed Sunday and holiday afternoons.

ST-CÔME

Chapel. – Ask for the key at the farm nearby.

ST-DEGAN

Ecological Museum. – Guided tours early July to mid-September, afternoons. 10F.

ST-ESPRIT-DES-BOIS

Old Farm. – Guided tours (time: 1 hour) Sunday afternoons, early May to late October; daily, early July to mid-September. 5F.

ST-GEORGES-DE-GRÉHAIGNE

Miniature Mont-St-Michel. – Early April to mid-November (daily mid-June to mid-September, weekends only the rest of the year). 5F.

ST-GILDAS-DE-RHUYS

Church treasury. – Guided tours (time: 1/4 hour) July and August, mornings and afternoons. Closed Sundays and holidays. 3F.

ST-GONÉRY

Chapel. – 2F.

ST-GUÉNOLÉ

Finistère Prehistorical Museum. – Early June to late September, mornings and afternoons; the rest of the year, apply to the caretaker, ☎ 98 58 60 35. Closed Tuesdays. 8F.

ST-JACQUES-LE-MAJEUR

Chapel. – Apply at the farm, opposite the side door.

ST-JAOUA

Chapel. – Apply at the farm behind the chapel.

ST-JEAN-BALANANT

Chapel. – Apply at the house behind the chapel.

ST-JEAN-DU-DOIGT

Church treasury. – Closed temporarily. Re-opening: summer 1986.

ST-JOACHIM

Church. – Open only for services.

ST-LÉRY

Church. – Enter by the small door.

ST-LUNAIRE

Old Church. – Mid-June to mid-September.

ST-LYPHARD

Belvedere. – Guided tours (time: 1/2 hour) July and August, mornings (except Saturdays and Sundays) and afternoons. 5F.

ST-MALO

St-Malo Museum. – Mornings and afternoons, daily (except Tuesdays in autumn and winter). Closed 1 January, 1 May and 25 December. 4.50F.

Quic-en-Groigne. – Guided tours (time: 3/4 hour) early April to late September, mornings and afternoons. 12F.

Aquarium. – Mornings and afternoons (all day early July to mid-September). 12.50F Exotarium: 12.50F. Combined ticket: 22F.

National Fort. – Early June to late September and also Easter to Whitsun. 8F.

International Museum of Cape Horn Vessels. – Easter then June to September, mornings and afternoons. The rest of the year apply to the St-Malo Museum. Closed Tuesdays, 1 May, 1 November, 25 December and 1 January. 4.50F.

ST-MARCEL

Museum of the Resistance. – All year. 14F.

ST-MATHIEU Point

Lighthouse. – Apply to the keeper.

ST-MICHEL-DE-KERGONAN

Abbey. – Services (Gregorian chant): mass 10am, vespers 5pm weekdays, 4pm Sundays and holidays.

ST-NAZAIRE

Panorama-Terrace. – Open mid-June to September. For further details apply to the Tourist Information Centre. ☎ 40 22 40 65.

Ste-Anne. – Apply at the presbytery. Closed Sunday afternoons.

Notre-Dame-d'Espérance. – Open for services on Saturday evenings and Sunday mornings.

ST-NIC

Church. – Closed 11.30am to 3pm. Guided tours Friday afternoons July and August.

ST-NICODÈME

Chapel. – July and August. The rest of the year, apply to the town hall at Pluméliau.

ST-NICOLAS

Chapel. – Apply to M. Joseph Robic, Kerviguen, at Priziac.

ST-POL-DE-LÉON

Kreisker Chapel. – Mid-June to mid-September, mornings and afternoons.

ST-RIVOAL

Museum. – Guided tours (time: 1/2 hour) early June to mid-November, afternoons. July and August all day. The rest of the year by appointment only. 6F.

ST-SERVAN
Ste-Croix. – July and August.
International Museum of Cape Horn Vessels. – See under St-Malo.

ST-TUGEN
Chapel. – July and August except Sunday mornings.

ST-VENEC
Chapel. – Apply to Mme Cariou, at the Jubig farm.

ST-YVI
Church. – Apply at the presbytery.

STE-ANNE-D'AURAY
Treasury - Basilica. – Early March to early October afternoons, and also mornings from early May. 5F.
St Anne Diorama. – Guided tours (time: 1/4 hour) early April to mid-October. 10F.
Nicolazic Museum. – Mid-May to mid-September afternoons, and also mornings July and August. 5F.
House of Nicolazic. – Early May to early October.

STE-ANNE-DE-KERGONAN
Abbey. – Services (Gregorian chant) 11.30am and 6pm weekdays, 10am and 4.30pm Sundays and holidays; also May to October 3.15pm Thursdays.

STE-ANNE-LA-PALUD
Chapel. – Easter to 1 November.

STE-AVOYE
Chapel. – Apply to the caretaker.

STE-BARBE
Chapel. – Mid-May to mid-September mornings and afternoons, daily. The rest of the year Wednesdays, Saturdays and Sundays only.

STE-CHRISTINE
Chapel. – Apply to Mme Le Gall.

STE-NOYALE
Chapel. – Apply to M. Jubin, cabinet-maker, in the village.

SEIN Island
Lighthouse. – Mornings and afternoons.

Les SEPT-SAINTS
Chapel. – Apply at a house nearby.

SEVEN ISLANDS
Tour. – Early June to mid-September: boat services from Trestraou beach (3 hours including stop-over).

SIZUN Cape
Bird Sanctuary. – Mid-March to late August, mornings and afternoons. 6F.

STIFF Point
Lighthouse. – Guided tours (time: 1/2 hour) afternoons in principle. ☎ 98 48 80 93.

STIVAL
Church. – Closed November to Easter.

SUSCINIO
Castle. – April to September, mornings (except Wednesdays) and afternoons; the rest of the year, Tuesdays, weekends and holidays only, mornings and afternoons. 8F.

t

TINTÉNIAC
Church. – Apply at the presbytery.

TONQUÉDEC
Castle ruins. – Early July to late August, mornings and afternoons. 6F.

TOUCHE-TRÉBRY
Castle. – Guided tours (time: 1/4 hour) afternoons July and August. Closed Sundays and holidays. 7F.

TRÉCESSON
Castle. – The inner courtyard may be seen on request.

TRÉDREZ
Church. – Guided tours July and August: apply at the town hall. Altarpiece removed for restoration.